NEGLECTED BOOKS OF THE 20TH CENTURY

Sybille Bedford, *A Legacy*

Elizabeth Bishop, *The Diary of "Helena Morley"*

Elizabeth Bowen, *Bowen's Court*

Jane Bowles, *My Sister's Hand in Mine*
  (an expanded edition of *The Collected Works*)

Paul Bowles, *The Sheltering Sky*

Mary Butts, *Scenes from the Life of Cleopatra*

Italo Calvino, *The Path to the Nest of Spiders*

Caresse Crosby, *The Passionate Years*

Ford Madox Ford, *Provence*

Cecily Mackworth, *The Destiny of Isabelle Eberhardt*

THE ECCO PRESS

The ❦ PASSIONATE YEARS

Caresse Crosby
The ❧ PASSIONATE YEARS

THE ECCO PRESS
NEW YORK

Published in 1979 by The Ecco Press
1 West 30th Street, New York, N.Y. 10001
Published simultaneously in Canada by Penguin Books Canada Limited
Printed in the United States of America

Cover design by Loretta Li
The Ecco Press logo by Ahmed Yacoubi

LIBRARY OF CONGRESS IN PUBLICATION DATA

Crosby, Caresse, 1892-
    The passionate years.
    (Neglected books of the 20th century)
    Reprint of the 1953 ed. published by Dial Press,
New York.
    Includes index.
    1. Crosby, Caresse, 1892- —Biography.
2. Poets, American—20th Century—Biography.
3. Publishers and publishing—France—Biography.
4. Americans in Paris. I. Title. II. Series.
[PS3505.R865 1979]   818'.5'203   78-31388
ISBN 0-912-94666-0

LIST OF ILLUSTRATIONS

LIST OF ILLUSTRATIONS (continued)

Plate.

LIST OF ILLUSTRATIONS (continued)

C
A
HARRY
E
S
S
E

*To the secure years of childhood,
to those years unblemished by fear,
unscarred by war—to the cambric
years of fun and faith, this book
is gratefully dedicated.*

FOREWORD

I have written these pages the way they live in my memory—
I have never kept a diary or a scrapbook, or subscribed to a
clipping bureau, so I have no data to refer to except those
"lined upon the tablets of my mind." If I have put unsus-
pected words into the mouths of my friends, I admit it could be
my memory, not theirs, that is at fault, but I believe the
characters in this human comedy to be my friends with only
a few exceptions—in those cases I have made sure that the
quotes are verbatim.

One or two personalities who are now in public life may
feel I have forgotten them—but to tell the world that a man
remains magnificent in a woman's memory might complicate
his career as much as if she were to say the contrary.

Each artist, however, is plentifully identified; for I have
observed that no matter how good or how bad an artist may be,
he believes that his every expression, public or private, is
history.

I can vouch that these remembered years are played straight
—and I hope, as every wishful mummer must, that they will
be played to a full house. May I thank the cast, one and all,
for making this wish possible.

C. C.
Delphi.

The PASSIONATE YEARS

CHAPTER 1

I'll never forget the day I was born—born to myself, that is. It was snowing big soft flakes, soft as vacuum—the feel of snowflakes melting on my cheeks was the first sensation I remember. Later I remember the taste of mitten thumbs mixed with ice, stiff and sweet to suck. I remember, too, how I looked the day I was born. I wore a corded cream silk bonnet edged round with swansdown and my cheeks were tight and rosy, and my eyes dreamily content to be alive. But perhaps it was only the day I *believe* I was born, for there was "no precipitation whatsoever" at 5.00 A.M., April 20 of my year nor at any other time during the round of the clock. "Perfect spring day," the weather bureau has chronicled, though I remember the edges of the duck pond in Central Park just below my nursery windows were still rimmed with frozen grasses and with the imprint of double runners and flexible flyers, but this too may be chronologically wrong for I recall that the first "flexible flyer" could not have left its print there until I was nine or ten, and that what I really remember was the slender track of my elegant Brewster baby sleigh of white enamel, with its cosy double-faced fur mound, the outside of squirrel for the public, the inside of ermine for me; and Delia from Cork in a smart blue cadet-like surtout with white high-laced boots pushing me proudly from shore to shore while my mother looked down from the bay window of my nursery above, as I took my first remembered journey. This was at Fifty-ninth

13

Street and Fifth Avenue and my nursery existed where Room 440 of the Plaza now floats in air.

When I think of my mother as she looked then, I fondly remember her lovely oval face and black hair with its delicate peak above the forehead, framed in a window, or reflected in a mirror; or over the banister at the top of a long steep stair. My father was head over heels in love with Mama. They had met in snowy weather too, at a skating party on Dickerman's Pond. He was her victim from that day until the day he died.

I was the first child, I should have hated not to be. I was the first granddaughter, too, although my father was one of seven; four brothers, two sisters, each one more delightful and lively and prolific than the last; known in and out of town for their fine wit, good temper and charming manners. That my father and his brothers had been brought up to ride to hounds, sail boats, and lead cotillions may not have helped them to fame and fortune but it did supply me with a crystal-chandelier background and if some of my most vivid memories are intermingled with the faint aroma of Dean's luscious pistache cake, the heady twang of Grandpapa's Andalusian sherry and threaded with the sweet scents of Black Starr and Frost silver polish, Mark Cross saddle soap, and beeswax on linen, it is because I grew up in a world where only good smells existed.

My mother and father were never rich nor even well off. They married on an allowance provided by my grandparents. Father just could not make money. Everyone he did business with loved him, honoured him and fleeced him. He didn't know at all how to economize. To eat duck without Burgundy or ices without champagne seemed utterly foolish, and not to eat them at all, impossible. My mother has told me since, that many of their economizing dinners planned for two in "some tiny restaurant" turned out to be enormous follies at the Lafayette —where inevitably Napoleon brandy appeared beside the after-dinner coffee cup and the homemade bow on Mama's shoulder was replaced by sky-pink camellias. She said her tears at that point often mingled with the brandy—but Father felt he couldn't offer her less than the "best." Of course during all this time, I was extravagantly languishing in my bassinet watched over by a highly paid nursery maid. My grandparents lived a few blocks away at 614 Fifth Avenue. Their brownstone front where Rockefeller Center now stands was the gathering spot for the carefree youngsters of the family and their youthful parents. It was from the bay window of my grandfather's study that I and my cousins watched Dewey return from Manila, and on the seventeenth of March we gathered there for the St. Patrick's Day Parade. The house was almost opposite St. Patrick's Cathedral, the old St. Patrick's.

The lure of 614 started on the outside. From the brownstone steps one's nostrils were assailed by the spice of baking cookies. Annie, the dream-cook of childhood, was forever baking cookies and they were always overfilling the terra-cotta dragon jar on Grandpapa's desk, the one that matched the dragon umbrella-stand, a monstrosity that stood by the front door where, unless the gas was lit, it was too dark to see it clearly in the hall and that is why I came upon my uncle kissing Aunt Lisa the day they were engaged. They were just going up to tell the family. He stepped onto the step above her and it was a kiss that sealed their future life. I realized it was a kiss too sacred to be watched and so I had to hide unhappily behind the terra-cotta monster.

This aunt was a beautiful Amazonian girl and my uncle was small and delicate but the incongruousness never seemed to mar their relationship. Only once in my life have I believed myself in love with a protagonist shorter than myself, but I found it so physically heartbreaking that I succumbed in a flash, trying in order not to hurt his feelings, to put a gesture of Cleopatra voluptuousness into an act that was pure funk—yet I have never known a swain to be too tall.

When I was two months old we moved to East Island for the summer and there the magic in my life began. My first "Season by the Sea" was lived in a shell cottage, entirely built of pink and saffron sea shells, walls, ceilings and doors all of shells. Tiny mother-of-pearl shells were encrusted in the white plaster so that the effect was of a fine mosaic, and up through the centre of the roof grew a spreading locust tree so the shells glowed cool in the shadows of the leafy branches or glowed red as the sun struck low across Long Island Sound and into our living room.

15

In this enchanted cottage crickets sang at evening and locusts droned on the hot summer days. Rose-coloured sand crabs traced pebbled trails across the wide board steps and fireflies gathered there on blue-black nights, while the salt waters of the Sound lapped the beach in front—like a lullaby. I spent all my summers there until I was seven.

It was a feudal island reached by a white-railed causeway with a keeper's lodge half-way from the mainland. If, on reaching the island, one turned to the left and skirted the bayberry bushes and pungent sedgegrass, one swung around the waterside of the island and arrived at our shell cottage. But if one drove spankingly up beneath the lindens that edged the driveway one arrived at the carriage block in front of the big house, where Grandmama and Grandpapa spent their summers. Here, unlike the cottage, the house was built of damasked walls and polished floors with huge mahogany tables and armchairs drowsing in summer gloom caused by dark shutters, Nottingham lace, and heavy satin curtains smooth and cool, and each room had its special approach.

Into "the den" one went only when invited by Grandpapa; into the "east parlour" when invited by Grandmama; in the "west parlour" we gathered before meals and in "the library" we gathered after dinner to drink coffee with rum in it. There were always a dozen places laid at the table. This was the rule of the house. There were more when needed but never less than twelve, so that bringing someone home to meals was a certain and delightful privilege. Annie was below in the big kitchen like a duchess in her realm.

There were three miles of white pebble paths on the island and they were raked every day. The song of the rake and the song of the locusts made a summer duet that enchants my memory still.

I do not remember very truly whether it was at 614 or at East Island that the humiliating experience of spending the night with my youngest aunt occurred. Delia must have been ill or on vacation and for some reason (I hope it was a cotillion) my mother and father asked my aunt to take me for the night. That year, my aunt, at eighteen, was a debutante and a great deal of importance was given by the family to her parties

16

and her beaux and her friends. I remember she had a school-mate staying with her, and the friend, for that one night was given the guest room at the top of the stairs next *le petit endroit,* while I was put to sleep in an extra bed in my aunt's room at the back of the house. I was told I must not budge until she came to hear "my prayers." This terrified me. No one ever heard my prayers. Prayers were a private and personal matter. I said them to myself and to my Maker, rolled into a kind of cocoon, my nose buried under my arm, and I always ended my prayers by kissing my armpit before "amen." So I was waiting trembling in the big bed wondering what I could do about it when my aunt and her best friend entered and turned up the gas.

"Now kneel and lean up against me, Pollykins," she said as she stood plump and pleased beside the bed.

"I always say them alone," I answered.

"But kiddies don't do that," said the friend.

"I'm not a kiddie," I almost sobbed. "And I don't want to say them to anyone."

However, in a truly heroic effort my aunt drew me close against her soft little bosom. I looked down into that warm fragrant heart-cleft with interest—my feeling was of wonder rather than of expiation. The dress was pretty, too, and so was my aunt, but suddenly I must have felt I was yielding for I pushed her violently away and burrowed beneath the bedclothes sobbing wildly.

"Please go away—please go away—I'll say them to myself—"

I saw tears spring to her uncomprehending eyes. I knew I was being a selfish little brute, cruelly I had caused her to fail in the presence of her best friend, but my privacy was worth fighting for. It always has been. After they left me, the window open, the gas turned down, I leapt from the bed and, a repentant sinner, fell to my knees upon the cabbage-rose rug, and prayed.

"Please, God, forgive me, please, oh, please." Then I jumped happily back beneath the covers and was immediately asleep with "Josie and the chipmunk" in the Wonderful Forest of Oz.

Thinking of this episode now, I wonder if children are often stirred by the pretty bosoms of their mothers as they say "Now

17

I lay me" and I wonder why the peekaboo seed does not flower more luxuriantly in the consciousness of "the kiddies." Perhaps it does—or perhaps all good mothers wind their charms in sackcloth and drop ashes in the cleft before the good-night prayers.

We used to swim every morning and every evening at East Island. The family and guests came down from the big house and there were latticed dressing rooms under the veranda for their use. We cottagers undressed in our own rooms. I remember the last summer spent there. I was seven and I had my first really grown-up bathing suit (made by Mrs. Foley, the seamstress who made all my clothes). It was of heavy rose alpaca with top and bloomers in one piece and a very full skirt banded with white piqué that buttoned on over the bloomers at the waist. The square neck was cut high and the sleeves came to my elbows and the heavy wet folds of both bloomers and skirt weighed me down. In the water I was allowed to drop the skirt, pull it off over my feet and fling it onto the wooden pier that jutted out to where the rowboats were made fast.

My grandmother, who considered herself too matronly at fifty-four to go in bathing, used to pick up the skirt and have it ready for me at the water's edge when I finally emerged. Screened by her billowy dress, I could button it on and scamper with decency to the cottage a hundred feet away. We were a decorous clan.

I think that from my grandfather's picture you can guess that he was not a very sharp businessman. Having been brought up in Chale Abbey on the Isle of Wight, where the Jacob family "Misterie Men" (for Mister) had lived for one thousand years, first as the Allardyce family and after the War of the Roses as the Jacobeans or Jacob family, they were (and still are) men who live for and love the graces and honest flavours of life; any worldly success must be acquired in spite of these qualities.

The tomb of one of my ancestors in the Chapel of Chale Abbey shows him in effigy completely hidden in armour, even visored, but with his poor legs twisted back and forth like convoluted stems, for he, Sir Thomas Oglander, had gone to one Crusade (the legs crossed once) and then because of more

wrongs to be righted, went straight back again (another crossing of the legs), so there he lies "a goodly Knight" and beside
him within the tomb lies his wife, the Lady Dousabelle. That
Uncle Len once named a cow Dousabelle has always seemed
to me lèse majesté.

And in one of the earliest numbers of *The Sporting Magazine,*
October, 1812, there is a spirited description of a stag hunt at
Chale run with my great-grandfather's pack of stag hounds.
To this hunt a royal party came across the solent from
Windsor, and knowing my forebears' virtues, I am sure that
the visitors received a royal welcome. It's fun to think of those
banquets, while one opens the cans in the kitchenette. I've never
asked, but I don't believe wild boar comes in cans?

To get back to my grandfather, he left Chale as a young
man and arrived in New York to seek his fortune. One of his
first acts of independence was to marry an American, Miss
Emma Lawrence of Trinity Place, New York City. Grandfather dived right into the finest flowerpatch on the Island and
came up with the first award, my grandmama. The Van Vech-
tens, the Clasons, the Schuylers and other cousins looked rather
askance at the procedure, for was the Isle of Wight really part
of England and who ever heard of a real Englishman with the
name of Jacob; but Grandfather was as convincing as he was
charming, for with the advice of Mr. Lawrence he began to
buy up quite a parcel of Manhattan. When he died he left
large tracts of real estate in and around Fourteenth Street,
Fifth Avenue, Cathedral Heights, Flushing Meadows and East
Island, but as at the time of his death, 1905, all these looked
like "duds" and as they had probably been unloaded by his
in-laws on poor unsuspecting Grandpapa, his sons went to work
to get rid of them as quickly as they could, at unusual losses.
Of course, Fourteenth Street is still no bonanza, nor Cathedral
Heights—but Flushing Meadows, and East Island!

And then there was the distaff side—how well I know the
implications of that word. It means in our Anglo-Saxon moral-
ity that one is not allowed the family crest on one's wedding
silver, that one does *not* inherit the family portraits or the
mahogany sideboard or the Aubusson carpet, not even the
"second-best" Chippendale. It is really too unfair being on the

19

distaff side of a family fence, especially as my grandmother's papa was well loaded with this world's goods—it all came from the carriage trade.

Riker Lawrence manufactured gentlemen's carriages. Broughams were his specialty. Our Manhattan rolled on distaff wheels, that is before the motor car did us in. The Lawrences had property on Staten Island too, and on the ferry Great-grandpapa would cross in his victoria or coupé twice daily, and, as he often quipped, he could loll comfortably "while old Vander-bilt did the ferrying"—

Mama's background was quite different except that it, too, was well padded. She was born Mary Phelps so I was chris-tened Mary Phelps Jacob. I am glad I bear my maternal fore-bear's name as well as my father's, for the Phelpses had de-veloped sturdy and puritan qualities to offset the popish attributes from overseas.

My great-great-great-great-grandfather, Governor Bradford, came over to Massachusetts in the *Mayflower* and became first governor of that state—this in the genealogy of Americans bears such tremendous weight that the title of D.A.R. is assured to all his female descendants direct in line. (Mother was bored by the idea. Should I do something about that?) Through her I am also descended from Robert Fulton, inventor of the steam-boat. I believe that my ardour for invention springs from his loins—I can't say that the brassière will ever take as great a place in history as the steamboat, but I did invent it, and perpetual motion has always been just around the corner.

My own grandfather, Walter Phelps, fell heir to a coal and iron fortune in Irontown, Connecticut. His mother had a fine house in Troy in which my Mama was left shut up like the storybook Princeling in the tower whenever it pleased her parents to travel. And there were other fine family houses, very jigsaw, turreted and cupolaed, scattered all over those regions. My maternal grandmother was a Schenk of Phila-delphia, and at the time Eliza married Grandpapa, her own father was the first U.S. Ambassador, 1866-1872, to the Court of St. James. As mother grew older she was sent to school both in England and in France as a young lady should be, but that was after the Civil War or "war between the states" as I learned my manners to call it in Virginia when I lived there over half a century later.

When the North and the South clashed in the 1860's, Grandfather Walter Phelps volunteered and became a dashing Captain of Cavalry in the Irontown Militia. "The Iron Brigade" it was called and he was, before the war's end, promoted to Brigadier. General Phelps led the Brigade at the Battle of Antietam. There he received wounds, decorations and a very honourable discharge and returned once more to the Connecticut hills to "puddle" ore.

He died the following year, a result of his wounds in battle, and my mother who was only six (a war baby) did not remember very much about him, she remembered more about his horse, Billy—the white charger which carried him into battle and which, in peace time, became the locomotive stand-by of the widow's family. Old Billy was driven from Limerock into Goshen for mail and supplies twice a week. On going in he limped pitifully but once his head was turned toward home it was as if the bugle had sounded again. He charged homeward at a breakneck speed (one wonders in which direction he was going at the Battle of Antietam).

Grandfather's dress sword always hung in my mother's living room under his handsomely tinted photograph in full regimentals—his soft, kind gaze looking as un-warlike as the begilded and tasselled weapon on the wall.

Aunt Annie was years older than Mama, for as I said, Mama was a result of the war. This may account for the belligerent and caustic spirit that endeared her to her family and friends, for my mother was a wit with a terse New England view of life. She was difficult to persuade and impossible to fool—and she never avoided an issue. "I don't see why you stand for it," was one of her sayings. She had no notion of winnowing the chaff from the wheat, if there was any chaff at all the wheat was no good.

My father, on the other hand, could pick a grain of wheat from a barrel of chaff—and of these two opposites I am made.

Mama, at eighty-three, had become very deaf and nearly blind but she never lost her "spunk" and ruled us all with the rod of impatience; "so stupid" was the phrase most often on her lips.

I remember ruefully how only a year or two ago, when I had flown in from Europe to breakfast with her in Seventy-second Street at 9 a.m., she said quizzically looking at me over her morning coffee, " When did you leave Paris?"

"At five yesterday afternoon, Mama," I answered, rather satisfied with myself.

Her instant retort was, "What took you so long?"

At such a moment the pleasure of homecoming was a pricked balloon, but later became an endearing memory. She was childishly eager for news and could stand the most lurid details without batting an eye. Incidentally, she mixed the driest martinis in Manhattan.

Mother died only a few months ago and as I write this page on an English terrace at Ardleigh Park, where the lawns roll out before me like silk-by-the-yard, I look up at the rose-hung windows of my Aunt Em's bedroom where she too, autocratic to the end, rules this little kingdom as some feudal queen-mother in lands forlorn. The old ladies of recent decades, brought up in ease, and living out these devastating years well guarded in the bosoms of their devoted families, are of a strain apart, a strain that is dying out. Despots, darlings, sorcerers, ladies of steel.

CHAPTER 2

From the New York flat we moved out of town to a house in New Rochelle, then more country than suburb. My first act of independence was taken on the day we again transferred from the high-bosomed structure at 126 Pelham Road to a far finer abode with our own driveway and a circle in front, and with several acres of meadow which reached down to the fence along Orienta Creek.

This new house was only a quarter of a mile away from the old one, but it was shingled a soft grey and had a wide piazza all the way round, a childhood prospect for happy days. I could hardly wait to move in—I was five and my brother Len only three, while Buddy, the baby, was hardly out of swaddling clothes. I had a number of possessions of my own which had to be moved, and the packing of these I undertook myself —six or seven dolls and a precious collection of sea shells and sea stones (picked up on the beach at East Island), also an invention that I was at work on, perpetual motion, but well in hand due to some very fine clothespins and a pulley or two garnered from my father's knockabout—also, and this was my top secret, a pair of real scissors quite against rules, my most prized possession.

Mother and Delia and Katie were running up and down stairs, calling and carrying, ordering and obeying a confusion of assignments. Len was closed safely in the nursery, but I was instructed to watch Buddy's carriage, which was pushed to one side under the shade of the horse-chestnut near the gate. My first remembered journey was across the duck pond with Delia, but my second was on my own.

It was May—my own properties and wares were tightly packed into doll's pram and toy wagon—I couldn't see why the grownups took so long. Buddy began to whimper.

I asked for the eleventh time, "When can we move, Mama?"

"We'll go when we're all quite ready," she replied in a nervous flurry.

But I *was* quite ready and I saw no reason why I shouldn't move right then and there and get it over with—I knew the way well, it was only a very little distance down Pelham Road to where our own new gateway was swung open for us. I had by now three vehicles for which I was responsible—Buddy's perambulator, my own doll's pram and the express wagon, which measured a good three feet, and was piled high with treasures. I had to invent a suitable method—so the perpetual-motion machine was dismantled. To a toy harness I attached a pulley, this in turn was attached to the wagon and the wagon to the doll's pram. I then stepped into' the harness and heaved—the convoy moved—I took the handlebar of Buddy's pram firmly in my fists—my eyes just about their level, pushed, and magically we all were in motion.

How we made the turn into Pelham Road I do not know but the struggle and the strain of the perambulator and the trailer were much too much for my five-year muscles, yet like the rescuer who carries three times his weight from a burning building or the swimmer who knows he must reach the shore or drown, I was given super infant strength—the teetering, swerving line that I piloted meandered toward my goal, but when one-half the distance had been accomplished I suddenly became panicky, for my trailer was jammed at a dangerous angle across the highway and I had come to an uphill grade. Buddy was yelling with terror and disapproval and I was all wound up in harness when to my horror I heard clattering toward us over the rise ahead the din of the iceman's wagon. I knew the iceman and I knew his team, Girlie and Gus. They were to my mind behemoths of speed and might—we were to be galloped down in cold blood (I could feel the horseshoes on my neck). There was a clang and a roar from Mike and a grinding of brakes.

"Well, what the devil," he said, and the lumbering wagon swerved and jerked to a standstill just in time.

The boy with the tongs jumped down from the back step and took charge of the chargers and Mike took charge of me. He wanted to turn us round and return us to No. 126, but on that subject I saw only in one direction—*Avanti!* And so with his big friendly fists upon the handlebar we straightened out, advanced, made the gutter and wheeled freely down our new driveway to the steps of our new house.

Papa was there, a hammer in hand, Tony, the Italian handyman, at his side. Mike explained with gestures and promised to carry the word of my safe arrival back to Mama. Papa gave me a big, hurried hug, but I felt he would have liked to rap that hammer sharply on my noddle, and Mike left with the ominous pronouncement, "Just as well it wasn't Malstead's that piled into her."

At this my heart stood still, for indeed I could imagine the awful results had Malstead's coal truck come along. It was three times the size of Mike's and it was drawn by three black percherons—I visualized a flattened version of my convoy—gorily spread like jam over the broad highway. There were no automobiles as yet—the coal wagon was the juggernaut of our roads—I had indeed been fortunate.

Papa loved the new house and I think Mama did, too, at first, as for us children it was paradise. Here we had plenty of room to romp, and to play such games as "Run, Sheep, Run."

Keefer's fish market was at the foot of the hill and his catboats mosied up the creek at evening, bringing in the day's catch. It was a delight to be taken down the rocky side-path by Delia to stand at the edge of Keefer's wharf and watch the nets being emptied into big wooden buckets—shiners, crabs, star fish, white and blue and black fish and lots of lovely, long slippery seaweed glistening like patent leather. Father's little knockabout was moored in midstream. Sometimes we were taken for a sail, but the cockpit was tiny and I, for one, was of a roving rather than a sedentary nature.

When Father came home at night he always drove from the station in Barney's hack. It had a fringe on top and smelt strongly of the livery stable, that pungent combination of manure, wet leather and sweat. It was a loosely hung rattley vehicle and Barney's horse was as ramshackle as the rest of it. Barney wore a rakish bow tie and a bowler hat tilted over his

nose, a nose always supremely red. He loved and admired
Father almost as much as I did. The last time I saw Barney
was at Father's funeral; he and I mourned loud and un-
ashamedly.

In those days when evening fell, and we heard the rattle of
steel-rimmed wheels on the gravel drive, we children would
swoop down to greet Papa crying, "Catch the fox! Catch the
fox!" He always played the game, running round the circle
until one of us held and nearly strangled him with kisses. "I've
caught the fox, I've caught the fox," the lucky one would shriek,
and as reward be carried piggy-back into the house. Sometimes,
Papa coughed and swayed, but we dug our heels into his flanks
and urged him on. He never once said "don't."

In the mornings he took the streetcar, it cost less, and it
started from the end of Pelham Road at 7.50. It was horse-
drawn and it had a stove inside for nippy mornings. The seats,
which ran down each side, were covered in gaudy bright car-
petry. The foot-bell clanged like one on an ice wagon. When
snow flew of a winter's day, the horse-car looked and felt like
a snug little house. We children walked Papa to the car every
pleasant morning, snow or shine, but when it rained Barney
came to fetch him.

Papa never liked being a businessman. I wish he had never
had to be. I loved him so.

One, two, maybe three years passed in this happy spot, with
midsummers on East Island, where all the family grand-
children joined for heavenly basking holidays—only a few
highlights blink the past of Pelham Road. I remember one
beautiful ritual held at dusk on the big, flat, micaed rocks that
pushed above the lawn down in the far corner by the fence.
This always took place when Mama and Papa were out for the
evening, maybe because we were not supposed to stay up after
dark, certainly not "outside," but on these romantic occasions,
Delia, whose uncle had sent her from the old country a huge
and impressive package for her birthday, would go secretly to
her room while Katie, the cook, herded us out to the rock.
Then Delia, more like a priestess than a nurse, would emerge
from the kitchen door and, held aloft in her hands on Mama's
best platter, there would rise a square of sod, sod of Ireland,

lovely, black and luscious peat from the bogs of Eire—a little fire of twigs and leaves would be kindled on the rock and in this the sacred peat would take fire and glow, a curl of smoke rising like incense against the shadows of the miasmal creek below, and Delia, her fiery hair agleam in the greenish light, chanted us tales of old Ireland that made our blood tingle and chill by turns. Her fine rich brogue and her vestal-like quality made of those happy childhood evenings ceremonies never to be forgotten; but sadly enough I do not remember any one of the legends she told.

Another blink from the past was the death of "Postman," our white bull terrier. I believe he was a "pit dog" though we were not supposed to know about that, any more than we were supposed to know about the fighting cocks that Papa kept in roomy barrels in the cellar and carried forth at night, hooded and spurred, to some subversive ring. Dog fights and cock fights were then, and I suppose still are, against the law, but in those days gentlemen had to have such sport and I recall that when Katie, our cook, on one occasion, instead of going out in the cold to the hen house to fetch a fowl, beheaded and stewed "Checkmate III," it caused more consternation at the dinner table where Mayor and Judge were our guests than the un-American activities they knew were being carried on behind our furnace.

The death of Postman still gives me the creeps. Perhaps from over-fatigue in the ring or due to a nasty jaw wound on his throat, one day about two in the afternoon when we three children were supposedly taking naps in the nursery with the faithful Postman to guard us, he suddenly got to his feet, let out a dismal howl and began spinning around on the nursery rug. We all stood up in our cribs to watch and then since Postman couldn't stop we clambered out.

He was foaming prodigiously at the mouth and whirling like a top despite the fact that we tried to cajole and calm and pat him. Finally he stiffened, bounded into the air and fell over dead, while we three, bare-toed in our flannel nighties, rocked back and forth on horror-stricken heels and closed in as near the corpse as we dared. The fact that in his fit of rabies he did not turn on us and bite us every one is a miracle for

27

which St. Francis is to be praised. The foam particularly fascinated Buddy, he wanted to taste it, but I held his fingers tight.

Another tight hold that saved my life though it nearly did for me too was taken by Len while we three were playing on Keefer's wharf as Papa bailed out his dinghy a few dozen yards away.

We had been trying to fish for minnows at the upper end of the float; we'd lie down on our tummies to scoop them up as they hurried by, caught in the rush of the waters. But I was getting nowhere until I spied a long bait hook lying on the wharf—it had a handle twice as tall as I and the net at the end was large and sturdy. Although it was unwieldy, I dragged it to the float's edge, then when I saw a school of minnows approaching I professionally lunged out, but the net filled quickly and dragged the handle deep beneath the stream. I held tight but with a rush it disappeared under the float and I went with it head down.

Len, who was on his stomach at my feet, grabbed hold of my ankle just as I was being sucked under. Frightened, he wound both hands around my foot and held on to me while Buds valiantly held on to him. By that time my head was under the tide and theirs so near the water's edge that Papa sloshing away at the other end of the wharf could hear no sound.

Finally Papa straightened up, turned and grasped the meaning of the tableau behind him. Len's frightened cry, "I can't hold on much longer," was just about true—another second and I would have been let go down stream, as it was I had lost consciousness. Papa hauled me out, and he believed I was drowned. With frenzy he called some Sunday idlers to his help and together they began to give me artificial respiration.

By now Len had run up the hill to the house, Mama had telephoned the fire department and before long a rescue squad with a pulmotor were at my father's elbow. They worked frantically and systematically to bring me to, it was difficult for I didn't want to come back. When my head had plunged beneath the water's surface, I took one long frightened gulp and I never got another breath of air, my lungs expelled once and refilled with tide water. The blood rushed from my toes to my nose and suddenly my head seemed to expand and explode, but softly as though it were a cotton ball fluffing out and out and out. Into my ears the waters poured strange sea lullabies and little by little, there beneath the flood a dazzling prismatic effulgence cleared my vision—not only did I see and hear harmony, but I understood everything. And slowly, as a bubble rises to the surface, I rose to the surface, rose up through the wooden platform, rose to where I could dominate the whole scene spread out beneath me. I watched my father at work on his boat, my brothers deathly frightened hanging to my spindly heels and I, my hair like seaweed, pulled flat against the submerged bottom of the float. Thus, while I drowned I saw my father turn and act, I saw my frightened brother run homewards, I saw the efforts to bring me back to life, *and I tried not to come back.*

It was the most perfect state of easeful joy that I ever experienced, then or since. There was no sadness or sickness from which I wished to escape, I was only seven, a carefree child, yet that moment in all my life has never been equalled for pure happiness. Could I have glimpsed, while drowned (for I was drowned), the freedom of eternal life? One thing I know, that Nirvana does exist between here and the hereafter—a space of delight, for I have been there.

From then my childhood flew on carefree and joyous wings —I lived almost completely in a world of make-believe. Tree houses were forest strongholds—the sloping space between the attic walls and the dormer roof was a kingdom all my own. One climbed in over the silver-trunk and then on hands and knees crawled through a narrow opening from crossbeam to crossbeam on to the far corners of a half-lit world where warriors and maidens waited to do my bidding. These hidden spaces were gradually furnished from the discarded treasures of our household—"an arras of gold" from Mama's silk petticoat, "a sumptuous service" from the dis-handled cups and chipped saucers pushed out of sight on the pantry shelf—"a rug of finest texture" from Grandma's plum-coloured carriage robe that had caught and torn beyond repair in the brougham door—and cakes and cookies were smuggled there, though I was warned not to leave crumbs about to attract the mice. In spite of this I helped my favourite mouse to rear a fat and lively family on Huntley & Palmer products.

29

We went to Keyport when I was eight. I learned to ride Mama's bicycle that summer, standing on the pedals, the saddle boring into the small of my back.

Our house faced the main street down which dray horses thundered, and the roll of varnished wheels on private equipages rattled the shutters, forever closed lest chintzes fade in the glowing sun.

Keyport, New Jersey, was a children's paradise. We rented a big white frame house with screened porches both up and down and a latticed enclosure around the kitchen door, which created a very special territory, peopled by handymen, icemen, grocery boys, and all sorts of interesting backyard implementi. From the kitchen a flagged path ran down the length of the garden through a thickly shaded grape arbour whose emerald depths were as eerie as a funnel under the sea and led to our own little beach upon the Jersey shore. This was inleted with tidal pools and tufted with sedge grass and cat-o'-nine-tails, and here and there the ebbing tide left cold wet ruffles of sand for squidging toes to scrunch. A whiff of sedge grass to-day sets me longing for those halcyon Jersey summers—my enormous lie that summer was the only cloud upon an enchanted season.

We children rarely left the shore and garden. When Grandma Jacob came to stay at the nearby Beach Hotel, and brought with her the landaulet and her prancing bays I used to be scrubbed and curled and buttoned into a starched pinafore that prickled my neck. Perched upon the little folding jump-seat, my back to the coachman, facing Mama and Grandma and their obliterating parasols, I spent many a wasted afternoon, but though I inwardly fumed envying Len and Buds their castles melting into sand, I never showed it. I was very well brought up, which did not however prevent me from learning to tell and to keep a very black lie.

The previous Christmas I had been given a string of golden beads, they were just loose enough around my neck to push up over my chin and be sucked into my mouth like a pony's bit. I could not resist chewing them and it became a habit for which I was continually reprimanded. I chewed the silk string so assiduously that one day it broke and the gold beads bounced upon the bathroom floor. I was frightened, but I told. The beads were recovered and carried to the jeweller for restringing.

I was severely scolded and warned that if it ever happened again the necklace would be taken away from me. This threat haunted my every hour, my former pastimes became a mental strain, for chew I had to—the temptation was too great, the sensuous feel of golden globules between tongue and lip was like a drug. I became an addict, and one day the necklace broke again. This time I dared not tell but with saliva-covered fingers I tried to roll the frayed ends together so that the grubby string would hold. It did hold for a day but Mama noticed the rather dirty knot and asked how it happened to be there. "I don't know," I lied. "I haven't chewed at all."

"If they break again, Polly, they will be taken away from you and given to someone who can appreciate nice things."

I was cold with unreasoned fear. That afternoon, squatting upon the beach chewing on my golden cud, I knew that I must protect my own even to the point of calumny. I sucked hard until the string gave, and I cupped my hands to hold the yellow spill. I needed something now to wrap them in, but there was nothing on the smooth wet sand and so, in desperation, I turned my thoughts to the pocket of my pinafore. I had never wilfully destroyed property before, but now I ripped the pocket out, I knotted up the golden beads into it and looked about for a hiding place. There was an old abandoned well at the bottom of the garden and into this I dropped the laden sack. They went *plump* beneath the iridescent slime, they would never be taken away from me now, and though I knew I could never revel in them again, I also knew they were forever mine. I heaved a sigh.

That evening I lied—deliberately and well. The beads I said I had put dutifully away in the nursery drawer. I wouldn't wear them any more that summer but keep them safe until we went back to New Rochelle. No one thought to look and when at the end of the summer they were found to have disappeared, movers and maids were suspected but not I. I was sick with deceit and grew thin with shame. To this day I am guilty of a pocket full of gold at the bottom of a Jersey well. I never told this to a living soul, and I don't remember that I lied again.

31

CHAPTER 3

Until I was eight I did not go to school or even to kindergarten—I do not remember ever being deliberately taught anything or asking questions. The world seemed to unfold before me rather simply—I accepted what I saw and what I heard, and what I thought or felt about it was my own intuitive response to living. I was very reticent about asking questions, always fearful that in some way I would embarrass the grown-ups or receive inadequate explanations. I was never read to; I doubt if my mother ever considered such a boring idea—no "Mother Goose," no "Peter Rabbit." The very first poetic rigmarole that I remember was "Henny Penny" or "The Little Red Hen"; this was told me at bedtime for a week or more by my Aunt Lily who, because of some parental absence, came to stay with us children. In my imagination the story built itself up into magnificent theatre—but it was recited, not read to me. After that I remember Father on Sunday evenings, a glass of port at his elbow, and with me perched on the arm of his big Morris chair, reading with smacking delight "The Bagman's Dog" and other entrancing Ingoldsby legends. He read the Bab Ballads too, with such savoury joy that for me the lines, "She long has loved you from afar, she washes for you, Captain R" and "It was a litter, a litter of five, four were drowned but one left alive" still fill my heart and ears with rapture. I longed to read, but there was no one to teach me.

And then a new world opened for me. My Cousin Ben Barnum, a few months my senior and a delicate and sensitive

1. I was the eldest : I should have hated not to be, 1898.

3. Me and Mama, 1900.

2. " Buttoned into a starched pinafore that prickled my neck ," Keyport, 1899.

4. I was taken to Mrs. Flynn's for my clothes, 1902.

5. Dick Peabody in France, December, 1917.

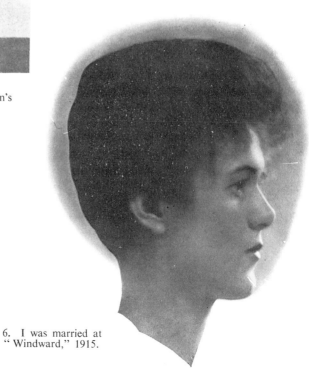

6. I was married at "Windward," 1915.

little boy, the youngest child of my Aunt Annie (Mother's sister) and Uncle Will Barnum, was to be educated at home, even day school being thought too rigorous, and a delightful young English woman, Blanche Kimber, had come out from London to America to seek her fortune as governess, and through her uncle Sir Henry Kimber, M.P., she had been steered to my aunt's door and at once accepted. But a little boy alone, especially in an enormous house with so many diversions such as ponies and stables, tree-houses and ponds, was in need of a playmate and fellow student as well, and I was the logical one. I was his age and my education was about to become a problem to my parents. "Windward" was only a few miles away, so the arrangements were made. I was to spend from Monday morning to Saturday morning at Windward and the weekends at home. My aunt and uncle offered to educate and care for me in return for my companionship to Ben.

When on the first Monday their smart trap drove up to our door with a liveried groom holding the reins, I was hopping with impatience to be in and off. My minute Vuitton trunk and hand bags were stowed under the seat and with hurried kisses to Mama and Papa and no thought at all for Len or Buds, I was off in a spurt of gravel.

Some weeks later I overheard Mama tearfully telling Papa that she felt as if she had bartered her daughter in the market-place, this because it had been announced on Saturday that the groom would call for me Sunday afternoon instead of Monday morning, and I had heartlessly cried, "Oh, goody!"

At Windward I had my own little room especially decorated in dotted swiss and garlanded chintz. My windows looked out over the kitchen circle at the back of the house. The laundry door and the buttery door were there, too; the kitchen garden and grape arbour just over the driveway and a continual stream of back-steps life going on beneath my inquisitive eyes. There was a big bathroom across the hall with a thick cherry red carpet delightfully soothing to bare toes. The bath was shared by Miss Kimber and by the green guest room. The pink guest room beyond the stairs had a bath of its own and was known as the "best room." Aunt Annie and Uncle Will lived in their wing and Ben shared a room with his elder brother next the schoolroom and the playroom. This was important because he had access to the playthings early in the morning; but I was a lazybones anyway and have always loved to linger in bed of a morning holding tight to the unravelling web of dreams.

As soon as I came under Miss Kimber's nimble care, the story books of childhood were opened for me. She read to us every evening in the library after our early supper. We began with *Captains Courageous* and *Scottish Chiefs* (why?), and then *Ivanhoe*. From this moment I entered another world, the world of romance. My hair became "tresses," my pinafores "silken robes" and Mary Sodan, the upstairs maid, and the waitresses and cooks and laundresses, "sweet servitors."

I had not been at Windward long before the most exciting event of my life took place. *I learned to read.* I had been trying with all my might to master the lessons in our schoolroom but for a while the printed page did not come alive, until one rainy afternoon as I was sitting cross-legged on Miss Kimber's chaise longue underneath the canary cage with "Rose, Tom and Ned" opened in my lap suddenly the eighteen-point words connected! Rose was actually saying something real to Tom, and Ned was running down the hill to join them. I was electrified. I turned the page to see if the spell would fade—but no, Ned and Tom were helping Rose over a fence, into the pasture. There were no pictures and yet I could see it all. I jumped to my feet. "Oh, Miss Kimber, Miss Kimber, I can read," I cried, and suddenly tears gushed from my eyes. I fell sobbing on her shoulder. "There, there," she soothed, "of course you can, and I am so glad for you, dear." That night with Rose, Tom and Ned beneath my pillow I was wafted around the world and back, but to the grownups' dismay, reading now completely absorbed me. I carried a book everywhere, dipped into it at every odd moment, gobbled my meals so I could get back to it, woke early in the morning so I could read before breakfast. Then headaches began. I was forbidden to read except for an hour after supper. I was so frantic that I tried to devour several books at once, spreading them about me on the rug; then luckily spring came and out-of-doors was more beguiling. The after-supper hour was devoted to croquet and chasing fireflies or playing tree-house under the Japanese willow on the lawn and so the fever subsided.

"Hillandale" was a neighbouring stock farm for the breeding and training of young trotting horses, and lay just across Quaker Ridge Road.

It happened that when I was about ten, a race track was built at Hillandale, and of early mornings the trials were clocked and the young thoroughbreds conditioned. Lou Dillon, as I remember, was a filly foaled of a Kentucky sire and a Hillandale dam. With every trial spin, she became more and more swift, more and more exciting to watch and to handle.

I had known her and petted her in the fields from her infancy. She was my favourite. She was to be sent to Louisville for the big race that June, and her timing was kept a top secret. I had been allowed now and then to drive the sulkies at a walk, up and back before the judges' stand—my feet did not reach the leather foot-rests but were tucked in under the sheep-lined traces, my spindly legs stretched wide as a nutcracker's.

It was the morning before Lou Dillon was to be shipped south. I went over early to bid her Godspeed, she was harnessed and waiting for a final spin, the stable boy at her head. I climbed onto the spidery seat of the sulky as I so often did and begged to have the reins. "They'll be coming along soon," said the lad, looking anxiously over his shoulder toward the stables. But it was still very early. "Just let me walk her up and back," I begged. My accomplice nodded. "Clock me," I called, as I gathered up the ribbons and started sedately the slow way round. But when I turned Lou Dillon's head, the goddess of speed seemed to nip her in the ear. Like a jet, she went into her loveliest stride. I hung on, hair flying, the ground rolling by below my opened knees which were stretched to the aching point. The boy shouted to no avail, we were off to win.

She did not break, around we went like Lucifer and would have gone around again, but I believe the agonized plea in my "whoa-ing" voice reached the thoroughbred ear, for suddenly, just past the judges' stand, she broke and slowed to a docile halt.

Of course I knew I weighed many pounds lighter than her regular jockey, but the lad insisted that Lou Dillon had never done the mile so fast before. A world record, he assured me, had been broken that morning (maybe even faster than the world record she established at Louisville a few days later). But we three have kept it a secret until now—the lad, Lou Dillon and I.

May was full of hidden mystery that year. Miss Kimber was reading us *The Faerie Queen*. Sap that penetrated the roots of oak and willow—daffodil and trailing arbutus—seemed to tingle my roots as well. Instead of the froglike tummy of babyhood, I was slimming at the waist and rounding at the thighs and my hair was turning from ash to gold. I was alone one sunny noonday perched on the stone wall at the far end of Hillandale pasture. The young thoroughbreds nuzzled at their mother's flanks and scampered through the daisy-filled meadows with such animal joy that I was inevitably drawn to their playground. This far corner of the farm seemed peculiarly their own. Here the horses were at ease, and I was the intruder—but a welcome one I sensed. I tried to lure the mares and their babies to me with lumps of sugar, but they were jumpy and so easily flustered that I had to content myself with sitting there swinging my bare legs and sucking the sticky bribes all by myself.

From this contentment I was startled that noontide by an urgent whinny behind me and the quick thrashing of hoofs on twigs. Turning, I looked straight into the dilated eyes of a coal-black yearling. He was trembling and I began to tremble too. I took the wet bit of sugar from between my lips and proffered it, tempting him to me. His nostrils wide, he approached tentatively, one foot pawing his desire. I swung my legs over to his side of the wall, which sent him stampeding backward almost sitting down upon his quivering haunches, then gingerly he approached again. I saw flecks of foam at the corners of his mouth. I was both frightened and fascinated. Some monstrous force was pulling us together as the moon pulls the tide—and once again I heard the unearthly singing of cosmic harmony as I had heard it before underneath the tide of Keefer's wharf. We looked at each other entranced and then he sprang toward me, pawing the wall. Frightened

36

into reality, I somersaulted backward landing ignominiously in a bed of nettles and cow dung. For one awful second I saw the wild hoofs flaying the skyline about the wall, but he was too near to leap it. I took no chances then. Grabbing a handy stone, I hurled it with all my might and main. With a whinny of fury and heartbreak, the animal pirouetted and fled away through the echoing woods. By this time all the mares and foals were racing excitedly around and around the meadow. One of the stable men hearing the commotion ran down the field to see what was amiss. He found me scratched and dirty with a twisted ankle and in tears. I had fallen off the wall, I said, that was all. He listened to me unconvinced but helped me to hobble home, while I looked warily at every quadruped I passed. I crept in through the laundry and up to my room without being seen, then I locked myself into a blessed hot bath and scrubbed and scrubbed, my hair, my feet, my arms, my heart.

I always went alone to the trotting track, but when tree-houses were to be built, or a homemade raft to be launched on Dickerman's Pond, we were numerous. There was Ben, although he was never the leader, and the Steerses—Harry and Coster—who lived on Quaker Ridge about three miles away beyond the golf course and who were the bane of my young life. Pulling hair, jumping down on me from trees, pushing me into a corner to be smackingly kissed, were all horrors these two indulged in. Once at a birthday party, bewitched by patent leather, bow tie, and sash, Harry Steers became timid and I became self-conscious. The game of Post Office brought us shyly to the border line of inhibition, but luckily healthy exhibitionism won the moment. The building of tree-houses and hidden house-keeping had stirred strange hormones from their slumber. I was growing, too.

It was during these years that I learned to skate and that I learned to ride; both were considered necessary accomplishments. It was at Dorland's Riding Academy on N.Y.'s west side (a part of town only suitable for horses) that Belle Beach Bayne, the equestrienne par excellence of our day, instructed little girls in the elegant ritual of horsemanship.

First, de Pinna made me a very fine bottle green riding

habit—long flowing skirt and smart box jacket—I wore a small brown bowler and brown leather gauntlets and boots. At first I walked my mount around the tanbark ring sitting as straight as a ramrod should, the next lesson I was allowed to jog on the end of a leading rein and finally to reach a really brisk trot round and round. It was at the eighth lesson only that I was taken to the park, still on a leading rein. Eventually, by the eighteenth lesson I trotted proudly by myself and cantered demurely around the reservoir in company with two or three other pupils. These lessons cost a lot, one had to take all eighteen, but when later on I hunted with the Quorn I appreciated that I had been well taught at Dorland's.

The skating lessons took place at St. Nicholas Rink where Saturday morning classes were as hard to get into as into the needle's eye. One's name was put down, considered, voted on by dowagers and if approved, one's governess accompanied one there on Saturday mornings and sat behind one like a witness in a court room. Wabbling ankles and a tendency to clutch at the side rail were with persistence overcome. Each little girl or boy had five minutes' exclusive attention given them by the instructor and I remember music, mittens, and muffs, but my ankles were weak and I never did learn to skate properly. I wished I could remain on double runners with the tots in Central Park, but accomplishments were the progression of my education. I could not retrogress.

The same winter I went to dancing school. "Mr. Dodsworth's Dancing Class for Young Ladies and Gentlemen" or Dodsworth's, as it was more informally spoken of (although this gilded institution was never slightingly alluded to), was the kind of mauve-decade exaggeration that could only have existed in the same city and era as Jay Gould and Diamond Jim Brady, Mrs. Astor and Barnum and Bailey. Mr. and Mrs. Dodsworth were superbly cast and undoubtedly had cast themselves in their role, possibly as escapists from some rural fair grounds. Their approach to their problem was beautifully theatrical and their set-up has become historical. I am sure many of my readers can remember it all quite vividly, even to the ten golden rules, gilt-embossed upon Tiffany's heaviest pasteboard. Rule Number 9: "Ladies should finish dressing before entering the ballroom."

That is why one's Nanny followed one to the very portals of red damask, twitching one's sash behind or one's belt before, so that emerging into the spotlight of one hundred maternal eye-power one would do one's home team credit.

First a curtsy to Mr. Dodsworth, who stood by the door. Mr. Dodsworth returned the curtsy with a bow from a waist so elegantly slender and perfectly appointed in crispest tails that a mere bob would hardly have done it credit. Then wobbling slightly, skirts held wide above lisle-stockinged knees (socks were ruled out), one advanced as at the Durbar to a raised dais of red plush, on which regal elevation was seated in a Cleopatra chair (a piece of furniture easily recognizable from history books because of the serpents) a presence so sumptuously adorned and plumply smiling that like Cleopatra or Queen Victoria, once seen it was never forgotten. Mrs. Dodsworth had a beautiful ageless appearance, as if preserved in syrup. Her low-cut evening dresses (of which there were seven) always showed a well-embanked cleft descending. Her dimpled arms were ganted in shoulder-length white kid (Rule Number 6, "In the ballroom ladies and gentlemen should always wear gloves"). In her symmetrically waved hair their blazed a tiny diadem or crescent—not too large. Her satin slipper just protruded far enough beneath a satin hemline to show a large *diamanté* buckle, and a glittering fan played an important role. In other parts, she was hung festooned and ringed with brilliants. This was *Ballroom* at its most splendid and into our small intelligences (into mine, at any rate) was thereby wedged a very real awe of pomp and ceremony. After a very low obeisance (in which one's panty buttons nearly gave) one took one's place, upon a chair, to the right of the throne. The goat-boys went to the left, as on the Day of Judgment.

As a grand finale, the boys were asked to walk (not slide) across the polished floor and hand on stomach invite and lead forth a partner to the dance. This number never went very well. There was always a good deal of giggling, some pinching, and deliberate bumps and several damsels woefully left in distress (for the girls naturally outnumbered the boys). To have to waltz about in the hands of another little girl was utter hell.

At the end of the season a graduation contest was given by

39

invitation. I don't know where Mr. Dodsworth procured his social list, but no error was ever made (public relations councils were not then invented, or the name of Dodsworth would now be written in the sky) and Jews or their affiliates were weeded from his patronage like dandelions from the front lawn, which goes to show that Mr. Dodsworth's dancing class was even more difficult to enter than the orange and black confines of "the Book." Some of the little girls appeared that day in rather richer ruffles than usual, but not I. My smartness, Mother and Aunt Annie were sure, was due to my tailored Russian blouses with crimson embroidered collar and cuffs and wide black patent leather belt. My hair fell below my waist and was tied painfully right on top with an enormous black taffeta bow. I danced in black pumps and long black lisle stockings. My costume did have style, but at the age of nine I yearned for eyelet ruffles and corkscrew curls and Viva Fisher had both. It was humiliating. In spite of my starched and frill-less skirt, I managed to win the awarded gold badge, but I took no pride in a decoration that could not be pinned upon a furbelow, and my dancing-school days got me as nearly into uniform as I ever care to be!

I was taken to Mrs. Flynn's for my clothes. In those days one did not buy things ready-made; even little girls were measured and fitted and fussed over by competent dressmakers or the family seamstress; and we were always *completely* clothed, even on the beaches. To wear a sun-suit next to one's skin, or to drive or to ride without coat and hat and gloves, was unheard of. Mrs. Flynn had made me, for afternoon walks in the park, a beautifully tailored tan velveteen coat with large Irish lace shawl collar. My floppy hat was of layer upon layer of accordian-pleated black chiffon. The elastic under my chin held it firmly in place; so firmly that when I took it off it left a round red line like a knife wound encircling my throat with a redder spot where the chewed knot rested and rubbed.

Via *St. Nicholas* Magazine, a guiding light, we joined the Saturday Club, which was invented and run by the artist Walter Russell and his wife. Each Saturday some member of the club invited the others to play and picnic at their country house, wherever it was—Long Island, Staten Island, New Jersey or Connecticut. Our first outing was arranged by Natica Nast's father Condé (Editor of *Vogue*); the second by the redheaded Lanes from Brooklyn—their cupolaed pile was on Brooklyn Heights; enormous grounds with rolling lawns overlooking New York. Walter Russell took these opportunities to sketch the young at play—the expensive young—and that is why his book *The Sea Children* was glamourized by such elegant little models as Helene Demarest, Natica Nast and Polly Jacob. If you get hold of a copy you will see what I mean.

Charles Dana Gibson turned up at one of these Saturday frolics, and he too has chronciled our pulchritude. He even persuaded my family to allow me to pose in his studio in my velveteen coat and ruffled hat. In one of the published albums of his drawings, 1904, you can see me being dragged up Fifth Avenue by an enormous St. Bernard, my governess at my heels. He called it "The Younger Generation." There were other scenes in which I appeared. When *Life* Magazine recently reported that the artist's widow was the only Gibson Girl extant, I nearly came forward, but then thought better of it. The vintage had reached its lees—bringing back to light old likenesses can often encourage sorcery. About 1935, *Town and Country* republished several society "shots" from an issue of twenty-five years before, side by side with present-day pictures. Mine was among them. The comparison was not too hard to take because in 1910, we all wore poodle fringes over our eyes and baggy shapeless garments hung straight from the shoulder —in 1935, at least the brow and shape emerged. I was rather pleased with my progression, but such chronology dates the victim.

The real Gibson Girl prototype was of course more grown up than I. My mother, my aunts and many others, typical Gibson Girls, wore big pompadours, sailor hats skewered on with devilish-looking hatpins and high starched collars with bow tie to fasten their finely pleated shirtwaists. Tennis and golf were played in *long* white linen skirts and starched petticoats that dragged the course and went into the laundry with bright grass stains bordering the hem's edge—one wonders now how the family laundress, without "Tide" or "Duz" or "Surf," ever

41

managed to get them so pristine white again. In those days a laundress in the house was as usual as salt in the ice-cream freezer. It was still 1904.

During club outings I had a decidedly biological reaction to the handsome redheaded Brooklyn Lanes—not one in particular, but all three. They were very well mannered and very well groomed boys. They wore Eton collars and long trousers. Harry and Coster Steers were not nearly as exciting to hide with.

The Saturday on which the club visited Windward, I was in a state of happy terror—it was my first taste of the heady estate of "hostess." I suffered agonies of apprehension. Would it rain; would they come; what would we play? But once the party started I enjoyed it to its fullest—and to this day I still do enjoy my own parties best. But Miss Kimber and *St. Nicholas* taught me how.

It was during Lent that I first fell in love. The family had a pew in St. Thomas', the fashionable Episcopalian cathedral on Fifth Avenue, where Dr. Stires, then nearing thirty and very handsome and dramatic, though unwittingly lust-provoking, preached on Sundays to a congregation of enthralled ladies and perturbed gentlemen (only the children were indifferent). My Aunt Lucy, lately widowed, was one of the faithful lambs who swooned with devotion. Our pew was way up front under the lectern and I usually sat on the end so I could see better; also I could almost touch the clergy and choir as they, hymn singing, swung slowly up the aisle to take their places beyond the pulpit railing. It was on my third Sunday that I felt a nudge from a cassocked elbow as a freckle-nosed choir boy brushed past me. I was amazed that such a thing could happen in church. I glued my eyes upon him. He sat on the end of his row, too, and I was certain that as he genuflected he winked. I knew then that he was a man I could love and I, like my aunt, became an ardent churchgoer. I asked to be allowed to attend evensong with her during Lent and I joined a Bible class on Sundays—anything to keep me near the object of my love. He never missed nudging me, he always winked, but at service's end he filed with the others out the vestry door beneath the arch, and though I got out as quickly as I decently could, we never met. Because of him, however, I was confirmed that

42

Easter, packed layettes on Thursdays, went to church twice on Sundays and once on weekdays; and while Dr. Stires, with his rhetoric and his profile, moved his grown-up parishioners, I took fire from the choir's sensual proximity and my heart was lifted to exaltation in the power and the glory of that cherubic wink. I believe his voice changed before the autumn and so the church lost not only a heavenly tenor but also a most ardent disciple, for I stopped going altogether (except on Sundays) and instead, fell in love with the coalman's son from New Rochelle —Robbie Mahlstead. I found no charm in the sons of family friends; that is, until Ben went off to boarding school and Miss Kimber took me to spend a week end at Westminster to see how he was doing. The school was at Simsbury, Conn. It was run by Mr. and Mrs. Cushing and their sons, Bill, who taught something advanced, and Tom, who wrote and directed rather surrealistic school plays. Each time I attended chapel, and it was a church school, I noticed that Hymn 602 was on the hymn board. And as soon as we rose, "I Need Thee, O I Need Thee" in all its adolescent agony rang forth while two hundred pairs of eyes were riveted on my burning cheeks. Tom Cromwell, a bespectacled first-grader, whose duty it was to list the hymns, told me, years later, that when I appeared he always supplied 602 for the eyes and throats of my otherwise mute venerators.

That summer I accompanied my family again to East Island. It was the summer that Father discovered diamonds on the beach. East Island Diamonds, we called them. Some of the stones were as large as robins' eggs and when faceted and set were for all the world as fine as Kimberleys—for all our world, at any rate. Father had hatpins and veilpins and earrings big as chandelier drops cut for Mother and for all the aunts. I unfortunately was too young to wear diamonds and so missed out on the visitation, for it *was* a visitation I am sure. During a year or more along the several miles of beach, diamonds would appear washed up by the tide. Some merchants pooh-poohed them, some were thrown into a state of wild excitement, but one and all admitted it was hard to tell the difference, and what they were was a mystery. Had some deep-sea current dashed a rock of crystal to bits against our beachhead or had some sunken galleon from pirate days spilled its treasures out

43

upon our shores? But the spell was broken when we sold the island. The same current must have swooped them up again, for when my Father went back a few years later with an assayer to visit East Island, which then belonged to J. P. (Uncle Jack) Morgan, every trace of the diamond jetsam had disappeared. To think that with a little pail and shovel I might have changed the course of history! For I always believe that had I had diamonds enough to finance the dreams I have dreamed, much that is wrong with the world would never have come to pass. But we used our pails and shovels for digging clams instead. Dosoris Pond was full of clams and there was a big sluice pen under the bridge by the keeper's lodge where the hard-shell ones were dumped for fattening. They were big and sweet and cold in the running tidewater. One of our privileges was to take off shoes and socks and climb down into the pen, scooping up handfuls of the lovely mollusks. They were hard to open, stubbornly sucking their sides together, but the keeper helped with his clam hook and once open, it was heaven to sip their icy juices and nibble at their cold firm bellies, our feet in the rushing sluice. We went to bed by sunset light; there was no time at all for reading.

That winter Aunt Annie and Uncle Will took a "brownstone front" on the corner of Fifty-seventh and Madison Avenue—still properly residential—and that is where with Ben's help I published "The Madison Avenue Gazette." It was a gelatin board production, the ink was very purple and quite runny; the circulation leapt from ten to twenty copies in the first month and I believe that that progression would have continued indefinitely had my staff stuck with me. The editorials, society and sports columns, the poems and the serial had to be written by me. That is, I composed them; transferring them to the gelatin and from thence to the sheets of the Gazette was a mere manual task though a very necessary one. But after two numbers master-printer Ben lost gumption; in fact, struck. Mary Sodan helped me on her afternoon off and Miss Kimber came to my rescue to save the fourth number from oblivion. But after that, though struggling valiantly for life, the publication flickered and went out. I have a copy before me; the date is December, 1902. The leading editorial is on the joys of skating.

The serial is embarrassingly reminiscent of *Hans Brinker or the Silver Skates*, and the Society Column begins with the frigid item, "While skating on Dickerman's Pond last Sunday, Mr. Henry sat on a tack and tore his new trousers. Miss Kimber sewed him up." Perhaps the "one-man" approach to publishing is what ruins such ventures, and how unsparingly history repeats itself. Could it be that *Portfolio* has lately languished for the self-same reasons?

That winter Miss Kimber subscribed to *St. Nicholas* for us, and our horizons ramified. There were story and poetry contests and photograph contests. No need for my own publication now, I could go on to country-wide renown and I toiled valiantly every month to do so. The nearest I came that winter was honourable mention for a drawing entitled "My Pet." It was, I recall, of a lizard in a bottle. That summer I won the gold medal for a snapshot "Our Picnic," but I received one horrid blow because of a matter of vocabulary. There was to be a June award for a poem of not more than fourteen lines on "Spring" by contestants under ten. At Windward in May of that year I had written with exuberance and many heart throbs my ode to the joy-packed season. I did my composing half leaning, half sitting against the terraced bank below the tennis court, hidden on one side by the back net, bursting with crimson rambler buds, and on the other by the branches of the great willow's frond-trailing fingers to curtain my retreat from the lawn behind. From here I could see but not be seen. Only a few feet above me Miss Kimber's window gave onto the lawn. Bits of conversation like broken biscuits fed my subconscious; my own world was snug around me like a chrysalis, but the vista before me had no bounds nor limits. Here I chewed my pencil, rhymed "love" with "dove" and was perfectly happy. And here I had composed my first poem. It began, "O wonderful, beautiful Springtime world." Now that *St. Nicholas* offered me recognition for my opus, I decided to turn it in. But I wanted it printed in proper form, businesslike, as it would appear in a business letter. I asked my uncle how I could get a poem "printed." I thought he would say, "Why, my dear, I'll take it to the office and have Miss Moody do it for you." Instead he said, "I think there is a little printer over on Sixth Avenue at about Forty-eighth."

One afternoon with Mary Sodan I went forth, in laureate spirit. We easily found the modest shop, W. H. Smith (I don't think the "& Sons" were affixed at that time). I showed Mr. Smith my poem, blushing deeply, and asked if he could "print" it for me. "Certainly," he said. "How many copies?" "Two, I guess," I gulped. "But my dear young lady, two will be very expensive for you." "Then only one," I compromised. So he explained that he meant anything less than one hundred would be about the same price. I was astonished. "How much will it cost?" He couldn't really tell, but I settled for twenty-five copies and was worried when he told me it would take ten days. The contest closed in ten days. I persuaded him to do it in eight. He took my name and address solemnly and, as a parting puzzle, questioned, "Shall I include who it is printed for?" "Why, yes, of course," I said, not knowing what or where he meant. I had a letter to *St. Nicholas* ready when I went to fetch my order the following week. The job cost all my savings, and to my disappointment was not "printed" at all. That is, it *was* printed in W. H. Smith's best Goudy italic, but what I wanted was a "typed" copy. The word type had not yet entered my vocabulary, and I had not known how to explain! I folded up the formidable, sheet, at the bottom of which in small block letters appeared "Printed for Miss Jacob of 571 Madison Avenue, New York City." It would have to go that way. The poem I still believed was a *chef d'oeuvre*.

When almost immediately after that an impressively "typed" envelope from *St. Nicholas, a Publication* arrived for Miss Jacob of 571 Madison Avenue, my fingers felt for the gold medal before tearing it open. Instead, my poem dropped out, and in a terse letter Mary Mapes Dodge had reprimanded me, "St. Nicholas does not accept published material!" My eyes were swollen with tears and red as port by suppertime. The fact that "Spring" constituted my first limited edition as a publisher and thereby added twenty-five years to such standing (les Editions Narcisse's *first* was in 1927) could not at that time justify the hurt.

CHAPTER 4

In my whole life I have never gone hungry, except once, when I was ten. Then I had a sudden attack of appendicitis and for four days the doctor prescribed a diet of rice and cambric tea (hot water, milk and sugar). I was allowed to eat all the rice I wanted to, so by Chinese standards, I was still well fed, but by my own I was being starved. Even if I had known then that two-thirds of the children of the world were truly starving, I doubt if my plight would have seemed either more or less doleful. The hungry children of the world were never brought to my attention; unlike to-day the East was very remote in 1905.

In spite of my four days' fast, another attack came on, and I was hurried into town to Roosevelt Hospital on dingy West Fifty-ninth Street where I was hovered over by family and nurses and attended by fiery-bearded Dr. Brewer. And there I was separated from my simian appendage—when it was brought to me in a bottle I felt not only sick to death, but I burst into a barrage of tears. I have often thought it would be fun to wag a tail, but never an appendix!

Alice Roosevelt (now Longworth), daughter of President Theodore Roosevelt for whom the hospital was named, was having hers out at the same time—she was almost grown-up and "a perfect hoyden" the nurses said—I remember that when she was convalescing and able to propel herself around in a wheelchair, she used to race down the inclined corridors, scattering internes right and left. I could hear her whoop past my

47

door and admired her very much, though *I* wouldn't want to behave like that!

This was in June. Appendicitis was a new and major operation then, my scar was six inches long and it itched. In July, I was taken to Kennebunkport, Maine, for the rest of the summer and because I was a convalescent, Uncle Will hired a black nag and a four-wheeled buggy for me to get about in. I did the driving myself. I had learned to drive at Hillandale, and I was the envy of every little girl in the place—the boys pretended not to care.

Back at Windward Ben and Miss Kimber and I used to drive Kim, the pony, in the governess cart, a two-wheeler with a square fluted basket body, entered from the rear—if it had had a hooped handle over our heads, it would have looked very much like a flower basket, and when these carts were filled with flower-faced children, they did, with a governess stuck in the middle, stiff as a trowel.

One of the delights of town was the Burton Holmes lectures. That year Ben, Miss Kimber, and I had season tickets. Once a week during the winter we took part in the life of other lands —lands as exotic and as fabulous as ancient Troy or Crusoe's Isle—were it Paris or Pekin, Tibet or Timbuctoo, Burton Holmes with his seductive voice and necromantic wand, brought such a surreal quality to the colour plates reflected through his magic lantern that no realer voyage could ever surpass those taken in Carnegie Hall.

The memorable afternoon that, seated in a dangling basket, we were pulled up the purple crags to the fabulous heights of a Tibetan monastery, I can hear Burton Holmes' chilling pronouncement as we swung in air, "What if the rope should break."

I nearly fainted then and my heart beat like a drum; before we left the hall I walked away with awed eyes, too transfixed to talk. I never have visited Tibet but I hope I never do; one land should remain for ever as I knew it then—the Never Never land of the magic lantern.

I heard Caruso sing *Butterfly* that winter and I saw William Farnum in *The Squaw Man*.

Uncle Will and Aunt Annie kept open house on Sunday

evenings. We often went out to Windward for week ends but came back into town for Sunday supper. Lobster Newburgh, hot biscuit, cold meat and salad and for dessert, pistache layer cake oozing with chopped walnuts and cream—the menu never varied, "Thanks God," as Mr. Enke used to say.

Mr. Enke from Germany spent a winter with us especially to paint Uncle Will's and Aunt Annie's portraits and the big panel of a woodland glade over the fireplace at Windward. Mr. Ezekiel, sculptor, from Rome, came too to do the family busts; in these family duties I was not included ("Thanks God").

When Ben went to boarding school I was enrolled at Miss Chapin's and I became one of the privileged neophytes of learning in a brown Holland apron. We all wore aprons; they were cut square at the neck with long sleeves and full pleated skirts and buttoned on over one's other dresses.

The school, that first year, was in a brownstone house in the East Sixties. Miss Fairfax taught mathematics, Miss Wheelright taught Latin, and Miss Chapin taught everything else.

The halls were narrow, the stairs steep, and our desks crowded into dark little rooms without proper ventilation, but it was a good school and very fashionable. I learned easily but could not make friends easily.

In my class were Vera Bloodgood, Ursula Brown, Gwen Condon, Lisa Stillman, and daughters of other well-known New York families but I, unlike the others, never had a "best friend."

I remember only two incidents in all three years. One when I was called upon to give first aid to Miss Chapin, the ceiling having collapsed on her head, the other during Easter vacation when a forgotten roast-beef sandwich went atrociously bad inside my desk and smelled so putrid that I didn't dare lift the cover for fear someone else might get a whiff of the rotten cache. I suffered agonies for days, having to get on with lessons as best I could without books. Finally, I made some desperate excuse to stay after school and while the classroom was deserted, I crept back holding my nose. I managed to whisk the sandwich out and wrap it up in my Holland apron. This I carried home with the excuse it had to be laundered, and I managed to shake the awful thing into the gutter behind Mary Nash's back as we crossed Madison Avenue. I was mortally afraid of being apprehended when I did so—to be responsible for this bad smell was to me a criminal offence and I imagined myself a lifer at Sing Sing if ever I were caught. That sandwich looms as the greatest horror of my adolescence. It was not that sandwiches were against the rules, it was not that I deliberately left it there to rot, why then did it affect me so? To this day I prefer a toothache to a bad smell and a stone to a roast-beef sandwich.

We used to spend our summers at Southampton, Long Island. It was July, 1906, I was fourteen and discovering golf and tennis. I had been swimming and my hair was wet, hanging in dripping ringlets. I couldn't have looked worse. My jabot had lost its guimpe and my white duck skirt had a big grass stain over the knee where I had slid into the bunker on the sixteenth hole earlier that morning. Then, coming up the path that led from the tennis court to the dunes, I met him face to face—a god in flannels—Apollo in a blazer. He wore a towel for a muffler as Englishmen do and he was swinging his racket viciously at the goldenrod that grew along the path. He was an older man, at least twenty-two, and I dropped my eyes in humility as I brushed by. And then in some incredible manner the ribbons of my leghorn entangled his racket—we were literally tied in a bow-knot.

"Oh, I say, I am sorry," he apologized and pulled.

"It doesn't matter at all, it's an old hat." I blushed.

"But a ripping one," he said, and it literally was at that moment, so we laughed and he said, "I think I owe you a new hat instead of an apology."

"Oh, gracious no, please," I stammered and fled. He watched from the end of the path, for I looked back from the bend in the hedge, and it was just exactly then I knew that at last I was really in love.

The rest of the day dragged by on leaden feet. Would I meet him again? I didn't see how, for he was surely one of the magnificent team being entertained all over the place, while I was still too young to go out at night; that is, to grown-up parties.

I passed by the tennis court three times for the mail that afternoon. I swam again at two and at five, but no Olympian, only an empty, overwhelming ache in my astonished heart.

I couldn't eat dinner and started early to bed, so that I would be alone to hug my agony—and then the miracle happened. Uncle Will called up to say that he and Aunt Annie had an extra ticket for *The Wizard of Oz* at the Town Hall and could I go to celebrate, for it was to be quite a gala evening on acccount of the tennis. They would call for me in twenty minutes. I never dressed so fast or so frantically before. *He* would surely be there—would he like my yellow organdy or my dotted swiss best? They both seemed inadequate. The dots won and I added a dab of dorine to the end of a sunburned nose, feeling very unequal to such an occasion.

The play was so enthralling that the ache in my heart was calmed, but only until the curtain went down at the end of the first act. And then I suddenly remembered—the elevator sensation came back. I looked shyly around me but he wasn't there. The seats next to us were vacant to the aisle. I had a great desire to slip out and run away—I scarcely knew where. Then the lights dimmed, the Prince was singing of love again, when suddenly I knew that *he* was there beside me in the dark. I turned my head just as he turned his and our faces nearly collided.

"You," he whispered.

I looked quickly back to the stage in a sort of unhappy ecstasy, and then I felt his fingers closing on mine. I was too dizzy to know what went on on the stage, but I kept my eyes glued there in fright.

"You look even more adorable than this morning," he whispered again, as the lights went up.

I was so afraid that my aunt or uncle would notice that I deliberately turned away and talked to my cousin Laura, knowing there was another act to come. It did come, and this time long, strong fingers caressed my knee. I shivered. I shook. I was nearly in tears—but what could I do!

The play was over now. The final curtain. Love was ending now. The lights came on, when abruptly Uncle Will leaned across and said :

51

"Why, hello, Archie. You *are* Skeffington-Jones' boy, aren't you?"

And he *was*. Archibald Skeffington-Jones, 3rd, Singles Runner-up for the visiting team. Oh, joy, oh, joy—and before I knew it Uncle Will and Aunt Annie invited us all to their house for "refreshments" and I was skipping down the driveway to the Brewster Wagon properly introduced to the man of my dreams.

Uncle Will had rented the most wonderful house on the island. Everyone knew it. The gardens were famous. So when Skeffington-Jones asked if I would show him the gardens by moonlight everyone said, " Of course, only don't get lost." And blushingly I found myself leading him away into a world of unreality. The moonlight drenched the roses and heliotrope; the katydids sang in the dense shadows of the box; the warm sea air fanned our cheeks and in the summer-house beyond the lily pool deep shadows wound around us as his arm wound around my waist and his eyes drew closer and closer to mine.

"Oh, you mustn't," I protested, and I said it again. But his free hand tilted up my chin and then, and then . . . . It was my very first kiss—that kind—and I didn't know what I should do. But he held me away at arms' length and looked at me for a long minute so gravely and so tenderly that this time it was I who lifted my face to his and flung my arms around his neck. In that moment I gave all of my heart, my past and my future. I was weak and trembling when we drew apart.

"I love you so," I said.

"You funny kid," he answered.

"It will be forever, won't it?" I was suddenly afraid, and again I wound my arms around his neck. But he pushed me away roughly.

"Don't be a foolish child," he answered me. "We must get back to the house."

"Oh, no, I can't go back now." Tears were in my eyes.

"Well, stay here, then. I'm going anyway. You come along when you want to." He dragged my arms away and strode angrily down the garden path.

I was shaking with sobs and my heart was breaking. Later

Miss Kimber found me all in a heap on the summer-house floor.

"We were worried about you," she said. "Archie told us you had lost something and couldn't find it in the dark; he went off to fetch a flashlight but he hasn't come back."

"It was my gold heart," I answered with my fingers lifted to an imaginary locket. "I'll look for it in the morning. Oh, Miss Kimber, I am so unhappy." She drew my arm lovingly through hers.

"That little heart would be a great loss," she said tenderly, as she led me safely toward the lighted house. "But I think I understand. Let us go around by the stables and say good night to the puppies. Perhaps that will make you feel happier."

I nodded through my tears, knowing that she was wrong and that I'd never, never feel happy again as long as I lived. And for at least ten days I didn't. Then gradually the gulp in my throat subsided.

In August I won the mixed foursome Junior Golf Tournament with Henry Rea for partner. At the age of sixteen Henry had to shave twice a day and he owned a Stutz Bearcat. Although I no longer believed in men, I was fascinated by his masculinity and also by the fact that his parents were not in the Social Register because "they came from Out West." His background and his beard both smacked excitingly of the hinterlands. His Stutz to me was a full-blooded mustang and although our friendship was one of austere propriety, I felt that it was a very reckless affair indeed, even leading me one evening after the Lawn Club dance to an inland night spot where we ordered ginger ale, and Henry, though not of age, poured gin into his from a pocket flask. It was all terribly daring, and this helped me to forget my heartache through September.

I met Cole Porter at my first Yale Prom. It was during my second year at Rosemary and I was in a state of nervous delight at having received the coveted invitation. I was actually sixteen, but as shy as a periwinkle, withdrawing into my shell with the periwinkle's timid twink whenever I came face to face with the sophisticates of the world—of which the graduating class at Yale was made up.

I was allowed by my family and school to accept the invitation, provided a chaperone went with me, and as my Cousin Walter Barnum had invited a Southern debutante to the Prom, it was arranged that we both should go to New Haven under Miss Kimber's fluttering wing.

My aunt and my duenna chose my Prom dress (my mother was in Texas). I was taken to Mrs. Flynn's for it. I had nothing to say, nor would I have dared disagree. They decided on a white eyelet embroidery with voluminous ruffled skirts like a petticoat and a square ruffled collar with a high boned guimpe of Valenciennes lace. The skirt came just above my ankles and as usual I wore a black taffeta hair ribbon on the top of my head, my hair hung down my back as it always had, and of course there was no question of powder or lipstick.

My travelling suit was of blue serge, double-breasted like a boy's. I felt miserably unglamorous, and when on arrival we were whisked off to tea in one of the seniors' rooms, which was crowded with dazzling damsels and their swains, I huddled silent and miserable behind Miss Kimber in a corner, wondering how Buster Brown, my host, had ever dared invite me. He stood by the door as tongue-tied as I, and I guess he wondered too. At the Prom that night I appeared like a kitten among vixens. The other girls wore long slinky silk, cut low in the neck; they piled their curls on top of their disdainful heads and openly smirked at my appearance.

All during the grand march I wanted to break and run, but Buster and I plodded through it as though we were tramping the snows of Siberia. When the line broke up I returned miserably to my chaperone and my chair. Then to my surprise and consternation I was sought out and invited to dance by none other than the great Cole Porter of Glee Club fame. He led me forth with such a flourish and we tripped the boards with such swirl and grace that even the Southern beauties turned to look. When he handed me back to my chair, a line of partners was already forming. Of course my cotillion card had been made out weeks before, but now the encores were being split four ways. I was a success—I couldn't understand how or why, but I was. Cole Porter must have been responsible. In fact, for the entire week end little Polly Jacob, chaperoned and shy, had a fine time, and at the station I had more "men" to wave me good-bye than any other two girls combined.

Cole had asked me if I ever managed to get to New York on Saturdays. He said he'd like to take me to a matinee. This was the apex of success. I didn't dare dream that it would actually come to pass. Then one happy morning during spring term I received a letter inviting me to meet him for lunch at the Belmont and afterwards the theatre. He had just written "In an Old-Fashioned Garden"—everyone at school was humming it. I was quite overcome by the invitation. I replied I would love to come. "No chaperone, please," he had postscripted. This was really life. The letter was passed up and down the fifth-form table. I was the envy of the entire school.

Saturday dawned and with borrowed finery tucked under my Rosemary uniform I was shepherded into town with the others and left on the steps of the Belmont (I often met my family there for lunch). As soon as I was alone I slid into the ladies' room and released the crumpled chiffon from the confines of my middy blouse. I pulled off my beret and attached an ignoble (but suitable, I thought) confection of osprey and black satin, lent me by a worldly six-former, to my pate. I must have looked a sight.

He was waiting for me in the big lobby. He wore a carnation in his buttonhole and had already reserved a table for two in a window embrasure. I was bewildered and my powers of conversation were decidedly stilted. I did not dare ask him what we were going to see. *Mrs. Warren's Profession,* perhaps, or *Mlle. Modiste* with Fritzi Scheff, I hoped—it was sure to be a sophisticated choice.

Finally Cole drew the tickets from his pocket. "I think you will like what I am taking you to," and he smiled a man-of-the-world smile. "I've managed a box for the best thing in town, 'Jumbo,' at the Hippodrome."

Happiness, courage and conversation all oozed away. My bubble burst, the day deflated; tears smarted my eyes as I almost wailed my "How nice!" In imagination I was already back at school among my inquisitors. How could I ever say,

"He took me to the circus," just as though he had been an uncle or an aunt. The girls would laugh, but I would probably never laugh again—at any rate, it was no laughing matter. I sat grimly in the box, never cracking a smile. It wasn't amusing at all, not any of it—and how I hated Cole!

It was at Rosemary the autumn of 1910 that I was initiated and named the first Girl Scout of America. Sir William Baden-Powell was on a visit to this country to organize an American Boy Scout Unit. The idea had only just grown into actuality in England, but under his administration was spreading as quickly as a Scout fire shouldn't. Lady Baden-Powell, while her husband went to Washington, came to Rosemary at Miss Ruutz-Rees' invitation, and I am sure it was in exchanging modern ideas over the after-luncheon coffee cups that they, together with Miss Lowndes and Miss Lewis (both as British as buns) brewed the scheme for instigation of a Girl Scout movement right there at Rosemary. In England it was the Girl Guides. Anyway, that evening the senior class was invited by the faculty to a campfire hike. Hiking at Rosemary was one of the most indulged in of sports. We often started off for long week ends on foot, our packs on our backs, swinging along, arms linked, chanting:

> *Camping, tramping, sun and rain*
> *Both are pleasures on the road*
> *Hill and valley, wood and lane*
> *These are our abode.*

Some returned by cart but most of us hiked all the way. We wore full black alpaca bloomers, heavy black stockings and white middies—so campfires were easy. We had had a lovely hot supper of grilled chops and potatoes and encircled the embers like a ring of virgin druids, when Miss Ruutz-Rees clapped her hands for attention and the plan was unfolded. We all agreed that anything *that* modern should start at Rosemary. Miss Ruutz-Rees looked like Mark Antony in skirts and her eyes were china blue.

Lady Baden-Powell said we ought to initiate a leader that very same evening in a sort of symbolic ceremony. I was a ten-bar girl (highest honour in self-government) and I was chosen. My name being Polly, laughter and cogitation were needed to work out an Indian soubriquet both symbolic and lyrical— Policumteenawa, Little-Possum-By The-Fire, or some such whimsy title was chosen. I was crowned with an eagle's feather and invested with an Indian amulet. A blanket of many colours was placed upon my shoulders by Lady Baden-Powell, who recited in real red-Indian an invocation that sounded blood-curdling. Then I was pronounced the Original Girl Scout. That evening was the greatest fun, but I soon forgot. The Baden-Powells sailed away and I don't believe any record was made of my priority; if so I must one day find out.

All in all, I was neither happy nor unhappy those years at boarding school. But it never occurred to me that I myself could influence or change the course of my life. I rebelled but once—at the discovery of Mabel B's terrifying "crush"—but my utterly false position of acting as school chaplain, unbeliever that I am, the unintuitive teachers and the unimaginative scholars all irked me. I wanted to be alone under a tree to read, and the track team, of which I was captain, the hikes of which I was leader, and the Shakespearean plays enacted in the flowering orchard, and of which I was heroine, are the only memories that have not faded.

I learned almost nothing at Rosemary in the scholastic sense, though I kept ahead in my classes; even had the second highest marks in school. It was history that kept me from being first—the past has always seemed a thing to be left there. For me, events of last year or yesterday have lost their contact. Only *persons* are memorable and once they grow listless are soon forgotten. I remember only three girls with any clarity, and those friendships have not survived. I must have been singularly uninhibited, with no roots in reality. My life was mostly dreams, and adults were the pale untouchables.

The next few years passed without great sorrow or great joy. Winter vacations were spent at Windward or Watertown. Summers in the Adirondacks or on Long Island, with boys and girls bathing and dancing, sports and flirtations. How remote that word flirtation sounds. It is a Victorianism that has no actuality in the life of to-day. To flirt is not to "court," nor to "go with" nor to "chase." Flirtation is the minuet of love. It took grace and precision and a time of ease to flirt. It was sometimes a prelude to true love, but not necessarily. It could be carried on with skill and thrill and still end in mutual admiration.

It was the words written on the cotillion card—the sleigh ride to Fraunces Tavern, the handkerchief cherished, the flowers pressed, the stolen kiss at the foot of the staircase. One could flirt with a dozen admirers at once. To-day the "going with" narrows the field and excludes such frivolous delights.

I never smoke and never have but once, so when people exclaim *how wonderful,* I tell them why it is not wonderful at all.

I was seventeen at a hunt ball in England. I had spent the week end with a delightful horsy family in Hertfordshire—and on Friday and Saturday we had been mounted and out in the frosty dawn, keen for the hallali of the horn and the *gone away* of the hounds. I loved those early mornings meets, everything seemed laundered and crisp, even the mist and the resilient earth. One came in tired but oh so finely tuned—and ravenous.

That Saturday there was a hunt ball given by my hosts in their candle-lit manor house as a bright finale to the week, and I with cheeks like apples, in my very first long dress of billowing tulle, was in fine fettle for adventure. I loved my new dress passionately, it meant many vistas of joy and fun and it was my very first ball dress.

I ate supper behind a screen of potted palms in the conservatory. My cavalier was a dream—and happiness went to my head. When he dared me to try a cigarette, there, where no one could see, and lured me on with the taunt that an American girl always took a dare, I succumbed. No lady ever smoked in those days, least of all a sub-deb—it was my first—he lit it for me and of course I choked.

I looked him firmly in the eye and puffed again.

"Good girl," he said but his eyes seemed more important than his words. I gazed and gazing, knew not what I did. As his arms went around me I forgot my cigarette, it slipped into a nest of tulle and suddenly it kindled. I was ablaze, flame, smoke, fright and pain. I sprang to my feet, which fanned the tiny tongues of fire, heroically my cavalier tore off his fine pink coat and wound and beat me into the most cindery of Cinderellas. In tears I ran from the conservatory out into the garden, around to the back stairs and up to my room where, dishevelled and dishonoured, this daring American sobbed out her humiliation.

The dress was ruined, my pride was felled, and my distaste for cigarettes became a lifelong habit. I never smoked again.

CHAPTER 5

My hat rolled down the garden path and the King went running after. It happened at a royal garden party at Windsor in the late spring of 1914. That was a beautiful breezy afternoon and the season of Merry Widow hats. Mine was merrier than most, for it tilted its beribboned brim like a jib in a gale, and off it blew just as I was curtsying to their Majesties. The King with princely agility dived to retrieve it, but it cartwheeled away down the garden path with His Majesty chasing most gallantly after. I don't know whose face was redder, His Majesty's from exertion (though he did not "break his crown"), or mine from embarrassment. But we both grinned when I jammed it on backwards, the streamers falling over my nose.

Only those persons who had already been presented at Court were invited to this very special reception. It was given every year in May at the time when the Royal Gardens are loveliest. Windsor with its picture-book battlements, its vast meadows, edged with Nelson's oaks and glimpses of Eton's toylike halls down by the printed river, was a page from a story book. At that party all the English were either noble or important. The women were delicious with parasols, posies and pearls; the Eastern potentates wore exotic dress, flunkeys and beefeaters in doublet and hose lined the paths and terraces, and in several gaudy marquees, reminiscent of Barnum and Bailey, ices and cakes and tea and punch were handed round in silver cups and on golden trays. The banners and ribbons curveted in the breeze, the royal band played stirringly, decorations were worn and the Star and Garter shone in the sun westering beyond Boleyn's tower just over the way.

In a few months all the men would be off to war, though we didn't guess it then; but in May and June it was still Merrie England and I remember one evening almost too perfect to describe. Nijinsky and Company were dancing in London that season. His opening night had been a triumph. I watched from Sir Otto Beit's box, but the night he danced in the Rothschild garden was the memorable one for me. The Rothschilds owned a house on the Thames on the outskirts of London. Behind the house an apple orchard, all in blossom, stood like a chorus of ballerinas on the polished lawn that stretched down to the bank of the river. The evening was mysteriously opaque, the fireflies looked big and bright under the trees, and the water was a velvet backdrop. As the animated guests who crowded the steps and terraces heard the opening notes of *The Swan,* their voices hushed and, as though emerging from the river itself, Pavlova on fanning wings advanced in the spotlight's beam up the legendary glade between the flowering trees. The music swelled, and a miracle was achieved—Pavlova and Nijinsky enchanted us beneath the moon.

I had been presented at Court that season. It was the last diplomatic court before the war and it was held at night. All the royal family, the statesmen and the princes of Empire, Eastern potentates and their retinue attended in full regalia. Mrs. Whitelaw Reid, the wife of our Ambassador, was to have presented me, but the Ambassador had died suddenly a few weeks before, and because of the mourning it was not protocol for the First Secretary and Mrs. Phillips to present me. Instead, the wife of the Doyen, Mme. Merry del Val of Spain, accepted the duty of taking this young visitor "from the States" under her wing.

I was the only American debutante to be presented at that court and the build-up was terrific. I was taken first to Paris, to Boué Soeurs, to have my gown made. It was of white brocade shot through with golden threads, very décolleté, with a huge swirl of tulle around the bodice. The train and the headdress were to be made in Bond Street by a Mrs. O'Connor, who specialized in court dress. This train was eight yards long, by command, and somewhere near the end an enormous rose of tulle was centred. The rose made it most difficult to manage, folded back and forth over one's left arm, as one stepped from one's coach and trod the crimson carpet into Buckingham Palace. By royal command, in my onduléed (first time) hair sat three little white ostrich plumes (Prince of Wales feathers). My beautiful kid gloves from the Rue de la Paix reached almost to my shoulders, and I carried a bouquet of yellow roses.

My Uncle George Elin (I was visiting my uncle and aunt at the time) drove to the palace with me, and he had to get into full evening dress just to hand me from the carriage to the steps. It was arranged, however, that I was to be accompanied home by a young and dashing secretary of the American Embassy, Hallet Johnson, who seemed to like me quite a lot; at any rate he took very good care of me while I danced and chattered my way through the evening. But when my uncle drove off and left me to reach the room of a hundred chairs by myself, my knees wobbled. I entered first a white-and-gold antechamber with rows of gilded dancing-school chairs (the kind that Sherry used to rent) drawn up as though for a prayer meeting. That is where one sat until called into the Throne Room, and that is where I found Madame Merry del Val, but she soon had to leave me while I waited for my turn, alone. I suppose an actress experiences the same anguish on a first night, before the curtain rises. I felt I just had to scratch my back, but I couldn't.

Then from the door a resplendent lackey called, "Miss Jacob." I got up, overturning the flimsy chair, but I had presence of mind enough not to pick it up and thereby lose control of my eight yards of train, and my bristling roses, and my card clutched between thumb and forefinger. First there was a corridor, all mirrors—it was endless, and a chorus of "oneself" seemed to be crowding into it from every direction. I was passed along this passage while "Miss Jacob," "Miss Jacob," was cried every ten feet, until the door of the Throne Room was flung open and, like a prestidigitator's trick, two liveried magicians with big wands lifted the folds from my arm, flipped them up and over like pancakes, and spread them beautifully out behind, in one perfect operation. Then the chamberlain announced loudly, "Miss Jacob of the United States to be presented to Their Majesties," and in I sidled as I was taught in Bond Street, making first an obeisance all the way to the floor to the Queen and then one to the King; next a bob to the young Prince of Wales as I passed; making curtsies down the line of royal personages, and all the time politely doing a side-step so as not to turn my back on all the other kings and queens behind me, which I didn't. I was told I performed very gracefully, too, even managing to give my hosts a big smile.

Now that I was properly launched, I went out a great deal. There was the Caledonian Ball, at which I danced with lairds and lads in tartan, and the embassy balls at which I flirted with prince and barrister. I went down to Oxford for Eights Week, and I lunched on top of gaudy drags at Lords to cheer for Eton at the Eton-Harrow match. I rode to hounds and I chased after harriers. I hunted and I punted and I had a fine time. But although London had taught me many a lesson in worldliness, I was growing homesick, not for my country or my family, but for my friends. I had almost forgotten the Yale boys I had danced with, the Harvard boys I had skied with, the Princeton boys I had flirted with. Only one stuck in my heart, a Bostonian, Dick Peabody. We had been engaged for six whole years, but before I left for Europe we had quarrelled and then life unfolded so absorbingly across the sea that I had hardly given him a backward thought. I do not think I was heartless, only forgetful, and my life in London and in Queen Anne's Mead, that royal cottage at Windsor where I spent an English spring, was crowded with as many experiences and mixed admirers as only an American debutante could muster —but a day came when the rain fell and my spirits with it. I wrote to Dick.

I suddenly wanted to go home. What I wanted usually came to pass. I do not know how or when it did in this particular instance, but it was soon, for by July 1, I was in the U.S. again —and just in time. At the end of July, Europe went to war.

The night that war was declared, Dick and I were together, engaged once more, for I had let him know that I was coming

63

home to *him*. I feared that by now he must have found some other love, but he was faithfully there when I landed, and I was immediately whisked off to visit his family on the North Shore, that stronghold of Back Bay properness where summer residences line the coast from Nahant to Gloucester—not farms, not cottages, not even plain houses, but glorified summer palaces in which family and servants are transferred from Beacon Street and Commonwealth Avenue during the months when tennis and golf are the most enjoyable and the days long enough so that bankers and brokers can catch the 4.52 for a swim on Singing Beach before changing into dinner jacket in time for dinner at eight. It was into this milieu that I was taken by my fiancé. It was daring of him, for I was a New Yorker, and I might just as well have been a Hottentot.

Dick and I had met when we were fourteen and he was at Groton, I at Miss Chapin's. That was the summer of 1906. My Uncle Will and Aunt Annie Barnum had rented the Townsend Camp on Upper Saint Regis in the Adirondacks—a luxurious and beautiful spot and a fantastically plutocratic one as well. There were not more than eight or ten "camps" on the entire lake, each one protected from its neighbour by virgin waterfronts. Not even a footpath led from one to another. The approaches were by water and every one of the summer campers owned a boathouse, well filled with speedboats, sailboats, rowboats and canoes and an occasional scull for the collegians. Each guest had his own cabin, consisting of living room, bedroom and shower. We bathed in the lake, but we ate terrapin from Maryland and lobsters from Maine in an octagonal log cabin overhanging the water; the kitchen, the servants' quarters and the guides' tents were beyond. One clapped one's hands for service, for the camp chores were never done except by guides. We were not allowed the joy of gathering firewood or baiting a hook, but life was fun in spite of luxury. The air reeked of pine, mountain waters gladdened the palate, lake water refreshed the body, and terrapin tastes good anywhere.

One of the first sporting events to take place that summer was the Idem Class race for junior skippers. The Idems were twenty-two-foot knockabouts built for speed and manœuverability; the nervous little craft were top-heavy with canvas

"I was bringing up my children in the shadow of disaster," 1917.

8. Polleen and Billy, 1921.

9. I made up the stage name of "Valerie Marno" for my movie career, New York, 1921.

10. The first time I saw Harry Crosby he was in field service uniform, 1921.

and when heeled over could be kept skimming the surface only by the weight of all three crew members slipping down the upturned side and standing perilously on the keel. The races were contests of skill and spunk, and every camp owner owned an Idem. On this particular Saturday it was the sons and heirs who were to do the sailing. The Rauch twins, big ungainly boys like overgrown pups, Ralph Earle, the eldest of the Earle tribe (later Governor of Pennsylvania), a McAlpin, a Vanderbilt, a Stokes—and last in size, but not last in place, a Peabody.

Dick Peabody was a wisp of a boy who wouldn't begin to shoot up until the following summer; but his appearance, even at fourteen, was one of great charm and grace. His middle was slender, his hips were tightly set, and he wore for that race his first pair of long trousers. They were of white duck and his brown ankles, which showed above whitened sneakers, were as finely boned as those of a mongoose. One of his front teeth was broken on the bias and, although he looked shy, he spoke with perfect poise and a fascinating indifference.

We campers were out on the water in launches or rowboats that afternoon. The course was twice around the lake and we bobbed about the finish line in a stiff breeze. On the last lap the Idems were well up in the wind. The crews were over the side for ballast, clinging by their fingernails, till a sudden puff hit them, and one after another the boats keeled over, flat on their fluttering sides. But still running, nose and nose, sails taut, on the final leg came the Rauch boat and the Peabody boat, ballooning out. Rudie Rauch strained at his tiller; Dick, perched like a fly on a race horse, held his tight against his stomach. It was a gallant burst of speed as Dick, the pint-sized skipper, sprayed past the flag to victory. Bang! went the judges' gun, and bang went my heart. When we met at the clubhouse my emotion was overwhelming, and I choked on my macaroon.

Dick proposed to me that summer at a Saturday night dance at Paul Smith's Hotel on Lower St. Regis. We had all converged on the resort in immaculate white launches that made the lake's surface look like a duck pond. Dick danced very badly and stepped all over my feet, so we sat it out on the veranda railing in the moonlight. They played the *Blue Danube* and he asked me if I would marry him when he finished college. He was going to Harvard in three or four years, so we'd have to wait seven, but I said yes. I love to say yes.

We were too shy to kiss then, but we did on the way home, and he sat with me in church the next day (everyone returned to Paul Smith's for church on Sunday, no matter how late they left on Saturday night) and we felt solemn and scared. Dick had worn long trousers for the second time the night before.

And so it was that in 1914, I returned to Richard Rogers Peabody. That most fateful of all Augusts found us on the North Shore. To announce our engagement, the newly wed Bayard Warrens had invited us to a dinner of Dick's most intimate friends. I wore a pink organdie with a V-neck and found to my embarrassment that the other young women (Lily Warren was twenty-two) were in low-neck satins and lace. At Windsor my organdie would have been quite fitting, but not so on the North Shore, where dinners even for the very young were impressive affairs, given at home, and the circle of guests was always intimate and restricted. One dined out, but never so far out as a roadhouse.

The following night, the fatal third of August, we were dining with the Oliver Ameses and this time I donned my presentation gown. It was a dinner of ten, mostly Ameses, but I was not overdressed. I sat on Mr. Ames' right, his eldest son on my right. I was the visitor in their midst and he was the father of our friends: E. for Elise, O for Olivia, Dicky the musician, who was the odd duckling in that impeccable family, and Ollie—Oliver Ames, Jr.—who was possibly the handsomest, most envied young man in Boston. Ollie was just over twenty and he seemed to have everything; intelligence, wealth and position. Next to him sat Kay Fessenden, a charming blackhaired beauty of the same age and the same background.

At the table we heard the news that England was going to the aid of France and had just declared war on Germany. It can't last more than a few months, said the elders. "I'd like to take a crack at those Huns," Dick Peabody said. Charlie Codman, the modern, said, "I'd like to help them fight it out in the air."

"Wonder if we'll get into it?" Ollie said.

"Certainly not," replied the father. "The British'll clean them up in no time. It will be over before Christmas."

In 1916, Kay became Mrs. Oliver Ames, Jr., the first war bride in our group. In 1917, Ollie was killed at Château-Thierry, where in 1920 as at Verdun the war memorials cried, "They shall not pass" and where in 1939, those first war graves served as sign posts for the conquerors to pass once more. Dick was at Château-Thierry too, but that night they were still undergraduates.

CHAPTER 6

"Booze," as the grain was termed, had played an active and dramatic part in the academic and the social life of Harvard College, 1914, and not a few of Dick's classmates drank boisterously day and night. There was a great deal of road-house life, in the company of "floozies," that loomed important in the undergraduate pattern. For them, "nice girls"—sisters and sisters of their friends—were not supposed to know or even suspect the goings-on at Ferncroft on the Boston Pike. Only when some flaming youth "fell for" some Boston virgin, the exposé of his double life and the plea for forgiveness and promises of reform became a classic means of courtship—to believe that one had snatched the wayward swain from the jaws of Ferncroft by a promise "to wait for him," gave to one's love an evangelistic aura—I myself was pledged "to wait for" Dick—the frequent recital of Flossie's or Shirley's comradely, though unprincipled, wiles, of Hazel's moral laxity, "great sport" though she was, was not only spellbinding, but incentive to reclaim the object of one's adoration from further contamination. Nevertheless, Dick's drinking worried my family. The New York boys were far better behaved.

Dick and I were so enthusiastically betrothed all that summer that he decided not to return to Harvard in the fall. Instead he took a job with Johns Manville in New York, hoping we could be married soon after. I was living again at Windward, my aunt and uncle's country place on Quaker Ridge, where I had been brought up during the years that my parents were in the South because of Father's health.

My father died in Texas while I was in school at Rosemary Hall. It is to him that I owe my indestructible idealism. I do not believe my mother ever understood the gossamer mantle in which the visionary must wrap himself for protection; a garment that can be as strong as faith or evanescent as a dream. That my father dreamed of, believed in, and planned for, a better world for rich and poor alike I know now, but his disastrous building project on Lake Avenue in New Rochelle, where there was as yet no lake, and his idea of community ranching on the Brazos in Texas, where the landowners were dead against him, were spoken of as "Will's crazy ideas." The idealists are all crackpots until they become heroes or saints, and it is no wonder that Father hid himself in his gossamer mantle. "You are just like your father," the remark so often made by Mama, was reproof rather than approval. That he died before I really knew him is one of the great losses I have suffered. Up to the time I was eight years old he was my world, but from eight to fourteen living away from home and learning to learn, separated us and temporarily obscured his importance to me. He returned to Texas for the last year of his life. It was only there that his asthma was bearable, and he died in San Antonio in December, 1908, while I was at Windward on vacation from Rosemary Hall. Early that autumn he had been north for a few weeks (I hardly saw him) but just before leaving for the South he came to school unexpectedly one Sunday afternoon to say good-bye. "Your father is in the drawing room" was as great a surprise to me as if the maid had announced The Lord himself. I was flustered unreasonably.

I saw at once that he was very ill, very sad and very cherishable. A great surge of maternal love washed over my heart—I wanted to draw his head to my shoulder and comfort him; instead, I catapulted into his arms, mine around his neck in a wild uncomprehending kiss. He had in his hands a purple and white wicker basket of white and purple grapes—it was October and he offered them as though before some altar. I felt the sacrificial implication as intensely as I felt my maternal love.

Father died that Christmas. It was not until years later, Paris, 1928, to be exact, that I was able to put this meeting into words. It was then I wrote my only epic, *The Stranger;* "For

69

that once all of love was given, purple ribbon damson grapes with tears above" are the lines that sum up the moment. Taking the basket into my neophyte hands, I knew I had accepted a gift more precious than sapphires, more ancient than wisdom.

After Father died, Mother went to live in Watertown, Connecticut, and built a little house there to be near my brothers. Bud, the younger, was a day scholar at Taft School, just up Academy Hill, and Len was a boarder not far away at Westminster School in Simsbury. But I preferred to wait for Dick at Windward, where I was always welcome, and where I was much nearer to him.

Windward where I had spent so much of my childhood, belonged to Aunt Annie and Uncle Will Barnum. It had started, when first purchased, as a modest country house on a hillside back of Mamaroneck, overlooking Long Island Sound, and it ended, when the architect, the builders and the landscape artist had turned their hands to it, as a rambling but supermodern estate (1900) with stables and greenhouses, gardeners' cottages and cow barns. But down the hill in the lower left-hand corner of the property, like an initial on a handkerchief, was an old chiselled stone cottage where various members of the family lived, loved, and were quarantined from time to time, and where family brides and grooms began their married lives. When he saw Dick and me looking too longingly at the cottage, Uncle Will pocketed the key.

In November the family moved into town, as usual, to spend two months at the Home Club, at 11 East Forty-fifth Street. The Home Club was the name of the de luxe experiment in community housing that my Uncle Will and several of his Wall Street partners had founded, on the premise that it can be a pleasure to economize under one roof if one meets the other economizers only at dinner. For the communal dining hall, two brownstone fronts were knocked into one. It made a spacious attractive room and the Home Club chef and the maître d'hotel, both chosen by Ootto Bannard, the bachelor in our midst, were superlative in their rôles. We lived very well but, contrary to the prognosis, not frugally, and the dream dissolved after a few years' trial. One trouble was that most families are not up to a symposium seven nights a week. My

uncle had, I am sure, visualized himself in a toga, but not I
—I was more modern. It was at the Home Club that I had
come out in the winter of 1913. It was also at the Home Club
during the same winter that I invented the brassière.

When I made my debut, girlish figures were being encased
in a sort of boxlike armour of whalebone and pink cordage.
This contraption ran upwards from the knee to under the
armpit. Over the top of it was firmly hooked a corset-cover
of muslin or silk, slightly boned and having small caps or puffed
sleeves, cut high or low according to day or evening wear.
These garments were forever having to be tucked or pinned or
pushed out of sight once one was dressed for a party, and they
were hellishly binding as well. If petting had been practised
in those days, it never could have gone very far, for even to
get one's own finger beneath the corset-cover took a lot of
wriggling.

It was not a determination to ease this virgin state that
motivated my invention, but rather a desire to move and sway
and dance in comfort. That season I had allotted to me for
my own personal attendance a pale and unprotesting French
maid. Marie's hours had to coincide with my hours, for in
those days, one kept one's maid in vigil all night. No
matter how late we danced, I can still see the gallery at Sherry's
or the Plaza or Delmonico's and the long-suffering line of
hollow-eyed ladies' maids in little black suits like a row of
sleepy crows crouched upon the railing far above the fun,
waiting for their birds of plumage to give the signal for departure. Then one's servant would shake herself awake and
stumble down to the dressing room, there to hold one's wrap
and kneel at one's feet to tie the ribbons of the velvet snow
boots, and follow out-of-doors like a clinging shadow under the
porte-cochère, where Mr. Sherry himself saw to it that each one
of his young ladies was stowed away in her special hack, her
trusty maid to guard her. No boy was ever allowed to ac-
company one home, unless, of course, he was a member of the
family.

I remember the scandalizing night that the Steele twins eluded
their duenna and, accompanied by two Harvard freshmen, were
driven in a public conveyance up Fifth Avenue from the forties

71

to the seventies, just as the sun was rising. Mr. Sherry telephoned their family in consternation to report this breach of social pattern and we all heard it whispered about next day that Mr. Steele was waiting on the doorstep when the foursome turned up twenty minutes behind schedule; and that the boys were denounced as "no gentlemen" and the girls were kept home from all the next week's parties.

I danced at from one to three balls every night that season and my usual hours in bed were from four in the morning to noon. Marie's were four to ten. At twelve I was called and got ready for the customary debutante luncheon, and then again to and from Sherry's or Delmonico's (which we had quitted only a few hours previously), Marie walking eight paces behind up or down the Avenue. We always stopped at Huyler's for ice cream sodas. Sometimes three or four girls would band together for a stroll in the afternoon and would combine on a single domestic to follow after, while the other maids trotted dutifully home to press or sew (or perchance to dream).

One rainy afternoon I was alone at the Home Club helping Marie refurbish a wreath of silk roses that I was to wear in my hair that night to match the rose-garlanded dress laid out upon the bed. I remembered how the, last time I had worn that dress the eyelet embroidery of my corset-cover kept peeping through the roses around my bosom.

"I'm not going to wear that thing to-night," I announced. "It spoils the entire effect."

"But, Mademoiselle cannot go without a *soutien-gorge*," Marie wailed.

"Bring me two of my pocket handkerchiefs," I ordered, "and some pink ribbon . . . And bring the needle and thread and some pins into my bedroom."

There before the glass I pinned the handkerchiefs together on the bias and Marie stitched the pink ribbons to the two points below my breast bone. The ends of the handkerchiefs I knotted round my waist and then Marie, grasping the idea and the ribbons, pulled them taut and made them fast to the knot behind, the practice being to flatten down one's chest as much as possible so the truth that virgins had breasts should not be suspected. *My* brassière did this neatly and eliminated the buttons and bones and hooks that had offended me before. I slipped my dress over my head to try. The result was delicious. I could move much more freely, a nearly naked feeling, and in the glass I saw that I was flat and I was proper.

That night at the ball I was so fresh and supple that in the dressing room afterwards my friends came flocking round. I gave them a peek and outlined the invention and promised if they'd supply the hankies, Marie would make up models for the trade. From then on we all wore them. But it was only when a stranger in Boston wrote enclosing a dollar and asked if Marie would make her one, that I decided I had something to exploit. So I inquired about a patent lawyer and even hinted to one of the Harvard Law School boys what I was after. I got a name and with Marie and our samples we went to call on Mr. Jones. He was enthusiastic; in fact, so enthusiastic that I insisted that the bra be modelled by Marie over her uniform, and not by me. He got that idea, but nevertheless his imagination must have run ahead, for the very next day he called on me with a series of the most portrait-like and at the same time most scientific drawings I have ever beheld, and he wanted fifty dollars. That was impossible; I could give him five dollars on account and more when the patent was obtained. He acquiesced very generously and asked me what the garment should be called.

"It has no back," I said. "Let's call it the 'Backless Brassière.'"

He went to work to obtain the patent for a corset-cover without a back, pulling on the bias to fit the figure, with ribbon shoulder straps to hold it up. That spring I went to Europe, grandly leaving my attorney to carry out my wishes.

To my amazement when I returned a year later, the patent had actually been granted, so I began in secret to run a sweat shop. (By now the reader must guess that most of my extra-curricular activities had to be in secret, owing to undue prejudice about what young ladies could or could not do to turn a longed-for penny.)

I borrowed a hundred dollars from an ageing friend, I hired a room in the sweatshop district, I got hold of Marie as a side partner, and I rented two sewing machines and engaged two little Italian girls to work for me. As I look back I am sure they were not only underpaid but under age as well; but we did turn out a few hundred Backless Brassières, presented to the public in very superior packaging (the de luxe edition blood must have already been stirring in my veins).

I went to call on Mr. Stern, on Mr. Altman, on Mr. Ginsberg and on many others; each one magnanimously took a few dozen to try, but it was such a revolutionary idea that the public might not accept it, they said (I felt rather like an anarchist).

Either the public didn't accept the idea or the salesladies didn't get the customary inducement to push them, for almost all my beautiful effort languished on their shelves. Then I became engaged and absorbed in wedding plans and forgot all about my wares. It wasn't until after I was Mrs. Peabody that I ran into Johnny Field, a famous Yale quarterback, 1913, and a former admirer of mine, and when I asked him what he was doing, he said slyly that he was making "jewel cases." By further inquisitiveness I learned that he worked for Warner Brothers Corset Company in Bridgeport. I told him of my invention and he was so interested that I made an appointment to travel to Bridgeport the following week to show his boss my samples. The long and short of it was that when I produced the Backless Brassière *and* the patent,* the company at once offered fifteen hundred dollars for both. To me this seemed not only adequate, but magnificent. I signed on the line and went home in opulence.

I believe that it couldn't have taken many years for Warner Brothers to clean up fifteen millions or more on *that* jewel case! The first inkling I got that Johnny had made a profitable deal was when a few months later he married the boss's daughter.

* See Appendix.

74

CHAPTER 7

Dick and I were married in January, 1915, from Windward, and Uncle Cottie (the Reverend Endicott Peabody) came down from Groton to tie the knot. For the simple ceremony in the library and to please my Uncle Will, I wore the blue cotton dress that he particularly liked, the one with the sailor collar, and for the reception I changed into white pan velvet and Venetian point lace. It was winter, but so mild that we could be photographed out on the lawn with the Harvard ushers and the New York bridesmaids.

When the guests had gone Dick and I walked (ran when we were out of sight of the Big House) down the hill to the Stone Cottage. My mother and father had started their married life there and so did we.

Dick was commuting daily except Sundays to Johns Manville in New York. I was so busy with my new household toys that I hardly left Quaker Ridge. My uncle and his neighbours, the Dickermans and the Heatons, had built a private golf course just over the way in some of Mr. Dickerman's fields; the fifth hole was in front of our front steps. On Sundays we always began at the sixth hole and Mary Mars, the gardener's daughter, caddied for us; she was saving up to buy a silk umbrella.

My son was born a year later, February 4, 1916. His advent was cause for much celebration by his father, for we were the first of our set to produce a child. I think Dick felt rather like Merlin. I was left out of the fun. William Jacob Peabody was born in New York. When snow covered the course and the front steps were slippery with ice, we moved into town. We rented the Peter Hoguets' beruffled little apartment in Fifty-third Street. It looked like a very cheerfully gilded birdcage, and it was, but a hazardous one for me for its bars were not soundproof. Dick was not the most indulgent of parents and like his father before him, he forbade the gurgles and the cries of infancy; when they occurred he walked out, and often walked back unsteadily.

I had been under the care of Dr. Thomas, that aristocrat of the operating table, who for an immodest fee guided new-comers into this world through its socially immaculate, though fleshy portals. My mother had been under his care when I and my brother Len were born. My grandparents footed the bills then and, thank Eros, Uncle Jack Morgan came to our assist-ance now. Dr. Thomas's bill was a whopper—two thousand dollars as I recall—but then he had already established a new social order, much on the same scale as the Union Club or Groton—to be a Thomas Baby your parents had to figure in both the Social Register and the *Wall Street Journal*.

On April 1st, we moved back to Quaker Ridge. Dick switched to private shipping that spring and I invested my father's legacy in his business, but things didn't go very well. And then the Mexican Border trouble came to his rescue. He suddenly became imbued with patriotism or, as I believe now, escapism. He was a member of Battery A, Boston's crack militia, in which all his friends were officers too. The trumpet called and they were off. I was left holding my son on his grandparents' door-step like a wayward daughter who had fallen from grace (and not a legacy to stand on). Colonel Peabody agreed that it was Dick's duty to serve his country. I was too meek to protest. It was a soldier's world, not mine any more, nor Billy's.

My nest-egg was gone and so was Dick. There was nothing for Billy and me to do but to quit our harbouring cottage and take shelter with Dick's family on the North Shore.

The first year of our married life I was bringing up my child in the shadow of disaster, another war bride living under her father-in-law's roof, in a household run according to her mother-in-law's rules; there was no time to weld my own life together.

When Dick came back from the Mexican Border, my son

was only six months old and when a year later he joined up for World War I my daughter was still unborn. I was again under Dr. Thomas's care, but this time was watched over by my mother. Dick was in Plattsburg in training camp the day the baby arrived and he sailed for France before ten days were up. All those first precious years were distorted by conflict far beyond my comprehension. Many of my friends were caught in the same cruel trap. I was one of the lucky ones, for Dick returned. I had lived like a nun while he was away, but in France it was hard to live like a monk.

In July, 1918, he was still in France and Polleen was about to have her very first birthday. Dick had never seen her except on the afternoon that she was born, when he had managed a twenty-four hour leave from Plattsburg, one hour of which he spent nervously at my bedside. I suppose he took a look at Polly in her swaddling clothes, but I imagine he didn't like what he saw—a red-faced maggot embroidered with heat rash —and he took the other twenty-three hours celebrating her arrival. I was rather relieved that he didn't, as he expressed it, "stick around." I didn't like him to see me in this flimsy deflated state, and the thought of nursing an infant in front of my husband made me blush—we had been so ashamed of my hugeness during the months before that I was glad he was away in camp, and when I did go out I hid and camouflaged myself as best I could.

I remember once I had to cross the lobby of the Hotel Belmont deprived of a dissimulating cloak and my embarrassment was so intense that I burst into sobs while the check-girl was searching out the blessed garment. Dick did not enjoy his children until they grew up, and to him they made me less available. Ours was a boy-and-girl affair. I was supposed to remain the perfect playmate.

Dick left for overseas duty when Polleen was ten days old. I was feeling very wobbly still, but the doctor allowed me (I would have gone anyway) to travel from Windward to New York to meet, greet and bid him farewell. We had one night together, most of it spent in riotous company—it exhausted me and distressed him, but we were poor little puppets in the war lords' grasp—I could understand why he and his friends were protecting their inner selves with an armour of heroism, but though I tried, I found no solace in heroics. To me war was then and always has been a cruel and brutal form of exhibitionism, solving nothing.

When he left me at dawn (I did not go further than the door) we clung together like bewildered babes—no more sure of life than those in crib and cradle—but the shutting of that door marked the end of innocence. I returned to my uncle's roof, to my children, exhausted in spirit and body. It took me a long time to recover.

The autumn came, and I and my infants took refuge again in the home of my parents-in-law, as so many of my friends were forced to do. It incommoded Mr. and Mrs. Peabody and it was agony for me; nothing seemed to go right. I did, thank heaven, have an excellent nurse, a woman twice my age whose experience and training were the best. She took over the nursery, perhaps too completely, but at least my in-laws were spared the inconvenience of my ineptness as nurse and mother—the children were kept miraculously invisible and subdued—and I escaped the family atmosphere of eau de cologne and tiptoe discipline. Mrs. Peabody was more than ever an invalid and the Major (as he was called in military days) was preparing to get himself overseas too. War invaded every cranny of the house —huge maps in the hall, where blue and red-headed pins moved each day to mark an advance or a retreat—long-distance calls from Washington waited for—implements of war laid out like precious *objets d'art*. All the papers every day, with their big headlines. No one in that household tried to understand or share my misgivings and terror, for it *was* a season of terror— Dick might never return, and then what? I saw no further than the walls of my prison, I was stuck fast like a mussel to a mudbank and a mussel without money. Pocket money was doled out to me like war rations, very, very charily, for as a matter of course Dick's pay was deflected to bear the burden of extra family expense, for which it was hardly sufficient.

Dick's parents, the Peabodys, Florrie and Jake, when they were not in their Adirondack camp lived in Danvers, Massachusetts. It adjoined the town of Peabody, but Peabody now was full of factories. My mother-in-law had been a great beauty in the nineties, when as Florence Wheatland she had bowled over kings and then unsensationally become the wife of Jacob Crowninshield Rogers Peabody. My father-in-law was a stickler for polish, both of manners and minerals, brass, silver, copper, glass, to say nothing of boots and belts and other epidermi. Mary Buckley, their Irish factotum, was forever polishing, dusting and arranging. Her primary duties were toward my once very frivolous mother-in-law, who, since invalid days, had adopted the protective carapace of knitted bed-jacket or corded dressing-gown. Of these she had myriads, all grey, brown or black, but cut to one pattern, as were her nun-like dresses, and in bed or out she wore starched collars and cuffs as severe as piping.

My mother-in-law had been born a Wheatland and her parents lived on Salem's main street in a house so very New England that one could easily visualize the homecoming captain in from China Seas inserting his great key of ownership into the gleaming front door lock, his duffle bag over his shoulder bursting with ivory figurines, lacquer snuff boxes and painted silk fans for the ladies of the household. The Peabody Museum round the corner is full of such treasures. Dick's Grandfather Wheatland was a giant of a man with a white walrus moustache. His wife was tiny. Grandpa called her "Mouse" and so Dick called her "Grandma Mouse" and his grandfather in consequence became "Grandpa Mouse" not only for Dick and for me but for our children as well. Dick was the only grandchild and Billy and Polleen were made much of there. Visits to the "old house" in Salem were a delight and Grandma Mouse always had some fabulous toy brought down from the attic with which to charm the great-grandchildren. She was a darling, another "lady of steel." We saw all too little of her. Salem seemed many miles distant from where we were marooned.

The Peabodys lived a strange muted life, uneventful and unjoyful. The moments wore themselves away, blue with the burden of each passing day. The household ticked on trainlike schedule. Only the doctor and the grocer came to call, performing the daily visit like an operation. Once a season the Peabodys entertained sumptuously, though unimaginatively; otherwise each one kept to a different part of the house and

Major (later Colonel) Peabody's door was always closed. Dick was an only child who had never been allowed to play or cry, for both these exercises disturbed his parents. Mary's big-boned Irish body and warm heart supplied both reality and comfort to the little boy. Her household tasks were herculean, but she performed them with fanatic devotion. I was thankful she was still there when I married.

I remember how, on one of her days off, she went to her dentist in Salem, who pulled out every tooth in her head and sent her home to us half massacred. Any other woman would have been flat on her back dosing herself with whisky and codeine, but Mary, her jaws aflame, carried out her evening duties as sure as the *Evening Transcript*. It was weeks before she could swallow anything but tea, and then, suddenly one Thursday she burst back upon us with the jaw line of a mastodon and the molars of a dental shingle. I was even too frightened to laugh, which was fortunate, for she was as pleased as Pollyanna. It turned out to be worth the price, for it bagged her a husband, Joseph, the handyman.

The house at Danvers had been brought over from England, brick upon brick, by some ancestral shipowner plying out of Salem. It was pure Georgian and furnished with exquisite taste, but it was a lifeless edifice too often shuttered to be healthy and it stood at the crossroads of an encroaching community until gradually its woodland and pastures and gardens were squeezed down to a garden path and finally to a few feet of protective sidewalk that kept Route 27 from the door. It was as different from my own family's headquarters on East Island as a well from a windmill.

I never did have any idea of what was due me, and I rolled bandages until my fingers burned. Occasionally I was permitted to invite a fellow war-widow to lunch, which, otherwise, I ate alone, but all during that awful season no human being ever "dropped in," for our house was a forbidding one. The kindest word I remember was when Uncle Jack Morgan, who had been calling on my family-in-law, and who was Dick's godfather (he had paid the doctor's bills when both our babies were born) actually asked to see Billy! I led him to the playpen on the back piazza and he assured me that my son was a fine boy and that he "looked just like his father." This so touched my starved emotions (no other member of the family had asked to see Billy) that I burst into tears in spite of myself. Embarrassed, he patted my shoulder gingerly and lent me his enormous cambric handkerchief smelling wonderfully of beeswax and friendship.

J. P. Morgan first became "Uncle Jack" when I married his godson Richard Rogers Peabody in 1915. And I remember vividly my first visit as Polly Peabody to East Island, now called "Matinacock." As we crossed the familiar causeway in our snorting Stutz I was breathless to see what changes had been wrought on my childhood playground. I had heard that the new house was fabulous, the improvements magnificent, but the straight and shining driveway, with all the familiar trees and haystacks cleared from its path, that ran like a ramrod down the centre of the island to where a great angel cake of a house stood firmly unfamiliar, annihilated for me too many happy memories. My grandfather's house had been swept away like some cobweb fantasy and gone were the carriage-block, gone the pebbled paths, the iron deer and the spring house on the lawn, all the compact pattern of stable, kitchen-garden and duck-pond had disappeared; instead a long and level lawn lay before us hateful to my retrospective eyes.

The house too I thought was monstrous, formal and uninviting—no wine-damp cellar, no pungent attic I was sure. We had come down to pay our respects to Aunt Jessie and Uncle Jack, but happily at that hour we found them out and I was able to drag Dick away from the trim and garnished beach, for gone too was the little wooden pier of yesteryear and gone beyond recall the purple mussel shoals, the languorous seaweed and the sand-locked diamonds.

I returned there only once again, and that was after I was married to Harry Crosby who in turn was Aunt Jessie's nephew, for she had been a Miss Grew, a sister of Harry's mother, and so the Morgans still remained "Aunt Jessie and Uncle Jack." My two marriages had related me, often twice, to most of Boston.

That time we went down in fear and panic, for Aunt Jessie's life hung in the balance. The evening before she had thrown herself between her husband and the bullet of some crazed revolutionary who had pushed his way through the front door and on into the library and levelled a gun point-blank at Uncle Jack's heart. Aunt Jessie's instant interception had saved her husband's life, but when she flung her arms about his neck she had received in her shoulder the bullet meant for the heart of the "Robber Baron."

After World War II when the United Nations first met in Flushing Meadows and delegations from every land were looking for impressive and comfortable quarters, it was the Russians who took over East Island; but the Russians let no one pass the causeway. Replacing the watchman who dug clams in Dosoris Pond and lived upon the bridge, there now were guards who stalked that bridge with rifles, and I have been told that by the front door rose a glistening mound of empty Coca Cola bottles and by the back door a mountainous pile of empty tin cans.

Now, in 1952, I learn that the house is to be torn down, I imagine the island is to be divided into building lots. When the GI's return from Korea and Japan with Asiatic brides undoubtedly another page of the history of our times will be acted out upon the island where I once upon a time grew up.

Uncle Jack was a big-featured, top-heavy man, shy in appearance and softly economical of speech, but infinitely generous of heart. I will always remember Aunt Jessie and Uncle Jack as the true lovers they were, and I believe, strangely enough, he understood later why Harry died. Cousin Walter Berry would have understood, too; until his death Cousin Walter was our best friend in Paris. Uncle Jack never failed me and when I married Harry, it was he who bolstered the Crosbys' belief in my integrity. Of that generation, my father, Uncle Jack and Cousin Walter were my heroes.

Except for that visit from Uncle Jack, Dick's letters became my one hold on reality and I wrote him every day; would he never return? I joined the Red Cross and gave all my time to war work. I operated the switchboard. Harry Crosby's aunt, Mrs. Boylston Beal, a fashionable woman, for whom I had a great affection, was the head of the North Shore Division. She took me under her wing and praised my devotion to the cause.

When several years later I divorced Dick to marry her nephew, she was as emphatically against me as she had been pro, but I have remained pro "Auntie E."

And now Polleen was to have her first birthday, July 21st, 1918. I knew it would have to be a joyless affair, *and then the miracle! Long distance calling Mrs. Richard Peabody*—it sounded impossible. Whoever could it be? I took up the receiver on my father-in-law's forbidden desk (he had left for France).

"Hello," I queried.

"Pittans, is that you?"

"Dick, where are you?"

"I can't say yet, but you must join me tomorrow."

"Where, oh, where?"

"Columbia, South Carolina. Sit in the biggest hotel until I come."

"Are you wounded?" I trembled.

"Never better. For God's sake, hurry."

"Oh, darling, yes," I answered.

"How's Ma?" he added. And I almost resented that he had remembered her.

"Pretty well."

"Hurry, hurry," he repeated, "I've got to stop now. There's a whole line of men waiting to talk to their wives."

"Tomorrow," I cried, "as soon as ever I can."

"Hurry." And then the wire went dead and I came alive, the vigour of joy possessed me. But how to get to South Carolina was the question. I had never been south of South Philadelphia and I had no money. Immediately I thought of Uncle Will Barnum—he would help. All I had to do was to get to New York, I could manage that. Now, like the revolving statues in the circus the world wore spangled tights instead of black ones, joy, joy, joy!

The nurse rose beautifully to the emergency. She helped me pack and lent me back her last month's wages. I kept racing in and out of the nursery to kiss the children and to fling my arms around her neck. She looked just like Florence Nightingale, or as I supposed she looked.

I landed at six p.m. in Columbia, in mid-July—it was stifling. I was wearing a navy blue taffeta dress with a big bow at the back and a tiny blue Panama bonnet, adorned with pond lilies. My waist was thin and so was my purse, but my heart was as big and as bursting as the station. I looked in vain for Dick, there were soldiers everywhere, moving in and out. I had received a telegram before leaving, "Have managed a room at the Jefferson." So I found the hotel bus, horse-drawn, with a benign Negro coachman. He lifted me aboard as though I were a baby. It was not full and we jogged through the town in Southern style. Everywhere there were soldiers. When I reached the hotel I learned that the officer and his wife who occupied our room would not be leaving until midnight. No place to wash, no place to hide. I waited beneath the biggest lamp as fluttery as a moth and then Dick was there, beloved and bewildering, the handsomest man I have ever seen, then or since.

He had grown a moustache, which was new and startling, but his lanky body and handsome head were breathtakingly beautiful. My own live husband again, I was ready to swoon, and then the agony began, nowhere to go. The couple whose room we were to take over were saying their farewells, for he was moving out overseas, one couldn't disturb their last moments, and Dick had to be back in camp at eleven, although he was a captain now.

We could dine and talk and hope for refuge, which we did in the big, bright dining room. I remember his spurs on my instep under the table. I didn't even take a drink in those days, but that night he ordered champagne, and we drank to each other and to the end of the war. We laid a plot for the coming months. It was decided I would go forth the very next day to find us a place to keep house in, big enough for us all, and then return to Boston to fetch the children. That it might be hard on them to be whisked from a cool New England shore to a stifling Southern city in mid-summer never for a moment interfered with our plans.

When we finished dinner it was after nine. Dick went to see if the room was free yet. "They're leaving soon," he announced hopefully, adding, "but I've got to be in camp by eleven."

It was nearing ten before the red-eyed couple descended to

the lobby. We brazenly took the return elevator to their sultry shelter, ours at last. But when my luggage was deposited on the paper-strewn carpet and the light switch above the mute and rumpled bed showed an empty bottle of Dutch courage on an untidy dresser, I turned away, tears in my eyes. "I can't," I said, "stay here," and fled down the corridor.

"Nor I," commiseratingly; he had understood. "I'll be back tomorrow when it's all clear and all ours."

"Thank you, darling," I whispered as we clung hand in hand in the descending lift. I decided to drive out to camp with him and we hailed a barouche.

The camp was a mile or more from town, but he still had time to show me his quarters, and as we started to retrace our way to the gate, "Couldn't I possibly stay?" I hazarded, the thought and the urge were overwhelming. No one was near.

"Come this way," Dick whispered and pulled me away from the lights. "I know a place," he added. And we ran hand in hand through the palpitating darkness until we were well away from the barracks and the activities of the camp. "There's a trench near here," he said. "My platoon dug it this morning. It is deep and it will hide us and I'll go get a blanket."

In my high-heeled slippers I struggled after him along the edge of a wood. We were on manœuvre ground and suddenly the trench loomed at my feet. Dick jumped in and held out his arms to me. "Now you wait here," he whispered, "I'll be back as soon as lights are out. You aren't scared, are you?"

I was scared to death, but I answered, "No, but come back soon."

"I will," he promised, and was gone.

And there I sat on my taffeta bow, my gloves and my purse on my quaking knees, the pond lilies atremble above the edge of the trench. It was as black as prunes as one by one the lights went out—what if I were shot for a spy, what if Dick were ordered on duty. Little Miss Muffet was never so terrified as I, but in my veins coursed the mating courage. I waited and then I heard the dry earth echo to a footstep. It was my husband, wrapped in one O.D. blanket and carrying two others. We made our narrow bed beneath the stars and then we lay in it; the soldier's return.

Just before dawn, my deep, deep slumber was softly shaken by a tremor under ear. It grew louder, I sat up gleaming in the gloom. Dick slept on, but distinctly now I could feel a rhythmic rumbling beneath us. I nudged him awake, he tried to pull me down again, but now I was fully aware and frightened. The east was beginning to lighten too.

"What's that noise?" I asked.

"Ugh."

"Dick, wake up," and I prodded him with my elbow. Then he too sat up.

"My God, the artillery!" The din increased. "Quick, get down," he said, and dragged the blanket over our heads. We clung together in horror as over us surged a sea of hoofs. The caissons came rolling along while the captain and his lady lay quaintly cradled beneath their charging wheels.

"You should give a command now," I giggled, with my nose beneath his shoulder.

I'm afraid his aplomb was rudely shaken, I know mine was. "They won't come round again, will they?" I pleaded. He assured me they were on their way to the proving grounds, but "I should be with them," he groaned and began pulling on breeches and boots.

My hat and stockings looked very rakish as they hung on that earthy wall. Dick climbed out. "What do I do next," I inquired meekly.

"Get dressed and wait until seven, the main gate will open then, All you have to do is walk quietly out. The General's wife lives in the compound." I smiled wanly. It was going to be a long time till breakfast and a bath.

The sun was up now, but there I sat waiting for the zero hour, huddled and alone. When my watch said seven I went over the top, shook out my taffeta, put on my gloves and with lilies flying I marched primly forth feeling for all the world like some wayward "o'Grady" but looking, I hoped, like the General's lady.

The guard at the gates saluted but nearly dropped his gun.

CHAPTER 8

I went North a few days later to gather up my children, for I had found a Southern roof that would cover us all. It was the Mayor's roof; he was a bachelor and lived in a big square mansion in the finest street in town. Up the back of his house ran a ladder-like flight of steps which joined a sleeping porch —this porch and two rooms on that floor were to be the babies' —Dick and I would take over the empty attic, where I had installed matting, a big mattress and electric fans. I furnished the whole attic at floor level with Oriental taste and missionary expenditure. That division of the American army might just as well have been stationed in Malaya. I even found a Canton-Carolinian cook and, of course, I imported the nurse along with the children. It was a toy soldier summer. I was on my own for the first time since 1916 and I played at housekeeping.

It was funny how nonplussed the Mayor was the afternoon I invited him to tea. He climbed his attic stairs (I imagine for the first time) to find a Governor sitting cross-legged on the floor, for we were entertaining a relative, as well as the landlord, that day.

It was a sweltering summer and water was scarce, but we all thrived and Polleen's hair began to show, a growth that I had almost despaired of. During her first year I had to sew dolls' curls into her bonnet.

The only unpleasant events of that summer were the Saturday night country club "hops," to which were invited those officers who had been privileged to join. There was always a very liquidous and tedious wait for a badly cooked dinner, a lot of raucous highjinks as the other wives screamed with laughter, but I just couldn't laugh too, though I tried to join in for the honour of the regiment. I knew they all considered me a wet blanket, for after I left (always the first) I was told that "the fun really began." I naturally got the reputation of being "stuck-up," which is the last thing I ever was, but I did hate those *hops*—and spurs can hurt.

It was understood that Dick, who was instructing at camp because he had trained at Saumur, would return again to France the following spring—and then most blessedly and unexpectedly, the war came to an end. The False Armistice was like Mardi Gras in that Southern town.

By Thanksgiving we were back in Back Bay, this time on our own, for I swore never again to jeopardize our future by squatting beneath the parental roof-tree.

We took a house in Marlborough Street just opposite the Codmans'. Charlie Codman, Bostonian of Bostonians but looking more like a Balkan prince, was Dick's "copain" and Billy's godfather, also one of the dearest friends I have ever known. He had been a member of the Lafeyette Escadrille in France. It was there that he acquired a fine palate for French wine and French cooking. Charlie is now considered one of the greatest gourmets of our land and the Somerset Club is his Beacon Street bistro. That year he helped me through the stormiest of seasons.

The Marlborough Street house was as Boston as beans; it smelt deliciously of treacle and cardamom. We could have been as happy there as we were in South Carolina, but Dick was now out of uniform, work was hard to find, glorious memories of France obscured his vision. He was restless and frustrated and his health began to suffer. Whisky was so plentiful, jobs were so few, and he had not accepted the reality of marriage. (I have never had a husband who did.)

I too loved adventure and play, but I was aware of my maternal obligations, and I loved my children. I shudder now at some of the awful moments that had to be weathered that winter. Finally Dick had to have a special nurse in the house who kept watch night and day. I was too unnerved to eat or sleep. Dick's father was still overseas with the Red Cross, for which his duties outran the war. Dick's mother was immunized behind drawn blinds, I hardly knew where to turn, and then I thought of Uncle Jack, so I travelled to New York to see him.

It was just at the moment when the French mission was in the city arranging for a private loan through J. P. Morgan and Company and meeting every day in the Morgan Library or in the Wall Street Office; the papers were full of Uncle Jack and high finance. I rang him up and he must have known by my voice that I needed help desperately.

"Come to the library at 11.15," he said. It is only very big men who have time for very little people. I was there ahead of time and as the solemn financiers filed out I tiptoed in— I had been told that they were coming back at 11.45 to sign papers—but half an hour was mine. Uncle Jack heard my woes, attentively, pondered them as though they were as important as world currency, then gave me sure and straight advice. Dick was his godchild.

"Can you get someone to stay with the children?"

"My mother will," I hazarded.

"Can you get a friend of Dick's to go with you to camp?"

"Charlie, perhaps."

"Fine."

"Have you any money?"

"Not very much," timidly.

The buzzer—then two calls on the telephone, one to the Morgan overseer at the Adirondack camp, which was to be lent to me, one to his son Junius who was to see to railroad tickets. The buzzer was for a cheque to tide us over.

"I'm here if you need me," he said, then we solemnly shook on it—and I stepped out as France filed in again.

There were wolves in the forest and orchids on the table and the snow drifted to the roof. Charlie could not get there for a few days and I had to manage my overdepressed husband by myself. I couldn't lure him out of doors, and though I walked and I stalked, he sat morosely by the fire. My heart ached for him.

89

Then Charlie came and we fished through the ice (the holes were cut and seats placed beside them by the guides). Dick attempted it, but it was no good. We took long rides, too, in the fur-mounded sleigh drawn by the fleetest pair of pacers in the county. There were plenty of books, wonderful food, games galore, but Dick could not snap out of his depression. Finally, although Charlie and I watched like hawks, he managed to get hold of a bottle, for any stuff would serve; this one was smuggled in by the boy who had brought the mail. It was a dangerous moment, and Charlie, who had to go back to Boston next day, decided that he couldn't leave me there alone with such a very sick man, so we telephoned Junius—and we all three departed together. Dick in anger, I in despair. From that time on life was hideously difficult, and soon Dick had to be treated in a sanitorium. It was that spring that I met Harry.

When I had married Richard Rogers Peabody in 1915, I had stepped right into a bonded circle of Boston hierarchs. My clothes at the time must have looked heathenish to Beacon Hill, a red velvet cassock coat trimmed with monkey fur, high-heeled walking shoes and fishnet stockings, my haircut was sensational (the Castle bob) and worse than that, I painted my fingernails pink. But my tenue was impeccable and my manners without a flaw and those amenities saved me from ridicule.

I have always enjoyed a chameleon-like exterior, and in no time at all I even came to out-Boston the Bostonians.

I was accepted and soon had my followers; that I found I could play them like trout was a revelation, once I used this unstintingly to save my neck. It was when I was suspected of considering divorcing a Peabody that the entire "shore" ganged up on me and were plotting to move in for the kill. It was to be done this way. I was again asked by Lily Warren to luncheon in the self-same house in Pride's Crossing where Dick and I had announced our engagement. I had heard rumours that every "We All" would be there and that they were planning to show me just how and why I must not throw off the proper harness so wantonly. If I refused the invitation I was to be branded without benefit of trial; if I went I knew I must defend myself or sink.

I lay awake all that night wondering how I could turn the tide of onslaught. I decided on a deadly counterattack. I guessed who would be there, Lily, Fran, Elaine, Ruth, Dorothy, Margaret, and E and O. I listed each opponent, and opposite each name I noted the most vulnerable chink in her armour. I rehearsed a speech for each, loading it with compliment and praise. I realized that I would have to knock them off one by one before any two could get together. So I arrived early, managing with the help of talcum and hairpins to look pale and subdued—but I was dressed to perfection—even a new hat from Tappé, special delivery from New York.

My hostess first; I came in bearing gifts, calculated gifts. I poured on praise like perfume. When the first guest was announced, I congratulated myself that one victim was already in my pocket.

Number two was easy; I just repeated the compliments of every well-known beau in Newport. The third succumbed to adulation of her offspring. It was this one's clothes and that one's horsemanship that came next in line of fire. The flattery was so blatant that at each overpowering blandishment I felt like being sick—but it worked, my Lord, it worked. They all forgot about poor little me and my defection while listening to their own achievements. Before the coffee, always a dangerous moment, I took a hasty leave. I said I was to meet a man about a magazine, one for which I was asked to write an article on Boston's Beautiful Women, and I even got away with that.

This was such a shock to me that I swore I would never use flattery again as long as I lived and I never have. It is too easy and too ludicrous a weapon, but that once may I be forgiven, it did help me to keep my special standards flying and to hold my sacred ground. The next winter Dick and I were divorced, and I took the children with me back to New York, that highly amoral bourne from which unquestionably I never should have strayed.

I would not care to tell all this if I could not tell also of Dick's remarkable recovery after our divorce. He was shattered at first until he managed to take stock of his life, past and future—we were gone, but Charlie and other friends stuck by him, and it was through them that he came in contact with the famous psychologist and missioner, Dr. George Worcester, of Emanuel Church, Boston. Through him Dick recovered his equilibrium and began attending the church classes. Little by little he joined in the work and he, too, began to talk with and influence his contemporaries whose weakness for alcohol had been their undoing. This work took on more and more importance, and he himself effected some remarkable cures. He even came to be spoken of as "Dr." Peabody, and though he was self-taught and a layman, he decided to set up an informal office in Newbury Street. Patients came to him from far and wide. His advice was, "When you need a drink you need a friend. Come to me then, we will talk it out at any time, day or night." He was a fore-runner of the famous Alcoholics Anonymous.

The last two years of her father's life Polly spent her winters with him in New York, where he then lived, married for the second time. He was inordinately fond of Polly, and theirs was a gay and sympathetic friendship. Billy he saw less of because Billy was away at school during the winters and in Europe with me during the summers, but they too drew very close to one another. Dick and I remained devoted friends until the end. I was in Paris when the news of his untimely death reached me. Dick wrote a book called *The Common Sense of Drinking*, which was widely read, and Johns Hopkins University has dedicated a research laboratory to his memory. Dick died in the spring of 1935, in his early forties, but he left a name honoured by hundreds who knew him, and revered by increasing hundreds of thousands who now benefit from his experience.

CHAPTER 9

The first time I saw Harry Crosby he was in his Field Service uniform. It was in April, 1919. He had just landed from over-seas, and he and his mother and his young sister Kitsa (for Katharine) were having a heated argument at the top of the subway stairs in Copley Square. They had come out of the State Street Trust Company as I was going in. His uniform looked shabby, his puttees were sloppily wound and accentu-ated his bowlegs, he was white and he was thin, but in his restless eyes I caught a look so completely *right* that from that moment I sensed my destiny.

It is difficult to describe Harry completely, for he seemed to be more expression and mood than man—and yet he was the most vivid personality that I have ever known, electric with rebellion. Harry was frail, of middle height and had an almost ungainly look, but he was taut as a tangent, his eyes blazed like mica, his mouth was large and it quivered ever so slightly when he was nervous, and his hands were like a musician's hands, sensitive, compelling. I quoted of him once

> *Yours is the music for no instrument*
> *Yours the preposterous colour unbeheld.*

Immaturity of mind and maturity of spirit were the forces that warred within him. He combined the naiveness of youth with the wisdom of ages. He seemed like one who had taken on burdens from many former lives and discarded many along the way. The circle was nearly closed.

93

To know Harry was a devastating experience, and every one of his friends fell beneath the spell. It is no wonder that I was drawn into the golden orbit, as metal to the magnet by his magic—and as I look back now I see that there was never any question of escape. Not even when I ran away.

On the Shore, Harry led the fun, the escapades, the sports, the thoughts of his contemporaries; without Harry the days lost their shine. When I met him there were half a dozen girls in love with him. I believe it was my princess-in-a-tower look that appealed to him, but that morning in Copley Square I only sensed the music and the colours.

I don't believe he even noticed me then. He has told me that he saw me first at a charity bazaar in Beverly Farms a few weeks later. I was wheeling my baby daughter in her carriage, she with a blue bow under her chin and I with a black one. Harry said that I looked like a little girl too, and he thought I had only borrowed the baby.

The next day his mother called me on the telephone to ask if I would chaperone her son and his friends that same evening to Nantasket Beach. There would be about a dozen young people, she said. It was Harry's twenty-first birthday, June 4, and I was a married woman of twenty-seven, and properly aged for the rôle. They were to have dinner at a new roadhouse just opened, called Normandy Farms, and then go on to the amusement park at Nantasket Beach, Boston's Coney Island. Dick was in the hospital at the time, and I had been by myself a lot, so almost guiltily I said I'd love to. My heart skipped a beat as I hung up the receiver.

They were to call for me at seven, but "they" turned out to be Harry alone, this time in billowing plus-fours, the most unbecoming garment a man can wear. He got out awkwardly from behind the wheel of his mother's new Lancia roadster.

"I am Harry Crosby," he said, surprised, "Ma told me to call for a Mrs. Peabody. I didn't realize it would be you." And he took off his glasses and looked into my eyes.

I was dressed rather gayly in a not-too-matronly dotted Swiss with a big frilly collar and poke bonnet to match. He said right away how pretty I was—he seated me on his right at the table, quite correctly, but quite incorrectly he never spoke to the embarrassed girl on his left. His attentions embarrassed me, too, and they embarrassed everyone else, but not Harry.

Afterwards, when we drove to Nantasket, I was matronly about getting into the car with some of the others and almost pushed the slighted maiden into the Lancia, but it was no use; once at Nantasket, Harry never left my side. And when we whirled through the Tunnel of Love, "I love you," he said, and I believed it then as I believe it now.

There was a feeling of impending fate watching over us that evening. I think everyone felt it. Harry seemed utterly ruthless and I reluctantly enthralled, while the others grew uneasily aware of our predicament. "Can I see you tomorrow?" was as though he had said, "Can I see you forever?" and my reply, "Should we?" was also an admission of acceptance, for whether we should or we shouldn't, the tarots were already dealt. That night we hardly talked at all. It was enough to feel his hand in mine as we wandered out of the Tunnel of Love into the Cave of the Winds and from the Cave of the Winds through the Penny Arcade, until closing time came round and all of us drove home together quite strange and mute.

Having disregarded the dictates of Back Bay and associated myself completely with Harry, to whom in heart I was already wedded, I underwent a complete change of spirit. For the first time in my life I knew myself to be a person. I had dedicated myself to love in the true platonic sense—the sense that all love is right. In the New England atmosphere that surrounded my childhood, expressions of love had been aborted—my urge to fling my arms around the necks of all darling people was denied me early in life—for it was not permitted that we children kiss the Italian furnace man, although it seemed the only natural way to greet him at his warmth-giving offices. Now I had taken a step in a direction of my own and from that step on, I would travel forward.

That summer Harry and I went for picnics on Coffin's Beach. We walked miles along the deserted sand at the edge of the dunes, talking, searching, plotting in the sureness of our union, some way to fulfill our destiny, not only happiness for ourselves but for my children, his family, my husband. Was loyalty to

95

my marriage more right than loyalty to ourselves? Would denial help or mar the lives interwoven with our own?

Dick came back from the hospital that fall and seemed better able to cope with postwar life. He actually took a job in the State Street Trust Company where most of the directors were relations or friends of the family. The Peabodys allotted us a modest allowance and this, with Dick's salary, enabled us to live by ourselves but to live much more frugally than our friends did. I was so happy at the thought of being away from the in-laws that I determined to find us suitable quarters no matter what or where—and they were found over a fishmonger's on River Street, a slum section of Back Bay, off Beacon, right under the hill, in process of being reclaimed and remodelled.

It was a one-flight walk-up with two floors of our own, two rooms to a floor, with a flat roof above which was soon transformed into a windy wickery terrace. 37 River was just at the back of 95 Beacon, the Crosbys' handsome neo-Georgian house that faced the Common and looked down its nose at the Ritz. I was sure to see a lot of Harry although I had determined to be a full-time wife that winter and do my cheerfullest to help Dick over his psychic trouble.

I refused to see Harry alone, but he did not allow me to ignore him. Harry's mother and sister had gone to Switzerland for the winter months and Harry was finishing his second year for a war degree at Harvard and was living at 95 with "Steve," his father.

Friends of Mrs. Crosby's during her absence remarked upon the lack of flowers that every other winter had in profusion filled her rooms and banked the hallways—orchids, camellias, roses and chrysanthemums from her hothouses on the shore. Eyebrows were raised when it was reported that on entering the narrow portals of 37 River the fishy smells at street level were routed by the perfume of gardenia and lily; and an unexpected profusion of orchids, camellias, roses and chrysanthemums was found to be ever blooming above. Harry had managed to deflect the weekly crates, and one evening when Steve Crosby was giving a dinner party, his butler came running round to borrow back my potted plants.

11. Harry Crosby and his Bugatti, Paris, 1921.

12. In the height of fashion at the Races—Caresse and Edith Cummings, Longchamps, 1923

13. "In life-sized effigy upon a double marble bed." Montparnasse cemetery, 1924.

14. Polleen, " Corydon " and Billy, Etretat, 1924.

15. Caresse and Comte Francois
de Ganay, Longchamps, 1925.

16. Mrs. Crosby took us to St. Moritz in 1925.

Harry used to load the children with books and toys galore. It was really rather unfair to Dick, and Harry was free in the afternoons too. I couldn't escape him and he absorbed me in spite of myself.

It was at this point that Dick installed a fire gong between our beds. He made a deal with the fire chief so that every alarm above a two-alarm should be clanged into our ears, night and morn. It was unnerving. Dick kept a full fireman's outfit, hip boots, rubber coat and helmet ready on a chair. His Ford was in the garage below and he was contemplating a greased pole through the floor, when these private alarms were stopped. No more amateur fire fighters were to be encouraged. This was a real blow to Dick, who now sought excitement elsewhere. The elsewhere turned out to be the roadhouses. He began drinking again. That winter didn't work.

Spring 1921 came round—Dick, Harry and I were all three miserable. Finally, in the early summer instead of returning to the shore I took Billy, who had developed heart trouble after a severe attack of measles, to my mother's in Watertown and sent Polleen off to a friend's in the country near Topsfield. Both men were causing me worry that summer, and moreover I felt I had to earn my own living if I wished to be free. I couldn't accept anything from either Dick or Harry until my own course was determined. To be quite independent I naively decided to support myself and my children by acting for the screen, so, bobbing my hair, I packed off to New York in sweltering mid-July.

CHAPTER 10

I wasn't going to try the stage; I had a well-earned misgiving of the stage.

The year before I came out, Carol Kobbé, daughter of the musician Gustav Kobbé, was my best friend. We were inseparable; at football games, proms, house parties and the Junior League, and we were both ambitious—even to the vulgar point of making money—for our allowances never seemed to stretch past the halfway mark of the month; Carol collected ruffles and ribbons, which she was forever pressing, and I invented things. Both of these activities called for cash.

She was visiting me in Watertown, Connecticut, for a week in the spring of 1913—my brother Bud went to Taft School up the hill and my other brother, Len, was at Westminster School over the mountain. The nearest city was Waterbury, where Mama's best friend, Mrs. Driggs, owned a safety-pin factory. We were so well known there that the event I am about to describe had to be kept quite secret.

At the Waterbury theatre an evening a week was reserved for amateurs. Some of the acts were considered "hot stuff" and the Taft boys often sneaked out of bounds to see them. On this particular Saturday night we had been told by one of the more worldly Taft seniors that the theatre was offering a cash prize of $50.00 for the best performance by an amateur team, and why didn't Carol and I compete? Under assumed names, of course! The idea was intriguing, the prize seemed enormous and we were both flat broke.

"We'll do it," we said and asked our informant to make the necessary arrangements. It seemed we only had to hand in our team name and give a sheet of our own music to the orchestra, and then appear. We decided to call ourselves "The Maxixe Maidens" (it was the year of the maxixe craze) and we set to work in secret to concoct our costumes. They were gay and giddy and I must say we looked divine. We used the sewing machine while Mama was out playing golf, so she never knew.

On Saturday night our hearts were in our mouths. We pretended we were going over to the neighbours to play pingpong, but instead we stealthily met our friends at the trolley stop at the foot of Academy Hill. These swains must have included John Garfield, freckled, sandy haired, six foot three, grandson of President Garfield, Otis Guernsey, now head of Abercombie and Fitch, Pat Calhoun, one of the blueblood Calhouns of the Southland, and other members of the senior class. The boys had armed themselves with whistles, rattles and a large bouquet of brilliant vegetables to cheer us on to victory. We carried our costumes hidden in red flannel Tiffany bags. I felt positively seasick with apprehension on the swaying trolley.

The Maxixe Maidens were next to last on the programme which terminated with "Baby Grossman and His Mother," a team that promised no appeal at all. There was a dog act first, then two clowns, followed by a very clumsy juggler with a very bossy wife, and then our big moment was at hand. The board bearing the legend "Maxixe Maidens" was placed upon an easel, the orchestra struck up our special music, and we kicked our heels and ran prettily out upon the stage to the valiant applause of the first row. We had to do an encore and, thanks to the rattles and whistles of our friends, we got a far bigger hand than any of the preceding acts. We were sure we were in, the grand prize was in our pockets, for there were only that baby and his mother to follow—and then their round came up.

A fat and beaming matron rolled her child to the footlights with a self-satisfied flourish. The audience waited in silence. There was a roll of drums, she lifted a stupid-looking infant from his carriage, and his hand in hers, led him waddling across

99

the stage. The house went wild, they stood up and cheered from the second row to the last. Baby Grossman had three legs!

But now it was 1920, the early days of the silent movies. Movie stars, I heard, made easeful money. I would seek my fortune on the screen.

My uncle's family had moved down to Southampton, Long Island, for the summer, the house on Park Avenue was vacant, except for an old caretaker in the nether regions. The furniture was shrouded in dust sheets, the rugs rolled and tied, bed covers inside-out drawn over the naked pillows like shrouds over the faces of the dead. I asked if I might use one of the shuttered bedrooms and was given a key and a candle (the electricity was off) and I was warned not to drip wax on the mahogany.

It was spooky all alone there, more so because of the mumblings and shufflings below stairs, but I felt rather like a stage heroine and the place was in perfect key with my theatrical aspirations.

A former schoolmate of mine, Ethel Outerbridge, told me that her father was the attorney for two adventurous young brothers who were starting a moving picture company in New York, an outlandish idea, as outlandish as they themselves seemed to be—their name was Selznick, an impossible name, too, but if I really wanted to be a movie star, she said she would ask her father to introduce them to me (not me to them!). And so it was arranged, and I met David and Myron Selznick in Mr. Outerbridge's inner office. I was promised (I was sure in deference to Mr. O.) that a test would be arranged. But first, if I wanted to try an extra part, just to see what it was like, I could come over to the studio where they were "shooting" *Lilac Time,* starring Norma Talmadge.

I felt my fortune was in my pocket. I promised to be at the studio at 7.30 next morning (which sounded workmanlike, but well nigh impossible) and I was to wear a calico dress plus a sunbonnet. It was a World War I picture, so that was easy. I telephoned Mother to tell her the news. She was properly horrified.

"Don't let your Uncle Will know," she warned me. "He

would never allow such a thing. Why, Polly, you may have to kiss one of those awful movie heroes."

I assured her that only the heroine kissed the hero and that I was nothing but an extra, which somewhat mollified but also chagrined her.

I got into bed, my hair in curlers to be ready for that morrow, and by the light of my candle I set to work to invent a stage name, for no one must ever know that a Boston matron had strayed thus far from the Sheep Pen. After filling several sheets with phonetic gems I decided upon "Valerie Marno" and was so well pleased with it that I never noticed that wax already puddled my bed table's rosy surface. I blew out my light and I fell asleep with new assurance, the happy assurance of a career-woman-to-be.

The casting manager looked me over rather dubiously. I didn't somehow seem to suit him.

"Marno," he said, "your name is Marno?"

I assured him it was—if I'd only known that the impressive name of "Peabody" had already been heralded and that the studio was awaiting my advent with its neck craned!

The first scene was laid outside a country railroad station. The English lads were returning from the front, dozens of them, pouring from a third-class coach and, shades of my mother, I was told I was to be a one-girl welcoming committee and was to greet them one and all; kiss and take, retake and kiss, hour after hour; by noon, smeared with grease paint and frazzled, I was ready to admit that maybe Mama knew best.

When the long day was over and, battered and unhappy, I accepted my first day's pay I was on the verge of tears.

"Come tomorrow," I was told.

I was about to say "No thank you," when the director patted me on the behind and said, "You're good," and so I wavered and answered, "Yes."

"Tomorrow you'll get a 'bit' part," he added. "Bring a bigger hat with longer streamers. You will do Talmadge's little sister."

If my sense of humour had not been able to swallow those kisses I think I would have sobbed myself to sleep. It was not going to be so easy to make a fortune.

The next day was better. All I had to do was sit beside the

star in a jaunting-cart and look wide-eyed and innocent. I noticed humbly that whenever the word "camera" was boomed out, Norma T. leaned forward just far enough so that her big hat obliterated all of me but the very ends of my ribbons. However, my career was progressing, for the next morning and the next Mr. Selznick's own car and chauffeur called for me at the house and brought me back at the end of the day. Once the great man (for by now I looked upon this "impossible person" as a sort of Zeus) actually came for me himself.

"How would you like to play a real part," he asked, "in Hammerstein's picture?" (Elaine Hammerstein, Oscar's daughter, was the glamour girl of the moment.) I choked with emotion. "We're shooting up the Hudson, on the Palisades, You can double for her," he announced magnanimously, "if you can ride a horse."

"What else?" I thought, but replied modestly, "I've hunted with the Quorn."

"That's it," he said. "She rides off a cliff. It's hard work, you mustn't let us down."

"Oh, no," I agreed, and almost added "Sir" as I mentally curtsied.

"I have your number, we'll call you," and he grandly drove away.

For the next two days I hardly left the telephone, waiting for that call, and then late one night it rang, but it was a frightened voice I heard on the other end, the voice of the friend in Massachusetts at whose house my daughter and her nurse were staying.

"It's about Polleen," she said. "The doctor has just been here, and he thinks it's acute mastoid. He wants to operate at once. We are taking her to Boston to the hospital tonight."

"I'll catch the midnight, there's still time, but don't let them touch her till I get there." Intuition guided me. "Take her to the Massachusetts General," I instructed. "Please call Dick and ask him to meet my train at Back Bay, but don't operate, don't operate. Good-bye, I must hurry."

It was 10.30, so I still had an hour and a half. I called my own doctor, long distance, told him the story and begged him to be at the hospital to meet me at 7.30 the next morning. He promised, and I packed and was about to leave for Grand Central Station when I discovered I had no money, only five dollars, my last day's pay at the studio. I would have to sit up all night and I couldn't afford a taxi either, so I dumped my suitcase upside down and stuffed a few necessities into a silk bathing-suit bag and was off on foot up Park Avenue alone at midnight. In those days ladies didn't go out at night unaccompanied. The house was at Thirty-eighth so I had only a few blocks to walk, but my heart beat furiously with anxiety and emotion. Even if I could have afforded a sleeper I couldn't have slept. That train was the slowest one I ever travelled on, while visions of Polleen's lovely little neck being gouged by a scalpel were terrifying me.

"I don't believe it, I can't believe it," I kept repeating.

Dick was on the platform looking anxiously up at the sleepers when I climbed down from the day coach.

"Pittans, why didn't you take a Pullman?" he exclaimed.

"What about Polleen?" I answered.

"She's at the hospital, swollen like a boil. They wanted to operate at once, but you said 'Wait.' "

"Yes," I repeated, "I'm absolutely sure it isn't mastoid."

At the hospital my small daughter was a sight to behold. Her face five times its size, eyes disappeared, but thank goodness Dr. Y was there as I had asked him to be, and he began gravely to examine the balloon-like head, then he went into a huddle with Dr. X. Dick and I waited, my hand in his.

"We have decided to try a serum," Dr. X announced. "My colleague does not agree with the diagnosis."

Thank God, I prayed, for I knew then that the hurt was only temporary and they might have scarred her for life. Treatment proved that the child had been bitten by some poisonous insect, maybe a black widow spider. The swelling soon subsided, the poison was eliminated from the blood stream and by next day my darling little daughter looked almost herself again— no operation—no scar—the maternal hunch had proved correct. We brought her back to the familiar apartment in River Street, with Mary there to care for her. In spite of her tears and Dick's pleading, I entrained that night for New York. I feared that a reunited home with Dick in this fatherly mood would tear my heart in two. My decision had already been taken months before. It would only reopen the wound to stay now. It was one of the most difficult departures of my life. All my decisions seem to culminate in departures.

When I reached the shrouded house in the sizzling city I inquired at once of the old caretaker if there had been any calls.

"No," she said reproachfully, "only Mr. Kelleher, who thinks you must have forgotten you were to have dinner with him last night."

I picked up the telephone to explain and to make another rendezvous with Pat, but with a sinking heart I did not dare call the mighty Selznick. I would just have to sit and wait.

It was not until a week later on a Tuesday—the day my cousin Kathryn always came to town for shopping—that she announced casually, "By the way do you know anyone by the name of Marno? Last Tuesday some studio or other kept calling for her so often that I told the man to please stop ringing, stop annoying us."

My career! I could have bitten her! But I couldn't say that call was for me without giving away my secret.

"I do know her," I said. "If they call again please say I will take the message."

"I doubt if they do," she answered smugly. "I fixed them."

And indeed she had. And I discovered that all the week some other "double" had been riding my hopes away.

I did have one more chance to make good. It was staged in Myron Selznick's new leatherette office—the suggestion was that I do a lead part in the fall, but it so happened that this part involved a trip to Paris so that Mr. S could personally supervise the buying of my wardrobe.

"You know Paris?" he inquired.

Indeed I did, but shades of the Salons of Boué Soeurs, where with my uncle on one side and my cousin on the other, I had, in 1914, chosen my dress to be worn at Court, and the thought of Mr. S on those same gilt chairs threw me into a tizzy. I told him I'd think the proposition over, and I hastened to escape, but I never saw him again until ten years later at the Palace Hotel in St. Moritz.

"Why! You are the little girl I was so sweet on," he condescended.

"Who got the part?" I countered.

"Oh, that part, she's over there. Come along, I'd like to introduce you to my wife."

CHAPTER 11

That summer of 1921 began and ended my career as an actress. After six months of indecision I made up my mind to get a divorce. I had made a tremendous effort to forget Harry, even getting engaged to some other men, but it didn't work. Without Harry life shifted back into second gear. Once one has known rapture, security is not enough. Morally supported, I wrote to Dick that it was really over. I sought out a lawyer, and I went off in the fall of the year for an eight weeks' stay at Millbrook, to establish a residence in New York State.

It was the beginning of the hunting season, Millbrook was horsy. I lived at the Inn, which was packed and gay. The Thornes, the Comptons, the Phelpses, all helped me to forget my woeful state. For I was not allowed to see Harry at all— those were my lawyer's orders. It was a very silly performance and everything was arranged beforehand. The only thing not arranged was the money part. I remember the private hearing in Poughkeepsie and the Judge's fatherly interest in me. When he pronounced the verdict, he turned to Dick to settle the alimony. "Oh, no," I cried, "I couldn't take any money, you see, it was all my fault." This almost landed me back where I came from, but the Judge only gulped and asked Dick about provision for the children. "Do I have to," said Dick. "I imagine you will have to provide, if you wish to see them." Again I broke in. "I am going to take them to France with me when I marry Harry, and I don't want them to come back. So, unless I can have them entirely, I will just get undivorced again."

"It's okay by me," said Dick.

But the Judge was confused.

"Who is divorcing who," he seemed to ask.

At this moment my lawyer interrupted.

"Mrs. Peabody has asked me not to accept alimony, but I do think we should make some provision for the children."

"So do I," said the Judge.

So I let them have their way about it and make an arrangement with the Colonel and Dick. The children would, I knew, inherit the Peabody Trust.

The outcome was that this provision should not figure except as a gentlemen's agreement, but that both children's schooling would be paid for by the Peabodys and that each should receive an adequate allowance at the age of twelve. Also, that I would be repaid any money that Dick had borrowed for his shipping venture. I guess the Judge knew best. If Harry hadn't been nearby, I would have stepped from court honourably penniless—I then proceeded to have remorse about Harry—his family were determined we should not marry and much pressure was brought to bear.

Finally, miserable, bewildered and broke, I embarked alone for England. My Aunt and Uncle George Elin had invited me for a visit to straighten myself out. My passage was paid for with the smallest strand from my grandmother's legacy of pearls. As soon as I said that I was going and before his family knew the plans, Harry, with his mother's help, found a job in the Morgan Bank in Paris. The Crosbys were determined to steer him out of my orbit, so perhaps they thought it was I who followed *him*. The children stayed with Mama.

I was coddled and cosseted at Ardleigh Park. My cousins treated me as though I were as fragile as a soap bubble. I was grateful for the care and rest. It had been a stormy season.

A chaise-longue was placed for me in the garden with a plaid steamer rug and sun-faded cushions. The lawn rolled out to where the holly bushes edged the southern pasture, daffodils and hyacinths bloomed along the fence and in the copper beech the wood pigeons fluttered and cooed. I could

107

hear the whisk of pebbles against the gardener's broom. It was summer again in England.

For at least a week I was as tranquil as tea. I desired nothing —till suddenly desire reawoke. It was Harry's voice from over the Channel that did it. "Be ready," he said, "I am coming to get you." And indeed twenty-four hours later he dropped in from the clouds and swooped me up from the family nest like some mythological bird of prey, to carry me sunwards on beryllium wings to lands across the sea—Venice, to be exact.

This was the first time in my life that I deliberately did what I knew to be clandestine. I had defied convention many times, but never ethics. I yielded to Harry's insistence. But he literally had to tear me away. We could all hear the ties ripping as I climbed into the big airport Daimler. That car should have been tagged with the letter "A" for all to see, instead of its proper G.B.

The Elin family was scandalized but tactfully never referred to this departure in their reports home. Mine was an act too wanton to be put into words—yet what a beautiful adventure it made possible! Venice for the first time, in love, in June.

We found a small hotel avoiding the caravansaries. The balcony windows of the Casa Petrarcha overhung the Grand Canal. For mystification, we registered as the Count and Countess of Myopia. The great adventure had begun.

Harry's five-day bank holiday stretched to a week. Morgan & Company was checking up. So reluctantly we boarded the wagon-lit that bore the sign "Venice, Modena, Milano, Paris." Dinner à deux on the Rome Express is a classic prelude to Paradise.

Too many people knew us in Paris, so we were no longer the Count and Countess of Myopia. Harry shared lodgings with another boy at the Metropolitan in the rue Cambon and I found a tiny room atop the Regina, just above Joan the Maid's gilded lance-point. Harry worked at the bank all day but we lunched and dined together, in secret, until Boston trespassed into our Paradise again.

I had a visit from an indignant hyena-matron who told me that I was ruining Harry's life, that he loved her daughter, that they wanted to marry but that he couldn't break away from me. I was furious—told her I was leaving anyway and would sail for home the very next day. She asked me to put that in writing, and I, furious and reckless, did. An empty room and a freezing note confronted Harry when he came by to say good night. I covered my tracks with scorn. He couldn't find me.

Back in Watertown a week later, still furious, I stopped only a day or two to kiss my children and fled to Newport, there to abandon my hurt, to dance—and to foolishness.

I wore entrancing Paris dresses, I was radiant with rage. Admirers were plentiful, and then the cards collapsed. I had told Mother not to forward Harry's letters, but his seventh cable she telephoned to me. It read, "Enough of this hell. Sailing steerage *Aquitania*. Have engaged bridal suite for return trip. Say 'Yes.' *Signed* Harry." It was conclusive and I love to say "yes."

"You had better come home at once to get the children ready," said Mama.

My heart sang with joy. I left Newport that afternoon. Also fled a dinner party being given in my honour.

As I kissed him across the barrier of Pier 57, he announced, "We're getting married to-day."

"To-day?"

"Yes. I get a hundred bucks from Lou Norrie, if we make it before midnight, and I'm broke."

"All right. As soon as you clear the Customs."

He had nothing with him but a pipe. It didn't take long. City Hall closed at five and we just made it. Then to the pastor of the Heavenly Rest, who blessed our union in the nick of time. Norrie was standing by with the hundred 'bucks' for the honeymoon.

Len, who stood up with me rather nervously, treated us to champagne at the Belmont, and Harry and I took a room there. We had only forty-eight hours before the *Aquitania* sailed back again. I called Mother to bring the children down next day and Harry called his mother to deal her the blow. She was in Washington, D. C., visiting Harry's sister Kitsa and her husband Robbie Choate who had been a classmate of Harry's

109

at St. Mark's. Kitsa answered the telephone, and in caustic tones told him that his mother was too upset by the news to even speak with him. Harry was immensely distressed. He knew we would sail in twenty-four hours. "We will take the midnight tonight," said he.

"I'd advise you to come alone," warned his sister.

"Nevermore," said Harry.

And so, against my judgment, too, we both arrived in Chevy Chase for breakfast, after a saddened night upon the train. All of us were unnerved. It was a bad beginning. Harry's mother never addressed a word to me. Kitsa was cool; only Robbie was compassionate. We left on the three o'clock, nearly broken in spirit. Our glorious adventure had lost its shine. They made me feel like a two-year-old who had got into the forbidden jam pot.

My spirits rose when I found Mama and Billy and Polleen all smiles and excitement, waiting at the Belmont. The nurse had gone off to say good-bye to her family, so I took over the care of the children that evening. And this was Harry's Gethsemane. He disappeared, goodness knows where. What a misshapen honeymoon it had become.

When next morning the *Aquitania* slid out into the stream I collapsed into abandon. I had problems, but I had my love to cherish too.

CHAPTER 12

I became a rebel when I married Harry. By *that* act of emancipation and by the conquest of desire over obedience, opposing the code of a conformist upbringing, I, of my own volition, entered into a life of adventure, but adventure weighted with problems in loyalty. I believe now that that weighty ballast is what saved me from the demoralizing influences of the era, for life with Harry was a hedonistic adventure.

It was perhaps my willingness that our life should be rebellious that made it so. But if I had followed the Puritan pattern and, as one Boston cousin hopefully suggested, "whipped him into shape," I should have lost, at the outset, the happiness I was seeking. I have never been able to understand that sadistic practice so popular among New England brides, for I believe one marries a man because one likes him as he is, not as he will be if 'whipped' into some other shape. There was a similar suggestion made about me to Harry by one of his classmates, then studying for the ministry, who wrote, "Pray God you will be able to lift her up!" I suppose in his eyes I was a fallen woman, and to a creed-bound conformist the idea of a St. Mark's classmate marrying a New York divorcée was a tantalizing mortal error. Since then, the classmate and I have become good friends and I think he now believes that Harry did manage to mend my ways.

When I had left Dick a year before in order to be free, many of my friends and most of my family felt that I was acting with prudence, so when I took Billy and Polleen away from Boston and asked for a divorce, they insisted I was acting thus nobly for the sake of my children. I protested that I was not at all noble; that I left because I was in love with another man; that if I still loved my husband best, no "drinking" nor any other power could cause me to act thus. My love for Harry blinded me like a sunrise. From the first moment to the last it joined me to him indivisibly, like wind to the storm.

The Crosbys were unrelenting in their attitude until the year after, when Mrs. Crosby came over to Paris to visit us. Either she was convinced of my good grace, or she loved her son too much to risk an estrangement. The barrier dissolved and we have become fast friends. She is a truly remarkable woman, pure in heart, receptive in mind and relentless in activity, a very human being, at times transcendent.

On all our travels à trois (for she took us on many adventurous trips) I never felt any in-law restraint or irritation. She was the soul of warmth and tact and I, on my part, yielded many wifely prerogatives to assure to mother and son the same freedom of comradeship that they had always enjoyed. Whether luckily or unluckily, I am not a jealous woman.

When we first debarked from the *Aquitania* in 1922, we found temporary abode in a modest little left-bank hotel in the rue de l'Université. It had been in trepidation that I brought my children and Mary, the nurse, with us on our wedding trip —but it had to be that way, I would not leave them behind— Harry and I were actually escapists from the society in which we had been brought up and I wanted my children to be escapists, too. Harry agreed, but it was often a problem to put just the right emphasis on their demands when his demands were so much more desirable. I realized when I walked the gangplank in New York that here was a problem fit for a fissionist (or that's the way I would have thought to-day). I had to play both the lead and the sustaining rôle in my drama, and both parts were very exacting and very dissimilar. To be a spectacular bride and a devoted mamma, a sort of saint and sinner combination, on one and the same voyage, was complicated but exciting. I actually managed beautifully; when Mary took to her berth as nursemaids always do, I made a sort of hide-and-go-seek game for the children (aged six and four) and if Harry suspected that perhaps I said I had appointments with the hairdressers or masseuses more often than I looked it, he was happy and gallant enough to make no comment. Only two incidents marred our otherwise smooth crossing. The first was when Billy fell from B to C Deck, in his endeavour to wigwag a make-believe signal to a make-believe battleship; luckily C Deck lifeboats were on davits and into one of these swinging cradles he bounced unhurt. The other was when I discovered that the children, who were instructed to eat alone and early so that we could eat alone and late, had been ordering double portions of Beluga caviar at every meal. The steward said, when questioned, that Mr. Crosby had told him to give them anything that would keep them quiet. Apparently it was caviar. I am glad to report that, possibly because they came from a long line of seafaring gourmets, the children felt fine all the way across. The evening before we landed, Mary suddenly recovered, and so that took care of that.

But the Hotel de l'Université was not as glamorous as the ship. Our rooms were small, stuffy and too near together, and no caviar. I went apartment hunting at once. Harry had to return to his uncle's bank and do overtime to make up for his unpermissioned roundabout trip. Through the Carters, also of Morgan et Cie, I found fashionable housing in the rue des Belles Feuilles. The flat was situated in the most bourgeois section of Paris, a section comparable to the East Seventies in New York that fishbone up either side of Madison. It was neither in the jigsaw shadow of the Avenue Wagram's Luna Park, nor on the *gratin gratin* Avenue du Bois.

The dollar had risen from five to twenty-two francs that year and the rate was most advantageous to Americans. We moved in and stretched ourselves, glad to be out of our over-cramped quarters—but here another problem arose—how to keep the children out of sight when Harry was home, and he was home for breakfast, lunch and dinner. I finally persuaded them that to use the back stairs was an exciting privilege, and by keeping the door from the front hall to the nursery closed, they could place a Punch and Judy show against it. (This meant that to see my children I had to go out the front door and down a flight, then up to the kitchen and in by the back door.) Twice a week they were allowed to jump up and down on my bed while the maid changed the linen. These expressions of freedom, they have told me since, were the high spots in their winter. Now such thoughts bring ice to my heart, but at that time I believed I was managing rather well; until one Sunday afternoon when Harry with young Ellery Sedgwick, who was visiting us, had gone to the races at Longchamps. I said I was tired and thought I'd stay at home and read. They went and I quickly donned a lacy tea gown that the children remembered and liked, and called them into the salon; there with blocks and picture books we were spending a splendid afternoon when, unexpectedly, not only Harry and Ellery but three other hilarious, vacationing classmates, Eugene Reynal, Ben Kitteredge and Bob Coe, roared up the stairs. They had decided since Circus Lady had paid so well in the first, and since it was cold and rainy, they'd come back and get me and we'd all go to the Cirque Médrano together. Harry's face, flooded with disappointment, chagrin and unhappy anger when he saw me being motherly with my "brats," told me the awful truth, that he was ashamed of the domestic scene. He turned abruptly, pushing his guests out into the hall.

"Let's go," he said, and off they all marched volte face. Ellery told me later how badly they felt, but so much later that by that time I believed my beautiful married life was finished. Harry did not return for three days, though when he did come back he came laden with toys for the children and a cloth-of-gold mandarin coat for me, a negligé that had nothing at all to do with motherliness.

This episode determined me to find another solution to our housing problem. It was spring by now and I decided to send the children to a *pension* in Versailles where they could play out-of-doors to their hearts' content, but Mary spoke no French, and it seemed best that she should leave for home if I could find a suitable French governess to replace her. I looked in the advertisement column of the Paris *Herald,* and if ever a paper proved to be a gold mine, the *Herald* was one. From the minute Mme. Doursenaud (Doosenooze, we called her) in her widow's crepe and bonnet sat down in front of me and tendered me her references, I didn't even need to glance at them. Her eyes, which were deep, and black as shoe buttons, fringed with long, long lashes, were so full of the look of human kindness that I knew God was with me.

Madame Doursenaud stayed with us until the children were (I was going to say 'old' enough, but that isn't quite true) tall enough to be sent to boarding school, Billy at the age of eight, Polly the following year, but Doosenooze has ever remained for my children their *Petite Mère*. Circumstances being against me, I yielded to her understanding and wisdom (another problem in loyalty). I never forgave Mrs. M., who once dismissed Doosenooze under a cloud because, she told me, on her day off Doosenooze used make-up until she looked positively sexy and stayed out until nearly midnight with a very opulent Frenchman. To my simple mind this sounded quite intelligent. I am sure that a complete repression of the female instinct in governesses might lead to quite sadistic flare-ups in the nursery, but Doursenaud wore her war paint only outside the nursery, although I have heard my small son begging her to look picture-pretty for him, too.

When my daughter years afterwards crossed France during the German occupation, she visited Doosenooze in her home on the coast of Brittany where, with an "opulent Frenchman" as her second spouse, she had been leading not only a devoted life as a wife and mother, but a courageous one as a leader of the Maquis, taking care of English lads on their dangerous missions into France. For this she has since been decorated not only by the French but by the Americans and British as well.

So Mary was packed off and Mme. Doursenaud moved in. A week later she and the children were out of town and an American Radiator family took over the rue des Belles Feuilles, while Harry and I moved into a romantic balcony apartment hanging above the Seine on the Ile St. Louis. The lacy towers of Notre Dame were framed between the curtains of our bedroom windows. It was here that we really began to live like newlyweds with only one little *bonne à tout faire* instead of the retinue at 40 bis. I was happy as a lark and loved to go marketing in the twisty back streets of that tiny island. I proudly told my friends that I had found a butcher who was actually one-half the price of the butcher uptown, his name was Monsieur Chevaline. Neither Harry nor I at the time understood that the gilded horse's head over "Boucher Chevaline" meant "horse meat" in Paris, nor quite why our French guests slapped their thighs in delight, but declined the roast.

It was from this enticing spot on the Quai d'Orleans that every morning at 8.15 I jumped into my bathing suit and then into our red canoe and, with Harry in the stern and I in the bow, paddled downstream to the Place de la Concorde, where he debarked only a few steps from the Banque Morgan. Then I turned and paddled (good for the breasts!) upstream, the hard way, again, cheered on by whistles and applause from the bridges overhead, finally to tie the crimson bark to a willow branch below our windows on the Quai. I have often wondered why the Parisians use their waterway so little.

At the end of the summer we had to move again, but thanks to Harry's Cousin Walter Berry, Harvard '71, we were able to sublet Princess Bibesco's flat in the Faubourg St. Honoré while she and her daughter were in Rumania. Marthe Bibesco, like Cousin Walter, was a friend of Proust's. At seventy-six, Walter Van Rensselaer Berry was the epitome of elegance in the Jamesian manner; in fact the flavour of Cousin Walter runs all through the writings of Henry James. He was James's close friend and his pattern for manners.

He was enormously elongated, slim as a straw and as *sec;* his small head poised erect above a high wing collar was birdlike in its sudden turnings and its bright quick glance. His most usual dress was a morning coat of Edwardian cut, striped trousers and highly polished black button shoes. His arms long, and his wrists like pipestems, he could have been exhibited as a sculpture by Lipshitz. His fastidiousness was part of his general allure. His speech was witty, and his knowledge worldly; his manner with women was most gallant and wicked; and to me he was utterly delightful. I could well understand his amorous successes even with the young belles of the day. Proust was a close friend, too, and Cousin Walter fitted beautifully into the Proustian legend. *"A l'Ombre des Jeunes Filles en Fleurs"* is dedicated to him and that puts him high on the roster of Those Who Live On, for it is my belief that the poet or the artist is the longest life-giver in the universe. Great men and women who have died unsung have flickered into oblivion, even though their seed endures, but those on the contrary whose deeds, dastardly or benign, have been recorded by a poet may live till the world snuffs out. In this respect Harry and I laid two of the foundation stones for Cousin Walter's immortality— we published his correspondence with Henry James and *Proust's Forty-seven Letters to Walter Berry*, B.S.P., 1929.

This is number seven of the forty-seven :

Wednesday Evening.

Cher Monsieur et Ami :

I am very behindhand in answering your little note of the other day. But I am always expecting to dine with you somewhere and then, at the last moment, I always feel too poorly and am obliged to give out. If I am writing you to-day it is because the *Nouvelle Revue Française* refuse to give me another hour in which to send them dedication for *Pastiches et Mélanges*. It appears that if I delay this any longer the entire arrangement of the pages will be destroyed (which seems to me to be exaggerated). Therefore, instead of talking it over with you I submit to you the following dedication (which you can alter to suit your taste, only please send it back by *pneumatique*).

> *"To Monsieur Walter Berry*
> *Lawyer and Man of Letters who, from the*
> *very outbreak of the war, when America was*
> *hesitating, defended and won with unrivalled*
> *energy and ability, the cause of France.*
> *His Friend, Marcel Proust"*

I find two faults in this dedication. The first one concerns you alone; the word *"lettré"* corresponds perhaps in your mind to the English word "scholar." If so, I imagine you won't care for it very much. How would you like me to change it? You must choose the art wherein it seems to you most creditable to have displayed an "unrivalled ability." Is it eloquence? Is it style? You have so many intellectual gifts that one is confronted with the difficulty of making a choice.

The second disadvantage lies in the fact that inasmuch as the dedication will be placed in the front part of the book, which begins with the Pastiches, it is regrettable that the *"Ami des Livres"* aspect should not be emphasized. In the form which I submit it to you the dedication would probably assume more significance if put at the head of that part of the book which is entitled *"En Memoire des Eglises Assassinées,"* and includes *"Les Eglises Sauvées (Clochers de Caen, de Lisieux,* etc.), Ruskin *à Notre Dame d' Amiens, de Rouen,"* etc. and *"La Mort des Cathédrales."* But this didn't please me as it would have made it necessary to put the dedication in the middle of the book instead of on the first page and this would have made it look as if there had been a mistake made in the binding. As regards *A l'Ombre des Jeunes Filles en Fleurs* you never told me whether you would rather have it dedicated to you instead of the *Pastiches et Mélanges.* (I think however that it still could be transferred. But I have not written to ask the *Nouvelle Revue Française* if this would be possible, as you never expressed a preference in the matter.)

I have finally discovered that my new landlord's name is Monsieur Varin-Bernier (he is a banker) and that he comes from Bar-le-Duc. But I don't know his address (for he had his manager write me to ask for an appointment for himself). However, I am going to try to find out his address, as I intend to ask Guiche to go and see him and ask him various questions. As a matter of fact, d'Albuféra sent me an article which proved my right to remain here two more years after I had signified my desire to do so. This would give me temporary security and might help me to secure a substantial indemnity, in case of their putting me out (if they really intend to transform the entire house into a bank, they will have to begin to cover over the courtyard and I tremble at the thought of the building operations which are impending). I shall try to see Guiche.

If I spoke to you of a person of the type of Madame Lorentz it was because my "subconscious self" dictated the words. I did remember afterwards that, when I mentioned your armchairs a year or two ago, you said to me, "I furnished Mrs. A. in this way" (forgive me for the word "furnished" which, of course, is not correct but which you used).

Please accept, dear friend, my very devoted respects.

Marcel Proust

Because we were welcomed as family in the rue de Varenne Edith Wharton's nose was slightly out of joint. I could tell *that* as soon as Cousin Walter indicated that I was now and then to play the part of hostess at his table. Walter Van Renssleaer Berry was Harry's cousin and that made him my cousin, too. It was according to protocol that when I was present at one of his famous little luncheons I should receive for him. But Edith Wharton had been doing this for years. She and Cousin Walter were such closely harnessed friends that one spoke of them, in those international circles, as a team. Cousin Walter received at 53 rue de Varenne among his beautiful books and Eastern treasures (here his friends James and Proust used to foregather). Everything in that apartment was perfection. The little library where he worked communicated by a concealed stair with the floor above, which was Edith Wharton's Paris *pied à terre*. She also owned a small but charming villa near St. Germain as well as a place on the Riviera, and her comings and goings were intermittent. But, up to now, whenever she was in town she and Cousin Walter received their friends together, so my appearance as Harry's wife threw a monkey wrench into that smooth machinery. Of course Harry and I were the gainers, and I know Cousin Walter considered us an asset, but there is no doubt that Mrs. Wharton didn't, and a chilliness grew up between us that lasted, I am sorry to say, until the day she died.

The guests at those luncheons were always chosen with great discrimination; a purée of wit, beauty and bitchery, for I think Cousin Walter believed as I do that a woman without a touch of bitchery is like milk without Vitamin D. The popish element was not lacking, for Abbé—, a great friend of both Cousin Walter and Edith Wharton, was almost always included. (I believe he also acted in the rôle of confessor to Mrs. Wharton.) He was an endearing and gay little Episcopalian, full of phrases that charmed. I remember once when asking him if he liked animals as much as I did he replied, "My heart is one big zoo."

While we still occupied the Princess's apartment, a bizarre autumnal incident came about through Laura Corrigan's largesse. Arielle Grosvenor, a favourite schoolmate of mine, was staying with us. Arielle was half French and half Italian by extraction. The first half looked Valois, the other I guessed might be ghetto. Her black crinkly hair was worn parted in the middle over a wide camellia-white brow and her nearsighted eyes squinted shut when she laughed, which she did constantly. Harry refused to like her on two counts. First that he believed, without reason, that she had a touch of Sappho in her fingers. Second that she came from the Middle West. Any "middle" whatsoever was anathema to Harry, and once in a while the Boston prejudice showed through the chink in his European armour. Also she used to give me worldly Middle-Western advice about how I was entitled as Harry's wife to run up bills for personal pretties. This horrified me and of course I didn't tell Harry, but just the same he was aware.

Arielle, née Chicago Frost, had married a Newport Grosvenor.

Arielle had recently arrived in Paris and was being very nice to a widowed Mrs. Corrigan from Chicago. Jimmy Corrigan had piled up a neat investment in car-lines, and his widow was smothered in dollars and mink and having lifted her feet high from the Chicago pavements she came to Paris with a well-planned campaign in view. She was a self-admitted social climber and she knew that the handiest steppingstones are those turned out by the U.S. Mint, but once in Paris, where was she to begin? Presumably at the bottom of the ladder, and her eye fell on a friendly Chicagoan—Arielle, and from Arielle on to us. After all, Harry was the nephew of J. P. Morgan, and she had seen me appear in Cholly Knickerbocker's column —could Arielle arrange a meeting? Arielle begged us to, and

Harry said, "Why not ask her Thursday before Auteuil, she probably likes to play the races."

"Oh, no, she doesn't," said Arielle.

"We'll ask her anyway," I comforted, and so we did.

We were having sherry in the library, when the doorbell rang. As the maid opened the door I caught sight of a very much over-dressed lady and behind her staggering under a weight of four or five dress boxes and hat boxes stood a footman in uniform.

"Follow me," she beckoned him, and like a squall she entered the room. Before Arielle had time to introduce us, "I just brought along a few old clothes. Not really old, they were only ordered last week for London," she gushed, "but I'm going south instead, and since you so kindly asked me to lunch, I want you to have them."

I couldn't have been more nonplussed, but of course I couldn't refuse. One accepted one's guests at their own valuation!

"That is most generous," and I gushed with enthusiasm, "May we leave them here in the hall while we are at luncheon?" I think she would have preferred if I'd done a strip tease and tried them on there and then. Harry added, under his breath, "I wonder what size socks Mr. Corrigan wears?"

"Hush," I said, "he is no longer with us."

The meal was a funny one. Mrs. Corrigan's conversation consisted of "do you know so and so" and "the Duke said to me." Harry answered, "Have you met the Duchess of Malfi?" "Do you know the Dardanelles?"

There were many stories told at Laura Corrigan's expense in those worldly days, but when in 1939 war came to her adopted country, she swapped not only her jewels and her sables for needed supplies but gave her unstinting devotion to succour those Frenchmen who lay dying on the battlefields, going among them carrying cigarettes to whole regiments of wounded poilus who gave her the sobriquet of "the American Angel"—she had climbed as high as that.

Arielle at the time was engaged to Paul Rainey, American millionaire lecturer and White Hunter of international renown. It was he who first hunted African lion with English hounds;

he was big, powerful and keen too. The expression "rough diamond" applied to him more than to any other man I've known. He was rich, ruthless and wrong; that is, he was wrong when he refused to sit down at an official London dinner table with a "native" of South Africa, a visiting potentate, an incident which caused a scandal. Rainey was to return to Africa two days later, he boarded a ship headlong—but came off feet first. It was a story that never was fully told, and suddenly hushed up.

When Arielle received the radiogram "Paul Rainey died yesterday, buried at sea to-day," it was for her as though Atlas had sunk beneath the wave. Indeed, we all three felt the prop give way, he had been such a mountain of a friend and a very generous one as well. He had given Harry the big grey Farman car when he left us and it was also understood that we three were to visit him in Africa after Christmas. He had offered us the round trip as a Christmas present—he and Arielle would be married in Kenya—but in London he refused to break bread with a "black" and he had been "taken care of." This was our explanation. There was no reason except "sudden illness" given for his too sudden death.

Arielle left for America soon after. She and Harry never did get on, but Arielle was never a menace to my peace of mind. Not so Constance!

Constance Crowninshield Coolidge Atherton (when I first met her) is the C.C.C. of Harry's diary—being a Crowninshield and also a Coolidge and a Peabody she should have been "typically Bostonian," but no phrase could suit her less. To this day she has remained one of those rare gems of humanity—a pure, naive individual, and with more charm and humour than is usually allotted to any one darling of the gods.

Her worldly cousin, Lulu Norman, gave a luncheon for Constance at Larue's on the Place de la Madeleine that autumn (a ladies' lunch, which was quite unworldly at Larue's) and I being a cousin too was invited. Had I known it was to be a "ladies'" lunch I might not have gone, I might not have met Constance or brought her to Harry, or helped propel the chariot of chance—would it have been wiser had I spoked its wheels?

From the moment that she hurried in late, all sparkle and fluster, I was captivated. She had recently returned from Pekin where she had separated from her husband, Ray Atherton, (later U.S. Ambassador to Canada) while he was a secretary at our Embassy. She had been known in that society as the Queen of Pekin, more for her ability to dazzle than to rule. She had lived in a temple, raced Mongolian ponies, defied convention and was generally an exciting pagan. That day she looked just like her portrait by Augustus John; she was perfection. I, foolish and trusting, ran home to tell Harry about her—we invited her to luncheon on Sunday before the races. All that season the Lady of the Golden Horse was tangled in my hair—all through the Paris years she was my most formidable antagonist, but I could not help immensely admiring her. The only weapon worthy of such mortal charm is a more wily brand of the same, and "may the best woman win," was my consolation, for try to annex my husband she did.

It was about this time I had the first taste of Latin Quarter life. Harry was working at the bank every day and I with Paris in my pocket felt I should do more with such opportunity than housekeep, rhyme and dine. It was our second winter in Paris and I decided I would try to become an artist. Since Harry had begun to write, I felt that that branch of the arts could be left to him. So on our return from Etretat I, in true Bostonian fashion, asked the Morgan Bank where I should study. They advised Julian's Academy. It was the only one in which there was a section for men and one for "young ladies," this on account of the nude models. And moreover, the ladies' section was just off the Champs Elysées, not in the Latin Quarter at all, which made it much more *convenable*. That it was stuffy and mild and that the teachers were dodos did not bother the Bank at all.

After I had been there for two days, I realized I had spent my cultural francs in vain. I'd never get what I was after at Julian's (even though Marie Bachkirtsev had) so I went to see Maître X., who I was told by an Italian countess gave lessons in his Montparnasse studio.

Maître X. had a class in progress when I called but he said after looking at some sketches I'd brought, and also down the neck of my blouse, that he felt I needed private instruction. "Can I come at nine tomorrow?" I asked. "Oh, no," he answered, "Private lessons are in the afternoon, not here. I give them in my Vaugirard atelier." He wrote down the address and I promised to appear at three the next day.

When I entered his studio I realized why. It was reached by a long dark passage hung in murky velvet. There were two large couches taking up most of the floor space on either side of a small model's stand, on the stand was precariously placed a Mme. Recamier work bench. There was plenty of paint in evidence and a lot of very aphrodisiac painting on the walls. Other students and Mme. X. were notably absent.

"Sit here," he said, "we'll go over these," and he took up my sheaf of sketches and patted the couch beside him. He was not unattractive. I decided to play the game.

"I engaged a model for this afternoon but she does not come," he said plaintively.

"I can draw flowers in a vase."

"Yes, you can draw flowers, but I myself must get on with my painting for the Salon d'Automne." He wheeled a canvas onto the floor. The subject was classic.

"Perhaps I could help you out," I suggested. "I could take my lesson in the nude." He nearly dropped the canvas. I was enjoying myself.

"It would be a great help, but I must see first if you will do," he mumbled, his eyes popping.

I whisked behind a screen made of pasted playing cards and stripped. Then, clutching one of his silken props about me, I mounted the model stand. I was one ahead of him. He was slightly dazed, but he was sorely tempted and I in my pseudo-innocence knew that Harry was due at four precisely, to see what kind of a teacher I had fallen on. Harry was never late.

"Like this," I said, eyeing his canvas.

"Let me analyze the pose," he stammered.

I sat down, very firmly. He began to arrange my scarf and just then the bell pealed through the hall.

"That must be my husband," I cried joyfully, "I told him to come at four."

"The Devil! Put on your clothes," he shouted, pushing me toward the screen.

"But you asked me to pose." The bell sounded again impatiently.

"My God," he said, "I implore you."

"All right," I laughed, teasingly, "don't worry, but open that door or he'll go for the police."

He precipitated himself down the hall and before they returned (very slowly indeed) I was back in full dress, my sketch book on my knee.

I could see the Master go limp with relief, but I knew I had taught him a well-deserved lesson. "Imagine trying to lure innocent little Americans into such a trap," I glowered at him as Harry and I left together.

Next day I changed instructors and enrolled at the Atelier de la Grande Chaumière, where Léger taught painting and Bourdelle instructed the class in sculpture. It was there I met Giacometti and Apartis and Noguchi, all fellow students and all famous now. Maître X. and I subsequently became good friends. He was a very engaging man, though a bad painter, I decided. His technique changed, but his desire for romance remained unquenched.

125

CHAPTER 13

In the spring of '24, when the Princess returned to take back her flat, we found asylum in a miniature *pavillon* in the rue Boulard behind the Cimetière Montparnasse. I used to detour through the cemetery whenever possible just to look at that intriguing tomb where, in life-sized effigy upon a double marble bed, lie M. and Mme. O—Monsieur propped on his elbow, his long stone beard rippling down the marble counterpane as he grimly watches over Madame in ruffled nightie upon a ruffled pillow. Her hand caresses a little stone spaniel curled against her rigid knee. On a pedestal stands an alabaster candle forever burning by the couch to frighten away intruding ghosts.

Ours was *Pavillon* Number 1 and, like the other seven, had a picket fence, a wicket gate, a garden plot, a tree, a sundial, and a flagged terrace. The house, or cottage, was all front and no back and, like the rest of the row, leaned up against and seemed hooked onto the high wall of a towering factory. These *pavillons* were one room deep, the stairs running up along the wall as on a backdrop; in fact, the whole place resembled a stage set. When we arrived, all the houses looked more or less alike, picturesque but unpainted and unjoyful. I set to work—first, vines were cleared from the windows and trellised around them; then a complete whitewash job; then yellow-striped awnings at all the windows, mirrors on all the walls, including the outside walls; slip covers of mauve and yellow and pink on chairs and sofas, a canary or two in wicker

126

cages, in the garden, a dog kennel, painted like a Chinese pagoda, the flagstones waxed, a hammock slung under the tree —until it looked like the giddy toyland house that it was.

There was one difficulty—downstairs there were only two rooms, parlour and dining room, and upstairs only two bedrooms. Outside in a narrow lean-to was the kitchen on one side and on the other, propped against the high street wall of stone, a similar sort of storeroom, where the icebox, the wood pile and garden tools were kept. It was obvious and right that Polleen should occupy one of the two bedrooms and we the other, but after the first night, Harry objected. Polleen's hours were not our hours and Polleen's ears were not our ears; so with some misgivings I turned the tool shed into the nursery. It was only six by eight feet, about the size of a small Pullman compartment, but by dint of overhead pulleys and ropes it became quite a fascinating playroom. The icebox was set in the garden behind the lattice, an electric heater began to eat up the damp; shades, shelves and rugs were lavishly installed, and so was Polleen. That she did not catch pneumonia was a tribute to her cheery adaptability; the whole thing, I trust, seemed more like a game than a regime.

We engaged a maid named Seline, but we called her "Sea Lions." It was a difficult place to fill, for we needed her on two counts, (1) to take Polly back and forth to school and to walk in the park in the afternoons, and (2) to place and collect Harry's bets on the races. Seline had to be fond of children and also fond of gambling, for Harry gave her five per cent of his winnings, but deducted five per cent of his losses; they agreed to that. Unfortunately, she became so absorbed in the game that, as I discovered too late, she used of an afternoon to hurry Polleen into a sideshow at the Place Belfort where a permanent fair was in progress, set her down before some fascinating freak, or a baby in a bottle, and lope off to the nearest bar to hear the racing results come in.

I do not know if I would have discovered this state of affairs had it not been that demon luck turned against Seline. Harry had given her a big bet, two thousand francs à cheval (one thousand to win, one thousand to place) on Sun Goddess at 20 to 1. Seline's cronies in the bistro assured her the filly didn't have a chance and that she would do much better to play Attaboy, but Sun Goddess blazed home first paying four hundred francs for ten, which would have been two thousand dollars for Harry, Seline couldn't pay and she couldn't say she arrived too late to bet, because the two thousand francs were gone. The scene that took place that evening between S.L. and H.C. raised six different roofs of six different *pavillons*. She was dismissed and disgraced in the eyes of the entire *quartier,* but Polleen's general health improved immediately—though I often wondered about her dreams. From that time on we called my child "The Wretched Rat."

That spring, while I was studying sculpture with Antoine Bourdelle at the Grande Chaumière, Harry gave me and my fellow students a never-to-be-forgotten party. It was my birthday, 1925, and we asked twenty-five friends. The guests—artists mostly—represented fifteen different nationalities; there were Apartis, the Greek, Giacometti, the Italian, Noguchi, of Japanese descent, Sato, of Chinese (all internationally important sculptors to-day); there were Tina, the beautiful Italian model, and Myrka, the exotic Guadaloupese; also Betty Parsons and Gretchen and Peter Powel, Americans, and Gerard Lymington, English, the de Geeteres, Hollanders, Manolo Ortíz, Spanish; and there were French and German and Russian friends as well. It was a wild gesticulating group, for not everyone could speak everything, but everyone could make signs. Harry and I had chosen, because of its name, Le Canard Amoureux, a little tavern near the city marketplace; and the proprietor of The Loving Duck entered into our plans with gusto. We had ordered an enormous cake flying flags of all our countries. A very long table was bountifully set in the *salon privé* and wine was cooling in bins. Multicoloured paper garlands were strung from the chandeliers to the four corners of the room and in each corner stood provocatively an opened paper screen. Inquiringly, I peeked behind one; it hid a small towel, a large pitcher and a *bidet.* I turned, startled, to find the proprietor whispering in my ear as he pointed to the other corners.

"I thought four would be sufficient for a party of this size; I hope Madame is satisfied."

17. When Jean Jacques Rousseau lived there (from an old engraving, 1770).

18. The Mill when we bought it in 1927.

19. "Monsieur et Mme. Henri," Le Moulin 1927—1935.

20. Narcisse, Caresse and Harry on the beach at Deauville, August, 1927.

22. Kay Boyle and Harry Crosby, Le Moulin, 1927.

21. Caresse and Narcisse, Paris, 1927.

"Oh, quite," I replied and added, "If we need more I'll ring!" I felt that I had at last come of age.

With the liqueurs each guest made a beautiful speech in my honour. When Sato, the Chinese, became intoxicated enough to forget his Asiatic reserve, he too launched into words, but his was a singsong recital; it went on and on and since no one could stop him, we finally departed noisily and joyously into the street; but S. remained seated at the deserted board, grinding out his melancholy lay. "He must go on and on to the end," André said. "It is the custom of his country." I wanted to turn back then, but André heard the music of a carrousel in the nearby square, and so, arms linked, we all veered and swung that way—which was the custom of *his* country. *Si tous les gens du monde dansent en ronde.*

Harry had a big list of little people whom he loved and admired, he never forgot an anniversary nor gave an inappropriate or unthought-out gift, *"L'art de donner est acquis,"* he used to say, and he acquired it. I only remember one of his offerings to boomerang—it was a monster police dog, beautiful but monstrous to me, this was soon after meeting Constance. Harry decided she needed police protection, presumably against other admirers, and unknown to me he had bought her a canine cop.

When the salesman appeared on the threshold of our apartment in the Faubourg St. Honoré with the massive and alarming animal, saying, "He is Monsieur Crosby's so I brought him here," I was astonished. "I did not know," I said. But the dealer was doing the dealing. "Monsieur Crosby has got to take him, he is paid for, where's the garden?" Puzzled, I showed them across the salon, the animal was snapped off the heavy leash and leapt destructively into a petunia bed. The man turned toward the front door relieved of the consequences, and as he exited his punch line was, "The other lady didn't want him either"—I reeled.

But Harry usually met with success and gratitude. There was the Widow Biron, a darling old woman of eighty, who in spring sold violets on a corner of the rue de la Paix. Her customers included many of the wealthy bankers and shopkeepers of the quarter who, hurrying home to their wives or paramours, stopped to place a few sous in the delicately wrinkled hand, and receive a nosegay. Some April evenings were very nippy, some were rainy too.

Harry always brought violets home to me and when his mother was in Paris he bought white violets for her (her favourite flower). They had to be specially ordered the evening before, and the Veuve Biron would carry out the flower-market transaction with as much acumen and know-how as though she were assisting Winthrop Aldrich to buy Continental Can on the Paris Bourse.

Harry's presents to the Veuve Biron were many and they included a light folding camp stool with a back, ordered from London, and a daily cup of hot coffee from Chez Phillipe (the nearby restaurant in the rue Daunou), this to break the long exhausting hours of the vendor's vigil beside her sidewalk basket.

Isabey, the gentle, sparrow-like carpenter from the Vendée, who had served with Harry in the French Army during World War I, was always called in when bookcases were to be built or furniture mended, and Harry was godparent to his daughter, but Isabey was really too ill to work, T.B. we feared, war's heritage. Harry helped him with the doctor's bills.

There was "La Jeune Fille du Relieur" the bookbinder's apprentice. A tiny girl of ten. She scurried around our *"Quartier"* hauling unbelievably heavy bundles to and from the shop. Harry gave so many books to Luichon to be bound that the Jeune Fille was constantly darting in and out of 19 rue de Lille.

Harry did not allow the giving of old clothes or any cast-off possessions to his friends. La Jeune Fille soon blossomed forth in a jaunty reefer jacket from "Old England," new boots and fur-lined mittens—and in consequence was blessed with a new and unexpected prettiness.

For Mazie, the indefinite huntress, a little whip of purest white.

"L'art de donner . . . est acquis."

The summer of 1925 we spent at Etretat and lived in a deserted gun emplacement on a cliff; it looked like a lump of sugar with curtains and was called Le Criquet. That is where I wrote sonnets and Harry, in envy, decided to give up banking

130

for iambic pentameter. It was also the summer when, in sun-bonnet, ruffles and diamonds, I played for the house at the Etretat Casino, and the summer when the puppy Corydon, *"mangeur des choses immondes,"* saved the children's lives with his warning bark and then, dauntless, was run over by a bus.

Some of the Etretat figures still cling to mind. There was Constance Martel, who was a professional scavenger and gathered fish along the beach. I wrote a poem about her and part of it read :

Constance Martel at eighty-two has work to do
Stoops she, turns she, picks she fish from off the sands.
And in her pail a rainbow swale of slippery snips and
rotting tips, and many a silver smear of sole, of
shark, of devil-fish she drops with joyful leer, from
fingers two. And almost blind, she gives a kind of
sniff and knowing peer at entrails twined, then grins
to find some good bits in the stew. You'd think her
back would surely crack to see her bending double;
you'd think that thirty francs a year were hardly
worth the trouble.

Then there was the jolly Comte Louis d'Hendecourt, the completely French husband of a completely American wife. She dressed for the Grand Hotel and he dressed for the market-place. When she went off to play bridge with a Pomeranian under her arm, he went to buy fish, with a basket on his. Choosing the right fish was like a daily apéritif for him. I timed my shopping tours to coincide with his. It was such fun to watch the flutter of anticipation in the buxom fishwives as Louis came down the line, prodding and poking into the baskets with his dog's-head cane, lifting a gill here or gouging an eye there to learn how long since Neptune had yielded up this silver. A sole that looked good to me would be flipped aside, in order to reveal some special mess of fresh sardines that would become a gourmet's dream when grilled. The envy, the curtsies, the ogles that followed Louis on his round were proof that he knew his fishes.

At the end of that summer we began looking for a fourth abode in a more accessible and orderly part of Paris, accessible for Harry, orderly for me. Finally, we nosed out a large handsome apartment at 55 rue de Lille, directly behind the Gare d'Orsay. It belonged to the Comte de S. and it was spacious enough and grand enough to suit both Harry and me, so we went with our lawyer to sign the lease. It was a three years' lease and the rent was very high, but the apartment was, we assured each other, just what we were looking for. That is why it was so strange, when on emerging into the street, our lease in our pocket, we both felt weighted down with despair. We sauntered along the rue de Lille trying to look happy, for each other's sake. As we approached the far end, hardly aware, I glanced up and sighed, "I wish our place had such a lovely gateway."

We were in front of No. 19. There was a massive door between two carven columns, each column topped with a large sandstone urn overflowing with fruit and garlanded with chiselled flowers. I looked at the high windows to the left.

"Why," I exclaimed, "this wing is empty!"

We ventured a few steps inside the gate and encountered a formidable concierge. We were about to retire mutely when she demanded, "Do you come to see the apartment?"

"Let's," I said.

"Yes," said Harry, but we knew we were treading on dynamite. She unlocked the hallway door.

"It's very large, three stories," she announced, looking at us commiseratingly. We were allowed to go up alone and it was then that we knew me must live *there* and only there, no matter what. The other lease was sticking out of Harry's pocket like a dagger. Suddenly our apathy left us and we flung our arms around each other "We'll do it," we promised ourselves. Down we raced to the concierge and gave her five hundred francs to hold the place; then we hurried into the street to No. 55, light as feathers, our depression gone.

The Comte just couldn't understand. We had had a difficult time persuading him in the first place; we had bribed him with more than he'd asked and now, a few minutes later, we offered him six months' rent if we could get out of the lease. *"Les*

Américains, les Américains," he groaned; but it was *une belle affaire* and so he accepted our retreat.

On the gallop we rounded up our lawyer again, who also was nonplused; but that evening we had a lovelier lease in our possession and this time it stuck out of Harry's pocket like the folded wings of a dove. Into 19 rue de Lille we soon moved, there to remain in sybaritic residence until the very last.

This was the Faubourg St. Germain, the *gratin gratin* section of Paris. It was the aristocratic left-bank quarter nearest the Seine, where Proust's characters had lived, loved and entertained. If one followed the Boulevard St. Germain on the bias away from the river, one came to the Place St. Germain; if one caromed off up Raspail to where Boulevard Raspail intercepts Boulevard Montparnasse, one came upon Bohemian locales; but the rues de Lille, de Seine, de Varenne, de Verneuil were all lined with handsome, ornate "hôtels" (as town houses are called in France) and those mansions of the eighteenth century still belonged to the *beau monde.* Many of the hôtels during the century had been sliced into one-floor apartments and part rented at a handsome profit by the ageing proprietors. The rooms were lofty and crystal-hung, the woodwork was often delicately sculptured and from the windows in the rear one looked out upon small formal gardens, statue-decked. Our find at No. 19 belonged to another nobleman, who could have been the Baron de Charlus himself.

Harry and I between us had various titled cousins and aunts living in this quarter, relatives whose American dollars were ever so politely holding up the crested portals of Lutetia. We did our best to avoid their tea parties, but now and then we were roped into some affair where one of us was introduced as dear so-and-so's child or *chère* Natalie's cousin, we who did so want to be known as ourselves. Then, too, my costume, the long-sleeved Vionnet cloth-of-gold evening suit, with its short gold skirt, was a startling innovation at a Faubourg dinner party. A French lady of fashion might be allowed to launch such an unheard-of-style, but an unsophisticated little American, never —and Harry's black button-hole gardenia, made expertly in the rue de la Paix, was too Proustian a gesture to be tolerated in a youth so definitely American. We were treading where the placards read *prenez garde*. By our background we were privileged, by our actions we were ostracized; but we stood stubbornly on ground which we knew to be our own and which gradually came to be recognized and envied, even *au gratin*.

We were not rich by plutocratic standards, but the dollar was mounting and I have always had a knack of making the pennies glow, in our case, the *sous,* for French coppers were still in circulation, and the huge bedraggled sheets of paper now in current use were scarcely even seen. A thousand-franc note, which to-day is worth not much more than half of a five-dollar bill, at that time was worth fifty, and of fifties we had few.

I remember that I received from Harry two thousand francs a month (about £25) to run my household. My personal expenses, which were small, were defrayed as they turned up and I could count on being with Harry when restaurant checks were presented. I also had a modest income of my own, which I used for the children.

Our greatest splurge was on the races. Some seasons we came out on top, but more often we did not—I believe all in all we lived very grandly, racing included, for well under ten thousand a year, but on that point I am vague; I only know that what I wanted usually came my way. I never tried to balance a budget in my life unless I'd added the necessary heading, "Experience and Fun."

There was the terrible day when Harry decided to spend principal, a dastardly deed in State Street. He telegraphed his father "Sell ten thousand, we have decided to live extravagantly," and we both signed the message. The guided missiles that were launched back at us showed what fundamental laws we had broken. The result of the reproaches, not of our extravagance, was disastrous.

Steve's third polemic was on the breakfast tray. Harry said to me, a bit unstrung, "Perhaps we *are* careless. Perhaps we should have respect for property. Perhaps we'd better start by locking up your jewellery in the bank, it's not insured."

"Oh, no," I wailed, "What good can it do me if I bury my treasure. And, besides, I haven't lost a single thing since I've been in Paris!"

"You might," and with Steve's typed admonitions under his

nose, Harry urged me to put all my trinkets together so he could take them to the bank that very morning. I had quite a lot—a pearl necklace given me, pearl by pearl, on birthdays and holidays by my Grandmama Jacob; three diamond bracelets, wedding presents from the first time; three great bar pins of square-cut rubies, sapphires and diamonds and several other clips and brooches, as well as some beautiful pear-shaped pearl earrings. I only kept out one little necklace and a clip. Then Harry, in masterful manner, stuffed it all into a red flannel Cartier bag and started forth on his errand of prudence.

Alas and alack, at the corner of the rue Castiglione and rue de Rivoli he was hailed by giddy Molly Cogswell, a cousin, now a Washington columnist, Molly Van Renessalaer Thayer. Harry jumped out of the taxi, unluckily in front of the corner bodega. "Wait for me," he instructed the brigand at the wheel, "I'll only be a minute," but Molly had lots of dazzling news to tell and porto flips are time erasers. Suddenly Harry remembered the taxi *and* the jewels, but when he emerged blinking into the sunlight, both the taxi and the loot were gone—everything I owned, flipped into oblivion and not a clue to go by! The police tried, I cried, Harry invoked St. Christopher, but to no avail. To my mind Molly was the devil's bait, but Prudence was the culprit.

The first time I saw modern and ancient art side by side was in the de Beaumonts' salon. The Count and Countess de Beaumont were Proustian characters and their tea parties even more in character than they, not only Charlus, the host, and the Duchesse de Guermantes were there, but every other prototype as well. The de Beaumonts invited Harry and me to tea one afternoon shortly before cousin Walter died, he was there too, but when I walked in with Narcisse Noir, our black whippet, dressed in his best gold necklace, his toenails lacquered gold, even cousin Walter was a bit startled. The Count almost immediately asked me if I would like to see the garden in the hope I think that I'd leave my whippet there, but instead Narcisse sat himself down upon a silken settee like a delta dog on a royal sarcophagus and waited in boredom for our return. He didn't even glance at the Picasso over the fireplace or the Clouets along the wall. Everyone else did however

135

and the Picasso was both extolled and denounced. Not so the Canaletto, on *it* everyone agreed, even wishing they themselves could be part of that Venetian frolic.

The most delightful Canalettos I have ever seen however were in the Crespi's palace in Milan. I was there at another tea party in 1947. The two huge companion pieces had been carried off and hidden during the war in safe keeping from the U.S. bombs and had only now been returned from some remote estate and this was the very week that they had been cleaned and rehung. In the huge reception hall of the Palazzo Crespi both paintings were especially floodlit and the impact of this work was so brilliant and alive that other masterpieces in other rooms seemed half dead in comparison. These two in their unapproachable setting seemed perfection in bloom. Like Tintoretto's *Susanna and the Elders,* or the Gobelin *Lady of the Unicorn.*

At the de Beaumonts we met that fascinating "femme fatale," Lady Abdy, and Harry fell completely under her Muscovite spell. Her domineering and sophisticated charm was too perfect for me to vie with. The best I could do was to quietly annex her cavalier. It turned out that I couldn't have put my foot in it more successfully for Manolo Ortíz, the blue-blooded Spanish gypsy who had come with Iya Abdy, was supposed to remain on with our host, but left with me instead! I made a double scoring, much satisfaction to myself, but it cost me that rung on the Proustian ladder.

Billy was growing as fast as wheat. His stiff shock of hair was the colour of wheat and his sturdy independent nature and complete trust in mankind endeared him to one and all, especially to me whose instinct was to overwhelm him with affection and whose wisdom of the heart warned me to temper my love with reason, first because of Harry and second because of an intrinsic fear that I might do him a disservice. How many times in his early years have I held down my arms when I so longed to enfold him—have answered with studied parismony the little-boy questions that made my heart ache and sing.

When I took him away to boarding school the first time he was only eight, and in a strange land too, as well as among strangers. He was the youngest in the school. I am not even certain now that he felt sure that I was still there when I'd said good-bye, or that I could be called back if needed, or turned to if in doubt. For I never dared unfathom half my love.

I remember a terrible morning after Easter vacation. I had brought him back to the Rosay, the school was near Lausanne, and after dining with the head master, Billy had asked and been allowed to return with me to spend a last night at the Hotel Beau Rivage—I had a big double bed and he fell asleep on my pillow almost before his head touched it but in the morning while I was still drowsing, I felt his fingers combing my hair at the nape of my neck. Startled, I turned; he was cuddling close. "I love you," he teased.

"It must be time to get up," I remonstrated almost savagely.

His lip trembled, "I don't want ever to get up," he said, "I want to stay here always."

The anguish that clutched my heart was so great that I pretended to somersault out of bed and fled into the bathroom where, on my knees, my head against the tub's edge, I tried to stifle my heart's sobs.

My next visit to the Rosay ended more successfully—it was graduation for the top class—families filled the school house and paraded the grounds, lots of excitement, lots of fun. On the last day there was a gymkhana and the final event a Mothers' Race, a hundred-yard dash.

I knew enough to borrow a pair of track shoes from a lower classman and to hitch up my skirts—I was Billy's mother, I intended to win—and I did—by fifty yards. He was as proud of me as if I had been awarded a degree, prouder I believe. Sometimes I think that this was the most I have ever been able to do for my son.

CHAPTER 14

"Yes," and never "no" was our answer to the fabulous twenties. We built a gossamer bridge from war to war, as unreal as it was fragile, a passionate *passerelle* between a rejected past and an impossible future. Perhaps no such span of years (only two whizzing decades) have ever so amazed and disurbed a generation. Harry Crosby and I briefed the pattern of our times and, unknowingly, we drew the most surrealistic picture of them all.

In 1927, Harry had left the bank. We had decided that life was too beautiful and days too short to devote three-quarters of them to that unimaginative place. He had asked me if *V* really wanted to become the wife of a partner of J. P. Morgan and Company, which we felt certain, with influence and work, he could be, or did I want to be the wife of a poet, which we felt less certain he might be. One course led to a fat income and a life on the Park Avenues of the world; the other certainly would not increase our inherited incomes whose dozen thousand dollars were carrying us along very nicely. However, we were sure it would furnish immediate joy and maybe fame. I, of course, chose joy. Money has never been considered an end in my estimation. I have never had much and even in those days we were not rich by Park Avenue standards and Harry's salary in francs at the bank amounted to less than £25 a month. But then as well as now, money weighed very little in the balance of my decisions, and to actually sacrifice joy for cash would have been very bad indeed. Our families protested, of course, but we were a united front three thousand miles from Boston. They accepted the inevitable and Harry resigned from the bank and we took Uncle Jack Morgan to Foyot's for dinner to break the news to him. He didn't seem to mind.

Up till 1927, we had lived in furnished flats, except for the *pavillon* which was almost too small for furniture, but in the rue de Lille we had space galore, the ceilings were lofty, the rooms immense and our few possessions brought from the rue Boulard were scattered and lost in those spacious quarters.

We were determined that our bedroom should become the heart of the house, and so before moving in we had haunted the antique dealers on the Left Bank, as well as the Salle Drouot on the right, to find the fabulous couch that we felt we must possess for our entry into such a dream world. I designed beds on paper, we went through the museums and châteaux looking for the perfect model and then, on the very eve of our moving, Harry telephoned me away from my packing to ask me to meet him in the rue de Seine.

In the dim recesses of an overstuffed second-hand shop I saw a headboard towering above the bric-à-brac like some Blakean torment. It was of ebony, massive cherubs entwined its posts—this was the top, the rest was hidden in the the cellar—I demurred nervously but Harry was so enraptured that I let him and the dealer have their way. It was to be assembled and put together by a neighbouring carpenter and be delivered and set up the next afternoon, ready for our first night in our new home. I took the dimensions and raced off to the bazaar to buy a box spring and mattress to fit—they had to be colossal. Next day, after many exhausting hours of unpacking, I was taking a bath when the new springs arrived and were stood on end in the adjoining room, but when finally we went out with friends to eat oysters at eight the bedstead itself had not materialized. Fortified with oysters, we came back two hours later. The children and the servants were asleep. All was dark and quite still, but on opening the unfamiliar door to our new room and switching on the light, Harry and I clung to each other in sudden panic. There in the centre of our rose and grey *chambre,* which had looked fresh and spacious until then, reared one of the most horrifying monstrosities I have ever beheld, a four-poster as large as a tumbril. From each post winked and smirked the most hideous imps of hell, not cherubs at all; the fruit seemed to burst with poison, the peacocks' tails reached out like tentacles. Upon the framework high off the floor were riveted the brand new springs and flowered mattress. I fled from the room and Harry quickly shut the door and locked it firmly from the outside.

"Will it walk," I whispered, for I was frightened.

Trembling, we stole hand in hand to the library above and there, on the familiar bosom of an old pink sofa, we clung together until dawn. As soon as dawn showed, we bribed the carpenter back again to undo his dreadful work. At daybreak, we carried the monstrous frame through the deserted streets to the edge of the Seine and from the Pont Neuf we let each hideous cherub plunge beneath the flood and gurgle away into oblivion. I swear the last one thumbed his nose as he went under.

Harry's library was on the top floor. It ran the length of our wing with a narrow balcony all the way round onto which three French windows opened out. Here the first afternoon after taking possession, he and I were having a breather, our elbows resting on the wrought-iron balustrade. The street was so narrow that the mansard roof of the building opposite almost bumped our noses. Out onto the other ledge before that window emerged two delightful-looking boys. They called "Allo"; we answered "Hello" and began to exchange information. We discovered they were Beaux Arts students learning to be architects.

"We are house-warming; come on over and have a drink," Harry invited, "and bring your friends."

"*Tous?*" they asked.

"Of course, *tous*," I replied, imagining a possible half-dozen teen-agers still hidden within.

"*A toute à l'heure,*" they grinned and waved, and so I went off to order champagne and biscuits for eight.

A few minutes later Harry called nervously, "Come out here, little rabbit."

There was a soft humming and tramping sound welling upwards. To my consternation, I saw a procession, two by two, crossing the rue de Lille to our gateway, an oncoming snake or *monôme* of students—big and small, light and dark, tramp, tramp, tramp, I counted thirty-two before I rushed back into the house.

"Ida," I cried, "run to the bistro and ask the *patron* to come quickly with a barrel of wine and all the glasses he owns."

Tramp, tramp, our own stairs began to shake. I stood at the top of them wringing each youth by the hand : *"Bonjour, bonjour, bonjour."* Soon the divans and chairs were overflowing and the floor began to fill up. Sixty-six, and they continued to come. We began with our two jeroboams from the cellar, but switched to Algerian red as soon as the man from the corner bar came to our assistance.

They were very gay but very polite. They won our hearts and we must have won theirs, for they elected me mascot of their atelier; and when spring came round, we were accepted as part and parcel of their activities. The Quatre Arts committee invited me to ride in the dragon's mouth—a papier-mâché monster constructed in our courtyard, and in whose jaws I sat stripped to the waist, an Inca princess, on the night of the famous Four Arts Ball for our atelier, Defrasse et Madelein.

Before the ball, we had invited the entire atelier to dinner, boys and their girls; also we were allowed to invite a small number of our own friends. The coveted invitation, so difficult to obtain, carried certain restrictions with it. To be dressed in the same costume as the rest of the atelier—this meant ochre paint and fabulous headdresses. The girls were naked to the navels, the boys to the loins. If one tried to enter the hall clothed they tore all camouflage away.

Since we served champagne at dinner instead of the usual student beer, our group arrived at the Salle Wagram in finer fettle than most. We marched practically undraped and wholly uninhibited up the Champs Elysées. I rode a baby elephant from the "Helen Scott will get it for you" agency. I particularly remember the antics of Gerard Lymington (now the Earl of Portsmouth) as he danced savagely, lance in hand, before my swaying pachyderm. Once admitted to the hall (and one first had to pass a rigorous questionnaire) the scene was wildly ritualistic and super-Inca. One stepped over the entwined bodies of couples rapturously climactic. One returned ardently the ardent kisses of the passers-by, and seventh veils slipped down. I remember one Brave who, kneeling in my path, embraced my painted knees and covered them with kisses. I felt deliciously pagan.

Around the huge hall each atelier had built themselves a private booth. Ours was high off the floor on stilts like an African hut and was reached by a flimsy ladder. One gave the password and the ladder was let down and held fast for the ascent by two guardian Incas at its top. If an uninitiated tried to climb up, the ladder was loosened until it swayed outward and shook off the invader.

Harry wore a collar of dead pigeons around his gilded neck and carried a bag of snakes. He was delighted to find a young matron who nursed one flamboyantly. When the fanfare for the contest was sounded, all the best-looking models were lifted onto the stage, gleamingly nude as each atelier prepared its float for the triumphal march. I was hoisted into our dragon's paper jaws, and my hair (a long blue wig) draped over my painted shoulders. My figure was as evident as the prow of a ship. Overcome by all the shouting, whistling and applause, round and round the room I went, carried on the shoulders of ten handsome warriors. There were sixteen floats in all. Professional models adorned them, but I and my dragon, to my glory and the atelier's delight, won the first prize, a case of very bad champagne. My breasts helped.

Harry said he suddenly glimpsed a beautiful girl high above his head and shouted, "My god, what *nichons,*" he didn't discover until afterwards that they belonged to his wife.

The Quatre Arts Ball is a harmless frolic among boys and girls, crazy fun, with no vestige of real wickedness. I have seen more licentiousness and vice (and just as naked) smiling balefully across the dinner tables of the Riviera as ever were dreamed of by those antic students. Ageing flesh had no place in Incaland, where a firm breast was worth a thousand lifted faces. I reached home later than Harry and found him with three pretty girls, all in a hot bath together, scrubbing off the paint. He was needed to rub it off their backs, he said, but I've never cared for pink soapsuds since. That crazy night our bed slept seven. We never knew who the seventh was, he wandered in, took off his loin cloth, and pushed over. He left early in the morning, too, pinning a little note upon the pillow saying he had to get to the department by nine—what department? We never saw him again. I wonder if he arrived at his desk in his loin cloth.

Harry now wrote for three hours in the morning and two hours in the afternoon. From 12.00 to 2.00 he went out alone, unless we had friends to luncheon. We usually had friends to tea and in the evenings we dined in bed and Harry read, sometimes aloud, especially the passage from Maldoror that begins, *"J'ai laissé pousser mes ongles."* Our life was divided into riotous hours of entertainment and secluded hours of work. We were never lax about work, Harry saw to that, but sometimes when very tired by a busy day, I would fall asleep, my head beneath his kimonoed elbow. Our bedroom light was very bright, but I learned to sleep in spite of it. Harry always read until one. Sometimes he would get up and dress as I slept and go out mysteriously alone. I was never invited, but he was always there when I awoke in the morning.

Ida brought us tea and croissants at eight. After breakfast I would go down to the nursery, plan our day and order the meals. We even indulged in fresh cream and real milk from the Necessary Luxuries Company, American necessities that the French never luxuriated in. And I often ordered banana ice cream and coconut layer cake from Gateaux Penny, more "necessities" the French did not know about.

I remember the Douglas Burdens just back from Africa, bringing their honey bear to lunch; he ate all the necessary luxuries before we others had a chance. Our table was one of the most satisfying in all the Latin Quarter, for we had a *cordon bleu* cook, and in addition to her achievement we were sent good things from home. Louise learned to fry chicken and make cornpone like a southern mammy, to cream codfish

143

and season chowder like a Gloucester house-wife, to serve brown betty and prune whip fit for the Pilgrim Fathers and, on top of this, we consumed a great deal of caviar. I never asked the price of anything; all I knew was that each week the kitchen accounts would be paid. I did try once to economize for a whole month and the saving was only a few shillings. You see, if you tell a French cook what you want and what she can spend per week, you will get all you desire, but if you order plainer food to economize, the accounts remain the same and she will grumble. They always spend the limit, good or bad.

We were sitting up side by side in bed, books piled all around us, Huysmans, Poe, Rimbaud, Mallarmé, Flaubert. Harry was engrossed in Poe's magic formulas and I was working on the proof sheets of my first poems, *Crosses of Gold*. The book was to appear at Christmas and was being printed by Albert Messin, Rimbaud's first publisher too (that is why we chose him).

The title page read Crosses of Gold, by————and then a blank for I couldn't make up my mind whether it should be by Polly Crosby, which sounded unpoetic, or by Mary Crosby, which sounded bluestocking.

"Why not a new name?" Harry asked.

"Why not," I agreed. I knew that Harry never called me Polly because he associated the name with Peabody; and my given name, Mary Phelps, somehow didn't suit me. No one but the bank ever called me "Mary."

"We must make an acrostic," Harry said, with Poe's formulas before his eyes. "Your new name must begin with a C to go with Crosby and it must form a cross with mine."

We looked up all the feminine C's in the dictionary, Carlotta, Charlotte, Clara, Clarisse, Catherine, Clytemnestra, Constance (decidedly not), Carmen, Caroline, Cara, Harry liked that one but   H   H   didn't quite do it, and besides Cara was

    CARA   A
      R   CARA
      R   R
      Y   Y

23. Harry came over to meet me. He had brought champagne, Croydon, 1929.

24. I brought back a bride for Narcisse Noir.
In the background, Auguste and the grass green Voisin, Le Bourget, 1929.

25. Mrs. Crosby, Harry, Caresse,
Temple of Baalbek, 1928.

26.
Harry, Bokara, Caresse,
Jerusalem, 1928.

27. Caresse with "Eclipse", Harry
on "Sunrise"—the donkey racetrack behind Le Moulin, 1928.

28. Harry and Frans atop the old stage-coach, Mai beside the team, Le Moulin, 1928.

29. D. H. Lawrence sunning himself at Le Moulin, April, 1929.

30. D. H. Lawrence with "Sunstroke" our race horse, April, 1929.

31. Photograph taken of C.C. by
D. H. Lawrence, 1929.

32. D. H. Lawrence and C. C.
" Season of Daffodils ", 1929.

a little harsh, we thought. "Your name should be more like a caress," he said.

"Then why not Caresse?" I answered.

"Of course!" and he joined the names upon the page but
H looked lopsided. Try it the other way, I suggested C
```
      A                                             A
CARESSE                                         HARRY
      R                                             E
      Y                                             S
                                                    S
                                                    E
```
and it worked!

We neither of us thought of spelling Caresse without the final e, so now I had a French name. It was one that we knew was sure to scandalize, but I was already committed; and so under "Crosses of Gold" I added "by Caresse Crosby"—and that was my very first title page.

Immediately Harry wrote a letter to his family announcing the birth of his wife, Caresse Crosby. In as long as it takes to reply we were bombarded with scornful gibes and quips. I was told that my name was like "undressing in public"—Harry's cousin, Betty Beal, signed her letter of protest "Baiser Beal," and *my* family absolutely refused to accept the new name; in fact, I am still "Polly" to my own relations. I was made uncomfortable at first but I determinedly signed Caresse Crosby to all written words. In no time my Paris friends adopted the new name, and I soon made friends who never realized that I had had any other. I knew there could be no compromise, even to the final E; it must forever remain that way just as we promised it that night in the rue de Lille, "Do you Harry take Caresse?" Before dawn I had added a final sonnet to my book, so that it ended "Forever to be Harry and Caresse."

CHAPTER 15

Gretchen and Peter Powel had become our closest friends. Like us, they were escapists from a Puritan background. Peter was one of a solid line of Rhode Island Powels. I had met him years before when I was invited to my first school dance, at Cloyne in Newport.

Peter Powel went to St. George's, but came to the Cloyne dance as a Newport native and so we met, I as Bo-Peep, he as a pirate. It was fancy dress, but Peter was a pirate at heart. I cared nothing at all for Bo-Peep. Now, in 1924, he and his Texan bride were living in Paris. Peter was doing exciting professional photography in a very unprofessional manner. Gretchen, like me, had joined Antoine Bourdelle's sculpture classes at the Atelier de la Crande Chaumière. Harry named them "The Crouchers" because when Peter crouched for photographs Grechen crouched beside him.

I recall the first evening that the Powels dined with us. We were going to the opera and we had said "dress." Peter, who had left his evening shoes on board his boat, came in a brand new pair of shiny black rubbers over bedroom slippers, to toe the line. In the entr'actes we persuaded him to take his rubbers off—style or no—and so he appeared at the opera in tails and beaded moccasins.

Gretchen was hazel-eyed and blonde with a lovely Texan figure. Like me, she wore her hair in a Castle bob, boyishly short with a big wide bang. I was dark, my eyes were blue and in Paris my figure was known as *spirituelle*. We luckily never

146

appealed to the same men and so got along beautifully. Peter's witticisms were a delight and his own laughter at them infectious. Each one of us held to our special brand of enjoyment. We often went adventuring *à quatre*—I should say *à six,* for we and our dogs were inseparable. It was in the autumn of 1927 that we took our trip through the towns of one syllable—Zulu white as suds with his Powels, and Narcisse black as tar with his Crosbys—all in the Powels' vintage Citroën, where there was no room for luggage. Harry always travelled with his finger in the Bible and stuffed the pockets of his mink-lined coat full to bursting, so he fared the best. Peter carried a toothbrush tucked away somewhere, Gretchen and I were allowed only a large sponge bag and a small hat box apiece. (Hats seemed so necessary in those days.) The dogs had a change of collar.

We started by heading west toward Brittany. The fun was that we swore we would only stop in towns of one syllable, for meals, for lodging and for luck. The first we struck was the village of Dreux, about one hundred kilometres from Paris; because we were getting thirsty, we drew up before the village pub, where we found ourselves the only customers. In the dim interior, the host stood back of a long zinc counter, which supported a comforting keg of good draught beer. On our side stood his wife, a great strapping girl with breasts like ripe melons. She had a tankard to her lips, a naked infant at her breast and as she drank the infant sucked and as he sucked a jet arched from between his fat brown thighs and splashed unheeded upon the sanded floor. They were all three wreathed in smiles and this liquid chain from barrel to father, from father to mother, from mother to son and from babe to the sanded floor is a picture I shall never forget.

From Dreux we continued to Dives for lunch. There at the *hôtellerie* of William the Conqueror we stuffed ourselves with and liked capons, everything was so good, especially their specialty, *Gaufrettes Coeur de Crème* and marmalade of quince. A *trou normand* (a big swig of Calvados—applejack—taken right in the middle of a Normandy meal to settle what has gone before, for what is to come after) helped us through. Continuing on our monosyllabic adventure we made for

Tours, but our car had worked itself into a frenzy. We had left Blois behind and had to go very slow. It was dark now and each town we came to had at least three syllables to its name. Even on our map no monotown appeared.

Finally, spluttering, wayworn and cross-eyed, we came upon the unsavoury hamlet of Bu. It boasted a post office (closed) and a tavern (closed), a garage (abandoned) and a red brick hotel, Les Jumelles, marooned on a deserted highway with rank fields at its back. It was as unprepossessing a set-up as could be imagined; but we were all too weary to care and the hotel did have a faint beacon light in its fly-specked window. We banged at the door until someone came. No rooms, they said, no rooms at all. We explained our plight so woefully that finally a compromise was reached. We could have the corner room on the ground floor where the grandfather and his eldest granddaughter were already asleep. They could go out to the barn, the lady of the inn assured us. The bed, she said, was big enough for four, and she had washed the sheets that very day. The dogs began to whimper, but we silenced them and all six of us, as soon as the family *déménagement* was effected, rolled gladly into the huge featherbed to which linen, damp and heavy, had been magnificently added. The dogs curled up at our feet; when at dawn a cock crowed, they both leapt like projected missiles over the footboard, through the window, over the garden wall and gave chase to a noisy hen. But we were too sleepy and deep in feathers to care, and presently they came leaping back with fresher feathers between their teeth. We had to wash at the garden pump, but the breakfast was divine : blood sausage, omelette and honey, and strong tea laced with rum.

The village blacksmith and his friends had been tinkering with the car. It looked sheepishly ready and waiting for another day, so we waved goodbye to Bu and were on our way to Luynes. The whole village came out to see us off, grandfather complaining bitterly of a pain in the back.

We wandered through Touraine visiting its lovely châteaux. Everywhere we went we met old women in starched lace bonnets, pretty old ladies in embroidered kerchiefs and aprons. I made up a song about them—

148

I love the old ladies of Langeais
The ladies of Luynes are divine
The ladies of Loches and Chenonceau
Are dressed like a nursery rhyme.

If all the old ladies of Langeais
Of Loches and Chenonceau and Luynes
Should each give a hand
To circle the land
What prettier sight could be seen!

It was the morning of the third day of our pilgrimage when, as we were heading homeward from Bluebeard's castle, we passed the imposing gates of a temptingly inhabited château. It stood half a mile from the road on a vineyard-skirted hillside. Peter stopped the car abruptly.

"That's the Genous' place," he said, "they make the best wine in Anjou. Let's pay them a call."

"But they don't know us," Gretchen protested.

"They know my brother," Peter answered. "Gerard and Harford roomed together at Harvard. In this forsaken part of the world I guess they will be damned glad to see anyone—especially from Boston."

It was noon, a very proper time to make a call, and we decided we'd risk it. If we didn't like them, we would come right out again, we assured each other. So we backed around and beetled up the well-kept driveway.

We left the car on the gravel circle and rang the bell which echoed loudly. The place was peacefully drowsing in the noonday sunshine. Presently distant steps sounded and a very old butler close-upped toward us from the far end of a polished hallway. He was deaf and we had to shout to make him understand that we were friends of the family from Newport, U.S.A. He looked dubiously at the dogs. We showed him they were well in leash. He ushered us then into a big sea-green salon shuttered against the heat, a beautiful room filled with beautiful objects. Each piece of furniture was placed just so on a floor waxed to mirror brightness. Huge jars of dahlias brightened the room. It was quite perfect. As *pièce suprême* a delicate spindle-legged tea table stood in a French window that opened out to the garden. On the table a full set of loveliest Sèvres china was arranged as though for exhibition.

We felt rather untidy in that room and poised nervously on the edge of our Louis XVI chairs. The dogs lay quietly at our feet, the silence deepened, the minutes passed. "Let's get out of here," Harry said, "we can leave by the garden, they'll never know we came." We all rose quickly, the dogs, too, but Zulu was on one side of the exhibition table, Narcisse on the other, their leads knotted, and as we made for the egress, with a seasick wave of warning I saw the leash catch the spindle legs right in the middle. Over tipped the table, off slid the tray, down crashed the Sèvres in a hundred pieces, reflected into a hundred more on the mirror of the polished floor. We stood stock-still in our flight, from the other end of the passage we heard light footsteps approaching and our host and hostess walked in. It was the most appalling moment of my life. We had to introduce ourselves over the ruins of their most prized possession.

Only a very great lady could have acted as Madame Genou did. She took one look, turned white, and then said calmly, but ruefully, "This calls for our rarest vintage, Gerard." And our host nodded. "We can drink better in the wine shed," he winced, stepping over the debris. "Let's go." Through the garden to the sheds we filed, numbed, and there we stayed sampling vintage after vintage until we were all quite intoxicated. We wept into our Anjou trying to cleanse our breaking hearts. Anjou is that sparking white wine that they serve at Pruniers—now each time that I taste it I hear a crashing of porcelain in my ears and feel a prickling at the nape of my neck.

When we returned to the salon not a trace of the holocaust remained. We stayed to drink, we stayed to dinner, we stayed the night. The incident was not referred to again, but we all slept badly in spite of the civilized and humane behaviour of the "friends of the family." There was absolutely nothing we could do to replace their Sèvres but there was something we could do about three little nursery-sized Genous, and on our arrival back in Paris we ordered a large portion of the *"Nain Bleu"* shipped off to Touraine.

I often wonder into what different encounters towns of three syllables would have lured us—just as one wonders "if I had walked up Fifth instead of Madison would I have met him?" or "if I'd been out when when she telephoned would she have taken that fateful plane?" and a bus that holds one up for a split second can sometimes hide heaven from view. Chance is such a busy servant to Destiny.

From our new life we banished newspapers, magazines (all except the *Nouvelle Revue Française* and *transition*) and until the Mill, gramophones (there were no radios to banish then). This was in the escapist tradition, we swore that they were Philistine instruments, and we avoided all home ties (except letters and money).

We made a point of not calling on our Ambassador or, indeed, on any officials—Harry did go once to the Embassy the day after Lindbergh flew the Atlantic. Steve Crosby was visiting us and he and his son made a formal call that morning, but I stuck to tradition-in-the-making and only acknowledged in verse the thrill of the day before. It had indeed been a spectacular and heart-pounding event.

When the *Spirit of St. Louis* took off from the United States with its solo pilot the news had been flashed to the world, most fully to France, and the French, always a touch and go people, were immediately touched and off they went—by train, by bus, by car, by foot to the flying field at Le Bourget where it was announced that from 5 p.m. on, Paris could expect him.

With thousands of others, we converged upon the Route de Flandre, the highway over which Joffre had led forth his taxicab army in 1914 to stop the Germans at the Marne—but this time it was a holiday army, everyone in high spirits, the afternoon was fine, the visibility fair. When we reached Le Bourget barriers were already up to keep the crowds off the runway, which was well marked with little white flags and later with little white flares. Myron Herrick, our Ambassador, was waiting in the signal tower and with him the French air officials and other greeters—there was a military band and the inevitable vendors hawking mats to sit on and boxes to stand on, and as time passed, of *petits pains aux jambon* to bite on.

151

Peter, who had been an ace in World War I, got us through the police cordon onto the field and there we waited in the lee of an emergency fire truck. About seven it began to grow dark, no sign of Lindbergh yet, he had no radio to call us on, only his compasses for dead reckoning.

Le Bourget was a commercial as well as a military field and from time to time we could hear the far-off drone of some scheduled air liner as it approached from the northeast. Everyone then craned their necks skyward, hopeful, until the loud speaker boomed.

"C'est Londres qui arrive," or *"C'est Strasbourg qui rentre,"* then the crowd relaxed as astonished pilots and passengers glided into the midst of that tense and nervous mass—but still no word, no sign—the early diners were getting impatient and a few cars around the edges began receding toward Paris. A report went out that the lone birdman had flown off his course, had been forced to come down in Ireland—but the crowd refused to be disillusioned, they stayed with him every air mile of his way.

My ears, which are unusually keen, of a sudden picked out a delicate hum of lightest calibre away up in the clouds, which were now scudding across a misted moon.

"Listen!" I warned as others heard and listened too. A small clear burring as of a toy, and then it was lost in the thickening clouds. Everyone heaved a sigh and sat back, "He's circling the field," and suddenly there was a silver flicker like the fin of a darting minnow out of one cloud, into another.

"C'est lui," the cries grew. *"C'est Lindbergh."* The crowd rose to its feet and prayed. Suddenly from the nearest cloud the bright wings flashed and veered downward, straight and sure to that waiting lane of flare-lit faces.

He hit the runway precise and clean. The *Spirit of St. Louis* rolled sweetly and silently to where we jumped for joy.

"He's done it, he's done it," yelled the crowd. Floodlights were turned upon the man and the machine. When the pilot started to climb from the cockpit the crowd broke from its boundaries and surged over the field to reach the hero whom they lifted to their shoulders and carried high. He looked boyish and tousled and very much like Harry. I heard a Frenchman say, *"Ce n'est pas un homme, c'est un oiseau"* (it is not a man but a bird).

Lindbergh, who had flown three thousand miles in loneliness, was now surrounded by thousands in triumph and carried to the signal tower, there to be officially welcomed, and when he spoke into the loud speaker his myriad fans were silent in awe before him. He said only a few words huskily in halting French, then he waved and smiled once and turned and left quickly, driven away in the Embassy car to bed. The disappointed people understood how tired he must be and turned again toward the little plane which was still smiling valiantly. Around the *Spirit of St. Louis* a thousand fingers strained to touch its luminous resting wings; it was like a candle to which their moth-hands flew.

It took us till midnight to reach Paris, for cars were still pushing out to see, as the others went streaming in.

On another occasion Harry and I took a sea voyage with the Powels. Peter had bought the *Emilie,* a Breton harbourmaster's craft, and he was having it fitted out at Brest. It would, when finished, sleep four in two double bunks. A butane galley stove and a pump toilet were to be installed as well. They had been fussing over this boat for weeks and at last we received the awaited telegram "tomorrow, Hotel de la Tempête. Bring chocolate bars and riding lights." We also brought a sack of lemons against possible scurvy. Harry wore his blue suit and overcoat; sneakers were his only concession to life at sea. I was properly nautical in dungarees and middy blouse, espadrilles upon my feet. However, I motored down in a Patou print and so we arrived the next evening at the Bar de la Tempête looking like Sunday at Longchamps. We found the Powels with tar on their noses, blisters on their feet and flea-bitten to boot, working hard. Of course, nothing was really ready, but we had expected that, and were also armed with literature and paper and pencils, and the Bible and a handsome Log Book especially bound in oilskin by Strobansk. The Powels already had maps galore of tides and shoals and winds and waters tacked up on the café wall. One corner of the bar had become their own. We drank rum (lemon improved it). The two prostitutes who shared the room above stuck to port.

153

It seemed that the marine toilet especially ordered from Amsterdam didn't quite fit—or flush. It had to be ripped out and another installed. Visions of a large hole in the bottom of the *Emilie* appalled us. We realized it must be filled in some way, so we settled down to do our own work and let the Powels do theirs, Harry writing, I translating Gerard de Nerval. The bar was picturesquely alive with *putains* and *matelots*. The thumping that went on overhead from dusk till dawn was proof of the jolly business carried on there.

We had instructed our chauffeur Auguste to keep himself and the limousine out of sight. He sneaked in now and then looking more picturesque than the St. Malo dope runners. We discovered later that he had organized a kind of ambulatory bordel in the back of the car, idling up and down the Brest waterfront after dark. (Luckily it was much too expensive for the clientele of the "Tempête".)

The first day we were there was very fine, with a gentle off-shore breeze. The next evening a storm blew in from Jersey. The third day it rained steadily; the fourth day was clear with following winds. It is all recorded in the Log, for Harry, suspecting that the barroom floor was the only sea we'd sail, had charted our voyage in his oilskin book. According to it we set sail at eight the morning after our arrival. The long trip into Lisbon is duly noted down. The tides, the winds, the sights we saw, and what we said, or could have. On the sixth day out, we summoned Auguste, got back into our Longchamps clothes and took leave of the Powels and their ship and their nautical problems. It had been a fine voyage. We were saturated with the smell and the jargon of the sea, and though many shared it with us, the toilet *at the Tempête* had worked!

Reading about the imaginary storm off St. Sebastian in Harry's diary, I was glad that I had weathered it so well.

CHAPTER 16

One of the very best things about our marriage was that Harry and I always enthused about people and places at the same time but as soon as one of us lost interest the other did too. We walked out of the same restaurants, we wanted to leave parties at the same moment and if an entertainer did not appeal to one, he or she never did to the other. However, we were each free to do as we wished, alone if not together, but *alone* was never really as well as *together*. We were restless out of one another's sight and Harry was forever telephoning to tell me where and why he was where he was, and neither of us ever came late to a rendezvous with the other. Only the devil or death could keep us waiting. My confidence in Harry was so complete that I never questioned him and he in return believed that everything I did or said or wrote was right. If I composed a sonnet before breakfast he would have it in print before dinner.

After his early sonnets Harry had struck out in new directions for himself. Experiment in rhyme was our most domestic game. He would call to me over the banister to come quick and I flew up the library stairs to hear some novel paraphrase—or I would buzz the buzzer and he would come leaping down to praise my newest couplet—and while I wrote in my own room I could hear his light pacing overhead, it was as though he were training for the big race, his steps had a good thoroughbred sound. I was sure he was going to win, my bets were already down.

In 1927 the Black Sun Press was born, the foal of Necessity, out of Desire. Ever since I had had my first work accepted by one of the little English magazines and Harry had begun to write sonnets under my guidance at Etretat, we knew that some day we must see our poems in print—it did not occur to us to submit them to a publishing house—the simplest way to get a poem into a book was to print the book! What we needed were the poems to be printed, the model to go by and a printer to print them. We had the first two. Each of us was ready with ammunition for the initial salvo, but as yet we had no printer. We wanted one who would follow our dictates, not we his. The three books that we chose as models were especially lovely editions: *Héloïse and Abélard,* Brussels; The *Boussole des Amants,* Paris, and the Bodley Head edition of John Donne's poems.

One of our very first publications was *Sonnets for Caresse* by Harry Crosby, a small oblong format, printed in Astrée italique. Nothing could have been simpler, but nothing could have been nicer, especially the margins. Typography is largely a matter of spacing and a correct mathematical margin. Like sculpture, it is the space that surrounds the object which gives it its balance—these things and many others I learned that year, before the Black Sun Press was born, for our venture was first edited in 1927 under the imprint "Editions Narcisse" (named after Narcisse Noir) and I designed the pool-gazing Narcissus for our first colophon—but that was not until we had finally run to earth—in his case I should say "scampered" to earth—the perfect printer.

We were hunting through the intricate little streets on the left bank of the Seine in the very heart of the Latin Quarter, when turning into what seemed to be and was the shortest street in Paris, we found his shingle hanging at the bend of the rue Cardinale—there was only room in all its narrow length for that one bend—"Roger Lescaret, *Imprimeur*" we read, and squeezing close in the narrow passage to study the display in his workshop window, we saw that he was a master at *faire parts,* those lugubrious though steady jobs, black-banded as deep as a cuff, that announced the death of the departed. Two big blue flies were buzzing in the warmth of the enclosure

156

and others had festooned and crisscrossed the sun-bleached display with their traces—as we looked, there was a frantic ringing of a bicycle bell at our backs, and the answering yap of an expectant animal within the shop, and with a side-slip and a jangle a bird-like little fellow in a black printer's smock came to a very sudden stop, his front wheel driving us flat against his wall. To the handle bar was strapped a large wire basket in which he was carrying his day's orders, on contact with the wall the whole thing erupted and papers flew and slipped and blew across the pavement. He bowed quickly, apologized and bent down bobbing hither and thither retrieving the scattered sheets. We also set to work and taking fire from his sudden activity whirled like spinning mice bumping each other head on tail.

"There," he beamed, straightening up. *"C'est fait."* And he looked as pleased as Pierre and patted the bundle beneath his elbow as though it were a naughty child. A fringe of unruly hair hung over his clouded glasses, behind which we noticed that one eye was decidedly *à travers,* there was a smudge on the end of his nose but he seemed quite unaware, and with a conspiratorial "ha ha," as though he were Bluebeard about to enter the seventh chamber, he took a huge iron key from the folds of his black alpaca and opened wide (that is as wide as it would go) the door of his domain.

"Enter," he said and we did. Roger Lescaret scuttled in at full height but Harry Crosby had to stoop to avoid the slanting beam overhead. There was a desk almost bang up in front of the door and three straight uncompromising chairs grouped about it for consultation, but each of these was already occupied by toppling piles of printed matter and he deposited his bundle upon the desk like a barricade through which he peeped and winked at us in delighted anticipation; our consulting was done standing.

"You do your own work?" Harry asked, looking over Lescaret's head for a possible assistant.

"All," he said proudly, "except for the young girl."

We gazed around. *"En haut,"* he grinned, pointing one upright finger significantly toward the ceiling. "She wraps and she cooks"—from the amount of unwrapped merchandise lying about I thought her job could not be arduous. There was an almost perpendicular ladder at his back supposedly leading to a heavenly region.

"And you print by hand?" Harry continued.

"Entirely." His satisfaction was so great that when he whisked the black cloth from off his mute and gleaming accomplice it was as though he were performing some feat of legerdemain. He beamed, "I cannot just yet afford another," but the satisfaction in his voice implied that it would be a sad day when he could.

"Fine, fine," Harry said, "we have some work here for you."

"Ha, ha, a marriage perhaps," looking at me.

"I'm afraid not," I apologized.

"A christening then?" He fairly danced with delight.

"No," we chorused, "it's a book."

"A whole book," he replied; his ego seemed faintly to deflate. "A whole book is a lot of work."

We asked him to try it and finally persuaded him to give us an estimate.

We had brought with us one of the newest limited editions de luxe of a famous Paris firm; it sold for a fabulous price and had been oversubscribed before publication. We asked him if he thought he could copy it in layout and typography, handing him Harry's set of sonnets written in long hand.

Lescaret's confidence returned. He could copy what he saw, he was on safe ground again. "Beautiful, beautiful," he commented, "but it will be *trés cher* the paper alone, and *Astrée italic,* we must buy some special type, you know."

"It will be hand-set?" queried Harry.

"Mais oui, mais oui"—by now our new-found printer was jumping up and down in his excitement.

We said we'd return at the end of the week for proofs.

"I can send them by the *jeune fille,*" he rubbed his hands together, "ha, ha, ha," it was as though at last he had found her an occupation worthy of her hire.

We backed from the confines bowing and smiling, he followed doing likewise. With his "ha ha, ha ha," in our ears— the door bell jangled stridently and we went out.

As we emerged into the sunshine, we heard a yap overhead

and looking up we saw the doggie peering over a crooked sill, the one that connected with the ladder, but from where we stood we could not see that Lescaret's pet had only three legs.

Two days later while we were at luncheon the maid announced "The Printer of Monsieur and Madame," it sounded as though he were attached to our court. The dining room was at the top of a long polished stair, he scrambled up it like a harried *sapeur*—waving in his hand our proof sheets, a signal to advance.

We offered him a glass of wine, he took it standing and smacked his lips, but with such impatience that we left the table and repaired to the library. You would have thought he had invented printing so proud and amazed he was at what he had accomplished—and I must say it looked to us as handsome as the model. The price of type face and paper was high but the printing cost was negligible. I think he would have been as unhappy as we ourselves if the job had been taken away from him. His pride in his output has always been his greatest commercial asset—one loves to do business with those whose gratification is in the work itself.

The sonnets looked Shakespearean. We were all three delighted and we tried to press an advance into our printer's hand. "No, no," he protested, "my credit is good everywhere in the quarter." No need to pay, only to print, and he wrung our hands instead—laughing and scurrying away.

His shop, by a devious route, was not far from where we lived and we could drop in several times a day just for the fun of seeing the pages emerge crisp and fair from the hand-worked press, and smell the good strong ink that permeated the place.

Sonnets for Caresse. Editions Narcisse Paris XXVII was such a great success and the typesetting, the paper choosing, the outlay and the binding were all such fun, done in this intimate and delightful manner, that we went on to greater and more complicated achievement. *Red Skeletons*, illustrated, was our next and with Lescaret's help we found excellent associates in the lithography line. With Poe's *Fall of the House of Usher* illustrated by Alastair, the Hungarian artist, the Editions Narcisse broke into the English and American markets—and on the credit page the colophon read "Printed on the presses of *maître imprimeur* Lescaret." This edition was so admired and reviewed that others followed. It was then we changed the firm's name to Black Sun Press because black was Harry's favourite colour and he worshipped the sun. Lescaret remained the master printer—it should have been master copyist, but the results were as good as the models copied, and if it was I who set the margins and planned the pages and Harry who chose the material, it was Lescaret and the young girl who worked the press.

It happened a year or two later, when we had a dozen or more titles to our credit, among them *Forty-seven Letters of Marcel Proust, The Escaped Cock* and *Sun* by D. H. Lawrence and *The Bridge* by Hart Crane, that a learned and professional group of typographers came over from England to visit the presses of France—through dint of our personal contacts, copies of our editions had reached the London critics and libraries—the Black Sun, an important press to visit, was on their agenda and the *"maître imprimeur"* was listed as a noted typographer to be consulted. The committee was slightly perturbed when neither the Bibliothèque Nationale nor the telephone company had ever heard of Roger Lescaret or the Black Sun Press, but they decided to visit the plant nevertheless. A dozen or more dignified gentlemen arriving before the fly-blown window could only believe their eyes, for the swinging sign *"imprimeur* Lescaret" was rattling overhead.

They walked in as a freshly inked title page was being spread out about the shop—on desk, on chairs, on the ladder's steps—and the continuous clank , clank of the foot pedal heralded the work in progress. That it happened to be part of James Joyce's *Work in Progress* duly impressed the visitors, the look of that page was first-rate too, but when the Master Printer greeted them with his gay "he he" and scrambled about picking up proof sheets but was unable to talk either coherently or intelligently on any aspect of the gentle art—they retired (backing) and in consternation withholding an embossed invitation to Roger Lescaret to address the group that evening at Foyot's (black tie).

Through the dozen years that the Black Sun Press functioned before War II, Lescaret's appearance, spirit and approach to his work never varied—he did, as more books appeared at our behest, acquire a bigger and better press, driven by electricity and not by foot. He acquired a typesetter, Madame Stessel, and an apprentice, Monsieur Paris, one of the most intelligent and tasteful young typographers imaginable—in fact Monsieur Paris secretly stole the show, but Lescaret never knew—and his office remained as unmanageably disordered and his approach to the publishing business as elementary as in the beginning. He was a little printer, an honest and happy one, he did not attempt to change this satisfactory status, nor did we.

The de Geeteres, bargees from Amsterdam, were our next lucky encounter. Frans de Geetere came to France the same autumn that we moved into the rue de Lille, dragging his barge behind him, and having manœuvred the dikes of Holland and the frontiers of Belgium and the northern waterways of France, he strode into Paris one summer evening towing his dwelling with Mai den Englendsen, his timid blonde bride, atop of it—he on the footpath, a stout rope about his lean and muscular middle. At twenty-one with sunburned torso, a crest of wild black curls, and snapping black eyes, Frans was a story book character and Mai, his Netherlands wife, was as frail and honey-golden as some *Princesse lointaine.* There were two tortoise-shell kittens aboard and a hold stuffed with paintings of flowers and nudes in profusion, for Frans had come to Paris for Art's sweet sake, not to study, because he was already confident and bold, but to compete in the marketplace with the greatest artists of the day. During one whole year he had been painting forget-me-nots on coal scuttles in Amsterdam to earn enough to make the trip. Mai's dowry had been the chunky little barge, and her family had packed it with cheeses and cabbages and fruits but the travellers had been three months on the way and the pussycats were meowing for milk and Frans and Mai were thirsting for the cool beer and juicy produce of France.

Until they reached their goal not one penny was permitted for frivolity. The toll for each lock had to be paid outright and along the wide river reaches they battened onto the long tug-drawn lines of barges paying passages as they went. Their story as they told it to us is as unforgettable as they are.

I met them one morning as they stood hand in hand looking up at the swinging sign of the Black Sun Press that now waved from my office window in the rue Cardinale, that street as slim and exotic as themselves—they spoke with a Dutch accent and asked timidly, when I stuck my head out into the sunshine, if they could order some calling cards to be printed. I would have steered them along to a neighbour printer had I not been curious upon whom and why they wished to leave cards. When Frans sidled into my tiny low-raftered office he unpretentiously filled it up, but as soon as he smelled printer's ink, his shyness left him. He had a good black pencil in the pocket of his open shirt and upon the white paper which I proffered him he sketched with such deftness and mastery that I knew him for a man of talent. It was a drawing of their "Gallant" craft at anchor at the foot of a long stone stair and behind her rose the lacy spires and apse of Notre Dame, the statue of Henri IV on his marble steed was glimpsed through a nodding chestnut bough—any Parisian would have known at once the exact location of the barge at the place du Vert Gallant and under this sketch he wrote :

Mai & Frans-de Geetere   Aboard *Le Vert Gallant*
Artists Peintres   Out of Amsterdam

as intriguing a calling card as I ever saw. I took the order and said I would deliver the cards myself. Frans paid in advance, counting very carefully.

So one September evening a week later, Harry and I and some friends made our first visit to the barge, carrying the cards with us. We had not warned them that we were coming but when we descended the long steep steps from the street and glimpsed the *Vert Gallant* through the trees at the water's edge, I could swear they had set the scene just for us. The lamplight behind the red curtain, Mai with a big bowl of cherries in her lap and Frans, stripped to the waist, cross-legged outside her window playing her a love song on his accordion. Stars were twinkling and the cats were purring, while these two strangers cosily cradled themselves in the very heart of Paris.

When they heard our hallos Frans jumped to his feet and

162

handed us by gentle fingertips across the narrow gangplank to the deck and down to the mellow-lit room where a big oil lamp swung above the centre table and turkey-red divans lined the walls. It was both stark and sumptuous, rather like the owners, and the place cast an exotic spell upon us—a great *bidon* of cider was brought up from the storeroom and we sank into the shadows along the cushioned walls, while the cherries were passed from hand to hand and the apple wine flowed as gently and as steadily as the river beneath us. Frans soon became a well-known figure in Montparnasse, leaving his cards of a morning on merchants and artists, on butcher and baker as he bartered for the day's supplies. One species of his currency was the good Holland cheeses from the hold (rapidly dwindling in number), another his ability, with pencil and paper, to make quick likenesses of his creditors. To Mai he always carried home a flower (I believe the flower vendor became the most portrayed man in Paris).

Mai seldom left the barge. She was very timid and she loved her river refuge. Frans had brought a crude wooden letterpress with him from Holland and was working on a set of woodcuts for *The Songs of Maldoror* which he was printing by hand on-board, and hunting subscribers by foot on shore. We ordered one and so did a number of our American friends, but toward the newcomer in their midst the Paris connoisseurs were wary—they'd have to be shown first—so Frans worked for fame and bartered for bread, met the world on its terms and protected his own on his.

We became fast friends and every Saturday morning they appeared in the rue de Lille for hot and soapy baths with their best clothes wrapped in a bright-covered canvas, and as soon as resplendent, we'd lunch together at some gay restaurant in the Bois and later go on to the races at Longchamps. Frans, when dressed in his blue suit and patent-leather shoes, was very proud of his appearance. "You see, I have become a banker," he used to say, and he played every race, the minimum, while Mai in suspense and trepidation clung to his arm. His excitement was so great when he won and he was so crushed when he lost that I realized what agonizing thrills he must be experiencing, but how glad I was that he was wise enough never to double his bets.

Then one terrible day, after a wild night of tempest, water began to seep in along the seams of the *Vert Gallant*—literally the bottom was about to drop out of their world! They might even find themselves and their hopes at the bottom of the Seine . . . Their friends rallied around and each one contributed in some way to help them save their situation and their boat. We arranged that the craft should be towed to the outskirts of Paris and there put on the ways, its bottom scraped and caulked and painted; but though we invited them to spend those two weeks with us, Frans said he must stick to his ship and help the men, and Mai wouldn't think of deserting her pots and pans and kittens or Frans—so they went on housekeeping in drydock. They were far from their source of supplies and from their merchant friends of the quarter, so the night before they quitted the shadows of Notre Dame we gave them a shipyard shower on the barge. Everyone brought something— wine, cakes, eggs, ham, cheese or fruit, and I remember that the Dolly Sisters, then dancing in Paris, brought a case of champagne which was consumed that same evening. A Maharanee, a prince and princess, counts and countesses, as well as writers and artists and models and students—all the friends, in fact, were there. It was a wildly successful party although the river kept rising about our ankles. At 4.00 a.m. the tug that was to tow them out of Paris whistled and chugged alongside, but by that time some of the guests were too happily unaware to notice and awoke at sunrise to find themselves, like cargo, being carried far from home.

The following year Frans gave his first exhibition on board. The painting, though less modern than those in most of the galleries, drew crowds to the barge and Frans realized several hundred dollars from sales. His first purchase was a new spring suit for Mai; I remember we were all invited to advise and help choose. That summer the barge was towed out to Fontainebleau and tied up to the river bank at the edge of the forest. There on Sundays we would gather for swimming, sunbathing and picnic lunches. We helped them to solve some of the problems of their life, but they helped us to add so many hours to ours that they overweighted the scales. No matter how many difficult and lean days were weathered, Frans' belief in himself and his intrepid ways were a heartening example to us all.

In 1927, Frans and Mai in the *Vert Galant* were anchored under the Pont Neuf only a few hundred yards from our front door—hardly a day went by that either Harry or I or both did not look in on the bargees—and when the weather grew warm, Harry started sun-basking on the cabin roof—that is why his summer tan got a head start on all of us. When there were special aquatic festivals, boat races or swimming races on the Seine, we were assigned front row seats. I remember on the day that Alan Gerbault's "Fire Crest" was towed to Paris from the sea, Harry climbed up into a crane to see her better.

I don't remember how we came in contact with the Jolases but I think it was through Kay Boyle. Gene and Kay used to meet us on the barge in the evenings—it is still the best place I know for romance. *Transition* had already been launched and was running successfully before Harry came into it, then the great moment arrived when the Manifesto for the Revolution of the Word was proclaimed. Harry and I both wanted to sign and we did, also Kay, Hart Crane and others. It is now an historic document. I was unqualified really, user of easeful cliché and well-worn rhyme, in fact I was flagrantly *démodée,* but the metamorphic spirit was strong and the pen was willing, and I did justifiably get some "hymnic" imagery into "The Stranger," which appeared in *transition* 18, and was published again in *transition Workshop* in 1949. I was sad to see that one word was still omitted, the line should read,

Where shall I find you
Or where shall I go

The Manifesto was also republished and I quote :
" EUGENE JOLAS Manifesto : The Revolution of the Word
TIRED OF THE SPECTACLE OF SHORT STORIES, NOVELS, POEMS AND PLAYS STILL UNDER THE HEGEMONY OF THE BANAL WORD, MONOTONOUS SYNTAX, STATIC PSYCHOLOGY,

DESCRIPTIVE NATURALISM, AND DESIROUS OF CRYSTALLIZING A VIEWPOINT . . .
WE HEREBY DECLARE THAT :

1. THE REVOLUTION IN THE ENGLISH LANGUAGE IS AN ACCOMPLISHED FACT.
2. THE IMAGINATION IN SEARCH OF A FABULOUS WORLD IS AUTONOMOUS AND UNCONFINED.

   (Prudence is a rich, ugly old maid courted by Incapacity . . . Blake)
3. PURE POETRY IS A LYRICAL ABSOLUTE THAT SEEKS AN A PRIORI REALITY WITHIN OURSELVES ALONE.

   (Bring out number, weight and measure in a year of dearth . . . Blake)
4. NARRATIVE IS NOT MERE ANECDOTE, BUT THE PROJECTION OF A METAMORPHOSIS OF REALITY.

   (Enough! Or Too much! . . . Blake)
5. THE EXPRESSION OF THESE CONCEPTS CAN BE ACHIEVED ONLY THROUGH THE RHYTHMIC "HALLUCINATION OF THE WORD." (Rimbaud)
6. THE LITERARY CREATOR HAS THE RIGHT TO DISINTEGRATE THE PRIMAL MATTER OF WORDS IMPOSED ON HIM BY TEXTBOOKS AND DICTIONARIES.

   (The road of excess leads to the palace of Wisdom . . . Blake)
7. HE HAS THE RIGHT TO USE WORDS OF HIS OWN FASHIONING AND TO DISREGARD EXISTING GRAMMATICAL AND SYNTACTICAL LAWS.

   (The tigers of wrath are wiser than the horses of instruction . . . Blake)
8. THE "LITANY OF WORDS" IS ADMITTED AS AN INDEPENDENT UNIT.
9. WE ARE NOT CONCERNED WITH THE PROPAGATION OF SOCIOLOGICAL IDEAS, EXCEPT

TO EMANCIPATE THE CREATIVE ELEMENTS
FROM THE PRESENT IDEOLOGY.
10. TIME IS A TYRANNY TO BE ABOLISHED.
11. THE WRITER EXPRESSES. HE DOES NOT
COMMUNICATE.
12. THE PLAIN READER BE DAMNED.
(*Damn braces! Bless relaxes! . . . Blake*)

> *Signed* KAY BOYLE, WHIT BURNETT,
> HART CRANE, CARESSE CROSBY, HARRY
> CROSBY, MARTHA FOLEY, STUART GILBERT,
> A. L. GILLESPIE, LEIGH HOFFMAN, EUGENE
> JOLAS, ELLIOT PAUL, DOUGLAS RIGBY, THEO
> RUTRA, ROBERT SAGE, HAROLD J. SALEM-
> SON, LAURENCE VAIL.

transition 16-17

It was about the time of the "Manifesto" that Goops came into our lives, that is he came into mine, he had already been in Harry's as a devoted batman during the days of the Ambulance Corps. It was he who used to tinker with Harry's machine when it didn't run or wash it bright when it had had a gory day. He was a self-immolated slave. He believed in Harry as in the Almighty, once all but disastrously.

Goops was as patently an underworld character as if he had been a movie director's product. He had fled to France out of reach of the legal arm and had joined the American Ambulance Corps both for salvation and protection—Harry became his idol. I never saw him in uniform but in mufti he ran true to type—the too stylish, too thin suit, the imitation-diamond stickpin, the checked socks, the grubby fingernails and the slight whine in his voice.

Harry encouraged his devotion—I was mildly frightened—he seemed to be so lately of the underworld, the most unsavoury section, but Goops' devotion to Harry overlapped onto me. I could not escape it had I tried.

Harry sitting with friends one stimulated noonday at the Rotonde Bar in Montparnasse said prayerfully that he was waiting for a lady relative to "kick the bucket." "Why," asked Goops. "Because it's full of silver." "Much?" he was asked again.

"All I need," said Harry. Goops was silent for a long time, suddenly, "I'll do it," he said, "that's my business. I bumped off Rothstein, just give me her name and address and a hundred bucks. Everything will be taken care of. I'll be back for Christmas."

We all laughed, but for some crazy reason Harry gave him the hundred dollars (as a going-away present).

Simenon, the famous French detective writer, was at the bar too, he sat there almost as thoughtful as Goops. After Harry's death I learned why. He went home and wrote one of his most wicked stories, *La Tête d'un Homme,* around this plot. Some of my Paris friends thought I should protest and sue, since Harry and I are both very lightly camouflaged, but of course I didn't.

In movie form it much later became *The Man on the Eiffel Tower.*

CHAPTER 17

The pace was quickening now. The following winter established an uneasy pattern of procedure that in time I believe I could have handled in happier fashion, but I was not given time. Five Christmases we had spent apart, I always spent mine with the children, to this I was pledged. Together Harry and I had greeted all five New Years, there were not to be enough. From now on I felt I was swimming against the current.

Harry was jealous of my children, there was no denying it and because of it I was jealous of the moments they had to spend without me; there were many times when my feet were in the Ritz and my heart was in the nursery; but one concession to Harry's demands I could not make, I had to spend Christmas with them, I owed it to them and to myself. Though I tried to persuade him to join us wherever we were, he always refused and made it terrifying for me by announcing beforehand with which lovely lady he would be drinking his Christmas coffee—there was one winter when he tried to compromise, God bless him, but it didn't work for him and it didn't work for me—the children, God bless *them*, were delighted.

Billy was for a second year at the Rosay in winter quarters at Gstaad (it was a movable school, the winter term spent in ski country), Polleen was at Marie José, a nearby "infants' paradise" so advertised (the Crown Princess of Germany, after whom it was named had gone there). I was able to have both children with me over the holiday at the Palace Hotel. The Christmas before we had spent in Mêgeve in the French Alps. I had had a whole week with them then and it had been fun, but this year they were in Switzerland and I arrived on the twenty-second with a trunk full of toys and a heavy heart—for Harry had begged me not to leave him alone, while I feline and predatory had urged him to come with me. I held Archie, whom we'd met at Joyce's party, and Ernest, met through Archie, out as bait, for the MacLeishes and the Hemingways were spending that winter in Gstaad. But Harry was uncompromising and as usual told me in what boudoir I could reach him if I cared to telephone. He would be waiting for me at home on the twenty-sixth as he had always waited, he said, and so we parted determined and miserable.

The Palace was overcrowded. I was lucky to get adjoining rooms, one double and one single, Polleen and I in the big one, Billy in the little one. In spite of my heartache I was happy and excited to be with them. On the twenty-third there was a mother-and-son skiing tournament—Billy and I entered, but that year I think Ada MacLeish and her son won—it was merry and gay, we all of us foregathered for hot chocolate in the hotel hall, the children were joyous.

On Christmas Eve in order to make a surprise I moved Billy into my room with Polleen and I took his little north room overlooking the laundry, not very attractive but adequate. After they were asleep I put up a small tree in my window. There was no fireplace so the stockings were hung by the heater with care and I sat up until 3 a.m. trimming and tying and festooning—on the radiator were spread the children's woollen underwear and stockings to dry. It had been a snowy Christmas Eve. I myself had taken that night to cold cream my face and put curlers in my hair—a luxury I never permitted myself at home, in fact the set-up was one hundred per cent mother. I fell so soundly asleep that even the clatter of fists didn't at first awaken me, then I flew to the door to see what was the matter—it was only half-past six, but there I found him—with contrition in his eyes—but when he pushed past me into that hopeless little theatre, I knew that my play was a flop—everything about it was wrong for Harry. My hair should have framed my smile like a halo. The room should have been vast and luxurious—there should have been a big double bed. I could feel those woollen leggings on the radiator boring into my back, my heart plummeted.

"My God, what a nursery," he said and turned away. "I'll see you at luncheon." It was then long before breakfast. For one desperate second I hoped to hold him, but the curlers threatened reunion like thorns, I crawled back into my narrow cot like a whipped puppy. I cried and cried and cried—praying the children would not hear.

An hour later when I put on my battle dress and went in to call them to see the tree and told them that Harry had unexpectedly arrived they were so thrilled that even Santa Claus's advent did not hold a candle to his, they hurried through their presents and flew down stairs to find him—he was the perfect Pagliacci, I was left holding the empty stockings! When later I did go down, I found all three in the main lounge playing a wonderful new game that he had taught them, the game of spattering ink on the hotel carpet. What devilish retribution—and I loved him so!

He did not want to spend the day *en famille,* so that afternoon while the children were skating we went for a walk in the forest. He walked just too fast, I couldn't quite keep up without dog-trotting (I did, then I didn't)—he led me miles through drifts and brambles, there was crimson on the snow where I'd stumbled to my scratched and wobbling knees. Finally as dusk was falling, he hurtled ahead like Lucifer afire— I reached the hotel just as his things were being loaded into a village sleigh. He was off, he said, for Paris, he would stop in at the village pub to have a stirrup cup with Ernest and Archie. The let-down was bewildering, the children were dismayed, and I was distraught with my thoughts on January.

I was born between Aries and Taurus. December is never any good for me. I'd like to tear December through.

January, on the contrary, I fold to my heart—January first always found us together and in January we usually went adventuring. That year it was to be a Corsican walking trip because of bandits in those hills—one in particular who was being glamorized by the Paris Press. So, united again, we took the train to Nice—there we had engaged passage on the Mediterranean steamer that leaves every evening from Nice's little square-cut harbour to the island and back. We had been singsonging "Tonga, Samoa and the Radak Isles" all along the way—so Corsica was a nearby compromise—and we realized just how disappointing a compromise the minute we stepped upon the gangplank. I say we but Harry carried me across for I had suddenly developed a fever and a dizziness—when he deposited me ever so gently on the berth I turned my head aside in weariness. It had been a long day from Paris and there was an awful smell of burnt olives seeping into the cabin—in an instant he was my Parfit Knight and gathered me up once more and carried me back across the quay, safe to land. They refunded only half the fare but that was enough to buy us a room above the sea, not on it or in it, and by morning I had slept my malaise away.

Then we decided to head for Italy by the coastal train—we took a local so that we could better enjoy the landscape—not realizing how populated and enclosed the hamlets were nor how very little one saw of sea and land—we were going to stop at Rapallo to call on Ezra Pound, but Rapallo looked too crowded from the train—so we went on and on. When we finally reached Pisa at dusk, we got off, (we had neither of us seen the Leaning Tower), it was already moonlight and we hurried to it fearful that the moon might set or the Tower lean too far before we reached it. Our packs were on our backs —in the twenties, Americans did not travel by foot, to-day we would have been a lad and a lass among thousands—but then we were pioneers at hiking and our outfitters not as expert as now; I wore the everyday tweed suit and low shoes, lisle stockings, lots of underwear and petticoats, a felt hat with a feather, and leather gloves—my pack was full of accessories— Harry's was full of books—we shipped our suitcases on ahead to the Grand Hotel in Florence. It was going to take us three or four days to walk that distance (one hundred kilometres by the River Arno). Harry was in tweeds too, bow tie and black patent-leather pumps.

We came upon the Tower, of a sudden, like the sea—more fastidiously beauteous than ever imagined—and sulphurous white in a moonlight as intense as neon. When finally we bid the

172

dream good night and went upon our way, we headed out of town along the muddy river. We dared not risk a morning glimpse since night had been so perfect—but it was late, our footsteps echoed in the deserted streets—when we reached the open country, we found it sound asleep. At the door of a primitive *hôtellerie* we knocked hard and long before the dogs barked and the innkeeper answered. He was really very angry at being dragged out of bed—we were shown into a sort of parlour with a couch behind a curtain and left without water or wine or welcome, but we were so tired that we collapsed upon the feathers and were soon asleep.

Next morning we were awakened by the police, three of them bristling with moustaches and indignation. How had we managed to get into town without their knowing it? Who and what were we anyway? Didn't we realize that foreigners couldn't just pop up in bed anyhow? Did we have papers?

We produced our U.S. passports and they were impressed but not mollified, we should have shown them at the barrier, they said. We told them we had walked the rails from Pisa the night before—no one was about. We were commanded to dress and appear at the *Questura* as soon as possible. All this seemed impolite but we agreed. By now not only the police but the innkeeper, his wife, his daughter and his livestock were all crowding into our ground floor bedchamber to get a better look. I buried myself under the covers. Harry sat up as pontifical as the Pope. It was difficult to shove the police out so that I could dress but eventually they moved on, leaving us rather mystified. We ordered a huge breakfast in sign language and asked for the bath—we might as well have asked for the swimming pool, so with a ewer of wellwater and a lovely Etruscan basin we made our scanty toilet.

When we emerged into the village street the crowd now gathered there heaved a sigh of regret. I believe they expected us to wear feathers and be striped yellow and red.

"*Inglese, Inglese,*" they muttered, disillusioned. As American savages, we were too disappointing.

We kept on along the Arno, all that day snow hovered in the air. Toward evening a slight coating fell upon the railroad tracks. Harry's pumps had begun to rub his heels and when we reached Empoli drops of blood were staining the track behind him. (I remembered the snowy path across the Gstaad hills) but this time he was going slowly and painfully, I had no trouble keeping up. That night I found bandages and warm water at the inn and bathed and dressed Achilles' smarting heels. I wanted him to buy a pair of good Tuscan boots but he wouldn't take a step outside of his own pumps, though they must have hurt him unbearably.

The afternoon of the third day we both flopped down on a trestle by the river, finally at the end of our energy. We were still ten or fifteen kilometres out of Florence and when a Tuscan cart came by laden with great straw-covered flasks of Chianti on its road to market we waved it down—the vintner's jolly family was with him but he took pity on us and made a place for Harry beside him on the driver's seat. Slim brown arms thrust out from beneath the flap at the back to help pull me aboard. I sat cross-legged on the floor and we sang all the way into town and that is how we came into Florence and drew up with a fine flourish before The Grand. The porter in a brass-buttoned coat reaching down to his heels was greatly astonished. We were a scandalous sight when we limped up to the desk; if it had not been that the Morgan Bank had announced our arrival by telegram and our Hermès luggage had already arrived I don't believe they would have let us in.

We had a beautiful gilded room with a sunken marble tub; we were soon in it and were served martinis by a conversational waiter across the bath's Pompeiian rim. Life was better than ever then.

It was early spring when we returned to Paris and because of Italy we were growing more and more restless for the smell of the country, not seaside resort or gaming racetrack but real countryside where one could bask and muse. It was in this uneasy frame of mind that we went to spend a week end at the Château of Ermenonville, invited by Comte Armand de la Rochefoucauld who had on his twenty-first birthday, just celebrated, fallen heir in June, 1927, to the Radziwill fortune and lands.

Armand de la Rochefoucauld bore one of the greatest names

in France—the ancestral maxim that suited him best was "one should never return to former loves"—Armand had no need to, there were so many ardent ladies in ambush on his path. His mother was a Radziwill and he had inherited the Château of Ermenonville from his uncle, Loch Radziwill, a very princely prince who had been known for his fabulous entertaining there, especially during the hunting seasons when the Château had overflowed with Lords and Ladies and Dukes and such. Armand began his reign with lavish hospitality, too, but his guests were, shall I say, less orthodox—they belonged to the international set—its gayest contingent.

Armand was short, sandy haired, full of love and the devil —his scrapes and peccadillos became part of the Parisian pattern—he was the most sought after young man about town.

He was a trial to his high-collar parents but he was his mother's favourite child, she helped him out of many a compromising cupboard. When Armand took over the Château he engaged a private secretary, a Monsieur Mathias, a dapper timid henchman—and a nudist to boot. From time to time Mathias and his party members used to go nudist in the Park —luckily there were gates that locked them in. At all other times Monsieur Mathias was as completely dressed as Wonderland's "White Rabbit" whom he greatly resembled.

Harry and I were among those invited to Armand's château-warming that June, and, though Harry balked, I had finally persuaded him to take me there. Nevertheless he had procrastinated so successfully that the house party was already at table when we finally arrived for the second try and walked into the huge gold and crystal dining room.

Harry had delayed in Senlis and there had bought revolvers for all the men—on entering he handed them round—for a minute there was a tense and horrified silence. Quickly I announced that we had been delayed by a country fair, and produced paper fans for all the ladies; then I slid into the empty chair on my host's right and conversation burst into bloom again. They had been awaiting our arrival with impatience. They all knew of Harry's fantastic and embarrassing ways. They were not disappointed.

This is how Harry describes our arrival from Chantilly via Senlis that Saturday after the races :

"Went with C to eat caviare and drink champagne in the Forest of Chantilly and we went to the races and I bet on Le Soleil in spite of there being a thunderstorm and he ran through the thunderstorm and won and the Sun came out as he passed the winning post and the Count was there and the Lady of the Gold Horse and we drank gin fizzes at the Manor House (how often one does the same things over and over and over again—I wish they were all as pleasant as this) and then C and I motored to Ermenonville to see the Rochefoucaulds and everyone went for a walk but I was depressed and went into a cold library to read again The Green Hat (how did it ever get there) and when they had all come back from walking I was very disagreeable and made C drive back with me to Chantilly and it was getting late and the 'Manor House' was cold and we were depressed and we telephoned to Ermenonville to say that we wanted to come back (this took courage) and we strengthened ourselves with hot rum grogs and I bought five revolvers in a bicycle shop so that they could shoot me for my disagreeableness and so back to Ermenonville and the Château and they were all at table and Ginetta sang and Erik Dahl talked of Heraldry and Evelyn told about the circumcision her friend had seen in Morocco and Barreto did his ventriloquism and there was a great open fire and much brandy and an enormous double-bed with monogrammes on the pillow-cases as large as birds." *Shadows of the Sun* BSP.

It was the following morning that on a tour of the property we came upon the abandoned and enchanted mill. Jean Jacques Rousseau had lived there when he was enamoured of the Duchess of Montmorency, and Cagliostro had worked his magic formulae beside the Moulin stream. The great water-wheel had been bartered away to some neighbouring miller but the millstones like mantic rings still waited on the granary floor. Honeysuckle choked the entrance. Four-leaf clovers pushed their way through the cobbles in the paved courtyard, doves circled about the tower eaves and the soft thunder of the waterfall made the lovely enclosure seem distantly removed from the outer world across the castle moat.

Harry and I gazed enraptured at the spot and then at each other. "Can we buy it?" he asked Armand who replied, amazed, "You don't want this old place. I have better houses in the village that I'll sell you." "Nothing could be better than this," we chorused and "How much?" asked Harry. "I haven't the vaguest idea," said Armand. "It certainly isn't worth a lot as it is. How much can you give me?" "I'll make you a proposition," Harry answered. "I don't really know what my bank balance is, but it's anywhere from forty thousand to four hundred thousand francs." (The franc was at 40.) "I'll draw you a cheque for the balance if you'll sell us your mill to-day." "Right now," said Armand, a little flustered. "Yes," said Harry. "I'll make out the cheque on anything handy—on Caresse's cuff," he crossed himself and ripped the white piqué from my wrist. Harry once wrote a cheque on a plate at Zelli's. It was cashed the next morning in the Place Vendome by an embarrassed barman, but Morgan & Company never turned a hair though we often wondered how they managed to file it.

Armand was game—back at the château he gave us a receipt —the Moulin was ours and happily Harry's balance turned out to be large enough to satisfy even the Rochefoucaulds' attorney!

The rest of that spring was ecstatically busy. We scooped out a swimming pool, fed by the waterfall. We whitewashed and we moved. We furbished the place in a manner reminiscent of Adirondack camps and Arizona ranches, but we left the thatch and the cobbles, the hayloft and the sheds just as they were, only adding a bathroom or two for comfort and each little bedroom (there were ten in the tower) was painted a different colour of the spectrum.

Once before in my life, I had lived on magic ground. And now I was to live in an enchanted spot again. When the hot weather came we were ready to move out of town and our friends moved with us.

CHAPTER 18

Henri Jacquit had been the local gravedigger for as long as Ermenonville remembered, that is before and since the battle of the Marne.

When "Monsieur et Mme. Henri" first came to work for us at le Moulin du Soleil, it was not Henri's ability to hoe or to dig that appealed to us, for he was well over sixty and gnarled and bent with rheumatism, but rather his saintly ways with the little whippets, Fleur and Kiss, and Sunday and Monday, and there was a look of tender admiration in his eyes when, almost apologetically, I showed him our "stable," consisting of six stocky Alpine burros, who then occupied the ground floor of the. main building. When I explained that I wished a log fire kept burning in the cobbled fireplace all during the winter so that beast and bird could pass the cold nights in cosy comfort, his understanding smile assured me that even when we departed at Christmas for several or more weeks in Massachusetts, Monsieur Henri would tend our hearth with as devoted care as if it had been the camp fire of his long-lamented *Capitaine de Cavalerie,* whose batman he. had been. The Captain had been the owner of the Château of Ermenonville, a prince of the realm and Henri's hero (because of the chargers, I am sure).

Henri's appearance while with us was unvarying. He wore under his bibbed apron of blue denim a baggy pair of striped grey trousers, obscurely of princely origin. His shirts were always snowy clean, due to Madame Henri, and to hide his collarless collarband he knotted a handkerchief *à la boyscout* around his turkey-red throat. This neckerchief matched the shirt and was evidently patched from pieces of the shirt's tail. As an outside coat, summer and winter, he wore a black-wool buttoned sweater, but his bulk varied with the seasons and with the number of garments underneath. To cover his white poll, outdoors and in (although he tipped it continuously) sat a porter's cap with a visor like a yachtsman's at a very jaunty angle. While he shuffled mutely about his work the big pocket in his apron, rather like a kangaroo's pouch, held a store of crusts and bones and sugar and grain for his animal friends.

I say his appearance never varied, but on the occasion of his granddaughter's wedding, when the village *char à banc* stopped at our gate to pick them up, he emerged in frock-coated regalia, looking more ducal than the duke of the realm himself—even to the high buttoned patent-leather shoes, and when he doffed his ancient bowler he returned it to his head at an even more rakish angle than the visored cap, but he never spoke a word.

We kept a string of burros for games of donkey polo, and the eight whippets for racing, the young schnauzers for frolicking, and Amanulla, enormous Afghan, king of canines, for keeping watch. On the week ends our guests brought their own pets with them, so that Monsieur Henri often had lunches to prepare for twenty or more, not to count Soucoupe, the little white goat given us by Kay Boyle, the two handsome cockatoos, gifts from sailor friends, the slinky and elegant ferret, the carrier pigeons, the loving ducks, Evelyn's Siamese kittens and the unpredictable cheetah, all shepherded happily into the wall-enclosed courtyard of our Mill. Their happiness and ours was due to Monsieur Henri—even when leading a stubborn donkey to the post or coaxing a screaming macaw back to its perch, he never lost his innate dignity or beatific calm.

We had engaged Henri and his wife to look after things in general—Madame Henri chose to look after us, Monsieur Henri chose the animals—and that is how it remained for ten years of comforting ministration.

To furnish their own apartment in the tower, where the

kitchens and storerooms were, they had brought their giant
armoire and their huge featherbed. Coming home late one snowy
night I found all the animals gathered as usual around the
hearth in the dining hall except the four youngest whippets.
Their mother and father could not tell me where they were so
I went to look. Knocking softly on Henri's door, I heard the
old man's heavy breathing and his wife's light footsteps as she
ran to open for me.

"I can't find the little whippets," I whispered.

"Oh Madame," she said. "I hope you do not object, they
sleep with us now." At that the eiderdown began to heave and
out from beneath its mountainous warmth wriggled Kiss and
Kent and Shadow. Henri slept on.

"It is all right by me if it is by you," I answered with a
smile, and I'm sure that Fleur's little black muzzle and beady
eyes just seen protruding from the foot of the coverlet returned
my smile most knowingly.

I closed the door then, realizing that the window was tight
shut, which must have made them all quite happy and much
cosier.

Monsieur Henri used to curry and brush the burros until
they shone like sons of Pegasus and when I tied ribbons on
their tails one gala Sunday, he took to braiding their whisks
daily in a most groomlike fashion. From then on, one of the
items in the monthly account book was *"ruban rouge"* or *"ruban
bleu pour les ânes."*

I think it was to Henri's great regret that we sold the donkeys
while they were all in perfect health. What magnificent graves
he might have added to the peaceful row beneath the willow.
For there was a row. In ten years' time in spite of most devoted
care certain of our canine and feline friends had been called
to face their Maker. When, just before World War II, I left the
Mill, the line of tidy headstones extended from the stream to
the starting-gate where the most tenderly dug and cared for
resting place was that of Narcisse Noir, "Monsieur Narcisse,"
as Henri respectfully called him.

Black Narcissus was my own special pet. He was the father
of all the whippets and his ego was as great as Henri's was
not. He was the only snob I have ever really loved. He went

everywhere with me, from one room to another, to the Ritz, to America. He never deigned to join his offspring under the Henris' eiderdown—a lace cushion at the foot of my bed was his sleeping accommodation. He remained aloof and uninterested in kitchen affairs and he always supped from silver by my chair. He was politely tolerant of Monsieur Henri's concern for the other quadrupeds but to my distress I sometimes thought that Narcisse snubbed the old man cruelly. Perhaps being addressed as Monsieur Narcisse had gone to his head, and he and Henri both knew that my wishes and his habits were unassailable. However, of the three I think Henri's manners were the best, and one black day proved what a truly noble haven was his heart.

It was June, the month of desire. One of my week-end guests, Felix Doubleday, was being driven to the afternoon train. Narcisse, who loved to ride through the village in state, was already erect on the back seat when the departing guest got into the limousine; if he had not been there for company I would have gone to the station too. "Don't let him out," I warned as I waved good-bye. Then I joined the others for a sunset walk into the forest. That is why only Henri was there when the corpse was carried home.

It seems that Narcisse had seen my guest off most politely, but, instead of climbing up beside the chauffeur as usual, he stuck to the cushions in the back, gazing out at the evening crowds like a county dowager. They stopped for the mail at the post office on the cobbled hill. It was impossible to foresee that just then a beautiful little bitch would cross the road, or that a magnificent Rolls Royce would catapult down it! Love and death must have been instantaneous. Those who saw say that the leap through the open window was as lightning-like as the chromium flash of the speeding car. The whippet was caught in mid-air. The villagers picked him up where he had so passionately fallen and in anguished haste he was driven home through the byways to the Mill.

Monsieur Henri must have sensed tragedy, for he was waiting in trepidation at the gates and it was he who carried the stiffening body into the twilit barn, where he laid him tenderly on a bed of sweet grass and hay. When I entered the temporary chapel he was on his knees winding a collar of ferns and daisies to mask the bleeding neck. "Take care of him, Henri," I said in tears, and went sorrowfully to my room.

All that night I tossed and turned thinking of my little companion cold and alone on his mound of hay. When Madame Henri came to wake me in the morning I asked for her husband, knowing how sad the old man must be.

"He has dug a beautiful grave," she said proudly, "deep and lined with flowers."

"I'm afraid he's very tired," I replied, thinking of the old rheumatic hands.

"Yes, he's very tired, Madame," she answered, "he sat up all through the night."

"In the barn? in the dark?" I asked incredulously.

"Oh, no, Madame, all the lanterns were lit. It was the last watch, he felt Madame would wish it so for Monsieur Narcisse."

Both with a sob and a smile for such simple devotion, I went to look for them beneath the willow in the garden. The burial was in the proper manner—Narcissus had been wound in finest linen (from their wedding chest) and lowered into the ground in a coffin of woven reeds—there were field flowers in profusion and as Henri's old shoulders bent to the heavy spaded earth, I saw tears drop from his tired eyes in unaffected grief.

"I can't thank you enough, my friend," I said.

"He was a noble animal," he replied. "He is buried like an aristocrat, I could do no less."

CHAPTER 19

Every Sunday at the races, Chantilly or town, we hurried to join "the Count." He looked like Santa Claus in mufti only noble and elegant as well.

Our friendship with Count Ulric de Civry goes back to a Sunday in the spring of 1925. It was at Longchamps, the great Paris racetrack, where day after day the elite of Paris joined (separated by barriers) the great mass of the people who followed this sport of kings with the enthusiasm of lovers. Harry and I, escapists still, were savouring all the proffered pleasures of life in Paris . . . among them *les courses*. We didn't know much about horses, but we were planning to have a racing stable of our own one day and were avid for information— in talking with one of the jockeys, Harry learned that the best place to see the finish was from the highest left-hand corner of the Tribunes, to the right of the President's Stand—it was a long climb and usually made at a run, for we always waited in the paddock until the bell for "Jockeys up" sounded, but once arrived in those heavens, we realized that it was indeed a vantage point.

That first Sunday we noticed a handsome old gentleman with a snow-white beard who stood aloof at the rail, watching the proceedings intently through a very superior pair of binoculars. Calm as a mirror and indifferent to his surroundings as though he had just stepped down from Olympus, the imposing, beautifully groomed figure stood his immaculate ground as though protected by a magic ring, and we noticed that no matter how many elbows stuck into our ribs and how much the public jostled and crowded each other, this nobleman, for we realized he must be noble, seemed to acquire elbow room with ease. We inquired of devotees of this vantage spot who he was, but though we learned that he always was there, rain or shine, they said he never spoke to anyone and no one so far had ventured to speak to him—but Harry, American, spoke to him.

It was just before the big race. We had played a horse *couplé* and we didn't quite understand what that meant, but it was imperative that we place our money on Sun Goddess who was running coupled with Astrakan. Harry, boyish and bareheaded, which was quite unorthodox in those days, edged in beside the old gentleman, and in his flat American-French asked politely if "Monsieur" would be so kind as to explain what *"couplé"* meant; would we win if Astrakan won?

"Did you play *gagnant* or *placé,"* inquired the Frenchman.

"To win, sir," Harry answered, horrified, for it never occurred to us that one would risk even the minimum except for the maximum. I think it was Harry's genuine horror that touched him for he smiled benignly and explained at length the intricacies of the French system (the totalizer had not yet been installed).

During the next race, we did not have occasion to speak to him, but during the last one when he saw that I held a ticket on an outsider, he turned gallantly toward me and said, "Madame is astute. Her horse will win." They were at the post already or I believe Harry would have careened down the many flights to place a thousand francs on Rock-a-bye, too, but my one-hundred-franc bet was indeed a happy one. The filly "rocked" home at 60-1 as the crowds went wild. I collected my six thousand with elation—the Count we decided must have played it also but his reckonings were with a bookie and he never divulged his losses or his winnings. From that moment Harry and I invested him with second sight and a rare knowledge of horseflesh.

The following Sunday he was there on top of the Tribunes and we humbly at his feet. He gave me a sweeping bow when we arrived and though not himself communicative he politely replied to each question that Harry posed—and again his "long shot" romped home. As we ourselves were both exuberant and gregarious, his fame soon spread among our compatriots. The following Sunday we arrived with a phalanx of eager young Americans. The Count seemed unperturbed, but the crowd was impressed by our daring. At the finish of that day, Harry said rather formally, "I would like to introduce myself, I am Harry Crosby and this is my wife, Caresse."

The other bowed low again and whipped out his wallet and handed us a calling card—Le Comte de Civry, rue de la Faisanderie, Paris, 16ième.

We apologized for our lack of cards but asked him if he would drink a glass of champagne with us after the third. He accepted as though for a banquet, and we all adjourned to the little bar under the flower-laden steps of the Jockey Club.

It was not until a month or more had passed that we summoned ample courage to invite the Count to luncheon. Sunday lunch before the races was a Paris ritual. The races began at two and we usually lunched at a quarter to one—so I timidly gave the invitation. He said he would let us know on Thursday. On Thursday he made a charming little speech, his white head uncovered and his soft beard like a drift of new fallen snow. It was a gem of *Politesse française*. But when I answered, "We will expect you at a quarter to one," the consternation in his usually serene eyes was alarming. "Madame, the races are at two. It is customary to lunch at eleven." "Will 11.30 do?" I countered, politely, thinking of our Sunday breakfast at ten. He looked dubious but settled for 11.30.

I alerted Ida and Louise as to who and why we would lunch before noon, but they took it quite as a matter of course. I could see that our habitual luncheons at one must have appeared barbaric to our kitchen. I will say I planned a rather lovely repast and Harry chose the wines and liqueurs with care. We were not going to let our new acquaintance take us for barbarians though we were Americans. That meal went beautifully, and by exquisite timing we reached our stand just as the ponies went to the post.

The next Sunday at the St. Cloud track, the Count invited us to dine with him the following Friday. He said he felt that to rush through luncheon was a pity (we silently surmised that our two-hour meal had been a hurried snack to him!).

He had invited us for seven and on arrival at his modest but glistening flat, we saw that it was resplendent with armorial trophies and the memorabilia of bygone splendours. We were ushered into a print-lined hall and I was asked to leave my wraps in the bedroom. I lingered a moment in this small gadget-filled apartment where every possible implement for masculine care and comfort was displayed—the top of the dressing table intrigued me most, and though it somehow seems a breach of manners to describe it here, I feel I should. There were four or more pairs of handsome crown-embossed hairbrushes—one solid gold pair, one silver, two more of ivory and six or seven little brushes for beard and sideburns as well. On a mahogany tray lined with red plush were at least two dozen sharp nail scissors, nippers, files and cuticle trimmers all with monogrammed handles, each one a different shape and weight; back of these stood a row of huge cut glass cologne bottles—six or eight each with a silver label around its neck . . . bay rum, lavender water, cologne, witch hazel, etc., etc., and along one side a row of pearl, ivory and silver-handled button hooks, jodhpur hooks, collar hooks. I have never seen anything to approximate that array—it was the dressing table of a court dandy. Marie, his servant, confided several years later when she came to accept and trust me, that the Count lathered his beard in Castile soapsuds every morning and she then brushed and combed it until it shone like silk and often trimmed the edges for him, as neatly as a barber.

When I joined the men in the study they were already poring over a table piled with albums of track favourites. We drank sherry until dinner was announced. That meal should go down in history not only for its lavishness, but also because of the royal manner in which the Count presided and the silent contest for honours displayed like a game between host and his maid, Marie. He ordered, countermanded, praised and scolded the poor woman until I should have thought her rôle as chef, sommelier, butler and busboy would have driven her to Borgian revenge. Harry and I had to take turns on second helpings. I one course and he the next—there should have been greyhounds under the table to throw the pheasant, lamb and venison bones to. After two hours we collapsed back from the table to the study, there to sip a variety of rare liqueurs—fit for a king, and it was then that we first heard the fabulous case of the Countess of Colmar versus the Duchy of Brunswick.

The Countess of Colmar was the mother of our friend and it was to justify her honour that he had for nearly thirty years contended in the law courts of France and Brunswick his succession to the throne and to the legal and honourable marriage of his mother to the deceased Duke of Brunswick. First and paramount, his mother's honour was involved—but also there was a matter of our friend's heritage not only to the crown, the castles, the wealth and the treasures, jewels, paintings, etc., etc., but also to a small standing army (at the time of the Duke's demise) and to a large racing stable.

The people of the country had on the Duke's death declared his widow morganatic and her children barred from the succession. The supposed disgrace caused the Countess to ail and die but her son swore that he would devote his fortune and his life to reversing the judgment and clearing her name, for she had been an honourable and devoted wife during the years that followed an ardent courtship and her subsequent marriage to the benevolent Duke. Charles Ulric Albert Ferdinand de Civry had spent his own fortune and for the last ten years had been retaining counsel on a contingent basis, the lawyers to divide the booty when the case was won. Already the standing army was on its uppers and certainly more than one castle had been pleaded into escrow but the Count assured us that the thoroughbreds still stamped in their stalls and that his mother's royal jewels and furs were just as she had left them. In the years that followed, whenever in a sentimental vein, he would gallantly offer me a diamond tiara or a sable coverlet, "if and when"—in the span of ten years I believe every elusive crown jewel in Brunswick was laid at my feet, for I am sure it was my credulous belief in his belief that softened the last demoralizing and pauperizing years of his life.

When his story was told and we rose to leave his fireside, the Count accompanied us to his room and took from the bedside table a miniature framed in an arc of rubies and pearls. "My mother," he said, his words weighted with pride and love. I gazed at the face of an exquisite lady who looked out at me with a gaze as noble and as trusting as his own and it was then I understood the burning devotion of such a son to such a mother.

During the racing seasons that followed, we saw him often. He helped us choose our own horses and jockeys and trainer when we, enthused by his interests as well as our own desire, decided to own a racing stable. He went with us to order our colours at Hermès. Royal rose for him, and a black disk for us. We never made a decision without the Count's advice. I believe our enjoyment in him and his enjoyment in our horses were factors that helped heighten and prolong his life; but more and more he was forced to change lawyers, to borrow and mortgage so that his case could finally reach the highest Tribunal. He was well over eighty and the strain was telling. He began to play the races with a desperate intent to win, and so to keep the unbelievers at bay.

He still looked impressively groomed but he became a little less opulent in his appearance. The benign eyes now and then showed their distress for he knew he must live long enough to clear his mother's name. We knew that he was being "pushed around"—even scoffed at for a hopelessly altruistic old gentleman who would not give up and who was getting the bad end of a ruinous bargain.

But he refused to surrender though now he realized that his means were such that he could no longer invite us to Lucullan feasts, and we saw him place his bets at the window marked "unite 100 francs," where formerly he had used the one-thousand-franc booths.

But from time to time we insisted on his dining with us at some well-known restaurant where we said we were only spending track money, won on his advice, and thus mollified, he allowed us to act as his hosts. He always chose the very best spots, Larue, Foyot or Voisin, and when he invariably, upon tasting some special dish cooked to perfection, would wave it away with noble displeasure and announce, "I wish a word with the chef," we knew that we would have to wait another half-hour till a second dish was made ready, but the chef ran to do his bidding with such joy and the waiters seemed to so approve this behaviour from a gourmet of his experience that we realized our rôle was to sit mum and be patient, which we gladly did—and I am quite willing on oath to affirm that the soufflés rose several inches between their first and second appearance.

The final hearing of the great case had been scheduled for early autumn and then put off, and off and off again, autumn after autumn and it was already November, 1934, when I sailed away for a Christmas at home in Connecticut. The Count and I had dined together the night before, and the next day he was there on the platform to wave me adieu.

When I returned in the early spring it was to learn from his brokenhearted maid Marie that at long last he had won his case, but that a few days later he had breathed his last. "Here," she sobbed, "in this very room," for I was standing beside his bed as I stood that first evening when I marvelled at the paraphernalia ranged upon his chiffonier, he had told her I was to choose whatever I wished as a keepsake, but there was nothing left, she said.

"What about the standing army?" I smiled to try to cheer her up.

"Everything is gone, everything," she wailed. I asked then if I might have the little miniature of the Countess of Colmar. "I hope it's not been taken," I pleaded, for the apartment had been completely dismantled.

"Those thieving lawyers—they took everything," she cried, "but the miniature I myself put into his coffin. It is buried with him, Madame, it was in his hands when he died, of all the rest nothing remains." But remembering a great gentleman and a gallant son, I knew that the riches he really fought for he had won. "Nothing," I said, "save honour."

But in the early days of the Mill there were no gravestones, only that of "Harry and Caresse." Harry had already prepared our marker.

During the years at the *Pavillon* we lived next door to a stonecutter and when I had adopted the name Caresse, Harry had hastened across town to have our cross engraved on a slab of dove-grey marble. This we carried with our first load of possessions to the Mill and placed atop the Tower where the morning sun struck first. We placed it at an angle so that the sunwarmed stone could be a back rest. We used the flat top of the tower for communal sun bathing. Its rampart rose breast high.

Days at the Mill were not always sunny. Sudden thunderstorms would gather and break. Sometimes the lightning barked our Tower, sometimes the wild electricity of the city needled our spirits into arson. Once I took night refuge at the château where Armand and his friends enfolded me, but heavy of heart I did not linger. Harry's diary says :

"The thunderstorm yesterday infinitesimal compared with the Black Storm to-day. Dark words and C went off with the Crouchers to the country and now the sun is gone from the dial and the *cramoisy* colour disappears and it is dark but in the centre I am undaunted with the Grey Princess (who corresponds to Gerard de Nerval's Adrienne) and I pray a grey and gold prayer into the centre of the Red Sun.

"To Chantilly with Mortimer and the Lady of the Gold Horse and we drank silver gin fizzes in the Manor House Bar and then the races began and no C and a great searching of hats and faces and legs and *derrières* but no C and I saw the Count and the first race and the Lady of the Gold Horse and the second race and the Lady of the Blue Pyjamas (the first time since the blue pyjamas four years ago) and the third race (Sun-Goddess lost) and more searching of hats and faces and then at last when black disaster seemed imminent C appeared all frail and delicate and there were dark words and tears and then the Sun and a great restatement after contrast *cramoisy* and gold and the Sun returns to the dial and the last hours of the twenties and I smoked my pipe and said a *cramoisy* and gold prayer and C's eyes are my towers of strength and now we have advanced another rung up the Ladder of the Sun."

CHAPTER 20

It was through Sylvia Beach that we first heard about James Joyce. She, to her glory, had brought out *Ulysses*. Her "Shakespeare and Co." with its olde shoppe signboard hanging in the rue de l'Odéon behind the Palais de Luxembourg was the gathering place at midday for book-minded Americans— my first encounters with Hemingway, Dos Passos and Eugene Jolas were, as I recall, *chez* Shakespeare and Co.—Harry and I were, of course, as excited as everyone else on the left bank over the publication of *Ulysses*, and Jolas, then editing *transition*, arranged through Stuart Gilbert, Joyce's amanuensis, that we should meet the great man. I am pretty sure we were admitted to the Joyce circle because we were Jolas's side partners. Harry and I were launching our Black Sun Press, and of course we yearned for a piece of the rich Irish cake then baking on the Paris fire.

That afternoon Stuart Gilbert was there and so was Nora, Joyce's wife—the Joyces lived near the Boulevard des Invalides, back of the Gare Montparnasse—the apartment was tidy but unimaginative, we sat in the dining room. I think I remember an upright piano and a goldfish bowl, I don't remember any paintings on the wall; but there was a rug by Marie Monnier depicting the waters of Anna Livia Plurabelle, a bright whirlpool on the floor. Also I remember that Joyce was uncommunicative and seemed bored with us, retreating behind those thick mysterious lenses until something was said about Sullivan's concert the evening before, then suddenly he came to life—talking all the while about great Irish tenors he led us

191

after him across the hall to his bedroom where he dropped to his knees beside the iron bedstead and pulled from under it an ordinary sized but very dilapidated leather suitcase and unlocked it. (I am not sure that the key did not hang around his neck.) It was stuffed to overflowing with clippings, bits of paper fully scribbled over, larger sheets of typescript like bulletins that had been five times through the machine, other miscellaneous odds and ends. "This is my desk," he said, on all fours, and smiled up at us through magnifying lenses, for the first time that afternoon. "It is all in here," and he pulled out one long clipping to carry back to the front parlour. I was hoping it would be his own poetic creating, but it was merely a journalist's eulogistic report on Sullivan—and Joyce beamed as he passed it around. Luckily we enthused with him to good purpose for he asked, in his soft Irish voice, if we'd be liking to join them after the concert the following week. You can imagine with what delight we accepted.

At that party there was much song and some ribaldry, I think we drank beer. Nora had cooked a special Dublin dish, a huge one, for those tenors' appetites were mighty. I remember Liam O'Flaherty and Leon Paul Fargue, also a young Swede, Hauser, who had just published a best seller, called *The Island,* and Archie and Ada MacLeish. Maria Jolas, whose private fortune launched *transition,* took turns with Stuart Gilbert at the piano, the barroom chords nearly raised the roof. The young Joyces, Giorgio and Lucia, were both there and a divorcée who later married Giorgio Joyce, and of course Stuart Gilbert's cosy French wife. Gilbert is best known as a critic of the twenties and also for his inspired translations of Proust, Gide, Malraux and others; he made his first translation in 1932 for the Crosby Continental Editions when I persuaded him to try Exupéry's *Night Flight,* first time in English for the author too.

Stuart wrote the introduction to my book *Poems for Harry Crosby,* B.S.P. 1931, an introduction that made me happier and surer than I had been for a long time.

It was several weeks before Harry and I plucked up courage to call on Joyce again, this time to ask him if we might publish

33. Hart Crane photographed by Harry
Crosby, Le Moulin, 1929.

34. Polleen, Jacques Porel, Caresse,
Le Moulin, 1932.

35. The gold suit with its foppish allure, 1929.
Portrait by Frans de Geetere.

36. Caresse Crosby—Hostess at Le Moulin du Soleil, July, 1932.

37. Max Ernst, Caresse, Jean Schlumberger, Nico Calas, Polleen, H.R.H. Ataulfo Orleans-Bourbon, Meraud Guinness Guevara at the Swimming Pool, Le Moulin, 1932.

part of his *Work in Progress*. Crosby Gaige had just brought out *Anna Livia Plurabelle* in book form, and we were determined to emulate it.

"How many pages would you be wanting now?" asked Joyce.

"It's the meat, not the water, that makes the broth," I answered, which seemed to please him.

"I'll think it over," he said. "I would be getting proof sheets, would I, and I could make corrections, could I?"

"All you want," Harry and I quickly answered. We left with a promise from Stuart Gilbert that he would deliver to us whatever manuscript was decided on.

"Mr. Gilbert," said Harry, "please tell Joyce we will pay him whatever he thinks is right for a single limited edition, and we will pay in advance."

"I think he knows that," smiled S.G. in his mischievously pedagogic manner. "He's heard about your press, and how beautifully it functions." We were flattered beyond measure.

Evidently Joyce dumped his suitcase upside down that evening, for the very next day S.G. appeared ready to do business for him—and so we began work on "The Mookse and the Gripes" and "The Ont and the Graicehoper." We suggested an introduction and Joyce agreed. He weighed every suggestion we made with the greatest deliberation. Finally, he himself suggested Julian Huxley, because, he said, only a scientist could deal with the material. I wrote to Mr. Huxley, but he could not give the necessary time just then, and *we* could not be held back! Luckily C. K. Ogden was just as happy a choice for Joyce, and so he was enthusiastically signed up.

Then the portrait. Harry and I wanted Picasso, Joyce seemed to care very much, so I went to see Picasso in the Faubourg St. Honoré where he then lived. Narcisse Noir and I climbed two flights of circular stairs. The artist called from over the top banister that I was to come all the way up to his atelier; at that time, he was not the world-shaking figure he is to-day, in fact very few Americans had heard of Picasso, although to the Paris intelligentsia he was the man of the hour, a title he has not yet relinquished. *Ulysses* had been published only a few years and not in French, Picasso was as indifferent to Joyce as Joyce was not to Picasso—I couldn't strike a spark. To begin with, Picasso said he rarely, if ever, made a portrait and never *sur commande*. I told him he would live to regret it, and I believe he must. He asked me though if I would like to look at some of his own work, which was piled against every wall, the canvases appeared shy with their backs turned, but once they turned! We had to step over brushes in pots and over dozens of match boxes, scattered everywhere on tables, chairs and on the floor. It was his practice to empty a match box and squeeze a modicum of paint into it. I don't know if he then ran from colour to colour, brush in hand, but the whole room seemed to be one big palette. I told him how Harry had telephoned me excitedly a few days before about the canvas in Rosenberg's window (downstairs), *The Game of Ball* painted at Dinard that summer, and how he had waited on the sidewalk gazing at it for three-quarters of an hour, until I joined him, liking it better every moment. He wanted to buy it, but Rosenberg, the dealer, said the artist didn't want to sell—so I now asked Picasso if he had changed his mind, but he smiled and shook his head, "It is my best," and when Kootz showed it in the winter of 1948, in New York, I asked, "How much?"

"Picasso isn't selling that one," he said.

"I know," I replied, "you see, it is his best."

Picasso showed me the work he had done at Dinard and much more besides. I was dizzy with new forms and new colours. My education in modern art was progressing at a gallop.

Narcisse began to yawn. "He's right," Picasso said. "I'm boring him, but wait, please, I want my son to see your beautiful animal, he loves dogs." And he ran downstairs to get the boy. The child was indeed fascinated, couldn't keep his arms from around Narcisse's neck, and I was terrified for fear he'd receive a nip on the nose.

"How can I get one like him for Philippe?" asked Picasso.

"Only one way," I answered. "He is fiancéed, but not yet married."

"When he has a son, think of mine," said Picasso.

I promised—but when Narcisse's sons and daughter were born, I was far far away in Hollywood, Narcisse was under a stone by the Moulin stream and all his sons were tawny. His only daughter turned out to be fragile and black as he, but I wouldn't have parted with *Fleur Noire—even for a Picasso!* As we went down the winding stairs, father and son leaned over the railing, waving and calling, "Don't forget. Don't forget."

So Joyce's portrait was still to be determined on. Brancusi was our next choice, but since he was a sculptor, and such an abstract sculptor, the question of likeness bothered us all. Brancusi agreed to do it, Joyce agreed to sit, but it was hard to get them together (and harder to get them apart!). The artist made several sketches, keeping only one, this one *was* a likeness, but I urged him with Joyce's *appui* to do also an abstract conception, and in this I believe I was wrong, for we decided to use the abstraction in the book instead of the likeness, now to my mind the first drawing proves vastly more interesting. I did not make the same mistake with Augustus John when I published the *Collected Poems of James Joyce* several years later. Some day, however, I should like to see the two Brancusis published side by side.

I became a frequent visitor to Brancusi's whitewashed atelier. It was in the rue de Vaugirard and was reached by a long thin passage as so many of these hidden work places are. It was *on* the ground, of course, with a small open area before it. The sliding doors admitted one to a fresh high-raftered room. Brancusi's work stood all about, much of it unfinished, and tools and chips and hammers were in evidence, Also in the centre a big white oven opened its door, and since it was autumn, it was red with coals. My first luncheon with him, *à deux*, was unforgettable. On his work table he spread a white sheet of crispest tissue paper to serve as tablecloth, in the centre to hold it in place one of his chiselled marble gems. A plump pullet was roasting on the coals, and huge potatoes baking there too. We drank Rosé from the Midi, and ended the feast with strawberry jam and "hearts of cream." He was a darling, and he cut up the pullet with a sculpting knife. He was in white linen, and I was in black velvet. Together we pulled the wishbone—I don't remember who got the wish.

Afterwards I drove away to the Press, in my sea-green limousine, Narcisse sitting haughtily next to the chauffeur, that was before I graduated to the yellow Hotchkiss with two young men on the box. It was all such fun!

The first proofs were ready for Joyce early in November and he said he would come to the rue de Lille to correct them one fine afternoon. We waited until dinner time. Just as we were sitting down, a note was handed me, it was from Joyce. He had come as far as our front door, but before Ida could open, he heard Narcisse's watchful bark from within and turned and walked right home again. He said he was very afraid of small animals for his eyes were so bad he might run into them —he had to tap his way with a cane and so could easily be tripped by our dog. He asked me if I would tie Narcisse up, then he would come back next day. I sent the proofs back to him by his messenger so that when he did appear the following afternoon, he had already gone over them, but to my horror they looked like a bookie's score card. Narcisse would never have understood being tied, but I did shut him into my bathroom and locked the door.

The fire was burning in the library. We went up, cautiously, by the bathroom, because Narcisse had yapped (I promised next time to muzzle him as well). Once ensconced in the biggest chair, Joyce changed his glasses and asked for a stronger light (later I ordered a special 150-watt bulb for these sessions). He picked up *The Mookse and the Gripes* and read the opening line, already rewritten beyond recognition.

"Now, Mr. and Mrs. Crosby," Joyce said, "I wonder if you understand why I made that change." All this in a blarney-Irish key.

"No, why?" we chorused, and there ensued one of the most intricate and erudite twenty minutes of explanation that it has ever been my luck to hear, but unfortunately I hardly understood a word, his references were far too esoteric. Harry fared a bit better, but afterward we both regretted that we did not have a dictaphone behind the lamp so that later we could have studied all that had escaped us. Joyce stayed three hours, he didn't want a drink, and by eight he hadn't got through with a page and a half. It was illuminating. When he left, Harry guided him down the slippery stairs—Narcisse was happily eating rabbit in the kitchen—and I started to mix some very dry martinis.

A final unexpected incident occurred after Harry's death, for regrettably, *Tales Told of Shem and Shaun* did not appear until the spring of 1930. (Harry had died in New York in December, 1929.) The pages were on the press and Lescaret in consternation pedalled over to the rue de Lille to show me, to my horror, that on the final "forme," due to a slight error in his calculations, only two lines would fall *en plaine page*—this from the typographer's point of view was a heinous offence to good taste. What could be done at this late date! NOTHING, the other *formes* had all been printed and the type distributed (we only had enough type for four pages at a time). Then Lescaret asked me if I wouldn't beg Mr. Joyce to add another eight lines to help us out. I laughed scornfully at the little man, what a ludicrous idea, when a great writer has composed each line of his prose as carefully as a sonnet you don't ask him to inflate a masterpiece to help out the printer! We will just have to let it go, I groaned and Lescaret turned and pedalled sadly away—but the next noon when I arrived at 2 rue Cardinale, joy seemed to ooze from the doorway of the Black Sun Press. Lescaret bounced out and handed me that final page. To my consternation eight lines *had* been added.

"Where did you get these?" I accused him.

"Madame, I hope will forgive me," he beamed. "I went to see Mr. Joyce personally to tell him our troubles. He was very nice—he gave me the text right away—he told me he had been wanting to add more, but was too frightened of you, Madame, to do so."

CHAPTER 21

Harry loved bed. In the rue de Lille, he liked to write in bed, to eat in bed, to entertain in bed. The consequence was that when we really "entertained" we gave lunch parties very grandly in our magnificent Sicilian dining room, but when we wanted to be entertained we received in bed, and near the bed one or two or three small tables would be set up according to the number of friends who stayed for dinner, but always at eight Harry would give the signal; it was bedtime and he and I would get out of our day clothes and into dishabille. Harry's Magyar gown of red and gold embroidery was extravagantly impressive and I had a number of hilariously gay furbelows to choose from. We always drank champagne and we almost always began with caviar. Our guests were invited to take baths if they wanted to, for we had a sunken marble tub in a black and white tiled bathroom that boasted a white bearskin rug and an open fireplace, as well as a cushioned chaise longue covered in rose red towelling. We liked to experiment in bath oils and bath salts. There was a great quantity of them to play with and most of our friends lived in Latin Quarter rooms where the plumbing was kept a dark secret. *Chez nous* martinis and rose geranium mingled in libation. We also provided voluminous bathrobes. Some evenings were rather Pompeiian. The bath could hold four.

We went to sleep by midnight and we worked busily all day. It was only the early evenings that were so gay. We went out hardly at all. I never owned an evening gown all the time we were married. Vionnet made me a cloth-of-gold evening suit cut like a man's dinner jacket over a short tubular skirt. With this I wore a vest of sheerest net and a big lace jabot, and on the rare occasions that we went out I wore that. Harry always wore a soft Brooks shirt with his dinner jacket and a black gardenia in his buttonhole.

I remember one stormy passage during a visit to Boston because of these eccentricities, for in those conformist circles our departure from the absolute was like a dagger in the bosoms of society. This time the Crosbys were asked by the Back Bay elders to entertain visiting Spanish royalty at dinner—The Infante and the Infanta Beatrice with their two handsome sons. Every lovely lady in Boston longed to be invited. New dresses were ordered. Beacon Hill was agog, but to everyone's consternation, especially my father-in-law's, our visit coincided with the Spaniards'. They could not very well ask us to leave the house but the thought of our informal evening wear and manners was inflaming the nerves of the already irritated Crosbys. Harry was implored to put on a stiff collar and to discard his black flower, and I to get into a nonexistent evening dress instead of into my exhilarating chic suit of gold with its foppish allure. If we could not conform as we were bid we could dine upstairs like naughty children. No one gave an inch. I did want to go to that dinner but I stood by Harry. Finally, at the eleventh hour I was told if I'd wear an evening dress, Harry could keep his *panache*. We capitulated. He wore his flower and was happy, but I had to borrow a wishy green chiffon from my sister-in-law. My "page-boy" bob, which looked divine with the golden suit, was all wrong with Back Bay tulle. Nothing fitted or matched. Every other woman there looked her best, I my worst. I was furious but polite as ice. I made up for my looks by flirting wantonly with the youngest prince, Ataulfo Orleans-Bourbon. Years later, after Harry's death, we became the greatest of friends and he told me that my conversation that night had quite rocked him off his royal heels, and that he met no one else on his whole trip who was half so exciting. I was as mad as mustard the entire evening.

It was a few days later during that same visit that the Powels and their dog Zulu appeared unexpectedly before breakfast at 95 Beacon Street. Harry had told them in New York that they were welcome any time, "just come along," and they had, on the midnight, complete with nine bags and a dog. There was a big room vacant on the top floor. Harry was sure they could have that one but it was sewing day and the seamstress was about to work there. Mrs. Crosby said "No!" she "was sorry." We then invited them to share our room. We had slept four in a bed before. Mr. Crosby said "No!" They could go to the Ritz for all he cared. Harry said, "Caresse, let's pack," and we did, adding more valises and a bag to the nine already in the hall. Harry went outside. "Your mother has taken the car and there's a taxi strike," his father shouted. Nothing daunted, Harry stepped onto Beacon Street and hailed a passing ice wagon drawn by percherons. He offered a bribe. "Sure," they said. The Statler was only a few blocks away. He and Peter piled all the luggage aboard, the traffic stopped and crowds gathered as the four of us took our seats on the blocks of ice. The dogs loved the fun and barked like mad. The Crosby shades went down in fury; the crowd cheered as we drove off. That night everyone in Boston knew what had happened. Besides the dozen suitcases we carried a block of ice to our rooms to cool the vintage wine from the Crosby cellar.

We might never have been forgiven but the market was rising and Contintental Can reached a new high next day—so high that Mrs. Crosby said she would take us to Egypt in January and I decided to sail immediately to have a long Christmas holiday with the children before leaving. Harry was to remain in Boston without me; this pleased Steve. Only, Harry didn't stay.

Halfway through December he became so homesick that he returned to the rue de Lille ship-haste. We all four hung stockings by the library chimney. That was the first Christmas since 1922 we all spent together. I was very happy.

It was that January '28 on our trip to Egypt with Harry's mother, that we discovered Lawrence and *The Plumed Serpent*. Harry found the copy of the first edition in a Cairo book shop and he read it as we churned up the Nile from Luxor to Wadi Halfa. As he sat hour after hour cross-legged on the upper deck, his nose between the pages, a native tribesman sat cross-legged on the lower deck brushing his teeth with a wooden stick hour after hour and his eyes never left his navel as he brushed. Was this a penance or a ritual? Harry's eyes never left the printed page. I hung over the railing, watching the women, "Mnemonic and maybe of centuries," winding down to the water's edge to wash their clothes, while monkeys chattered at their backs. I wondered had he been travelling in Mexico would Harry have been reading the story of Aknaton?

We had arrived a week before in Luxor, a trippers' paradise, very grand hotel and organized excursions to the tombs, donkey races organized by the hotel management and nautch girls dancing in the secret recesses of small cafés. There were the vendors of trinkets and rugs, the beggar women carrying babies whose sticky eyes were caked with flies, the guides with halitosis, and Moussa the magician with his bag of snakes, dust and dung and prattle and oaths—commercialized poverty in the raw. Children born into blindness and filth, the shame of our century.

We arrived at Luxor that evening by train from Cairo. A guide who told us his name was "Champagne Charlie" met us at the station and hurried us off to the hotel, hardly allowing us to crane our necks. The Banque Morgan had engaged us lovely quarters. Mr. Wynn had himself written to the proprietor, so that "Mrs. Crosby of Boston and family" were very welcome. But no sooner were we in possession of the key to our room than Harry and I raced off hand in hand back the way we had come to get a real look at the Temple of Luxor. It was magnificent in the evening light but Harry said he wanted to come back at dawn for he must be up on the topmost eastern ledge when the sun's rays struck there. I said I would come too. The sun rose at five.

We were late to dinner, too late to dress, as the English did, but no one minded except the maître d'hotel, who hid us away behind a screen. Mrs. Crosby had met two contemporaries, Mrs. Allen and Mrs. Norman, two widowed sisters from Boston, and was already at the roast.

The air from the desert was clear and cool. My sleep was as deep as Nephratiti's until just before dawn. Then a banging awoke us. The impossible guide had accomplished the impossible. "Sunrise at the Temple," I groaned as I prodded Harry under the missing rib. He blinked and crossed himself. "We have a rendezvous at sunrise," I murmured, and at once he was on his feet (always the right foot out of bed first). We could still smell the stillness of the night. The bougainvillea is not a heavily perfumed vine, but it has a bittersweet odour all its own. We dressed hurriedly. In the garden our guide, Charlie, was waiting, the curled rope in his hand. "Fine," said Harry, "that's just what we need." Through the dark streets we hurried, the light advancing like a tide across the floor of sand.

The Temple of Luxor was not far. It stands squarely in the town, the ground rising only a trifle beneath it. The western end appeared intact but the eastern pillars had lost their capitals. One of these had crashed in huge ruins to the ground, another precariously held a bit of toppling cornice that wedged apart the neighbouring columns and formed a kind of sloping highchair perched above the rest, and broken acanthus leaves formed an elbow rest for gazing toward the east. A perfect sunrise spot if only we could reach it.

"Champagne Charlie" must have been an adept at the rope trick for when he tossed the gyrating loops into the air the rope stuck there and moreover it held, what to us did not know, but Harry with one hand on the rope and a pushing and prodding from below swung a leg up and over and topped the broken capital. The dawn was breaking. We must hurry, so next I, too, was thrown up into the air much like a parasol about to open. I wound the rope around one wrist and pawed for Harry's fingers while he leaned dangerously down to help me as the loose cornice wobbled. I lifted my shoulders in one goddess-like effort and together we wiggled back onto the temple's summit and crouched together on the sloping marble rest, just as Ra, in all his glory, shouldered the eastern rim of the Sahara. Straight into our faces he flashed a greeting and as Harry moved aside to shade his eyes, lo in that space between our two heads the first ray struck upon a name carven there before us, "Rimbaud 1887" it read—our hearts stood still. Rimbaud too had watched the sun rise from here. Rimbaud had climbed here, to this highest spot. It must have been when he descended the impossible tides of the Nile on his first trip to Aden, when his vision was still filled with the poetry of discarded dreams. I am sure that both poets knew that it was from here and here only that their first Egyption sun must rise—and when Harry kissed me the carven R bit deep into my cheek.

We sat there kicking our heels and hymning the solar system until our innards told us that it was long past time for breakfast. We slid to the temple floor and raced each other homeward, but the hotel dining room was not open so we bought dates and oranges and went down to the Nile to watch the unloading of a steamer. Long lines of nubian stevedores were moving chain-like up and down the gang planks, black ants from an anthill, naked but for a sarong, they glistened at their work, chanting in singsong fashion the musical plaint of the River, like the drone of the waterwheel. This chant permeated the life of the Nile, this and the everwhining creak of the waterwheels.

We ate an enormous breakfast and I wrote a poem. Harry continued to read *The Plumed Serpent*.

With the help of Champagne Charlie and our own four feet we explored every niche of Luxor, drank coffee from the tops of old sewing machines, with every odd character in town. Mrs. Crosby and the Bostonians stuck to their Baedekers and camels.

The third day was Sunday. There was to be a *gymkhana* in Luxor. Laden donkeys and oxcarts streamed into town. We took a box. Such chattering and yelling as one never heard. There were horse races, donkey races, camel races, and bookies were as plentiful as bettors. At the halfway pause in the program a *visitors'* race had been announced. One chose one's favourite donkey and mounted and went to the post followed by a dancing, shouting, gesticulating mob of ragged admirers and backers.

Harry's feet dragged the dust on either side of Rosita's fuzzy white tummy. I was mounted on Blackie, known as the nastiest-tempered animal in the valley. But his master assured me Blackie was certain to win if he didn't kick me off. "I fix him," he leered at me with a wicked squint. I placed a large bet on myself and mounted, my skirts tucked well in under, above my knees. As we paraded by the grandstand I glimpsed Mrs. Crosby and the others using field glasses as though they were at Belmont.

There were about twenty entries. We (most of us) got off to

the bang of a pistol (some balked at the post). I must say the owner *had* fixed Blackie. It may have been a shot in the withers or a burr under the tail but we streaked ahead as though jet propelled. I soon realized what the man meant, we would win if I could stick on, so I wound my arms around the dust-caked neck and I inverted my toes twice around the stirrups. A bespectacled Grotonian was close at my heels, but he couldn't whip his steed neck and neck though once they almost came even. When Blackie arched his back and turned to bite my ankle, I kicked him in the mouth and from then on he decided it was better to carry me to victory. We came into the straightaway well ahead of the field and we went by the winning post and started around again so fast that I could hardly hear the applause from the stands. It took the entire populace to stop my mount but I was the heroine of the hour. It seems no other visitor had ever lasted to the halfway mark, let alone finished, and the odds were high.

On Monday we boarded the river steamer for Aswan and the second cataract. It was a serene advance up the Nile. The boat was comfortable and the air was fresh as we glided silently from shore to shore; we stopped en route at "The Lions," an exquisite little temple which the passengers visited on foot, and then rejoined the boat. We arrived at Aswan next day and decided to stop over on our way down the river again. The second cataract is at Aswan, thence one travels on to Wadi Halfa, where we were to be met by members of the Harvard Archeological Expedition, Dr. Reisner and his aides, who were digging ten or twelve miles out in the desert. At the quayside at Wadi Halfa there was really nothing for the tourist except one mud-hut café whose dim interior was painted with amazingly brilliant murals done by some gifted native. These primitives were of the most rich and imaginative kind. I asked to meet the artist but as our conveyance was waiting at the door, I had to leave. I regret that I never searched him out. I wonder if they were already there when Rimbaud passed that way? I was reminded of the work years later when I saw the murals done by Theophilos in a tavern in the hills of Northern Greece.

I said the Ford was waiting. It was a Model T with a bare-footed nubian at the controls, his (once) white burnoose tangling with the gear shift. The desert stretched endlessly ahead of us with only a faint cart track to mark the way. We were hardly seated when the chauffeur with a big grin plunged us into action and we swayed off from one wheel to another and made for the farthest oasis. Up dune and down delta we slithered and bounced. We were so banged and churned we couldn't speak. "Slower!" we gasped. "No slow," chortled our charioteer and flogged the chariot. We drew up finally at a muddy water hole with one bleak palm standing guard. The Ford was boiling over and we were too. "Try to make him go slower," Mrs. Crosby pleaded. She was nearly in tears. He filled up the radiator and we were off again, even more furiously than before. We clung to the rigging and prayed for our destination. Finally over the rim of a dome-like sand hill we glimpsed the tents and diggings of our friends. Shaken and unnerved, we drew to a grinding halt before the excavated entrance of the tomb. A very nice young man led us into the glareless and dustless interior of their main lodging. It was shaded and flyless. We collapsed in thanks into the wicker armchairs and accepted gin fizzes with praise and prayer. We had brought ice from the steamer under the back seat of the Ford. Dr. Reisner now appeared glowing from beneath the sands, a chip of a plate in his hands held as carefully as a soap bubble lest it break. The piece seemed inconsequential to me but to the team it was diamonds and rubies and four thousand years of history. Their entire findings laid out upon the table in the main building looked unimportant enough. Not one piece was whole, but the graverobbers seemed well pleased with their precious thefts, and if I had known more of the subject I would have thrilled to the treasure too.

How heartbreakingly often this happens in life : music in Aix this summer, ceramics in Vallouris, mathematics in Perugia, forests in Maine, and even of my own special subject, typography, I know too very little. Can there be a truly educated person to-day in view of the many specialties in every field? One cannot follow all the ramifications and to know one subject thoroughly, one must choose a single branch or particle of that subject, say diverticulitis in medicine, nineteenth-century miniatures in art, bouillabaisse in cooking, the letter O in printing; but if one learns all there is to know of one subject, then one is bound to know much less of the others.

We stayed in the diggings two days. Dr. Reisner's desert-tanned assistant drove us out in his own car. We were spared the Model T. Again on board the steamer we floated back to Aswan and debarked for the Cataract Hotel, one of the most luxurious in the world. There we lazed and worked for a week, hunting jackals in the desert at night. We saw one once but that was all and the frightened bleating of our tethered kid wrung my heart in pity. "A goat for delight," I allow, but not for bait.

Back in Cairo we found the Sun Ring. I gave it to Harry to be worn as a wedding band. It was on his finger when he died and now it is on mine. When I am buried I wish it left upon my finger. It was in Tutankhamen's tomb for thousands of years before us. Unless fission unfuses gold, it will endure forever. The eternal circle, the letter "O."

Dr. Reisner's young man followed us to Cairo and when he turned up on the terrace of Shepard's Hotel, Harry suddenly became jealous though I didn't see why.

We were to leave for Jerusalem the next day but first Harry wanted to be tattooed; a Sun between his shoulder blades. The English had made it illegal for foreigners to be thus branded, but Harry sought out a brigandish crew who said for a certain large sum they would do it in a sampan on the river after midnight. We pretended to go to bed early and said goodnight to Mrs. Crosby. Later I wished to Ra I had told someone where we were off to.

Under a willow tree at the river's edge we met our gang of tattooers, and like babes confidently stepped into the flat-bottomed craft. Harry sat amidships facing me. I sat down beside a bearded bedouin who held the tiller with one hand (the other unfortunately was free). We slipped out into midstream, the lights along the shore made the river's reaches even darker. In the bottom of the boat was a little kettle of *braise* and several sinister irons and needles. The tattooer himself looked like Svengali. Harry handed him a drawing of the sun as he wanted it to be transferred to between his shoulder blades just below the neck. Besides the artist who squatted amidships there were two brigands in the bow, each manning an oar, the

206

helmsman at my side, and a boy who crouched well astern—five to two.

Harry pulled his shirt over his head and hunched his shoulders ready to be tortured. Suddenly the oarsmen dropped their oars and one on each side they seized his arms and bound his wrists to the gunwale cleats. "No," he protested, "not necessary." "Sh," the artist warned and clapped a dirty hand across his mouth. "Untie me, Caresse," Harry gasped between his teeth. I started forward to do so and was pulled roughly back by the bedouin, evidently captain of the boat, who put a firm arm around my waist and pulled me down beside him. "Let go my wife," challenged Harry, and again a dirty paw was clapped across his mouth. "Silence!" they hissed and the boy in the bottom of the boat held Harry's feet. Meanwhile the Captain put his stained fingers down the neck of my dress and Harry nearly choked with rage.

"We asked for it," I said. "All we can do is keep calm." Harry groaned. The needles were puncturing his skin. We were floating down stream now, away from the protection of the lights. I was being mauled and Harry hurt and branded. I felt that with the least alarm they would cut our throats and toss us overboard. I decided to cajole instead of anger our captors. Instead of fighting, I made them laugh, agonizing all the while to see the sweat stand out on Harry's brow. The Sphinx beyond the river's edge smiled enigmatically at our discomfort. It was a dark night, only the stars kept watch.

Finally, the artist's work was done, our torturers relaxed their hold, Harry was released and I was asked to admire the results, which he could not himself see. The sun was there, an exact replica. "You will like it," I said to him. His face drained white and he collapsed forward on his knees. I scooped water over his head and I tilted his flask into his mouth. The boatmen looked scared. "Hotel," I commanded and they one and all set to, to scull us back whence we'd come. Harry sat up, his hand on my wrist like an iron cuff. "The pain was hell," he said, "but it was worse to see those dirty fingers molesting you." "I'm intact," I said, "let's treat it as a joke. A joke on them." But though the Sun gnawed between his shoulder blades, it was his heart I knew felt sorest.

CHAPTER 22

It was in Jerusalem that Harry met the little temple boy without a name. He had been brought there rolled up in a Bokara rug he said and so we called him Bokara. Harry left the boy five thousand dollars in his will but the executors could never find him, although they say they searched. I wonder if Bokara was only a lost child and mystified as well.

Since Harry would disappear at intervals I took to watching for him from my hotel balcony, overlooking the heterogeneous crowd milling around the Jaffa Gate. The police guard changed every day at five. Mounted on high-tensioned thoroughbreds, they rode and herded the multitude hither and yon like cattle, which at least half of it was, for the Jaffa Gate guarded the entrance to the city from the east and at sundown long lines of mule teams, camel caravans, sheep, pigs, goats and chickens would be driven into the biblically protective walls against the coming night. A dozen head of animals, a dozen languages, dozens upon dozens of multicoloured garments ranging from the black gown and stovepipe headdress of the rabbi to the patchwork cloak of the Syrian beggar, the tan robes of the holy men, to the white veils of the Arab virgins. My balcony was like the stage box of the greatest show on earth and besides the enthralling spectacle, romance pranced and pirouetted there before the Allenby Hotel.

The sun was setting (it was February). All the bells were ringing for muezzin. The human whirlpool beneath my window appeared unmanageable, the lone Turkish officer (since Allenby's occupation Turks policed the city), on his wearied horse, seemed at his nerves' ends when at the stroke of six a murmur arose and a path opened up before the snorting of a pure white charger on whose back straight and smiling rode the pride of the Turkish police force, a young man of flashing teeth and curling moustache, a veritable dynamo of passionate duty. Even those foot-tired travellers were impressed. He swished his horses's posterior back and forth like a new broom, the square cleared, the traffic unjammed, as a final gesture he waltzed his mount in one completely ballroom circle. I applauded from my balcony—at once he looked up, doffed his kepi and winked (as good policemen do), expanding his chest with pride. The crowd went wild. From that moment I realized that his duties were performed for me alone as though "on stage." He "trampled the beggars underfoot" and "made way for the old woman with her basket of eggs" all in true Hollywood style. I was hugely entertained. When Harry finally reached me I told him about it. "From now on I can feel you are well guarded," he smiled, all unknowingly.

The next afternoon was the same. My policeman even blew me a kiss! and pirouetted more than ever. But it was on the third afternoon that his ego burst all bounds. He kept watching my deserted balcony so avidly that I kept him waiting an extra quarter of an hour before I stepped forth. In order to frivol with a little fire I had put on a lacy gown as "boudoir" as I could manage from a suitcase. I crossed my legs and heard vociferous swearing as a chicken merchant lost a pullet under the charger's forefeet. I smiled, he beat his heart, but the crowd was a difficult one. He ought to have been paying attention to his duties. So I twisted loose a curl in my fingers. More tempered cries. I stood up and beckoned slightly, then slowly disappeared, and from behind the Nottingham curtains I saw him leap from his mount, throw the reins to a boy in the crowd, and good heavens, in a moment there was a clattering of spurs on the hotel stairway, my door opened and shut like a trap, there was I *en déshabille* and there was the Turkish policeman bursting his silver buttons. In a second his arms were around me, he was eating me up! I had not bargained for this. At the same moment I heard a furious pounding on the door and the voices of Hassem, our snoopy guide, and of my mother-in-law calling my name. The door was locked, he had been quick. Knowing then how safe I was, I flung my arms around his neck and pretended to swoon. "Tell them," I muttered in his ear, "that you saw me faint on the balcony and came to my rescue." He carried me to the door and unlocked it. I let my head loll pitifully upon his heaving heart. By this time the hotel manager and maids and bellboys crowded in. They all bowed low to the officer as he laid me tenderly but reluctantly upon the bed (this time it was I who winked!), and backed from the room. The uproar unchecked from the square was terrific—screams and curses rent the air. "He will undoubtedly be decorated for this," the proprietor pronounced pontifically. Just then Harry came in. "What happened?" he asked, frightened. "Caresse was rescued by this Turkish policeman," his mother replied. "She fainted on the balcony."

"Well, it's the only time she ever has," sputtered Harry, for he knew me well (and then he blinked), but he never left me alone with my police guard again.

The wailing wall in Jerusalem impressed me greatly. It was constantly in use. It gives, I believe, the same sort of *soulagement* to the nervous system that breaking china at a county fair or shaking an exasperating child must give. Just an untensed yell of nerves—the wall was so high and the wailers so small and the wailing reached such crescendo that I am certain it must be excellent cure for the blues. I wrote a poem about it and drew many pictures, one of them Harry published to illustrate his poem "Wailing Wall."

From Jerusalem we careened across the hills by car to Galilee via the Dead Sea. (I still have some of it in a bottle.) It was hot and dusty on the road. The other two took a swim in the *mer morte*, I refused, but said I would take a dip at Galilee that evening at the Mineral Spring Baths advertised all along the way in English and Arabic as health restoring and cooling with a large terrace for sun bathing. I pictured a sort of Cap d'Antibes and somehow I got it into my head that there would be music. Alexander's Ragtime Band maybe? It sounded much more civilized and pleasant than the Dead Sea. After a lunch in a fly-specked tavern we continued on. The hills unrolled biblically

210

before us. At each turn of the road it was like turning a leaf in Deuteronomy. We skirted the walls of Jericho. At the end of a dusty day, we drove into Galilee, which looked like a boom town in Florida. The hotel was on the lake. Mrs. Crosby got out, but before we let the car go I asked the hotel manager the way to "the Pool." "You mean the Mineral Pool," he asked nervously. "Yes," I said firmly, "I have come here especially for the baths." He turned pale but gave us directions and almost shoved us off. As we neared the place and then turned the final corner I saw what he meant. The pool was not very large and its edges were alive with bathers, but what bathers! Legs without feet, a face without a nose, lipless mouths, stumps of gangrened arms waving to us. A terrace was there where naked horror stretched. The signboard told us this was "it" but the bathing was for syphilitics, this pool was the last "resort" of the maimed.

Harry and I clung together in despair. With my Schiaparelli bathing dress I wiped the tears from my eyes. The rags were there, the ragtime somewhere else. That night by moonlight I bathed naked in the Sea of Galilee, with the tears still smarting my eyes.

CHAPTER 23

From Galilee we transjordaned into Syria. At Beirut we wound up in a quayside caravanserai as photogenic as it was uncomfortable. Ants in the bread, sand in the bed, but it was very Beirutian and we were ready to adore local colour. I remember best our side trip to Baalbek, that Mythraic temple so pagan and so huge. That beast of temples where each poor little virgin had been but a flower under cloven hoof or a tiny moth to the lucky flames of Taurian ritual. I had a vision while there. I saw it all, even felt the wrists upon my ankles as nubile, I recoiled before the onslaught of the bull. Was it in these hills that Christ wandered with Lawrence's *Escaped Cock* in his arms? I believe that it was knowledge of this land so wild and temple ridden that made us decide to publish the Lawrence fable, when one evening eight months later D.H.L. read it aloud by the light of the Moulin torches, and again the wrists were on my ankles.

We left Beirut by the desert road to Damascus, chugging up into the snow where the camel trains with their tinkling bells and burdens of frankincense and myrrh made me think of Christmas cards and kindergarten. We headed out across the sands into their monumental mirages. The walls of Babylon, "Triremes & Quadremes ploughing the known seas," wild horses in stampede, but always they were never there. An oasis was our toy, we took pictures and played with it, as one used to play with Noah's Ark.

"We are now entering the Street called Straight," murmured

Harry, and it was true. Damascus was badly lit, sinister in appearance that evening in February. The Street called Straight was not. As we entered the lobby of the only possible hotel we bumped into Parisian acquaintances in altercation with a Syrian merchant whose prehensile fingers held firmly under their noses a gorgeous necklace of gold and amethysts and emeralds. "Belonged to the Queen of Sheba, gentlemen," he was yelling, his prey nearly in the net. Our interruption was a godsend to our friends. "Harry, Caresse, wonderful. You will judge it," said Pepo, "but you are too tired now." And to the Syrian, "Bring it back after dinner." We were scowled at by the trader but beamed upon by Pepo and Chico. They were fabulously wealthy South American playboys of a category much in evidence in the Paris panorama of the twenties.

Chico could be typed as a playboy because he *was* nearly a boy, or looked nearly so. Pepo, on the other hand, was a well-seasoned dilettante, an *habitué* of the International Set of Paris, Rome, London, Madrid. He was floridly proportioned, slightly bald, impeccably groomed—lavish but not too imaginative. Chico was less imposing to the eye, short, plump, redolent of Lanvin's scent (for men) with an overdeveloped taste for the exotic, but it was Chico who had the imagination. We heard that he gave a stag party in London that spring so bizarre that the "bobbies" had to take over.

We had met these two at Armand's coming-of-age party. Now they welcomed our advent as enticingly as cheese does the mice—luckily our whiskers were nice and long too!

It was after dinner that we wandered forth with them into the moil of that trader's paradise, the Street called Straight. At Asphar's, internationally known dealer in beautiful loot, we looked again at the Persian necklace, it was really lovely. "It is for the most beautiful woman in Paris," Pepo said, "will she like it?" I looked again. "If she is part Sorceress she will," I answered. That summer dining at Cannes I saw the necklace wound round and round the arm of my most beautiful friend, but I had never suspected she was a witch.

It was Asphar who next day produced the gold cup, unhooded it, as though it were the Holy Grail, before our dazzled eyes. As soon as Harry saw it, we both knew it was *the* cup, *Our Chalice,* the one for the October of our chosen year, 1942. But two thousand dollars was a lot of dollars and Mrs. Crosby, who directed finances, suggested that it could be a fake. "It is real," said Harry, and I saw the stubborn wonder in his eyes. "It is unique," said Asphar. "Sh . . ." and he looked behind the doors. "It has been stolen from the ruins of the Temple of Palmyra. It will have to be smuggled out of Syria." "Then we won't touch it," protested Harry's mother, but touch it we did, with our fingers, our eyes, our desire, until it was ours. Mrs. Crosby gave a check to Asphar. We Bostonians were always treated with complete confidence in the matter of money. We must have exuded solidarity.

From Damascus our trip unwound eastward, along the Syrian Coast to Istanbul. Luckily (some would have said unluckily) we were just in time to take the first through train of the Orient Express from Homs to the Turkish capital. It was to have been an official, historic trip along the Orontes with flower-strewn tracks to mark the way, speeches by Turkish and French dignitaries, but the train was two days late in getting started and the star performers had dwindled away. Some city official pounced on us as the next best bet, relatives of the American Ambassador to Istanbul taking the first overland train route to join him; it sounded fine. We were pressed into service. There was no dining car, only a cooking caboose, where, over a charcoal burner, tended by a native of Homs, we were permitted to cook our wayward meals. Water, too, was hard to come by, but our special "wagon lit" was a fine confection dreamed up by the *Compagnie Générale des Express Européenes.* We shuttled along on goosefeather cushions though the linen was nil. But it couldn't have been more fun—and we stopped in every hamlet and homlet along the way. The only time that the "express" took it into its entrails to act like one was on our leaving Aleppo when Harry, who usually sauntered alongside as we crept out of towns, boarding the last car when we ever so slowly increased our momentum, was deep in the *Lusiads,* pacing evenly along behind, until, with an inelegant snort, our engine leapt forward, breaking off relations with the caboose and seeming hell bent for the Hellespont. I wept wildly at the window. Mrs. Crosby, with great presence and authority, pulled the emergency signal. We buckled up like a clockwork train crossing the nursery rug, dislodged all the passengers with a shake and came to a full stop. Harry by now was racing behind us, his head up, elbows in, as he used to do on the track in Cambridge. We stopped so short that he almost bumped his nose on the rear platform, as an afterthought the caboose was hooked up and again we were off. But once our engine had got the hang of the thing, our departures were violent and jet-like, no more pacing for our poet.

The desert villages looked like hornets' igloos (if you can imagine this), ranged like white chequers upon a prairie board. Not a tree or a bush or a rill or a hill in sight. They were lived in, we knew, because smoke rose from their conical tops like feathers from a dunce's cap, but no child played, no dog barked, no man sat in the streets. Perhaps some came out at night like maggots, but then it was too dark to see. Philippe Barrès, in his *Jardin sur L'Oronte* describes this mysterious land better than I ever could. To it clings the desperation of the desert, the deviltry of its siren coastline, the lure of its *Princesse Lointaine,* and over its crags by night the ghosts of Mithras and of the goat wander, pawing and unsatisfied.

In Homs we got out—there was to be a delay of several hours, no one knew why, least of all the officials—but Homs did not offer much to avid sightseers, except its vivid populace. I could have sat happily for those hours on a sun baked lozenge of public grass watching the ever-never-changing throng, but both Harry and his mother were yearning for exercise, so with a bamboo stick, Harry drew in the dust a race track alongside the station platform. Three lanes with starting marks were handicapped. Mrs. Crosby placed well out in front, Harry not so long before had won laurels on the Harvard track team and at Rosemary Hall I had once set a world record for women sprinters in the 220 yard dash, and I was placed accordingly. But this was to be a walking race, and long legs in tweed knickerbockers had the advantage over short ones in tweed skirts. To start us, Harry shouted one, two, three, go ! That race would have been a funny sight anywhere. Mrs. Crosby and I always wore proper hats and gloves and each of us was seriously intent on winning.

The Homsians were open-mouthed with astonishment. Soon the crowds began to thicken, bets seemed to be offered and taken, the applause increased. The contest was three out of five races. I can't remember who won, so it couldn't have been me, but a wonderful time was had by all, and when the Orient Express got going again, we could have been the U.S. Olympic team, so vociferous was our send-off.

When we steamed into Istanbul, cousin Joe Grew, every inch a statesman, lean, handsome and mellow, was there on the platform to greet us. The embassy limousine flying the Stars and Stripes was impressively U.S.A. They had invited Mrs. Crosby to stay at the Embassy, but Harry and I had rooms almost next door at the Pera Palace. As soon as we entered the lobby, there were Pepo and Chico again, but this time talking with a personality quite other than the jewel thief. I was introduced to Dr. Voronoff, the most talked of Russian surgeon who was the first to practice the exchange of old glands for new, his specialty being the glands of frisky monkeys. Harry had met him already in Paris. Mrs. Crosby was to dine at the embassy, *en famille* (Alice Grew was not very well), but Harry and I had begged off for that first evening and accepted their invitation to luncheon next day to meet a famous athlete. The lunch was in honour of our youngest cousin, who had just swum the Helles-pont. Dr. Voronoff would be there also, but that evening he and our Paris friends were planning a tour of the Continental bordels *en touriste*. I was invited, too. Chico was particularly pleased at the prospect of an off bounds house-of-pleasure where he had been promised a knothole on the arena. This was a little high for my scale of entertainment, so Voronoff suggested something more erotic and less pornographic. I went up to dress, which we did while our floor waiter peeled us ostrich eggs.

It was a gay evening, but the performance put on for our benefit in Stamboul's House of All Nations fell far short of Marseilles and Cairo; in fact I was quite bored and wanted to go on to where we could dance. Voronoff was a charming host and

216

expanded; he promised to reserve his prettiest white chimpanzee for me for 1950 (good Lord, it's past).

I don't remember a thing about the lunch next day except that Tom, an embassy secretary, was as attentive as embassy secretaries should be. He wanted Harry and me to dine that night at the gayest restaurant in town and he took me out to look at mosques—Harry went another way.

When we met at the hotel before dinner, I realized that Harry was excited. He told me that Cousin Joe's chauffeur knew where the Kurd shepherds danced their religious dances and moreover the man was of Kurd origin and would take us there that night. We had been offered one of the embassy cars for the evening. It was at dinner while the music played that Harry took out a lump of hashish and offered us each a bite. Tom was incredulous. "This isn't the real stuff, is it?" he asked as he popped a sizable bit into his mouth. I only nibbled at mine, I didn't at all need a stimulant, but Tom, the sceptic, and Harry, the tempter, argued it out. My one bite, I will say, transformed me into a dervish. I whirled as I waltzed. When dinner was done, we wafted to the car. "Kurdistan," we murmured and off we drove into the hills.

The hashish was taking effect, less on me than on the others, because I had had less. Nevertheless, the shadows outside the window formed a landscape unlike any other ever seen. It was over an hour's drive, but it passed like a single heartbeat. We circled down into a valley in whose centre was a ring of fire. And lit by the flames, an outer ring of dancers moving hand-in-hand very slowly from left to right, a man and a woman, a man and a woman, side stepping, "Mane sua in Man d'amante," rhythmically, from east to west, and their chant of ecstasy rose into the hills like fumes of faith.

We got out far from the fire and approached cautiously on foot. Our chauffeur, who had abandoned his cap and uniform, took on a different look, walking forward together he took my hand, very naturally, and beckoned me to give my other hand to Harry, then the three of us swung into the same singsong motion as the dancers at whose backs we moved. One, two, three, left; one, two, three, right; one, two, three, left; one, two, three, right; till miraculously the circle opened to take us in. Our guide pushed Harry and me gently forward. "Man, girl, man, girl." We now moved with the others. Presently we saw Tom and a gypsy partner join hands along the line. The motion and the chant never stopped. Our eyes on the sacred flames, the black hills at our backs, we felt as eternal as flame or hillside. Mesmerized, we never ceased our unending round. How many hours I do not know, but imperceptibly the dance grew faster, the singsong wilder, until just before dawn the pace became orgiastic and from hand-clasp to hand-clasp flowed the wild eroticism of that tribal blood. One could not break the passionate chain but one's whole body asked for the coupling of desire. Then suddenly the flame died, pre-dawn was felt, the ring dissolved into hushed and broken bits, each bit a man and a maid, scattering earthward in the final ecstasy of consummation. I, too, dissolved into Harry's arms. As the light grew we sought the cave-like protection of the car. Our Kurd friend delivered us safely to our doors.

At noon next day, Tom's valet phoned that he could not wake his master. "I'll be right over," Harry said, though he, too, was still somnorific. He found our companion out cold. He was scared. "Don't tell the Embassy," he warned the valet. "But he is due at luncheon," groaned the servant. "Then telephone that he has ptomaine, can't get out of bed. I'll be back." Together Harry and I went in search of Voronoff. He had flown that morning, but the Pera Palace supplied a Turkish M.D. who seemed to know his "stuff that dreams are made on" and the Embassy never guessed that their secretary had not been legitimately poisoned below the belt.

The trip home was kaleidoscopic—Belgrade, Prague, Milan, Lausanne, Paris, but we who had started from Tripoli felt we had initiated some far flung *Lusiad* all our own.

It was on our return from Egypt that Harry wrote most of "Mad Queen"—he had been reading *The Plumed Serpent* and he was in a spirit of tirade. I did the drawing of the "Mad Queen" that was used as frontispiece for the first edition. "House of Ra" is one of the most insistent poems Harry ever wrote, it moves with such ruthless momentum.

218

From "House of Ra" :

let the sun shine
(and the sun shone)

on the first Family Hotel
in the finest position
on the River Nile
(views of the Pyramids from every window)

on the recently remodernated
333 beds

on the fifteenth century court
in the interior of the Hotel

on the Salle à Manger
of the Hotel
on the Délice des Gourmets
on the Crème de Gigolette Germiny
on the Loup de Nile Grillé
on the Pommes Perlées
(they were pearls that were his eyes)
on the Dondines de Behague à la Régence
on the Asperges Géantes
(sauce Neige)

on the Cailles de Vignes sur Croutons
on the Tournedos Beatrice
on the Salade à la Citronelle
on the Corbeille de Pomone

on the Anges à Cheval
on the Café Egyptien
("Si ce que tu manges ne te grise pas
c'est que tu n'avais pas assez faim.")

on the Steam Laundry
of the Hotel

on the ladies' chemises plain
on the ladies' nightgowns plain
on the ladies' pyjamas plain
on the ladies' drawers plain

on the ladies' chemises silk
on the ladies' nightgowns silk
on the ladies' pyjamas silk
on the ladies' drawers silk

on the morning gowns
on the dressing jackets

*   *   *   *   *   *   *   *   ***

upon the front steps of the Museum
  in my ears
  in my eyes
  in my flesh
  in my nostrils

O Sun I in to you
the arrow of my soul
(under the sharp point
that pierces the flesh)

  let the sun shine
  (and the Sun shone)

Malcolm Cowley has told me that at a farewell party given in Brooklyn in November, 1931, for Hart Crane, by Cowley and Peter Blume, Hart kept reciting "Let the Sun Shine and the Sun Shone" with all Harry's rage and Ra's passion. Hart was off to Mexico, land of the Sun, his point of no return ("Harraburra", "and the Sun shone").

CHAPTER 24

Since our return from Egypt, Walter Berry had been encouraging Harry to write a life of Rimbaud and when, in October, 1928, Cousin Walter died we inherited his exciting library : "I leave to my cousin, Harry Crosby, my entire library except such items as my good friend, Edith Wharton, may care to choose," etc.

This clause was interpreted by Mrs. Wharton in such a sweeping manner that she indicated as "such items" practically "the entire library." We knew this was not what Walter Berry had intended and we fought her and her Grab Act, tooth and nail. Finally she relinquished all but about five hundred volumes and so the remainder were carried from 53 rue de Varenne to 19 rue de Lille, a distance of a furlong, by Maple's moving men with baskets on their heads, as welcome to our heated imaginations as baskets carried by *Vendeurs de Neige* to desert lands.

Whatsoever had been written about Rimbaud was there, but it was little. Only *Rimbaud* by Rickwood, and a biography by the poet's sister, also the sparse notes in the "Edition de la Banderolle." The next day Harry began his research.

It was for his final birthday, June 9, 1929, that I travelled to Brussels in secret to purchase as an anniversary surprise the first edition of Rimbaud's poems, published there by Verlaine, price one penny the copy—I paid many.

Messein of Paris published Rimbaud's next work and that is

why I, too, went to Messein to have my first book of verse, *Crosses of Gold,* printed. This was before we had established a press of our own.

Years later when I visited Henry Miller in Big Sur, the morning mail brought its usual copious correspondence and numerous publications to that man of letters. As he unwrapped the latest bundle from Switzerland, he said, "This makes the seventieth life of Rimbaud to date." Twenty years sooner Harry would have had the field all to himself!

Cousin Walter encouraged us both—when I showed him my second colection of verse, *Graven Images,* he read it very carefully and then, twenty-fours hours later, called me to his library. "I shouldn't change a word," he said, "but if I were you I'd send it off exactly as it is to Houghton Mifflin in Boston— they have just lost Amy Lowell." "But I'm not in her class," I gasped. "You're a lady poet from Boston," he said, "that's a beginning."

So I did as he suggested and, to my utter astonishment, received a cable back from Ferris Greenslett saying they wanted to bring out all my poems and, with my help they did. That following winter, 1927, 1928, the publication of *Graven Images* was timed for my arrival home at Christmas and not a word was changed since that summer day when I chewed my pencil on a cliff about Etretat and, as in the *St. Nicholas* years, rhymed dove with love.

I then had two titles to my credit, Harry was not yet in print, but in the spring we brought out "Red Skeletons" in our newly founded Editions Narcisse. Harry was steeped in Baudelaire at the time, Alastair's illustrations for this first edition were just as convoluted and lurid as the verse. The autumn before he died, Harry gathered together all of these books that he could lay his hands on and staged a shooting contest at the Mill, riddling each volume with bullet holes until not a word was legible, then he heaped them upon a bonfire in the court-yard and we, the Powels, the de Geeteres, the children, Harry and I did a snake dance around the pyre—but I still have one copy saved and undoubtedly a few others managed to escape. The poems were dedicated to me.

It was a few months before Harry's death that we inserted

222

a little slip in the October issue of *transition* (Harry was assistant editor) asking for any and all translations of Rimbaud's work. When a few months later, I returned to Paris alone, I found the answers had been piling up; there were a dozen versions of *Bateau Ivre* and dozens of *Vowels;* only a small number of the early poems, more especially the short ones, but no rendering at all of *Un Saison en Enfer* or of the more esoteric work.

One well-known English critic (I will spare his name) translated *Frissons d'Ombelles* as "Shivering Umbrellas" and so I gave up the idea of collecting translations that way, since most of the versions fell fathoms short of the originals, but I did want the B.S.P. to do a Rimbaud in memory of Harry, and I determined to find a translator worthy of the task, a Baudelaire-for-a-Poe combination, if it were possible. In this vein I wrote to Lawrence of Arabia—T. E. Lawrence—who I knew was working on a translation of the *Odyssey* for John Lane.

Private Shaw (as he called himself) answered my letter in longhand to tell me how much he loved and admired Rimbaud and how much he was interested in the Black Sun Press, but he said he just didn't have time for the job and he only translated for his bread and butter, though Rimbaud, he admitted, was different. Perhaps he would do it another year, if I could wait. I was sad, but thanked him and sent him my *Poems for Harry Crosby* just published. It was not long before T.E.L. wrote back, congratulating me on my own work and suggesting that I do the translation myself—anyone he said who could write "Sweet Leaves" was a poet and maybe I could find my Baudelaire-Poe combination in myself.

Excited, I sent him off my rendering of *Mirage*. Back came his answer winged like the shuttlecock. His version was inscribed —"Rimbaud out of C.C. by T.E.L." and I knew at once that I'd found the perfect Baudelaire for my Poe. Unfortunately, Private Shaw died, accidentally, too soon after. His brother's account of his death describes the tent in which he lived, incognito, with his regiment. On the camp table beside his cot were a few books—Rimbaud was there, and so were *Poems for Harry Crosby;* at "Sweet Leaves" there was a marker.

Like many other Americans I was amazed to find that the French considered Jack London our greatest author and Poe our greatest poet. Poe was indeed fortunate in having Baudelaire for amanuensis. Not only was Baudelaire a great poet too, but his macabre spirit was like a looking-glass in which Poe's image was truthfully reflected. The symbolist Mallarmé did Poe the same faithful service, but Baudelaire's rendering at times even transcends the original, and therefore, the French were wooed and won.

I have found in editing the review *Portfolio* that too often the translator does the author a disservice, and though I have made a rule never to publish the translation without the original, it is only just that the transition be true both in sense and sound. I am not one who believes that a prose rendering of a poem is better than an imitation of its sound as well. That is why I have too often felt obliged to withdraw foreign poetry from publication.

I refused to use the translations of the works of Séféris, the Greek poet, because they did not do justice to the originals and he thanked me for my decision. He said he had been shocked too. The rendering of his poems into French, on the other hand, was excellent. So, eventually, I used the French. My own poems rendered into French and Italian and Japanese have been, I'm sure, improved upon.

Jack London must have had an energetic Paris publisher, and a translator whose vernacular was loaded. The Yukon and its spell opened up new vistas to the adventuring French mind, and so Jack London became one of the most read and enjoyed of contemporary Americans.

Harry was made executor when Cousin Walter died, and in October, 1928, when the will was read, we discovered that Harry had also been made legatee to the bulk of his cousin's estate.

There were a few special bequests that were both glamorous and explosive, causing many hurt feelings, as well as the unexpected good luck. The bequest that caused the most excitement in the Berry group, that special charmed circle, was the one made to Comte Etienne de Beaumont, and this because Harry at that time did not pay enough attention to the difference between Picasso and *les autres*. It was well known that the

38. Caresse at the Marcel Archard fancy dress party in 1890 costume, 1932.

39. René Crevel, George and Nora Auric, Caresse, Pierre Colle, at the Mill, 1932.

40. Around the embers at a party, Le Moulin, 1932.

41. Below—personalities include Bunny Carter, Comtesse de Contades, Comte Armand de la Roche-foucauld, Henri Leui-Despas, Prince Hohenlohe, Louis Bromfield, André Dürst, Estrella Boissevair, Erskine Gwynn (U.S. Lines), Vicomte de la Rochefoucauld, Bettina Bergery, 1932.

Comte de Beaumont and Cousin Walter had disagreed in many spirited debates on the merits of the important artists of the day.

So when Harry, as executor, wrote to the Count that Walter Berry had willed him a Picasso *Harlequin* all Paris was agog, and the Count was verbosely delighted.

Etienne de Beaumont wrote to Harry in the grand manner that he would present himself at five o'clock the following afternoon to receive the bequest in person. It was a lovely day in November and Harry, the dogs and I decided to take a quick turn in the Bois. Harry put on a pair of muddy sneakers with his blue suit and an old St. Mark's sweater instead of his coat. When we were at the farthest point in the woods, we suddenly realized that it was ten minutes to five, and we ran back all the way to the waiting car, a matter of a mile or more, so that we arrived at the rue de Varenne hot, dishevelled and late, and as far as the Comte was concerned, in stocking feet. He had been waiting half an hour, his beautifully gloved hands resting on the knob of a cane that tapped the floor impatiently. We burst in with apologies, but he held himself disgustedly aloof.

"Please, my Picasso," he said witheringly, and Harry went into the study to bring forth the magnificent bequest, but when he picked up the frame, tagged with the Comte's name, he discovered to his dismay that he had made a slight error. Rather embarrassed, he emerged with the painting and a winning smile, saying, "I fear there has been a slight mistake. It is a Sert that my cousin left you."

The look that came over the Comte's face was one of blasphemous horror. "Sert," he shouted, "Walter knew how I feel about Sert. He *would* do a thing like this to me." And he swished the painting from Harry's hand with an angry brandish of his cane, as he strode to the stairs.

"But what shall I do with it?" called Harry in consternation.

"Burn it," cried Etienne, and slammed the great carved door behind him. Of course word got around and the story of the Comte de Beaumont's *Harlequin* became a "gem" at many Parisian dinner tables. The part that Harry had played was duly considered a boorish American blunder for there had been the two *Harlequins*.

225

Cousin Walter, in his will, had also requested that he be cremated, and in his own words, that his ashes "be chucked out anywhere." Through some embellished channel the phrase was reported as "scattered to the four winds," and just before the funeral Edith Wharton asked to talk with Harry. It seemed that she, with the support of the Abbé, had determined that the ashes would be happiest reposing at the end of her garden, underneath the rambling roses, where "dear Walter" used to sit, and it was her idea that a special Mass be read at her house before the final resting place was given him. As Walter Berry had seemed quite indifferent to what was done with him, and as Mrs. Wharton was his best friend, Harry agreed that he would bring the ashes in a special casket, provided by her, to her villa near Versailles.

When the coffin with the mortal remains was driven from the American church to Père Lachaise cemetery, Harry and I and the Powels (to keep me company) followed after in the cortège. Harry descended to the crematory, for it is the rule that one member of the family must watch until the body is reduced to ashes. It was a trying ordeal, and Harry had provided himself with a large flask of brandy and a copy of Baudelaire, while we sat in the car at the edge of the cemetery soberly awaiting his return. When he finally did come out with the urn under his arm, we dropped the Powels, first finishing off the brandy in the flask, and directed Auguste to drive us to the villa. During that trip I vaguely noticed that a black sedan was following us.

On our arrival, the Abbé, with Mrs. Wharton and her servants lined up behind her, was awaiting us. The shutters of the parlour were closed. The soft notes of a requiem seeped from under the stairs and a distinct odour of incense permeated the villa. In the parlour a small altar had been arranged with enormous silver candlesticks alight. I supposed then that Mrs. Wharton's church was very high indeed, which I knew was quite the contrary of Cousin Walter's. The casket was handed to the Abbé and we tiptoed into the improvised chapel.

Suddenly there was a loud banging at the front door. Everyone was startled. "I can receive no one," Edith Wharton ordered, as the maid flew to open the door. But the "no one" proved to be two of the most sinister-appearing gendarmes from *la Sûreté* that were ever beheld, and in brittle argot they asked, "What gives?" Mrs. Wharton, in her perfect French, tried to explain that we were gathered together for a very simple ceremony for the dead.

"And what's going to happen after that?" they asked.

"I am placing the ashes of my friend in the bottom of my garden," she replied.

"Oh, you are!" they continued in their rude vernacular. "Don't you know, lady, that it's against French law to bury anyone in unconsecrated ground? And you can't tell us that that garden is consecrated." The solemnity of the moment became ludicrous. The remains were abandoned while the argument waxed passionate. Finally Harry had to sign papers agreeing that he would be responsible for the ashes until they could be placed in a fitting spot. When the door had closed behind the uninvited guests, Mrs. Wharton was fighting her tears.

Harry said, "It will be all right now. I'll just leave the ashes here with you tonight."

"No, take them away," she moaned, "and please 'chuck them out anywhere'!"

That is why if Cousin Walter could have been at his own funeral he surely would have chuckled.

While floating down the Nile, Harry had sent off by over-land-camel an enthusiastic letter to D. H. Lawrence, care of the London publishers.

He wrote to the author of *The Plumed Serpent* about his own belief in the Sun God, described the impact of the Egyptian sun and asked Lawrence if he had any Sun story that we might bring out in a Black Sun Press limited edition. Harry offered, as bribe, to pay in twenty-dollar gold pieces, the eagle and the sun.

On our arrival in Paris in March our first visit had been to the rue Cardinale. There Lescaret handed us a big envelope postmarked Florence. It was from Lawrence and the Mss. of *Sun* was enclosed—that very afternoon the type was chorusing up the forms, the Holland van Gelder paper samples being pored over for texture. It was a Caslon job with margins as wide as a *faire-part,* the title in sunburnt red.

To obtain the gold pieces was more difficult. The State Street Trust couldn't send them, Steve wouldn't send them and so Harry wrote to Ted Weeks. Ted, who had been in the Ambulance Corps with Harry, was our first B.S.P. representative in America. Already he had sold our *The Fall of the House of Usher,* illustration by Alastair, and was excited at the prospect of a Lawrence item. His tastes were literary, his instinct right. That is undoubtedly why he is now editor-in-chief of the *Atlantic Monthly.* He promised to get those golden eagles to us somehow but it might take time. Lawrence said he didn't mind waiting, but we almost despaired and decided we'd have to smuggle them over on our next trip from Boston. Then, we had a surprise one autumn evening in '28.

We had come home from the Bois in the Powels' steaming Citroën, and piled out, dogs and men and girls into the echoing cobbled courtyard of 19 rue de Lille. We jostled up three flights of stairs, with nipped fingers and red noses to spread our hands before the blaze of the fireplace in Harry's library on the top floor—Narcisse Noir and Zulu yapping and excited—Peter and Gretchen bundled in polo coats, reminiscent of Harvard football days at home, Frans and Mai like story-book people, bargees as they were, and Armand, Parisien, full of suave mischief as ever.

We had been running the dogs at "le Polo," a smart French club near Longchamps that had recently gone in for whippet racing. It was late afternoon in November and we were ready for hot tea and strong drink. The spacious library lined, piled and glowing with the Berry books, with chintz curtains at the fourteen-foot windows and lioness and tigress skins on the polished floor, *à l'américaine,* was as pleasant and impregnable a spot that autumn afternoon as could be imagined. Conversation waxed very gay and slightly ribald. The cinnamon toast was luscious, the Cutty Sark had twang. We were enjoying hilarious fun when Ida came up the final stair to announce above the mêlée, "Monsieur Sex to see you, Madame."

"Who, Caresse, is Monsieur Sex," they all cried, but I had no idea. Harry had no idea.

228

"Ida," I said, "that can't be his name. Please go down and very politely ask again."

In a moment she returned. "Oui, Madame, Monsieur Sex. He says he is from Boston from friends of Monsieur."

"Mr. Sex must come up," they all insisted, so Ida was once more dispatched to usher him into the arena. We waited.

"Le Monsieur," she announced shrilly from the hall below, for he had outstripped her. A dark, curly head appeared above the stairwell attached to one of the most delightful young men I've ever seen. He was about twenty. He looked shy, but advanced with authority into our midst. It was a strange entrance.

"I am Bill Sykes," he announced, "and this is my introduction." With that he pulled off one of his low tan shoes and dramatically turned it upside down over the lioness on the hearth. A shower of gold glittered in the firelight. Off came the other shoe and more gold pieces shone and clanged and rolled and spread across the floor under the desk, behind the sofa, down the stairs. The dogs barked. Ida threw up her arms like semaphores, we all exclaimed and scrambled to retrieve the precious loot.

"Ted sent you? Fine. Fine," said Harry, shaking Bill's hand nearly off and turning to us. "This is the gold I promised D. H. Lawrence for his story *Sun*. Caresse and I are publishing it in the Editions Narcisse. Twenty twenty-dollar gold pieces— The Eagle and the Sun—let's find them before they roll away 'because they're round.' " Everyone set to. I pressed a glass of Cutty Sark into Sykes' hand. Soon the brilliant heap on the rug in the flamelight totalled up, and I made Bill sit down on the sofa between Gretchen and Mai and tell us all about it: how he had decided to became a painter when his father died and left him a little money; how he had to wait until he was twenty-one; how he now was twenty-one and had, like us, "escaped," from Boston to Paris; how he had promised Ted Weeks, our Press's representative, to deliver the forbidden bullion; how he had eluded the customs officers; how he had walked from the hotel to us on secret linings.

Harry, with his usual precipitousness, started to hunt for a box to send off the treasure. Lawrence was in Italy, it was nearing Christmas. Harry wanted to get the gold to him as quickly

229

as possible, but no one we knew was going to Italy. In his desk he found a small square Cartier box that had held rue de Lille notepaper, and he was busy wrapping each disk in cotton.

"The Rome Express leaves tonight at eight," he said, "what time is it now?" (He had no clock there to watch over him.) It was nearing seven. "I'll take the package to the train myself and ask some passenger to mail it in Florence"—the free circulation of gold was forbidden then as now.

"But it might fall into the hands of a crook," Armand protested. "It's too dangerous."

"If I can't tell an honest man when I see one then I deserve a crook." Harry crossed himself and went on preparing the package. He rang and ordered the car for 7.30.

Bill Sykes went off with him and he told us later that he and Harry arrived at the Gare de l'Est a few minutes before train time, Harry in his oversized mink-lined greatcoat that had been Cousin Walter's, the undeviating dark blue suit and grey spats, bareheaded as always. He hurried along the station beside the *wagons lits* through the confusion of a transcontinental *départ,* searching for his "honest man," but he hadn't found him when the guard called *en voiture.* At the final moment a distinguished Englishman with a schoolboy of about twelve at his side pulled down the window of one of the compartments on the Florence sleeper, and leaned out. Immediately Harry spotted him and called up through the din, "Would you help me out, sir, by mailing this in Florence when you arrive?"

"Glad to—not a bomb, I trust," as he reached down a friendly hand.

"No, it's gold," shouted back Harry as the train began to move.

"Then we'd better introduce ourselves. My name's Argyll," called back the man.

"Crosby," shouted Harry, "it's gold for a poet." They both waved a salute.

In a day or two Lawrence wrote us that the gold had been delivered in person by the Duke of Argyll. Harry had not mistaken his honest man.

In spring D. H. Lawrence and Freda, his wife, came to visit us at our "Moulin du Soleil." Lawrence, fugitive, strung taut

230

and full of wisdom—Freda, possessive and full of pride. I loved him at once. Lawrence was like a prickly pear when people wanted more. I wanted more of him because of Harry. Freda didn't want any of us. Lawrence used to sit for hours on the sun-warmed paving stones in the courtyard, his back against the ancient pillar, brought there from Chalis by Cagliostro when Cagliostro was in retreat at that nearby Abbey.

It grew more evident every day that the Mill was built on magic ground : Jean Jacques, Cagliostro, Lawrence and Harry, all felt the spell and from the mill stream at the foot of the tower little fishes leapt mysteriously twenty feet in air to land safely in the pool above, and there were tree trunks like tortured lovers in the forest. Once a flock of sheep had walked right through our thrice-barred gate. I have said we kept our tombstone on the sun tower and it was inscribed with our Harry-Caresse Cross, and with the dates of life and death. When Harry died, too soon, it leapt the high balustrade and exploded to a thousand bits below.

Varda, the mystery-loving painter of Greek descent, has a theory that if one founds one's house upon ground beneath which water flows, the house will be one's touchstone with magic. This explains, he said, how spiritually arid some houses are, others how full of invisible power.

Less than a mile from the Moulin tower and seen from its heights, a sea of sand had appeared five hundred years before and this has never been explained. Suddenly the forest opened and golden sand filled those hollows, Atlantis receding beneath the waves, perhaps tossed back a handful of her shores to keep one earthbound toehold. Some day the ocean tides may seep again into the *Mer de Sable* and transfuse their qualities, mermaids in the tree tops, wild deer under waves.

It was the season of daffodils and we went searching. Lawrence and I in the donkey cart, jogging down long aisle-like paths where no flowers grew. We hunted in the most unlikely places and with a shawl tucked round his knees, collar up and his soft hat pulled over his scorching eyes, we briefed each copse and sward, talking, talking, talking all the while, and Eclipse trotted briskly along urged on by my ear-tickling willow wand. We would return to find Harry still writing and Freda still playing the gramophone. On one of these occasions, Lawrence in a fit of exasperation, broke the record over her head and, I imagine, immediately felt "insouciant," a state he believed in. I was both chagrined and pleased for I hated that record, but Harry helped Freda to sulk a bit and promised to send to Florence a gramophone for her, complete wtih record, which according to Lawrence's letter to me from Bandol, October 15th, he did—I quote, "The gramophone is in Florence and will probably be sent on here—but it's quite safe"—*L'art de donner est aquis.*

That week end I had stemmed the usual onrush of Sunday visitors. Lawrence disliked meeting people, but Constance was not pre-warned. She appeared at noon with two swains, Merritt Swift, diplomat, and Felton Elkins, dilettante. Felton had never heard of D. H. Lawrence, but was an aspiring though uninspired playwright and insisted on telling Lawrence how to write a play. Lawrence, unfortunately, did not tell *him!*

The Aldous Huxleys were to come out for lunch one Monday, but we drove in to lunch with them instead, six of us in the rue de Lille. I remember the conversation was a delight, but what we said or why, I have forgotten. I had only met the Huxleys once before. It was at a luncheon given for them by André Germain; the guests were a brilliant lot, André Gide, Drieu la Rochelle, Maurice Sachs, Jacques Rigaud, and the Paul Morands, as I recall. I sat between Aldous and Drieu. Both were lanky, witty and satiric. (Were there four suicides at that table or only three? Sachs' death remains a mystery!)

When we returned this invitation André Germain, wizened and wise, requested several dates to choose from, like royalty. He also said he liked to rest before luncheon so that his mind would be at its keenest for the skirmish. He asked if he might borrow our guest room for his siesta. He would arrive three-quarters of an hour before the meal, and he would send his valet around early that morning with a dozen or more of the latest publications which he could skim through. The valet arrived as scheduled with books and a pair of party trousers— these props he said he would like to place at the bedside for his master's convenience. But our only guest room had a guest in it, so I arranged a Hammam-like couch in the petit salon.

At 12.10 precisely Monsieur Germain rang our bell and tiptoed after the maid to his retreat, the blinds were down, but the door of the salon he left a crack open since he was hidden by a screen, and as I went by I saw the trousers depending rakishly from the wing of our Venetian paravent! At 12.50 he reappeared, chirpy as a morning robin. At luncheon, he discussed the latest books, retrousered. The other pair along with the spent literature disappeared as if by magic.

Another salon where I met Gide and Germain, Valéry and Maurois was that of Natalie Barney. She received then, and still does, in her house in the rue Jacob. Her girlhood, the story goes, was fraught with blighted romance but she undauntedly picked up stakes and left her home in America to establish herself as a lady of letters and loves in Paris. It is reported that she once said, "Upon the disorders of my life I have built a throne." Among her many friendships one may cite the most beautiful and talented women of Paris and among those frequenting her salon were the best-known literary figures of the day. "It is her life that is her *oeuvre*," someone said of her.

To Gertrude Stein's we went but once. I do not recall that Harry ever met her again. We were only three or four. She wanted to look at our editions and we wanted to look at her Picassos. We did both. Her portrait is well known now, but then it had not yet met the public. The story goes that a friend complained to Picasso, "It doesn't look like her." "It will," he replied.

The next time I met her was in the Midi in 1934 at Mougins. We all lunched together at Sir Francis Rose's.

Francis was painting a portrait of me that summer. He had made many portraits of Gertrude Stein, whose protégé he was. I remember that the Escargots Provençales gave Billy a stomach ache and he was taken to lie down in Francis's pink and silver bedroom. It was wildly baroque and Billy told me later that the satin flounces and the gilded ornaments made him more uncomfortable than the snails. It was Alice B. Toklas who was the star of that luncheon. She was in top form and led us through many a merry adventure, as she told us tales of her travels with Gertrude while Gertrude sat smiling upon us all like a happy Buddhess.

The next time I met Miss Stein was at a party given by Carl Van Vechten, the year of *Four Saints in Three Acts*. Only that time the meeting was no fun, too much like an audience with the Pope or Elizabeth Marbury—each aspirant was led to the footstool like a mule to the well. Then there was the first time when the play opened in Hartford and Chick Austin gave *his* famous party for the occasion, and guests gathered from Boston, New York and Philadelphia. I went with Harrison Smith, who gave a house party that week end in nearby Farmington.

But the last time I saw her I liked her best of all. It was the fall of 1945 in Paris, just after the war. I was one of the first Americans to return. I did not bring coffee and rice to my friends but I had brought them drawings by the American artists Pietro Lazzari and Romare Bearden, and I arranged to show these at John Devoluy's minute gallery in the rue Furstenberg. I had invited friends and artsists by telephone; Paris was starving for contact with the American world of art and everyone flocked. Gertrude Stein came stalking in with her white poodle at her heels. She sat in the centre of the tiny room and almost stole the show, my show, but even when she walked off with the best-looking GI in the place, I forgave her.

As Picasso had foreseen, his portrait now looks just like her. That afternoon in '28 Harry was fascinated, but more by the portrait than by the subject.

CHAPTER 25

Christmas, 1928. We were all (children included) at the Mill but Harry left just as the Star of Bethlehem arose, for Kay's baby was wailing and he couldn't stand that. He spent Christmas Day with Constance. It was very hard for me to simulate a merry spirit. I was very unhappy.

But New Year's Eve again found us together. Harry returned to the Mill as soon as Kay's infant and my children returned to Paris. The weather was cold and crisp and fair, the fireplaces were crammed with blazing tree trunks. The evening walk to the Poteau de Perthe was made by lantern light. The myriad jackrabbits jumped crisscross before our lantern's beam. The forest was alive with them.

And on New Year's Day '29 the Mill was alive with guests, like rabbits too. We would rather have been alone, but there seemed to be no way short of bar and bolt to escape our eager visitors. The Mill had become the place of the hour. Our gates swung inward. It was exhausting.

With our closest friend, Lord Lymington, poet and peer, we formed a special trio. He happily arrived on New Year's night. The latchstring was always out for him, but Harry wrote, "Caresse and I are a little like shock troops in the war, who were often *en repos* because they often attacked." The next day guests ebbed away and we were *en repos, à trois*. Gerard was correcting proof sheets for his *Spring Song of Iscariot,* he had to be back to sit in the House of Lords on Monday. I was becoming rather restless under the strain of Harry's search for clandestine fires, but he made me believe that my children balanced our account. Though beleaguered, I felt safe, still centred in the widening circle of his interests, and I knew it would be treason to even wish for simpler love. But that winter I wrote down some of my uneasy desire.

One night there was a country dance in the village. I recorded my feelings at the time :

"Last night at ten, H and I rode over on donkey back to the Hôtellerie Jean-Jacques by the light of a misty moon—they say there are wolves in the forest, it is so very cold, and the sheep took fright and crackled 'up and away' in the dry frozen underbrush as we hooved softly along the edge of the snowlit pond.

"The Château was, and always will be my 'dim castle miming the sublime.' My heart aches for that night, how many nights how many centuries away! Last June only—and the turrets are as always, *mine*. Through the folds of its heavy curtains (sun-warmed velvet, I remember) the Bishop's Room showed a needle of light high up above the moat.

" 'All Paris says he is your lover.'

"Sunrise and Sunset made a pattering entry into the inn yard and Fiat and Citröen gave way—no Hispanos here—no shining Rolls—No grass-green Voisin—the Country folk (what a nice word for a horrid mixture) were making merry—three hundred of them—at fifty francs a head. A. will make money only I don't believe they spend much of anything, these glum young men and their unwashed maidens—what a smell! I feel ill. 'It has been such a hard winter' (never since 1870!). I suppose that is their excuse for hairpins and dandruff—thank God, we have emerged from the dank ages into the white blaze of modernity with its Crane plumbing in the open—

"A. welcomed us (le bon hôte). The parrot coachman took the donkeys and because we were not *en habit de rigueur* we assumed positions behind the bar with the barmen and barmatrons.

" 'They will think you are the cashier.'

"I felt like the panther in the Zoo—so many vapid eyes, so many would-be haughty chins—and when I danced with E. and A. turned his back discreetly, taking valiantly upon himself the

236

full breath of a halitosic Virgin—I loved him for his impusillanimity.

" 'Je n'ai rien negligé.'

Harry on the cellar stairs drinking red, red wine and I love him for his Quixotity. The Comte de R. was in full dress (He thought he had been invited to a dance at the Château). I ate a chocolate eclair and loved them all so much that I tasted the salt tears with the sweet. We soon left, amid applause, Sunrise and Sunset at a gallop.—(I didn't say good night to A.— I wonder if that is why all night I dreamed so badly?)

"Coming home across the Park, the Mill through the trees looked stark and lovely with its candled windows (portholes) and its clean white barricaded court and Harry said, 'I would rather have it than all his Châteaux' and I answered

'A million times'

and I wonder what I would rather have a million times—

Sunday :

"The dogs barked long and loudly at Mme. Henri bringing in firewood.

" 'Bonjour Messieurs, Dames,'

and then the sorties of the donkeys clattering like a troop of cavalry over the uneven flagstones out into the courtyard. And then the good news that the bathroom in the tower works is *dégelée et fonctionne.*

"I run for my slippers and grab a Berry dressing-gown. The water is even *Hot!*

"Hart Crane left behind him so many books and so many pictures of sailors, and victrola records that the yellow room is quite *meublée,* he had carried an armchair over from the *grenier* and a table from our bedroom and a bureau from the bathroom. I looked around among his things to find my mirror but it was rather like reflecting him unaware. I didn't look further. I like his voice best—it is a foghorn far at sea—and *The Bridge* is a masterpiece—I am so glad we are to edit it— Clytoris sleeps late. The Comte de R. asked me for one of the puppies when they arrive (when?).

"I put on a lot of lip rouge this morning and my Burberry

237

St. Moritz suit and a seagreen handkerchief around my neck and some jade green woollen socks—and Harry and I walked to the Poteau de Perthe and back, and we ran Narcisse—like lightning—black lightning—Harry suggested we go into town soon after lunch—I not so anxious to, all alive and sensitive to far sounds (ecstasy horns).

" 'They said they would come over for cocktails.' We climbed to the top of the tower, I looking toward the west, instinctive—on coming down to earth Marcelle reports *les messieurs ont quittés le Château pour Paris*—deflated bubble of attention! The brave green handkerchief and the rouge flicker and fade. Now I want to go back to Paris quickly—only to be nearer—though never yet near enough—I wonder why I am so afraid to be nearer?

"I read yesterday in Blake : 'Those who restrain desire do so because theirs is weak enough to be restrained.' "

One night that winter the Lady of the Golden Horse, as Harry called her, because she wore one on her wrist, appeared at our doorway in the rue de Lille just as we were about to turn out the lights. She was wrapped in a mysteriously dark cloak and her eyes had a look of childish fear and anticipation that enticed one to follow her even against one's better sense. "You must come with me," she said, looking furtively over her shoulder. "Everything is arranged—Pierre will meet us there."

"Where?" we asked.

"At Drosso's," she almost hissed. Harry and I, who were already undressed, leapt for our clothes. In one minute we were ready. I had put on a loose silver-grey dress, nothing under it and my big squirrel coat over it. Colours and fabrics and comfort would be important. We let ourselves out without waking the household and scurried across the murky courtyard.

The chauffeur tucked the monkey rug around our knees and we turned northward toward the Bois. "We will get out around the corner," Constance whispered. "The place is sometimes watched." Harry held my hand in his. We had smoked once before, but not at Drosso's. This was the one place in all Paris where the sumptuous rapture of the East was evoked by

238

the ease and luxury of the surroundings. Only a few habitués and an occasional new friend (we had met D at the races) were admitted. The ritual of the pipe was observed in its most sybaritic manner. No dissenting note ever ruffled the trance-like surface of one's "Kief."

We left the car around the corner and Harry made sure that no watcher lurked in the shadows of the chestnut trees. We pushed the iron grille of No. 30 and entered the vestibule like thieves. After we had tapped on the glass as instructed, the door swung open and we followed the tiny Chinese servant down a blacked-out passage. There was a tinkle of temple bells and through the folds of a heavy curtain, we stepped in upon a scene from the Arabian Nights. The apartment was a series of small fantastic rooms, large satin divans heaped with pillows, walls covered with gold-embroidered arras, in the centre of each room a low round stand on which was ranged all the paraphernalia of the pipe. By the side of each table, in coolie dress, squatted a little servant of the lamp. The air was sweet with the smell of opium.

We were shown first into an undressing room where one could choose one's own kimono and slip one's toes into soft glove-like sandals. Our host always wore one with a huge red and gold butterfly across the back; we called him "Monsieur Papillon." He looked like an insect with gaudy wings that were attached to a dry little body.

Pierre was waiting at ease, stretched out on a big black divan, one arm around a tiny French woman whose poppy-filled head drowsed against his heart. He did not stir but drew Constance down to snuggle at his other side. Harry and I found a place among the pillows near them. Drosso came to crouch at our feet, followed by a servant carrying a tray holding candied rose petals and tiny bubble-like cups of tea.

"We will prepare the next pipe for you," he promised. I settled back in Harry's arms to wait and watch. The pellet of black magic is rolled deftly between the ends of the long spatula-like needle; it is roasted in the flame of the tiny lamp until it glows red-hot; then it is wheedled into position on the flat porcelain or metal bowl of the pipe; ours was of jade and bamboo.

239

Opium is a drug that need not be more habit-forming than tobacco. It is the handmaiden of dreamful ease, the unraveller of pain, the nemesis of passion and deceit. I believe that it illumines the brain rather than obscures the reason. Cocaine, on the other hand, is a habit-forming drug and those who sniff it, I learned, are dirty and unkempt, sly and evasive. It gets into one's clothes, under one's nails, down one's neck. Hashish or marijuana is criminally dangerous—the violent cracking in one's brain, the rocking of one's surroundings, the desire to hurt, are all part and parcel of this wicked weed. An assassin is a hashishin, or hashish eater. The one time only that I tried it, with Kurdish shepherds, I saw camels underfoot and the Orient Express upside down in the sky.

My pipe was ready now. It was handed to me and I crouched above the tray. I drew the sweet smoke deeply into my lungs, then very slowly exhaled and breathed in again. With each indrawn breath, the little pellet glowed; cooled by the long jade stem, the smoke seeped into the crannies of one's heart. Another deep breath and the soft clouds wooed one's body, winding and unwinding its spell, holding one in a web of lustless rapture. Smiling, one relaxed and drowsed, another's arms about one, it mattered little whose.

Two pipes sufficed me, although the others smoked several. The night passed in confidence. When the first rays of light pierced the iron shutters, we rose to go. It was like dragging chains to leave that couch. Once out in the dawn-lit street, I felt sick and dizzy; so sick I had to lean against the outer wall while Harry went to find a taxi. It seemed as if I stayed there for days, clinging to those topless heights—then into the swaying cab, held tight, and home to a hot bath and to bed for a little sleep and a huge breakfast. I awoke with the appetite of a lioness and sang all that day.

For eighteen years I kept a blob of the sticky substance in a little silver *bonbonnière* on my dressing table, and when I wished to evoke visions of long past joys, I would take it out, heat it ever so slightly under the hot water tap, and sniff the poppy dream. At last, my zealous maid went on a silver-cleaning jag while I was out of town. When I returned home, everything shone dazzlingly clean, including the inside of my *bonbonnière!* Now

I must close my eyes to see again, *fermer les yeux pour voir*. I have never craved the drug but I am glad that visions remain.

Toward the end of January, I flew to London, ostensibly to purchase Cutty Sark at Berry Brothers in Regent Street, and rose geranium bath oil at Floris' in Jermyn Street and to find a British bride for Narcisse worthy of his beauty and his breeding —but mostly I flew to see my son and find out first hand how he was getting on in his English school, but this mission I dared not stress.

I had sent Billy to Cheam that year because the Milford-Havens recommended it for little boys and they sent their son, David, there too. The Marquess of Milford-Haven was the elder brother of Lord Louis Mountbatten and Nada, his wife, the daughter of a Czar. They were good friends of ours.

I had entrusted Billy to Gerard Lymington to be returned to school after the Christmas holidays but I had received a disturbing letter from the boy soon after. It said that he was awfully hungry at night because he "didn't have eggs for tea, just bread and butter and milk; only the boys whose parents made special arrangements, had eggs for tea." I was anguished and wired the school to supply eggs and whatever other extras were permitted. I was afraid he had dwindled away; he also wrote it was "pretty cold at Cheam."

On my arrival at the school, three weeks later, with tins of biscuits, chocolate bars, etc., I huddled over a tiny coal flame in the headmaster's parlour and then went up with Billy to see his room. This he shared with seven other boys. It was freezing. There was ice in the pitcher on the washstand; that, he said, was why they couldn't wash! I was again in maternal anguish but as he looked better, rosier and livelier at Cheam than he ever had before, I decided not to try to tamper with the English school system. I did not stay to lunch either. Billy warned me it was the day for "codfish eyes and glue."

In London, I stayed at Claridge's as usual and Gerard, as usual, was very devoted. He helped me find the perfect bitch. The whippet vendors assembled with their wares in the hotel's gilded hallway at noon. I chose the fairest and wired Harry that

I was ready to return. He answered that he'd fly to meet and bring me home—and he did. He brought champagne with him and it was at Croydon airport that we christened the little pearl pink whippet *Clytoris*. (We told Polleen that Clytoris was the name of a young Greek goddess.)

Once again, on the last day of February, Harry flew over to the London Cartiers' and back to buy me a diamond necklace. He saved two hundred pounds that way.

That winter catapulted into spring—we were hurrying. There were five books on the presses. I was very busy. These were Harry's birthday resolutions that year :

June (1929) : C and the invisible Sun and it is a grey morning (grey-cramoisy-gold) and our oneness is the colour of a glass of red wine and there is a gardenia and the frailest silks (my Lady's favour) and I am thirty and I make laws :

to read four chapters of the Bible every day

to read a book every week

to continue rites but to abolish superstitions

to be taciturn, not talkative

to be ascetic, not hedonistic

to be lean, not fat

to shave and take a cold bath every morning

to never take more than four drinks a day

to be inextravagant in everything except books and gifts for C

to be bright and delicate and gentle and chaste

to worship the Sun with a chaste heart and a chaste soul and a chaste body and to-day gold won the horsegame with cramoisy second and grey third and this is as it should be and to-day the Lady of the Gold Horse appeared and to-day there was a reading of the Bible and to-day there was caviar and champagne with C and to-day there were fire prayers into the red fire of the Sun.

I remember the headlong summer, while we still owned the green car, and before Auguste was fired, how one aestival morning we astounded the natives of the Ile de France :

I was spending a hot week that July in Cannes, getting sun-burned and rested. Harry remained in Paris to help Hart Crane out of jail and for other mantic reasons, but he had grown restless and had sent me a wire the day before : "Leave the *train bleu at Lyon.*" I knew that meant he would meet me there, and he did. I arrived at 6.00 a.m. Harry was on the platform, very tanned, too. He had been taking sun baths on the top of the tower at the Mill. Auguste, in a new white duster and wearing a very smart and rakish cap, was with him to take my luggage. Narcisse and I were very joyous and Clytoris, his wife, was trembling. We crossed the square to a nearby hotel for breakfast and a bath. The day was going to be a scorcher, so before we started we put the top of the limousine back, huge as it was, it actually did unfold. Harry decided to drive, and I sat in front with him. French roads were dusty, so we all five wore goggles—this included the dogs, and although Auguste had his cap on, Harry and I were bareheaded. When we reached the open country, Harry pulled his shirt over his head. He was a beautiful Inca red and he wore his Egyptian necklace to boot—and I had mine on. "Take your blouse off, Caresse, your arms are golden, too," he urged, and so I did. Harry was stripped to the waist, only our naked shoulders rose above the sides of the car, our hair blew in the wind, the necklaces flashed gold—and in the back seat sat Auguste, buttoned up to the ears and on either side of him, very straight and proud, sat the two whippets peering homeward through anxious goggles.

"*Les peaux rouges, les peaux rouges,*" shouted the villagers as we hurtled through their cobbled streets.

We stayed on in town that year. In fact we never did close up the rue de Lille, even after the *Grand Prix* in June. In August we went off to Deauville for the Yearling races. I remember arriving late the first Sunday, just in time to see a sparkling black colt canter to the post. I took one look and plunked my one hundred francs on his rose-lined nose, through which he was blowing like a happy porpoise. He came home at 100-1, so I was able to play at the big table at the Casino that night.

We had motored down from Paris with Nada Milford-Haven

and Evelyn Boirevain and we were staying at the Normandy Hotel, that is until we met Ralph Beaver Strausberger whose stable, Normandy Farms, was flourishing that year. We had bumped into him in the paddock the first afternoon and he insisted we move up to his place where a large house party was already in full swing. We said we were sorry but we were with friends; however, as soon as he caught sight of Nada and Evelyn, he could hardly wait until we were all four under his roof, so we promised to come the next day. But he whisked us up very late that evening for a nightcap just to show us the way, and let us hear the latest New York hits played by his resident pianist. "Just press the button for music any time of the day or night," he said, and press it he did. It was 2 a.m. but almost before there was time to mix a drink, in staggered the "music" in tails. His name was "Hutch," his head heavy with sleep. He must have gone to bed with his clothes on, to get to that fire so quickly. Down he sat and play he did on request, tune after tune until the dawn broke. I discovered when I was under the same roof that indeed he would and did appear at any time, at breakfast in Charvet dressing gown, at lunch in Lanvin shorts, at cocktails in Bond Street flannels, and at night in tails. It was an arduous life, but he said he didn't fret—just kept his mind on pay day, and his work on the "Lullaby of Broadway."

The house was filled with English nobility, though none so noble as Nada HRH, and yachts, cars, planes and horses were forever getting mixed up in the workings.

Just as twenty or thirty people were about to sit down to a mammoth lunch, prepared by the Strausberger staff, someone would suggest prawns at Houlgate or snails at Dives, or maybe a sandwich under an umbrella on the beach, or aboard a yacht in the harbour, and off we'd all go leaving the groaning tables and grim faces at the villa. "The Music" told me that on these occasions he had the place all to himself. Mrs. S. never appeared for meals, nor at any time. She lived on the other side of the garden.

As usual at Deauville we ran into friends and other people's friends from every corner of the globe. It was then and still is the "mecca" of the restless and the rich. One table of Baccarat started as high as five hundred dollars—at this time the Dolly Sisters and the Greeks (The Syndicate) were most in evidence. "The Greeks are here" meant the play would be fabulous. On Sunday nights when fortunes had changed hands one could see frantic ladies pulling diamonds from their fingers and pearls from their ears to toss them in desperation into the green baize arena.

In September we were back at the Mill—*en repos.*

CHAPTER 26

It was April '29 in Paris. Harry and I were living in town except for week ends at the Mill. Polleen was in Switzerland at boarding school. She was coming home for Easter vacation, and she had reached her eleventh birthday, an age when teddy bears and toy-boxes must be replaced by frilled pin-cushions and rosebud wallpaper. So I had had great fun that month doing over the two rooms which she occupied on the floor below ours. Her suite, I might say, was as fresh and dainty as a *bonbonnière* and awaited her return with not one muslin fold out of place. She was due the following Monday, but on Saturday Harry brought Hart Crane home for the night. We had no other guest room, and so he with his sailor's duffle bag and his hobnailed shoes had to be put in the *jeune fille* apartment. That horrified me in itself as I whisked away the rosebud cake of soap and put carbolic in its place.

Hart was stocky and bristly rather like a young porcupine. He had a lot of gusto and a Rabelaisian laugh. He even held his belly when he laughed. I think he had a moustache that year, his mouth looked that way. He was young and cocky.

We were aware of Hart's midnight prowlings and also aware, to our dismay, of his nocturnal pick-ups. He said he'd go out for a nightcap so it was with great relief that I heard him come in about two a.m. and softly close the stairway door. Then all was quiet. But in the morning, what a hideous awakening! Marcelle brought my morning coffee to me in hands that trembled with shock. "Oh, Madame," she said, *"quel malheur, quel malheur.*" I jumped from my bed and followed her down-stairs to see what was the matter. By that time it was ten o'clock and Hart had already departed, probably as silently as he had entered, but he had left behind him traces of great activity. On the wallpaper and across the pale pink spread, up and down the curtains and over the white chenille rug were the blackest foot-prints and handprints I have ever seen, hundreds of them. No wonder, for I heard to my fury that he had brought a chimney-sweep home for the night.

That I forgave him sufficiently to agree to publish *The Bridge* shows that my good manners as a hostess did not fail me—nor my good sense as a publisher.

But he was dynamite to handle—and Paris and Toulon proved so tempting to his Wildeian spirit that finally in desperation we carried him bodily out to the Mill and shut him up there in the tower while we returned to Paris. But first we took away his trousers and shoes and instead supplied him with writing paper and a case of Cutty Sark.

On week ends when we went out to Ermenonville we found him knee-deep in manuscript, but always knee-deep in trouble too—he had frightened the postman's daughter, or insulted the baker's son—he had also bought out the haberdasher, on the cuff (our cuff) and was gaudily dressed in corduroy and calico. He had put on becoming weight too.

We had installed him rather spartanly in the tower, but he had soon changed that. The most comfortable and best furnish-ings we owned had been transported from the other house, even my silken chaise-longue was weathering it out on the tower's top—but *The Bridge* was finally being riveted together and he was very pleased with himself.

We had arrived one Saturday a numerous band, Kay Boyle, the Jolases, Carlos Martinez, of the Argentine Embassy, who could play five games of chess at once, and Evelyn Boirevain, our most beautiful friend. Having been incommunicado all week, Hart was at the exploding point.

Kay had been working the winter before for Raymond Dun-can, selling batiks in his shops on the Boulevard St. Germain. It was there Harry had met her when he went in to buy me a scarf of curious design—she so fascinated him that he rushed home to tell me about her and forgot the scarf, forgot to pay for it too, which was unsatisfactory for Kay but not for me, I liked to share good news instantly—and Kay was beautiful news. That winter she was ill and she was worried about Bobby, her infant daughter, who was being boarded and cared for at the Duncan Centre in exchange for Kay's salesmanship. Kay slept there, too, in a big community hall with the baby, both rolled in a blanket on a kind of pallet on the floor, or so it sounded. Kay was desperate, being alone and without support, she assigned the baby to the House of Duncan for keep and keeps —but it was not a really happy arrangement. I believe she was hardly ever allowed to see the child—and never to cuddle it. That is how she and I came to kidnap it on Christmas Eve a year later, with the writer Bob McAlmon as undercover man. Kay is built like a blade—to see her clearly you must look at her from one side and then from the other; both are exciting. She wears her hair like a panache, it was black then and her eyes silver green, the colour of moss. Her cheek bones are high and her face oval and delightfully pointed. She looks like a Seminole maiden. Kay is always as neat as a needle. I have never seen "her hair down" not even when she tossed and turned with fever. She is like a breeze or a bird's wing.

Maria and Eugene Jolas were and still are grand, gifted people, with minds like new brooms, hearts like hearts. They founded, edited and published *transition,* the most famous mouthpiece of the Surrealists.

Evelyn Boirevain was a Parisian divorcée, half English and half French, with the complexion and form of a goddess and the mind and humour of a gamine. Carlos Martinez, now Admiral of the Argentine Fleet, was tenderly and truly in love with her, so truly that he once dragged her in a rage over the cobbles by the fine hair of her head—which only seemed to make it finer by morning.

Hart the poet, with an Otto Kahn fellowship, was exuberantly tight—and rather difficult to handle, so I took him with me when I went across the courtyard in the evening drizzle to look at the macaw in the icebox. I had only discovered the bird a few minutes earlier, while Madame Henri was at market in the village. Monsieur Henri had hidden him away, back of a screen of lettuce and celery. I had been told the week before that Faustus had escaped from his perch and disappeared into the forest, but there he was, stiff as the skewer that pinioned him to the tray whereon he reposed, cocking one glazed astonished eye at me, as I went poking behind the green leaves looking for olives. His beautiful multicoloured feathers had been bent double to fit him in, one foot with a bit of chain still clinging clawed at the ceiling of his frigid tomb.

Hart, who that afternoon had been bemusing his brain with pernod, clasped his head in his hands, and sat down heavily at the end of the kitchen table, sobbing that our bereavement called for another bottle, I joined him, first placing the defunct on a burial platter between us. Hart launched into an oration while beating his breast. If I remember, the verses he declaimed were his favourite Marlowe, "Cut is the branch that might have grown full straight," the farewell to Dr. Faustus.

While we were sitting there I heard Madame Henri's chirpy little voice calling in the dogs before she bolted the courtyard gates against the evening, then Lucien's light step upon the stair. Lucien was my new chauffeur, Harry had again fired Auguste for driving me too fast and I had chosen Lucien myself from a number of applicants solely because of his good looks—I took it for granted any chauffeur could drive, but very few could look like Lucien. He combined the elegance of a gazelle with the muscular charms of a Carpentier but was more beautiful than either. I should have realized the danger he now ran and should have flung a potato sack over Hart's head and led him back to join our more lucid guests in the *grenier* where drinks and talk were being served, but too late! Hart's misted eyes spied Lucien above Faustus' feathery bier. No rescue now. At that moment Madame Henri came in, in consternation threw her apron over her head and wrung her hands. "I didn't want Madame to grieve," she kept repeating, "so we pretended that Faustus had flown away."

"But why did you put him on ice? Why not bury him in the garden?"

"He is too beautiful," she wailed, "we could not destroy him."

"You could have eaten him," suggested Lucien politely.

249

"*Quelle horreur,*" cried Madame Henri and I together.

"Come along, Hart, we'll take our bottle over to the other house," I insisted.

"I must conduct a wake," said Hart, pontifically. "I will carry him to my room and Lucien must come with me to mourn."

I fled across the cobbled courtyard and up the narrow stairs to the loft where a huge fire was ablaze almost in the centre of the enormous room. I had designed the fireplace myself. Logs were laid like a campfire directly on the cement floor of the loft and a sort of huge funnel-hood depended from the rafters to draw the smoke up and out. Along three sides of this attic place were built low trestle-like divans. There were thick mattresses covered in natural burlap with a dozen or more big pillows—yellows and browns—on each couch, while cartwheel sections of tree trunks, highly polished, to serve as tables, stood at every probable elbow. The north side of the room opened out into space through swinging hayloft doors. I had had a stout railing made to save our guests from plunging to sudden death on the cobbles below—from here, a few weeks later, Douglas Fairbanks, Sr., swung by the hay pulley from cornice to column and from column, in a Robin Hood arc, to the stable roof. On the floor were scattered zebra skins and into the crossbeams holes were gouged for marching lines of candles that stretched from one wall to another. I loved that room.

Harry in stocking feet was cross-legged on one of the divans racing his lead horses by firelight. This horse game was his passion and no matter where we were, Cannes or Cairo, some time during the day, out would come the green flannel cloth marked with yellow track and out would come the tiny horses from the tooled leather coffer (one we had found on the Ponte Vecchio). Each horse had its name and its stable colours, but these changed with Harry's mood or his dilemma. In a notebook he kept a record of every victory, and important stakes were inscribed on the flyleaves of his favourite books. If any of these ever come to your hand you will undoubtedly find some *lutte acharnée* (passionate contest) recorded there in Harry's racy vernacular. Tonight it was the Bedroom Stakes and Frivolity was in third place, Concubine was trailing Fidelity.

"What's wrong, Little Rabbit?" he said as he saw my distressed face.

"Hart has commandeered Lucien for a wake in the tower. Faustus' wake, so there is no one to help Madame Henri serve supper." It sounded so absurd that we all laughed. Across the courtyard, through the tower window, came the sound of the chanted dirge, slightly on the bias. "He's having a good time," said Harry. "I'll call Lucien when we're ready to eat. Let's have another round of drinks."

Constance was throwing the dice for Harry. Kay Boyle was deep in discussion with Jolas and so I plopped down on a cushion by the hearth, where I could look up through the chimney out into the sky that was filling with stars, just as a theatre fills with people, two by two, one by one, until the place is a sea of nodding, twinkling heads, and now the stars above me were crowding the heavens that way. Are they the audience and we the actors? I wondered. If so, then night-time is the time to play one's part to perfection, and in the dark one should look one's loveliest.

When dinner was announced Harry fetched not only Lucien to serve it, but Hart to eat it. He was magnificently intoxicated by now and after dinner, with sweeping invective he flung Kay's recent book into the fire, a sea of red-hot embers, where it smouldered to ashes. Much as one loved Hart, his fits of excess ego were a trial to his friends as well as a bore to all. After this he staggered off to his tower bed, falling asleep with his candle still burning. Harry went over later to blow it out and to bring Faustus down to a final resting place in the moon-soaked garden. Monsieur Henri, always gratified to be called upon to dig a garden grave for deer or dog or cat or mouse, interred the macaw at midnight as no macaw was ever interred before (even in Inca land!).

Walking back to the house along the donkey track hand in hand, Harry and I saw seven shooting stars and stopped for seven lucky kisses.

There was a ritual that cycled round the Mill. A rite once

251

adopted became a part of our life there.

First was the walk to the Poteau de Perthe, once in the morning, once in the evening. The Poteau de Perthe was a huge wooden five-pronged signpost a mile away at the crossing of the forest lanes—once upon a time these lanes had been roads, but now they were paths overgrown with fern and trailing vine. From the gates of the Moulin one plunged directly into the thick growth of the forest—a straight bridle path led to the Poteau, from thence one could branch off to Chalis or the Table Ronde or the Maison de Chasse, or else circling it, touch the splintered Sun, hand-carved by Harry at its apex, say a silent prayer, and stride back the way that one had come. It made a two-mile turn-around and Harry walked it religiously twice a day. I always made it at least once, but even when we came out from Paris late and dark at night, Harry would light a lantern and penetrate the deep cathedral gloom, touch the crossroad Sun and then hurry home to bed. One winter there were wolves in the forest.

There was our guest book on the wall. From the cobbled dining room to the raftered living loft, a narrow stairway ran with whitewashed wall. On this wall, we asked our friends to sign their names. Upon a ledge by the newel post was ranged a rack of little jars, in each a vivid colour, and in a pewter jug was water and beside it an assortment of water-colour brushes. Our guests had fun emblazoning that book.

When I left the Mill the stairway was a kaleidoscopic pattern of multicoloured names; among them were both royalty and rogues but more were artists, and not a few of these, Surrealists. The fumes from master-chef Kurnonsky's *pot au feu* haloed the regal signature of "George" and D. H. Lawrence's Phoenix clawed at the embellished graph of Indira, Maharanee of Cooch Behar, Louis Bromfield and Salvador Dali interlocked I's for the only time in history and Hitler's Eva Braun, who once dropped in for a drink with a Viennese White Hunter, and Lady Koo who signed "jade", could have been sisters on that wall. I wish I might have taken it with me when I left. It was the German troops billeted there in 1940 who painted our world out !

There was a swimming pool on the stream side of the courtyard, around whose paved shores coffee and croissants were served on summer mornings from sunrise until noon.

There was a race track at the back of the garden, with neatly whitewashed railings—this for donkey races. Sunrise and Sunset, Eclipse and Sunfire at the post.

There was the old village stagecoach pushed under the shed; "Ermenonville-Plailly" was written round its red and yellow waistline. We pulled this gaudy vehicle into the centre of the yard on those festive days when a Ritz bartender came out from Paris to shake up cocktails within its bottle-bursting sides and to pass them out through its paneless postillion window.

And then there was the cannon, a marine gem of solid brass designed for yachting in waters where loud salutes were welcomed. We kept it on the hayloft floor at the granary window and fired it whenever special guests arrived or when we left for town on Sunday nights.

Those rides in at night were memorable hyphens between the Mill and Paris. We made a point of waiting until the last guest had gone before we snuggled down beneath the monkey rug in the back to drowse en route, Lucien at the wheel. Alone together then we travelled countless ways, and I have memories for a million days.

Harry had been learning to fly that autumn, "feet off the ground" was his hallelujah. "Sept. 9th. Seven orchids because we have been married Seven Years and various rites performed : into the swimming pool a walk to the Poteau de Perthe a firing off of the cannon and prayers into the Sun from the top of the tower. We took luncheon together at the Ritz—The orange-coloured cocktail and the gladness of good fun together. In the afternoon I flew Aviator Poet Lover all for the Cramoisy Queen." Each clear day he went out to the flying field at Le Bourget where Detroya, French ace, was giving private lessons, it was there he met "The Aviator", American ace, with a keen eye and a handsome foxy profile. Harry brought him home to dinner one evening and from then on we became active friends. He was a relation of the Vails but to us he was simply "The Aviator" —he was rich and he was worldly and he loved to dance, which Harry didn't.

Henri Cartier-Bresson was another birdman whom Harry

encountered during those flying hours but Henri unlike the Aviator was most unworldly. In fact he was really a bird *boy* and he looked like a fledgling, shy and frail, and mild as whey.

Polleen and I drove by the field one day to pick Harry up en route to the Mill. Harry had Cartier (we never called him Henri) in tow and he told us the story of their meeting while we sped home.

Le Bourget was partly a military field and Harry had been sitting in the office waiting to talk to the French general in charge when Cartier who was doing his military service was marched in under guard and interrogated; the conversation it seems ran like this :

Le Général: "You have disobeyed the rules."

Cartier : *"Oui, mon général."*

Le Général: "You have flown out of bounds and turned somersaults above the clouds."

Cartier (shyly) : *" 'Ne balancez pas si fort le ciel est à tout le monde,' mon général."*

("The sky belongs to all of us," my general.)

Le Général: "What's that?"

Cartier : "Cocteau."

Le Général: "And what is *cocteau* I would like to know— three days in the guard house !"

At that moment Harry intervened—he asked permission to incarcerate Cartier at the Mill instead of in the guardhouse for those three days. Permission was granted and the culprit was put in our charge, how, only the French can tell, and so Henri Cartier-Bresson came to visit us in the rôle of military prisoner.

Harry had just taken up photography—Cartier was fascinated and it was Harry who gave him his first camera that Monday morning when he left. To-day Henri is one of the greatest photographers in the world—perhaps the greatest.

CHAPTER 27

Constance of the Golden Horse had sailed from France with us on our last voyage to America; it was a nervous trip, three can be an awkward number.

It was the end of the football season, 1929—we were hurrying to reach home for the Yale-Harvard game (why, I shall never know). And all the way across, Harry was hurrying to finish a holograph copy of *Sleeping Together*—"these dreams for Caresse," the last poems he wrote. This book had just been published at the Black Sun Press and we were taking presentation copies with us for our friends and families and Harry was determined to make one fair copy in his own hand for my Christmas, and for this he had an especially beautiful binding done by Gruel of Paris, in rose vellum, gold embossed—into it were bound the necessary number of blank pages for the sixty-four dreams.

He swore he would not make one mistake in this fine copy, and though the ship rolled unmercifully not one blot or erasure mars his gift—he gave it to me before we left the ship (why I shall never know). I drew the frontispiece for the dreams too. I especially liked "In Search of The Young Wizard" :

I have invited our little seamstress to take her thread and needle and sew our two mouths together. I have asked the village blacksmith to forge golden chains to tie our ankles together. I have gathered all the gay ribbons in the world to wind around and around and around and around and around and around our two waists. I have arranged with the coiffeur for your hair to be made to grow into mine and my hair to be made to grow into yours. I have persuaded (not without bribery) the world's most famous Eskimo sealing-wax maker to perform the delicate operation of sealing us together so that I am warm in your depths, but though we hunt for him all night and though we hear various reports of his existence we can never find the young wizard who is able so they say to graft the soul of a girl to the soul of her lover so that not even the sharp scissors of the Fates can ever sever them apart.

"The Lady in the Yellow Hat" is one that is often cited—Myron O'Higgins, who taught contemporary writing at Fisk University in Nashville, Tennessee, told me many years later that he used it as the perfect example of the one-line poem.

NAKED LADY IN A YELLOW HAT

You are the naked lady in the yellow hat.

At 95 Beacon "Alley" we were given the best guest room, at the back of the house overlooking the Charles River—but Harry had had his mind set on the Chinese room—smaller but much more exotic—the wallpaper was a fine importation of flying cranes and dragonflies and great water lilies afloat, the furniture black-lacquered Chippendale with intricate pattern of gold—the lamps, the screen, the ornaments were all of Eastern origin—it was a rather dark room. I would have preferred the pink and river room with its bright ruffles—the one I always have now.

Harry's sister Kitsa was living at 95 with her babies; her recently divorced husband, "Beaney" Choate, lived alone in a little house under the hill. Harry went there often. I had no idea that during that visit Harry made foolish secret rendezvous, for when we were together we were happiest and at night the wings of the golden cranes hovered over us like ancient proverbs.

I must have been so full of trust that even the most improbable proverb sounded wise. I was only jealous of one rival, the imaginary "Jacqueline," the shepherdess of the Zorn etching

42. Party at Le Moulin, personalities—Billy Reardon, Gertie Sandford, Marquis de Montsabré, The Maharanee of Cooch Behar, The Duchess de Gramont, Evelyn Boirevain, Gerome Hill, Elsa Schiaparelli, Mai de Geetere, Frans de Geetere, Meeda Munroe, Comte Albert de Mun, Betty Lindon-Smith, Baron Chatto Elizaga, Comte Armand de la Rochefoucauld, 1932.

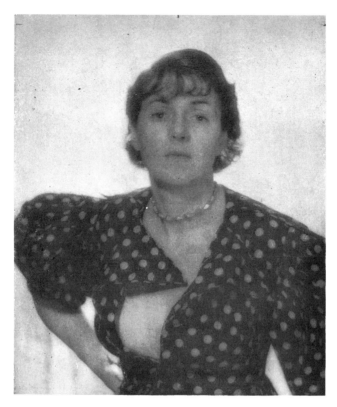

43. Caresse Crosby photographed by Dürst, 1934.

44. Salvador Dali and other guests at the Mill, 1933.

45. Our trip to Greece 1933—Jacques Février (" Covered Music "), Polleen, Caresse.

Val Kulla (the one that looked like Harry); the others, The Lady of the Golden Horse, Helen of Troy, The Tigress, The Lady of the White Polo Coat, The Sorceress, Nubile, The Fire Princess, The Youngest Princess, all were substantial props to the poet's dream (see *Shadows of the Sun*)—thus I accepted them, all except the image of Jacqueline—she *was* the dream— the girl of infinite mystery. She now hangs in the Fogg Museum placed there by Harry's last will and testament—the everlasting shadow—no other loves were quite as true.

Then came the final day of our visit to Boston and the sortie with Harry's mother and father to see the game. It was bitterly cold, Harry had a flask in his pocket, the one his friends "the Hounds" had given him in the Ambulance Corps and he and Steve passed it back and forth across my nose. There was one small white face in the crowd turned toward us, far off like an impervious ticking clock. I have hated football ever since.

Returning to New York from Boston, we took Room 2702 high in the Savoy Plaza. We could see the Fuller Building's shine and the Ritz Tower's shaft from our window. Harry was excited by New York. He met E. E. Cummings and William Carlos Williams, and Hart Crane and Archibald MacLeish. He was hurrying all that trip. He wrote daily and worked feverishly on the last volume of the *Shadows of the Sun.* He was happy when his mother came to New York and took the room opposite ours. Harry loved and trusted his mother completely.

We were to sail home to Paris before Christmas and Hart Crane gave a farewell party for us in his Brooklyn apartment hard by the Navy Yard, and the Cummingses, the Williamses, Peggy and Malcolm Cowley and Walker Evans, whose photographs illustrate our edition of *The Bridge,* all were present. Sailors too (one asleep on the stairs) and we drank a toast to Hart and to the Brooklyn Bridge, drawn like netting across his window, and they all drank to "Harry and Caresse," outward bound—it was a wild party. Harry's hair bristled like thorns and his eyes blazed like twin suns—I remember someone—was it Cummings—had a pack of cards and said to Harry, "pick a card" and Harry said "the Ace of Hearts" and crossed himself and he picked the Ace of Hearts—there was a silent second torn from a doomed tomorrow, as inwardly all of us crossed ourselves.

On the next day, December 9, he made the final entry in his diary and that morning as the early sun dazzled us :

"Give me your hand, Caresse," he said, "our window is open wide. Let's meet the sun death together."

"But why?" I asked. "Why, Harry, when we have so much to live for?"

"That is why, Caresse. There is too much. I cannot endure it all." He spoke with anguish.

"No; we mustn't," I answered, frightened, "but we must leave here very soon."

"Yes, soon," he repeated. "I'll call the travel bureau now for our tickets home." So that morning we were booked to sail for France on December 13.

"Let's keep on round the world, Little Rabbit, I don't want to stop," he said.

"Yes, let's," I answered, unaware of the danger lurking in the shining city beyond the sill. We kissed.

We had a full day ahead of us. Harry was to lunch with beautiful G. Hopkins from Philadelphia (I heard later that he never kept that rendezvous)—but first we went to see Kay Lane's sculpture of Narcisse Noir on exhibition at a Fifty-seventh Street gallery and at eleven in the morning we found the rooms already crowded. Harry and I on either side of the exciting statue of our beautiful whippet clasped hands across his cool metal haunches. "Kiss me, Caresse," said Harry, "before I go," and with his left hand he took off the big bone-rimmed glasses (he never kissed me with them on) and leaned across Narcisse's bronze flanks. Then he nodded, as he always did, turned swiftly and was gone. "I'll see you at five," he had said.

That afternoon, I had an appointment with Davis & Sandford to have my photograph taken for Christmas and that morning Harry had asked me to wear the new black velvet with the jade earrings he had given me at Thanksgiving. "I want a picture of you just as you looked last night," he'd said. At tea time we all three, Harry, his mother and I, were to meet at Uncle Jack's. Harry had had a special copy of *Sleeping Together* bound for his uncle for Christmas and I promised to bring it along with me. At seven, Hart Crane was to join us at the Caviar Restaurant for dinner. Mrs. Crosby was taking us all to see *Berkeley Square.*

She and I arrived simultaneously at the Morgan front door on the dot of five. At 5.15, Harry had not turned up. "That's strange," his mother apologized. "He is usually so prompt." "I think he is taking G. Hopkins to the movies," I invented for Uncle Jack's benefit, "I am sure he'll be here any minute," and I was. I did not know he'd been waylaid but when at 6.15 he was not there, Mrs. Crosby and I, both of us amazed, took our leave, saying of course something very unforeseen had arisen. I left the book of dreams, with its Merry Christmas card, on the hall table.

We hastened back to the Savoy Plaza, but Harry had not come in and there was no word. We went up to dress. It was 7.15. I was alarmed by now and called the desk. "I think Mr. Crosby tried to get you about four," the girl said, "but he left no message." "He knows where we are dining," his mother said to reassure me. "He will surely meet us there."

Dinner at the Caviar was an apprehensive eternity. Hart and Mrs. Crosby talked nervously together. I couldn't even eat, my heart told me that something was very wrong indeed. Harry never left me even for a few hours without some word. He had called me from many strange places at strange hours.

It was 8.15. I excused myself and went to telephone to ask our friend Stanley for help. He recognized the sheer panic in my voice and promised to leave his mother's table to search.

"He might be at your studio," I hazarded, knowing he often was. "I rang fifteen minutes ago; no one answered," said Stanley, "but I'll go over and look. I'll call you in fifteen minutes." I gave him the number of the restaurant. It was 8.30.

Back at the table, the room began to reel. "Telephone," said the boy. "That will be Harry," the other two exclaimed, but in my frozen heart, I knew that they were wrong. Stanley was calling me from his studio, over the wire I could hear the axe upon the final door, and I ran from the booth into the tragic night in helpless terror.

Harry died, with no compromise, by the hand he had reached out to me in supplication, only a few short hours before. I tried

259

to describe that morning in my *Poems for Harry Crosby,* and these, like his *Dreams for Caresse,* were the last I, too, ever wrote; it broke my heart to cry.

INVITED TO DIE

Our eyes were opened to a blaze of Sun
New York beyond the sill flashed form
That wed white structure to our dawn
And found us storied high, in wool and lawn,
Above New York
Our eyes strung level with the Fuller's shine
(Ritz Tower windows flashed your smile to mine!)
"My hand in yours Caresse, unblind?"
That morning knew
The sudden wave-length of my longing too.
"But we so strong so one so true" I said
"To seek the sunvast splendour through negation"
Pled the future
Flew the star-filled pennant of my hopes across our skies
Over the sun-hung cauldron of your eyes . . . .

Clean sunbuilt dawn the day we owned New York
Rose into noon, the day returned to dark,
     Your goddess flown.
     ("To tempt us less" you'd said).

     I did not guess
     I did not guess

That madder beauty waited, unaware,
To take your hand upon the evening stair.

CHAPTER 28

All the dancing figures of a world that had been arrayed in rainbow colours now froze into immobility. The prism dimmed to deepest black. Nothing was familiar, nothing sure, even to sight or touch. I myself was drained of life and hope, only faith remained, but faith can baffle reason. I had received a blow straight to the heart with sheer terror to the brain, but faith persisted—for me there was nothing to doubt, only an overwhelming enigma confronting me—my puzzle was to know what Harry expected of me—should I follow him? What signpost showed the way? No final note—no word at all—only empty reality. What could I turn to, where could I find comfort now? for it was he and he alone who had ever understood.

I saw no one—my mother and a few close friends passed before me like automatons upon a moving track. I had to decide alone and in limbo where my destiny lay. At last through a curtain of pain and peril a dim light glimmered. I weighed reason and unreason, love and desperation until I finally realized that "no compromise," no word at all was the only way that Harry could have assured me that still and forever we were "Harry and Caresse." To explain would have been to destroy, and only his supreme faith in me could have made this departure without words justified, and so with that as my life raft I pulled myself back out of the depths into the light again.

Harry had asked to be cremated. I carried his ashes wrapped in his silk Damascan robe in my arms when I boarded the boat on the thirteenth—Harry's mother travelled with me. I realize now how piteously little heed I gave to her grief, my own encompassed me so fully—and she was a veritable angel.

The Franklins, the owners of the line, had put their private suite on the sun-deck at our disposal but I had asked for and clung to an inside cabin amidship on the lowest deck. It was thither that I went carrying my only link with reality. Mrs. Crosby followed me and slept next to me, too, though I was told that our sun-deck cabin was massed with flowers and piled with cables and messages. I never left my sheltering cocoon except the last evening after nightfall when she and I walked the lower deck with only the stars for light. Alice Grew and her two daughters came to join our promenade. I had not seen them since Istanbul. They were beautiful people—I felt safe with them, not speaking, but gaining courage from the arm-in-arm contact.

At Cherbourg, Nina de Polignac and Armand de la Rochefoucauld met us. We four travelled to Paris together in the same compartment. It proved almost more of a strain than I could bear—that road had been travelled so many times before under such happy circumstances. I just shut my eyes and hugged my sorrow close.

At 19, rue de Lille, Marcelle my maid was waiting for me— she had come back from England where she had gone to join her family when Harry and I sailed away. She told me weeping that she had promised "Monsieur" to return to me immediately if I ever were in need of her—was this a prophecy?

The Powels and Bill Sykes were there too when we arrived. Sykes took a train that night for Chamonix to fetch Polleen home to me—he said he would try to explain what had happened. She was only eleven but I trusted him to help her. Gerard Lymington went to Billy's school near Croydon and it was he who broke the tragic news to my thirteen-year-old-son, and flew him back to me in Paris. Both children were desperately unhappy—they loved Harry and they loved me. They never knew the underlying heartbreak so wantonly at play between us on their account.

It was already December 22. I wanted to go down to Ermenonville for Christmas. There was a fine dry snowfall in

the air, the cosy and twinkling appearance of the Mill filled
my heart to bursting as we approached. Mrs. Crosby stayed
on with us and several good friends came too.

"The Aviator" appeared, he brought me some beautiful fox
furs for Christmas but Mrs. Crosby was so disturbed that I had
to give them back, Sykes and the Powels were there and all
the lovely frolicking whippets and the donkeys and the
schnauzers romping in the snow. I was at home. "The Aviator"
asked me on Christmas day to marry him quickly, so that he
could protect me from the cruelty of the world. I was amazed.
"I'll never marry again," I said, "I am still married to Harry."
In the months that followed not a few of my devoted and
chivalrous friends offered their hearts and their hands if I
would look aside from the dead to the living—but my whole
being had been torn and bruised. I wanted now to become
sufficiently whole to undertake my life pledge to the eternity
of *Harry and Caresse*—so I began to live two lives—one inner
life with Harry, one outer life with mounting distractions. I
turned about each facet of the day wherewith I might catch
some beam of light hoping to fix the gleam in the years that
followed. I doubt if any one of my friends questioned my inner
preoccupation. I was eaten by the moon, the sun some other-
where and while I kept the secret place alive and lighted, I
trod the hedonistic paths of play and the healing ways of work.

But before work and before play I shut myself away in the
fastness of the Mill, and while snow flew and fires burnt I
endeavoured to capture in my *Poems for Harry Crosby*, the
essence of   C   I wrote spontaneously and swiftly almost

       A
  HARRY
       E
       S
       S
       E

as though some urgent ghost were guiding my fingers.

When I went back to Paris at the end of January, the poems
were ready for the printer. Stuart Gilbert said he would like
to contribute a preface, and so having written and planned
the book, I left its execution to the skilful care of Stuart,
Lescaret and Paris.

While this edition was on the press, Billy, Polleen and I

joined Nina de Polignac and her small son Dalmas for a few weeks of Arlberg ozone in the Austrian Tyrol. Though Hannes Schneider was a champion and the best ski teacher in the world, St. Anton had not yet become the fashionable resort it is to-day; its one small hotel was simple and restful.

The children had learnt the sport at school in Gstaad. I was a novice and began my lessons on Angelica Hill where Schneider's handsome assistant, Matt, was forever shouting, "Bend zee knees." The children's bent so easily!

They were spontaneously happy. We stayed out all day and came in at sundown limp with fatigue and ravenous with hunger, gathering in Nina's room for hot chocolate and spiced cookies and nips of the big Virginia ham that was kept hidden under her bed.

I began work by editing Harry's collected poems in four volumes—and for each of the four titles I asked a distinguished man of letters to write an introduction. D. H. Lawrence for *Chariot*, T. S. Eliot for *Transit*, Ezra Pound for *Torchbearers* and Stuart Gilbert for *Sleeping Together*. Every one of these writers was a man of vision, but though Ezra was the only one who had not known Harry personally it was his critique I liked the best.

It is interesting to note that Cyril Connolly who is at present at work on an introduction to *Shadows of the Sun* (the diaries published twenty-two years ago in an edition limited to only forty-four copies) did not know Harry either, yet he seems to be the most understanding of them all. I believe he associates himself with Harry more than did (or ever could) the others.

Ezra, the man, was unknown to me except by the written word, but of these words I personally had already received not a few in regard to Gaudier-Brzeska whose drawings I wanted (and still want) to publish. Concerning them I have exciting letters in Ezra's own hand, interlarded with his vivid designs and graphic flourishes—but it was only after Harry's poems were published that Ezra and I first met. That was in the early spring of 1930. We Parisians were rigidly pale with winter, but Ezra arrived from Rapallo bronzed and negligé—there was a becoming saltiness to his beard. I asked him to dine with me in the rue de Lille, and afterwards he asked me to do the town with him. He wanted, he said, to savour the immediate flavour of Paris by night. I took him to the Boule Blanche where a remarkably beautiful and brilliant band of Martinique players were beating out hot music. We had a ringside table, Ezra was enthralled—I with my broken heart could not dance, which was perhaps just as well. As the music grew in fury Ezra avidly watched the dancers, "These people don't know a thing about rhythm," he cried scornfully, and he shut his eyes, thrust forward his red-bearded chin and began a sort of tattoo with his feet—suddenly unable to sit still a minute longer he leapt to the floor and seized the tiny Martiniquaise vendor of cigarettes in his arms, packets flying, then head back, eyes closed, chin out, he began a sort of voodoo prance, his tiny partner held glued against his piston-pumping knees.

The hot music grew hotter. Ezra grew hotter. One by one the uninspired dancers melted from the floor and formed a ring to watch that Anglo-savage ecstasy—on and on went the two, until with a final screech of cymbals the music crashed to an end. Ezra opened his eyes, flicked the cigarette girl aside like an extinguished match and collapsed into the chair beside me. The room exhaled a long orgasmic sigh—I too.

From that time on we became the best of friends and the following year the Black Sun Press brought out a limited edition of *Imaginary Letters* by Ezra Pound.

I've never been out on the town with Eliot, he's not that sort of a poet, but I used to call on him almost every time I went to London. I asked him to write an introduction to *Bubu of Montparnasse;* and since he was enthusiastic about an English version of this French classic of the underworld, it was probably not difficult for him to say "yes" when asked.

I remember at that interview that his long thin legs under his desk in the tiny office at 24 Russell Square were entwined with the legs and tails of four or five yapping Sealyhams. The pets were his wife's, he said, she was out of town, and he was looking after them. To find a Sealyham sitter must have been as difficult then as to find a baby sitter now.

Eliot congratulated me on my choice of titles for the C.C.E., he liked the entire Black Sun list, he said, no exception.

It was on this same visit that I remet Jim Ede, then curator of London's Tate Gallery. I went there on Ezra's suggestion

265

to inquire about Gaudier-Brzeska. Ezra had been urging me to publish something of the Polish sculptor's and Jim Ede had collected many of his drawings and some of his marble pieces at the Tate. Ede later wrote a novel about Gaudier-Brzeska called *Savage Messiah*. It became a best seller in U.S. I could do nothing at that time, but in 1944 when I was running the Crosby Gallery of Modern Art in Washington I tried to get hold of the many beautiful drawings that Ezra had collected and which were stored away during the war years in his villa above Rapallo. Though I looked, I never did find them. I believe they are still there. Gaudier did a very fine head of Ezra, too.

I obtained permission on that visit to the Tate to reproduce the Blake "Heaven and Hell" series which is to my mind the most magnificent collection in that Gallery, but I found later that the cost of reproduction would be beyond my reach.

Jim also rushed me through room after room to view Chile Guevara's portrait of Edith Sitwell, very excellent. The Chilean painter was a great friend of mine and later married Meraud Guinness, another great friend and a very fine artist, too. I am planning to show her work at my new World Gallery in Delphi this summer.

CHAPTER 29

On the title page of *Sleeping Together* Harry had inscribed this verse from *Ecclesiastes:* "If two lie together then they have heat but how can one be warm alone." It was a cold season that followed, only faith remained and faith can baffle reason. It was not until the second spring that I really began to come alive again. I found my lesson in the pages of the *Needlewoman.* "If a garment is burnt, it may be possible to embroider the edges to hide the damage."

Billy was back at school in England but Polleen was constantly with me, and a Mlle. Dutate installed as her duenna and governess—I soon found that Mademoiselle knew as little about "book learning" as she did about governessing and I decided to try the Paris classroom instead—but Polleen was determined not to go to school and although she was enrolled at one and then another "académie de jeunes filles," a few days, sometimes only hours, later she would be back in the apartment in such floods of tears that even the doctor advised that I keep her at home with me. Harry's death had bruised her too.

I went over to London for Billy's Easter holiday and took Polleen and Mademoiselle along, for we were invited to the Lymingtons at Farleigh-Wallop—Gerard and Mary's children were younger than mine but the great house with its miles of farmland, gardens, streams and pasture was an ideal spot for their holiday, I thought with gratitude.

I, myself, ventured off to London and took a room at Claridge's where the gaiety and giddiness of an early season

267

were already apparent. I felt that in this atmosphere my desperate weariness might end; I'd try theatre, take a look at pictures, hear music, even maybe dance.

Claridge's in London, like the Ritz in Paris, the Grand in Rome, Sacher's in Vienna, and the Adlon in Berlin, was one of the most sophisticated hotels in Europe, it combined elegance with intrigue and luxury with snobbism, so that the ordinary traveller gladly proceeded elsewhere, only *le beau monde* remained. Now, as then, the rarefied atmosphere persists.

Frank Crowninshield's brother, Edward, was staying at Claridge's too, and was most solicitous and attentive. He was older than Frank, perhaps seventy, and had a great *penchant* for feminine pulchritude—I, at thirty-seven, was much too elderly to attract him and much too deep in grief to supply the needed entertainment. But he was a dear and thoughtful friend and, during one rather late night of theatre and supper with Gerard and Edward they suggested I go to the private showing of Sir Siegfried Sassoon's collection at the Sassoons' town house the next afternoon. It would be a gala occasion, very mondain, and one to lift the heaviest heart. Rather against my better judgment, I said "yes," for I loved to say "yes." My widow's weeds were from Paris, my weight was down to 7 stone 4, my hair was piled high in auburn curls under a swirl of crêpe from the rue de la Paix, and it framed a small, lost face, white as the ruching at throat and wrist. As I mounted the great ancestral staircase in the Sassoon mansion, people began to stare at me as at a ghost. I grew panicky, wanted to turn and run, but my knees shook and too many other guests were surging up behind me. I reached the top step with apprehension. Before me was a crowded gallery, a mob of celebrities, a floor like glass that reflected the scene as in a mirror, then suddenly that mirror shattered and burst. The din in my ears became intensified. The stairwell whirled like a spinning top and I quietly wilted down beneath the toes of spangled slippers and the heels of polished boots. Quite inert and lost, my heart seemed to suffocate inside its bodice. I tried to pull open the high-boned collar at my throat—and then all was oblivion, heavenly oblivion.

When I came to, I was back in my room at Claridge's and a number of frock-coated Harley Street doctors, a white-capped nurse and other unfamiliar faces hung above me—only Crownie, bald and birdlike, was familiar—"Dear Crownie," I murmured, and slipped back into the protecting shadows. The next time I emerged, Gerard was there too and soon, Constance. She had flown at once from Paris. I did not know then that those frock-coated gentlemen of the medical hierarchy had prophesied my immediate demise—by use of stimulants and rest, my heart—they said—could be kept pumping for a month at most. So cables went flying back and forth across the ocean—with a broken heart, I hadn't long to live.

Now weakened into non-resistance, the tears began to come. All the pent-up agony of months surged through me as I lay inert, awake or asleep, the tears flowed on. I was taken to a nursing home, presumably to die. I didn't care, but miraculously soon my heart hurt less, my tears began to dry, the children were brought into town to see me, Narcisse Noir with them.

Mine was a therapeutic chintz-hung room, filled with sunlight. I began to think about living, and the doctors began to think I could.

I believe the first time I smiled was the day Rosa Lewis barged through the portals of the nursing home and swept down the hallway (my room was on the ground floor), her entire staff in her train and, in her arms at least three goggle-eyed yapping Pomeranians. Beyond the herbaceous border of her large and bristling headpiece, I caught sight of Edith, the devoted secretary and companion, her arms stacked with covered dishes and, back of her, old William, the doorman, creaking at the knees, his brass buttons gleaming, several potted plants waving above his snowy head. Rosa Lewis was a world-famed character, she ran the most exclusive and, at the same time, inclusive hotel in Mayfair. Rosa, when twenty-two, had been very special cook to King Edward the Seventh, and it was at those small, but Lucullan bachelor dinners that Rosa dished up the bird and bottle and invariably, following in the wake of the savoury, appeared golden-haired, blue eyed and curvesome to sip a glass of port with the royal gentlemen—or so the legend goes. She was always at Cowes for the yachting and her bouillabaisse was the equal of any in Marseilles. Lord —— admiration was lifelong and gossip has it, that had Lady ——

not persisted in the picture, he might have offered Rosa his heart and hand—at any rate I believe he helped set her up in Jermyn Street where at the Cavendish she created one of the most succulent atmospheres of the era.

On arrival at the Cavendish, one was always welcomed as a very special and privileged guest, and was soon ushered into the big oval drawing room filled with myriad tables, cushiony armchairs, flowers in profusion, canaries in gilded cages and royalties in silver frames. Rosa's greetings were effusive and one was exaggeratedly introduced to the invariable coterie of lords and ladies (on their uppers), and to the glamorous, though often world-worn band of youths and divorcées, out for fun and frolic.

At each new arrival, William was summoned and a champagne cooler wheeled forward, then everyone drank the newcomer's health—if the price of the toast appeared on one's bill, it was to be accepted in part payment of the frolic.

In 1910, I had been taken there by my Uncle Will Barnum and Mr. and Mrs. Percy Chubb, a most respectable company of continental trippers,—but then we never reached the oval room. On my second visit in 1913, I was alone and at the mercy of the "set-up." I had gone to Rosa's hotel because I liked her and, besides, it was the only one I knew. I was royally welcomed —a little too royally for my taste, since the wily Duke of —— seemed to go with my suite—that was the impression I got until finally I had to poke him out with my new Briggs umbrella. Rosa also had a handsome Rolls with an unscrupulous chauffeur, which she'd offer her guests for an evening to and from the theatre, or a trip to the airport, but the amount that appeared on one's "note" for "transporation" was staggering. What had sounded like a gracious gesture turned out to be a bit of business. As soon as one learned to refuse the champagne and to say "I think I'll call a cab, thank you!" the bills became quite respectable—it was always the newcomer who paid the piper!

During World War I, Rosa met many American officers on leave from France. Dick Peabody, Puss Smith, Charlie Codman, Phil Wharton and other Harvardites were a few of her favourites and were constantly brought to mind by Rosa's tall tales. She later met Harry Crosby as my husband, but I remain to this day "Polly Jacob" and am forever eighteen when year after year I enter the now bomb-cracked portals of the Cavendish to say "Hello!" to an old but dauntless friend.

Before arriving at my bedside that morning Rosa must have stripped the Cavendish bare—hall, and cupboard and cellar—for, bringing up the rear, was the boots, his arms akimbo with Lanson '21.

"Now Lovey," she cajoled, "you must have some of this," and planted an icy bottle of bubbly firmly on my chest—"a bit of lark too," she said as Edith uncovered the steaming dish of lark pie—and waving and commanding she distributed the plants and flowers about the room as though a curtain were about to go up in Drury Lane. The dogs yapped, the nurses rushed in, the wheelchair patients gathered at the door. In no time glasses were produced, corks popped, and Rosa Lewis in her stellar role, beamed upon us all. "Polly Jacob!" she cried. "How did you ever get into such a place and why aren't you at the Cavendish? Tomorrow over you come—Edith and I will fix you up in no time! You'll get nothing but slop here." I did smile then, even might have laughed if my memory had not suddenly stabbed my heart with pain—for I remembered the Lanson '21 with Harry in the enormous fourposter in Jermyn Street, during the runaway days—but that morning before Rosa was driven from the arena, routed by nurses and attendants, I had picked at a lark's wing and sipped of the grape and found them good—from then on I began to mend!

As soon as I could be moved I went down to the Lymingtons' at Farleigh-Wallop and from there by plane back to Paris—but under strict orders not to strain my heart by any effort whatsoever. I was carried everywhere and engaged an athletic young valet to act as my porter. He wore a striped black-and-yellow waistcoat with crisp black sateen sleeves—they smelt new, and oddly, of hope.

Harry's father and mother both came over that June and we all tripped out to Rheims, invited by the Marquis and Marquise de Polignac (Nina was née Crosby). The château was vast and Victorian, but the gardens were beautiful, the food and wine perfection, and the welcome warm. Polleen and Billy were with me. I was coddled and cosseted, I even attended a gala dinner for wine growers, at which each guest drew his own wine from a silver spigot in front of his plate, a silver pipe ran round the table in a loop, through which the Pommery sparkled and splashed into an array of crystal.

Before they left for Boston, the Crosbys made me a present of a very smart town car, a Hotchkiss with a special landaulet-body built by Labourdette—it was canary yellow with black leather trimmings and they re-engaged Lucien to drive it, providing him with a beige whipcord uniform and black leather leggings. He looked as rakish as a storm trooper on a holiday. It was early summer by now and Paris was in bloom. I was still carried up and down stairs and tended by a devoted covey of servants, but I was beginning to crane my neck this way and that.

Billy had sailed for Boston under the wing of an old friend, Connie (Mrs. Puss) Smith; he was to go to Lenox School that autumn. Polly and I left by car in mid-July for the French Riviera. The Phil Barrys, with *The Animal Kingdom* a Broadway hit, had rented a house in Cannes for the summer, and we were invited to visit. We arrived in Cannes ahead of our hosts who had stopped off in Germany to see the motor show and invest in one of the fabulous German cars then being put on the continental market. (*The Animal Kingdom* was piling up royalties.) I didn't mind being alone for a while. I loved the bathing and the quiet of the gardens, the house was on a hill overlooking the sea.

In a few days Phil and Ellen put in an appearance, soon followed by the new car, delivered straight from the factory. A car super-exotic, red as a pepper and so underslung in construction that on its first appearance not only did it do a belly-whopper at the entrance to their drive, sticking fast astraddle the community gutter, but it also brought the whole town out to watch it being pried loose—this got Phil into such a state of nervous indignation that it nearly cost him his *objet d'art*—he was all for "hacking the damn thing free." Finally it was extricated and stood with gleaming nonchalance before the Barrys' doorway. Someone said : "Let's go down to the Casino for an apéritif." The car was unduly long but unduly narrow too. When Ellen got in the back, Dick Meyer at 14 stone or more could hardly squeeze in beside her, and looked as if he were riding in a pram. Phil sat beside the driver to take an object lesson, and the other guests and I followed in the Hotchkiss. At first all went well, indeed too well for the Barrys' sangfroid, people stood still and stared, even whooped and cheered, but when they swerved smartly into the Casino driveway, bang! the underpinnings sharply met the curb again, the the concave gutter, shallow as it was, held and cradled the chariot tight. Traffic jammed, urchins jumped for joy, out the Barrys piled, but luckily this time, once the passengers were eliminated, Frau Mercedes did heave herself free of the gutter. From then on our friends took the precaution of getting down at every crossing and walking their driveways; such untimely exhibitionism was hard to take, even for the most whimsical of playwrights.

At the end of that summer, I met Jacques Porel, son of the famed French actress Réjane, that is I remet him for the first time since he separated from his beautiful wife, and I had become a widow. It was a Saturday noon of early autumn in Paris. I had gone to call for my mail at the Bank in the Place Vendôme and Jacques had been there cashing dollars. We met in the revolving doors and revolved together out into the brisk sunshine. "Won't you lunch with me?" he invited. "Oh, no, thank you." I answered. I hadn't been out to lunch alone with an admirer as yet and I realized at once that Jacques could be an admirer. "Perhaps another day?" he offered. "Maybe, Monday," I parried, in the vain belief that Monday was safer than Saturday—and then I visualized a lonely luncheon on a tray and veered suddenly, "After all why not to-day!" Jacques appeared slightly startled at the excitement in my voice but assured me "Why not indeed." So off we went down the rue St. Honoré to the Crémaillière, the most fashionable small restaurant in Paris, and once inside that revolving door I realized the die was cast—all eyes turned upon us, most of the lunchers knew Jacques by sight, he was the Beau Brummell of his day, and not a few recognized me—tongues began to wag at once—now that I was there I decided to enjoy myself and Jacques proved charming, witty and full of tact—it was welcome fun at last and when we left each other in the rue de Lille without even a hint that we meet again, I knew that we both knew that we would.

It had started with luncheon at La Crémaillière and went from good to better.

There was the evening when we took the little Bateau Mouche down the Seine to the Riverside Café beyond Versailles. We had chewy snails oozing with butter and garlic, and a bottle of Chablis, and double cream and wild strawberries from the woods of a nearby château. We sipped Armagnac as we plopped snail shells over the railing of the balcony into the smooth gliding river at our elbow. After this on the Champs Elysées there were fruit-filled sherry cobblers as tall as towers.

There was a luncheon in a thunderstorm at Melun, with Roquefort and Burgundy and the mechanical piano that played "Et puis ça va" over and over again while our toes touched under the table on the sanded floor and we talked of 'Eloise and Abélard' and 'Harry and Caresse' and when we finally ate our way out of Paris there was fish soup at a quayside table in Marseilles in the shadow of the ochre sails, while the tarred hulls of a fishing feet flocked all around us . . .

. . . and at night there was cold lobster and vin rosé on a balcony by an indigo sea.

Together that autumn in the library where the B.S.P. had been conceived in '27 we two mapped out a new venture. The Crosby Continental Editions, twelve francs or one shilling the copy, reprints of *avant garde* literature. Tauchnitz with reprints of the classics was the only English paper edition then in the field although very soon both the Penguin and the Albatross flapped their pinfeathers.

That is how Jacques Porel came to be associated with the Black Sun Press, and that is when such lovely books as *Grand Meaulnes, Diable au Corps* and *Vol de Nuit* came to my attention.

Although Jacques knew all the *jeunesse dorée* and the *jeunesse douée* of Paris, he was no better at finance that I was, and though Hemingway, Faulkner, Kay Boyle, Dorothy Parker and other exciting American writers appeared in the C.C.E. along with the best of the French, the C.C.E. took a big loss at the end of the year, and by 1935, had quite eaten itself up—but it brought me back onto the literary scene not with a whimper but a bang!

CHAPTER 30

That winter, "to hide the damage," I planned a semi-"embroidered" Christmas in New York. Billy was at Lenox School now and I was going to take Polleen across with me so that we could all spend his holidays together and I had ordered some lovely demideuil clothes from Schiaparelli. My mother had found a furnished apartment for me at 825 Fifth Avenue, it had a balcony overlooking the Zoo, we all loved that, I, not so much, because I was frightened to death they might fall over; as it turned out it was not the children I should have felt nervous about.

Roland Toutin, acrobatic movie star, who had crossed with us, did feats upon the ledge that made my heart curl. He knew how, but other guests seemed tempted to try too. One young man with a wounded ego was saved from a backward plunge by a waistcoat button.

The first dinner in my honour was given by Marie and Averell Harriman in Sixty-eighth Street where we were eighteen at table, with a Derain portrait of Marie over her shoulder and a Van Gogh of Van Gogh over the fireplace. The other rooms also held treasures.

I was the subject par excellence for speculation that season. How had I weathered fate's blunder? was the question. Was I as hedonistic as the old wives told? That evening a plot had been woven by my host and hostess of which I was quite unaware—Jim Forrestal had apparently been among my most staunch believers at the time of Harry's death and he was also a great friend of the Harrimans, but he never went out to dinner parties. This time however he was led to understand it would be a quiet evening à *quartre* and he had taken the bait, explaining that his wife Jo already had a dinner—"some big affair," he said, "I refused, so I'm free!"—he didn't realize that he was being invited to the self-same party. He hardly ever accepted and Josephine often went alone.

When I arrived one of the first, he was already there. I hadn't seen him for years, though I had known him well. We became engrossed in each other as the room filled up, then suddenly "Mrs. James Forrestal" was announced, her entrance was charged with electricity, neither he nor she had expected to see the other that evening. At dinner I sat on Averell's right with Jim on mine. Had the dinner taken place sixteen years later, in official Washington, I would have had to be a very V.I.P. to rate that place of honour.

After dinner, drinking coffee with the ladies, I chose a green mint from the tray while I stood before the fireplace. My low-cut black crêpe (Schiaparelli said it was the best dress she ever designed) was supplemented by a little white chiffon bolero, long tight sleeves attached to a great trailing sash. I wore Harry's last present, my beautiful diamond necklace (penance for Prudence) and my jade and diamond earrings, green mint was the perfect accessory to that *toilette*. I looked my best and I guessed that I was cresting the breakers of society's opinion. My path through that winter promised to be carpeted.

I saw a lot of Jim Forrestal for the next few years. It was he who first introduced me to Canada Lee. Jim rang me up late one night to tell me about the play at the Fourteenth Street Playhouse, *Stevedore* was the title and the rôle was played by an extraordinary Negro actor. Would I go with him the next evening? He wanted to see it again. So we dined together in the Village and went. I was just as enthusiastic as he was and back stage I met Canada. That winter I saw the play many times, even travelling as far as Chicago to be with the troupe when they opened there.

I have realized since that Jim Forrestal's friendship was one that I should have knit more closely during the World War II years while he was Secretary of Defense, instead of allowing it to unravel to such a tragic end. What I heard and observed in Washington made me both apprehensive and unhappy. I wrote him several times and tried to appeal to him through orthodox channels but he had already fled the open spaces and seemed to me to be hacking his way into a monstrous jungle of his own making. Just before I left for England in '49 I sent him one more message, together with the *Manifesto for Individual Secession into World Community* published by the Black Sun Press the spring before that in Paris—he made no comment and he died by his own hand while I was still in Europe.

While Polleen and I were in America that Christmas, Jacques came following after, he had presumably travelled across the ocean to visit his married sister in Boston but New York proved far too tempting. Jacques was so spirited and full of charm that he soon became the most sought-after cosmopolite in town. I was seeing a lot of my old friends and he and I drifted apart, he still possessed a key to the Press, but it no longer fitted my heart and when I sailed away, Jacques stayed on as the cavalier of a much publicized New York matron. I was rather dismayed, but he promised to be back in Paris when he was needed at the B.S.P.

So the return to France was unescorted, though it might have been with Scott Fitzgerald.

This is the story of Scott Fitzgerald and the chamois gloves— if I had not handed back the chamois gloves, he never would have left the ship.

"I planted them in your cabin just now," he said. "I only need one small excuse to sail." "I know," I smiled, as I edged him nearer the gangplank, and "as much as I want you to, it would be mad." "But I thought *you were* mad, Caresse."

This is, as I remember, our conversation as the ship's whistles blew and the gangplank started to sway on the evening of the one day I spent with Scott Fitzgerald. In fact, the only time we ever met.

It happened that Louis Bromfield and his entire family, which included Mary and the girls, George Hawkins, his genial manager, two nurses and a dog, were returning to France on the Baltimore Mail Line. He had told me it was much less expensive than the big liners and actually more luxurious, for the cabins were large and the food good, and the bartender, he said, was supplied with the best of ingredients. There would be so few passengers to bother about that one could relax for ten long days. I had had a hectic month in New York so the rest cure appealed and I was sure that Polleen would be happier in open-air luxury than in a tourist cabin on the *Europa*. So I switched our tickets and began to re-plan our sailing. The rub was that one had to leave from Baltimore, and no boat train. It was each for himself and baggage and bundles to be delivered to the pier at least three hours before sailing.

Polleen had a school friend living there and she and her governess were to take Polleen to lunch, and then on to the dock with all our luggage, since they could supply a station wagon and chauffeur. In the meantime I decided it would be a fine idea to call Scott Fitzgerald whom I had never met and arrange to lunch with him. On the telephone it went beautifully. He would wear a red carnation. He would meet me in the bar of the Lord Baltimore at twelve, he would take me to lunch, he would see that I reached the pier by two—I was delighted—and quite unaware of the hurricane signals that were already up, even on dry land.

In New York, Mama and Len saw us off at Penn Station at 8.30 a.m. and a rather strange assortment of friends turned up as well. I had no idea that some of my exotic midnight pals would look so wan at eight. I met a trembling Narcisse Noir there too, brought by the vet, in a new Abercrombie and Fitch travelling coat, and I accepted, besides farewell flowers and books, a case of champagne splits, delivered by Lehman Brothers where I had made generous friends.

The porters did a bit of grumbling, as porters will, but finally we managed to get stowed away and off on the first leg of our economical journey. At the Lord Baltimore my daughter's friends were waiting, the mound of bags and bundles were piled into their station wagon. I said I'd join them at the dock at two, and gave Polly her tickets so they could get things aboard as soon as they arrived; all was progressing well. I waved them good-bye and adding a bit of carmine to my lips and a bit of Bruyère des Alps behind the ears I confidently entered the bar. It was 12.15 but no Scott—so I sat down and told the waiter I would order when the gentleman arrived—but no gentleman arrived though someone who was no gentleman insisted on joining me. I got up flurried and went to the telephone. I had forgotten the number which I had had from a friend in New York. The operator could find no record of Scott Fitzgerald whatsoever. I was furious, and then I heard my name being paged. I was wanted on the telephone. My barroom friend retreated. It was Scott full of apologies, he had been working, he said, forgot the time, etc., etc. Would I jump in a cab and come to the house? Did I like beer? I didn't, but answered, "Love it." If it hadn't been for the barroom beau I'd have gone back and had a snifter by myself.

We drew up in front of a rather sinister-looking house, and as I remember, I had to go around to the back to get in. Scott answered the door in a flapping dressing-gown, hair tousled, but with a smile that unlatched my heart. "So you're Caresse Crosby," he said.

"And you are *you*."

He had a glass of beer in one hand and in the other, one for me. We sat down on a divan littered with books and papers. We both talked at once. He baffled me, and I believe I must have baffled him. He told me that Zelda was in the hospital and his little daughter came home from school only on weekends. He lived quite alone, did his own cooking, and he vowed he was going to cook me a lunch fit for a queen, but he never got round to it. He lured me into confessions and regressions (but no transgressions). I was getting a bit confused on charm when through the sympathetic haze I heard the long-drawn wail of a ship's siren. "What's that," I asked, alarmed. "Your Baltimore Mail calling its mate." "But it's hardly two," I said, looking at a static clock. "Does it go?" "I'll ask Central," he drawled. To my horror it was three-thirty. The boat was scheduled to sail at four, and I had told Polly I'd meet her at two. "I'll get a taxi," I moaned. "I must rush." "Impossible," he said, swaying slightly. "I will drive you myself in the family coach, but first I must dress." I was frantic, "In fact I will begin from the socks up," he continued.

It seemed he was bent on torturing me for he took hours over each decision as to the choice of socks and tie and suit. Finally,

280

he was ready and looked very smart indeed. "Now I'll 'chercher la car,'" he said. I asked if it were far, but he replied that it was waiting under the back shed, and there we found it—a real antique—and it took precious minutes to get it going; at last we backed destructively out and headed, it seemed to me, away from the sea. The ship's sirens were pleading again. "Hurry, please," I urged. "They won't leave without Caresse Crosby," he teased. "I'm not so sure," I retorted. Just then he slammed on the brakes. "My yellow gloves," he exclaimed, in just the same tone as the white rabbit in *Alice in Wonderland*, and he swung sharply around. "I can't see you off without my chamois gloves and my malacca cane, whatever was I thinking of!" And we were chugging back the way we had come. I could have yelled in exasperation.

In front of his door he leapt out saying he would only take a minute, and indeed he did reappear almost at once with a yellow cane and a pair of new canary-coloured gloves. "We were going the wrong way," he announced, "so we haven't lost any time," and then we headed harbourwards.

The ride seemed endless, it was nearly four-thirty, we should have sailed at four, and perhaps we had. "Relax," he told me, "they are holding your child and luggage on board as hostage." That was so, I thought, but just then we bumped over the railroad sidings and headed down the pier, deserted now except for one forlorn group of trunks and bags and a little girl perched on a champagne case, her arms around a trembling whippet. The ship's gangplanks were up, all but one, and everyone else on board. We tooted wildly and Polly waved and Narcisse barked. The ship's mate came running toward us and the ship's siren blasted an impolite welcome.

"I was all on," quavered Polly, "but they took me off again," and indeed the purser was very angry; however, I do think that the sight of the imposing figure by my side complete with cane and gloves, somewhat mollified the situation.

Scott insisted on going on board with us, though there seemed no time at all. He carried my dressing case to the cabin. "This is fine," he said, "I think I'll stay." A surge of horror swept over me, he might be serious; enticing as such an idea would have been at any other time, the thought of combining Scott

Fitzgerald with my promised rest cure was not for me. We went back to the upper deck to join Polly at the rail, the boat really was about to sail this time. I pushed him not too gently toward the gangplank. "I could go with you," he said, "I brought my cheque book." It was then I took the chamois gloves, that he had dropped in the cabin, from my purse, He accepted them with a sigh. "It has been a fitting occasion," he said. "I shall never wear them again." And he kissed me solemnly. The gangplank was already rising in the air when he landed on the pier and there he stood in farewell salute, leaning on the malacca cane, waving the chamois gloves slowly back and forth above his head.

Perhaps it was just as well that we never met again!

CHAPTER 31

While I had been in New York the list of potential C.C.E.
authors had mounted and I still continued to publish the editions
de luxe, *Alice in Wonderland* illustrated by Marie Laurencin,
Archie MacLeish's *New Found Land, The Bridge,* by Hart Crane
(begun in 1929) and *James Joyce's Collected Poems* were some
of the titles produced during the early 30's. It was sad that the
Black Sun couldn't have expanded then, but I had no capital,
although I had lots of encouragement. We circulated publicity
broadsides among prospective buyers that now are collectors'
items, one reason being that I went all the way to Berlin to
find the special inks, greens and browns, for this and other de
luxe jobs. The German inks were so good that a day after sheets
were printed they could be put to soak in a pan of water and
the impression emerged just as crisp and clear as when it had
left the press.

This inking process had been important in the printing, 1929,
of *Sentimental Journey* with engravings by Polia Chentoff, tiny
Russian artist. The text was in bistre but the titles and decorations, by Polia, in apple green. In order to print the green the
sheets had to be damp, so first we ran the bistre, then dunked
them and ran them through again for a second colour impression.

Harry and I had discovered Polia together at the Salon
d'Automne in 1928, where we both fell under the spell of her
painting *First Communion*. We bought it; it had won a prize.
But soon Polia became entirely Harry's as so many of our mutual

enthusiasms did—in the process she painted the strange portentous portrait which he reproduced as a frontispiece to his *Chariot of the Sun*. She also painted one of me and this portrait now hangs in my house in Washington where the poet St. J. Perse (*Anabase, Eloges*) drops in from time to time to gaze at it with concerned admiration. I promised several years ago to leave it to him in my will. He says he has never seen the distaste of one woman for another so skilfully and subtly portrayed. Harry's portrait exists no longer, for on returning to Paris after his death, I found it so metaphysically disturbing that I put it to the torch (as Harry had done to *Red Skeletons* a year before).

As I said, I flew off to Berlin to buy paints for the B.S.P. and this trip included two other missions, one to search out George Grosz whose drawings I admired and desired—we had never met, but I felt we should—the other mission, to enjoy Berlin in the company of Baron Berni W—U—, he had been an admirer for years but during those years I had been a married woman, now I felt free to amuse myself "under the lindens," especially as Jacques was still dancing his evenings away on the starlit roof of the Waldorf. He actually had the *culot* to call me long distance from his ringside table a few nights before, and it was in delighted retaliation that I boarded an "airlift" for Berlin.

All missions were accomplished, including a prophetic encounter that followed, but first I travelled attic stairs to find my coveted artist. No Narcisse Noir to tug the leash, no Picasso at the top of this stairway, but bleak shady hallways, with whiffs of Sauerbraten in the permanent air. *"Sieben,"* the suspicious porter had grumbled, then *"ganz oben"* he added in cheerful defiance, delighted at the trek ahead of me. I saw him leering out at me from the artist's canvases when I finally reached my destination. I had not let Grosz know I was coming, first because he had no telephone, I couldn't write German either, and also because a beeline is the quickest distance between two points.

He looked astonished when he opened to my staccato knock, but in two words he understood my errand. I always come to the point at once so much so that sometimes I omit politeness, due I think to a self-conscious desire not to bother or to bore.

My wish is to be welcomed at once or to get out, but if perchance I do encounter hostility it really whets my determination!

If George Grosz had set the stage for our meeting it couldn't have been more in character. He had the typical German-artist-in-an-attic look. His beret awry, his faded smock cobwebbed with colours; the cracked skylight, the riddled water pitcher, the cot-bed with its sagging springs, and the wealth of work, all were there—not like Picasso's, spread all about through half a dozen rooms, but pushed and piled, swaying and toppling from the four corners of this heavenlit garret.

I murmured "Flechtheim," who was his dealer—the best in Berlin or, except for Vollard, in the world—I produced my card with "Black Sun Press," in the corner and I fell at once into admiration before his work.

We talked in French, first about Paris and then about New York. At once my plan for a book of his great satiric drawings of Nazidom emerged. I looked at hundreds. I was excited and sure. He was excited, but not so sure *of me*. Indeed, I was a bolt from the blue or perhaps from the black—he would of course have to check with his dealer, but confessed that he very much wanted to illustrate Hemingway. He asked me if I couldn't arrange it with Hemingway, but I was not so sure of Hemingway. We promised to write each other, and I blew out as unexpectedly as I had blown in. (It was already lunch time at the Adlon!) That book of drawings did not materialize immediately, but it was finally accomplished in New York in 1934—*Interregnum,* eighty lithographs by George Grosz with reproductions by George Miller, printed by Joseph Blumenthal, introduction by John dos Passos ("Satire as a Way of Seeing") and edited by Caresse Crosby—it won a Graphic Arts prize as one of the fifty best books of the year—a tribute to those four geniuses whom I had so successfully bound together.

A prophecy I made on that trip turned up nearly twenty years later among my mother's letters while she was sorting them out one rainy day.

"Do you remember this?" she asked me. The postcard was dated 1931. And it was into the fascinating but not then famous face of Marlene Dietrich that I now gazed, and underneath it was the name of a Berlin night spot. On it I had written, "Berni took me to a dive last night, we heard this lovely creature sing. I told her she should come to America, I'm sure she would go far."

My mind leapt back to the kaleidoscopic evening, and the dubious entertainment along the Wilhelmstrasse, plenty of forbidden fruit was offered, both sweet and tart, but the pure glamour of Marlene's act, the husky fascination of her voice and those lovely legs, which strutted her about through the smoke and the din, had captivated me at once. Berni introduced us. That autumn in Paris I saw her in her first film, *The Blue Angel,* but it could not top the entertainment I experienced that evening in Berlin.

I flew back to Paris overweight with rainbow tubes of ravishing ink just in time to meet Jacques Porel's boat at Le Havre, for I'd wired, "I'll be on the dock," not quite in time at that. He was still sulking in his cabin when all the other passengers had gone ashore, but the proof of my industry and serious intent (those inks) while he had been frolicking in New York and lolling out at sea mollified and shamed him into contrition. In fact, Jacques was so contrite that he accepted the idea of carrying on at the Press by himself while I accepted the Embericos' invitation to be part of a glamour cruise to Greece and back, whither we would take off the very next week.

I had been installed in the Roussy de Sales' entrancing little *pavillon* in the rue Monsieur ever since my return from the U.S. a month before. It was as toy-like and as scenic as a Boutet de Monvel nursery rhyme—the maids wore mob caps and I'd inherited a tabby cat, a milkman with a horn, a carriage block and a very first Picasso—*The Bull Fight.* Count Raoul de Roussy de Sales (he was acting for me then as American distributor of Black Sun Books) had stayed on in New York to work and to write. I loved and admired Raoul, his wife Reine too, but above all, his transcendental courage and purpose. Though a young man when we met, he was a very ill one and he died only a few years later. His final book was an outstanding success and justified the difficult years he had spent upon it—but that spring they had rented me, practically given me, their enchanting Paris maisonette.

During the week that followed, between mornings at the press and afternoons at the couturier, I gave several well-planned little luncheons with Jacques as the guiding genius.

To the first one came the Aurics, George the muscian and Nora, his cherub-haired wife. The Bourdets, he the author of *La Prisonnière* and she his *mondaine* spouse. Also, the Dalis, Salvador the Catalonian surrealist and Gala, the erstwhile Madame Paul Eluard, and René Crevel, the gifted surrealist writer of *Babylone, Les Pieds dans le Plat*. Dali in his memoirs has chronicled that luncheon at which he and I met for the first time and which—he says—was entirely white. According to him, we ate cream of celery soup, breast of chicken with rice, little boiled onions, blancmange with cream and to finish off, marshmallows with white mint. He also said that I wore white shoes and *white* stockings, so of course, I don't believe the rest!

To another luncheon, as I recall, came Howard Sturges and Cole Porter, who lived in the adjacent rue Madame, Kit Wood, an English painter and world charmer, Vera Mazuchi, a husky-voiced White Russian, party-giver-and-goer, and Naps (Lord Napier) Alington, known as the most delightful man in the world, also Elsa Schiaparelli, already famed for finery, who had designed the clothes for my pending journey.

I really hated to sail away just then, but Hellas' siren voice was singing and Polleen's Easter vacation was at hand. Mrs. Crosby was giving us the trip for my birthday present, we would be back in Paris for part of May and all of June, and summer at the Mill was waiting to flutter the calendar round the corner after June. Days were full to bursting, the only time for loneliness was at dawn. "If two lie together" etc.

CHAPTER 32

Andy Embericos was one of the most sought after bachelors in Paris; his uncle owned one of the most important merchant fleets trading between Greece and Italy, and Andy had the genial idea of getting together, for enjoyment *and* exploitation, a group of Parisiens worthy to be internationally publicized! His plan was to arrange a voyage de luxe of about fifteen personalities to leave Paris, via Brindisi, for Athens and back—all of them together in one of his uncle's luxury cargo ships.

Parties were to be given along the way, a cameraman was to take pictures at every stop from the platform at the Gare de l'Est to the ledge before the oracle at Delphi—in order to embrace all coverages. Andy chose brilliantly, first (but that was the rub, each one of us felt we were first) among his prímum dons and prima donnas I am sure he placed Lady Mendl— she was such good copy in any clime—and with her, of course, went either Tony Montgomery or Johnny MacMullen (they flew to her side by turns). Next, Marquise de Joucourt, and Princess Faucigny-Lucinge always in *Vogue* or *Harpers* and reported at every chic event in Paris—her husband, Johnny, joined us in Rome—there were Marcel Achard, the Paris playwright then in the limelight, and Juliette, his gay and giddy wife; Jacques Février, pianist and composer and number-one snob of the Paris salons (he covered music). There was Raymonde Heudebert, socialite wife of a rich industrialist, and a sculptress to boot, a titian-haired beautiful lady, who added much glamour to our group. There were Professor and Madame Goldschmidt, for intellectual ballast, and last, but certainly indispensable, the representatives of the U.S.A., my fourteen-year-old daughter

46. Polleen, St. Moritz, 1934.

47. Kay Boyle, Caresse, Spring, 1935—
    ski-ing at Beuil above Nice.

Caresse with Maître Imprimeur Lescaret
    at the Black Sun Press.

49. Black Sun Press. Outside No. 2,
    rue Cardinale, Paris.

50. Hampton Manor designed by Thomas Jefferson. Winter, 1939.

Polly and I, the American widow and child (the Daisy Miller touch). You can see how astute young Embericos was.

As I remember, Antoine offered us *coiffure de voyage*—Hermès *mallettes de voyage*—Schiaparelli *manteaux de voyage*—Roberts *selles de voyage*—we were hung with offerings like Christmas trees. I am still wearing Schiaparelli's luggage brown tweed, twenty years later, which goes to show that such enterprise is not only worthy, but indestructible.

We left a sleety Paris to the clicking of cameras and arrived in Rome the following afternoon to the chirping of spring. Polly and I found it hard to resist the gallant advances of the Italian sidewalk dandies. In uniform and out they were resplendent and always awaiting our slightest glance to break into warm Italian smiles. We returned to our hotel loaded down with fruits and flowers and our tummies rounded with spaghetti. That night there was opera, and the next night Princess San Faustino was to give a ball in our collective honour —I had a beautiful new dress for such an occasion and I knew it was going to be a fabulous party, but when the Achards and the Goldschmidts said they were planning to leave at two for a night in Naples and would rejoin the party at Brindisi, I decided to forego the ball and show Polly Naples instead.

I had not been there since 1926, when Harry and I rowed out to meet the *Mauretania* and scared his mother and father pink as we bobbed about in the wash of the liner. Safe ashore, we had visited the aquarium and museum and then we four took the trans-Mediterranean boat for Palermo. I now wanted to revisit the perky sea horses in the aquarium and the *fa niente* gods and goddesses in the museum, and shop in the open-air market where island treasures and delicacies abounded. We had a full day there, all said, even managing a quick motor trip to Pompeii and Amalfi, where we lunched in a hanging garden above the sea and were not at all sorry to have left the Roman cavalcade behind. The Professor waxed very jocose on Amalfi *vino* and told some rare stories; the Achards were, as always, the best of company. Polly, rather like a colt at a country fair, pranced from one objective to another, her thin legs twinkling beneath blue serge and her long flying tresses reminding me of my own Rosemary school days in far-off Connecticut.

We returned to Naples to catch a four o'clock train for Brindisi, where we were scheduled to board the ship some time before evening, for she was to sail at dawn for Venice. When we reached the harbour, there was our carrier directly in front of the little quayside hotel, the Traveller's Rest, as I remember, or some such inappropriate title. We had had dinner on the train and, tired out, were looking forward to an early sleep aboard, and so was the Roman contingent. Jacques Février met us on the gangplank in pyjamas and a becoming Charvet dressing-gown, a glass of bromo seltzer (or its equivalent) in his hand—the ladies, he said, had already retired—Elsie Mendl having wired for a special masseur to be on hand was having her deservedly famous legs rubbed down as she did at every *étape*. Tony had departed along the waterfront looking for local colour. Bags of flour were being loaded by a silhouetted line of humming stevedores, the harbour lights beckoned sweetly in the distance, it was poetic and restful, so we all repaired to our cabins. Polly and I had a very charming cabin in white and blue and gold with a bath adjoining (the Embericos had done us well). We were soon in bed and "lights out" seemed to be the order all along the stateroom deck. It was about eleven p.m. when the first rumblings occurred, surely not Mt. Aetna in eruption, I thought, and then the boat began to vibrate gently as the strange sound grew. It was as though hard coal were bounding down a chute just underneath our bunks. This increased until the roar was deafening. I rang for the steward.

"We are loading cargo," he answered. "And what is the cargo?" "Nuts," was his answer, if it had not been in Italian, I should have thought he was being impolite. We twisted and turned. Polly stuffed cotton in our ears, but to no avail—the avalanche was infernal. Hard little hazel nuts, millions of them pouring into our bottom, and the dust that arose began to make us sneeze. There was a tap at our door—it was Jacques.

"*Quelle horreur,*" he shouted above the din. "I am going across to the hotel for a beer, I cannot sleep, can you?" We agreed we couldn't, and Polly and I, in proper dressing-gowns, padded after him down the gangplank. When we reached the hotel parlour Marcel Achard, a black necktie wound over his eyes, was already there stretched out upon a masochistic couch.

"They say it will go on all night, '*quel toupet.*'" One by

one in various states of undress, the others wandered in exhausted and mad as hornets. "Why weren't we told it was a nut ship?" said Juliette, and jokes ensued that were hardly repeatable. Jacques had roused a *camelieri* who brought us beer and then into our disgruntled midst, in majestic sequence, marched Lady Mendl, her head swathed in chiffon to cover the curlers, her gem-heavy jewel case held firmly against her stomach, followed by masseur, maid and midshipman.

"Where's Tony?" she demanded; unfortunately, we all could guess. "Find him," she said, pointing an accusing finger at the sailor, "and telephone for a limousine at once. I am motoring to Venice. I will join the ship there tomorrow. I will go mad if I remain here another minute." The nuts went on rattling like thunder in our ears, and re-echoed along the vibrant waterfront no matter where we hid. Soon Tony came dejectedly back from his midnight prowl and got busy on the wire. Somewhere, somehow, an elegant Isotta Frascini, complete with chauffeur, was uncovered. Elsie invited any of us who cared to to join her. It meant some seven pounds per person, and if I wanted to, we couldn't have, but Baba Lucinge did go along, which was fitting for a princess! The rest of us drank beer and dozed intermittently, windows and doors shut against the roar. At about two a.m. the Professor and wife arrived in nightgowns and quilted robes, looking more professorial than in the day. They brought with them their precious box of Sedebrol—a jug of boiling water was ordered, and each of us partook of a double dose of the soporific bouillon—soon after, our heads hung so heavily that one by one we slid back to our quarters. As each one left the parlour, he pronounced the word "nuts."

Needless to say we were already nearing Venice when we awoke the next day. There Lady Mendl and retinue joined us with such a horrifying description of their night that we all felt quite pleased with ours. At Venice, each one got off his own special brand of telegram to organizer Andy Embericos—(in the U.S. they would not have passed the censor). We only touched at Venice for we were to debark there on our return and all had planned to stay a week or more on our way home.

It was almost hot in Athens that week, and the first day we ventured forth in summer linens, I went hunting for the most international bookshop in town, and I found "Aetos" just under

291

the colonnade alongside our hotel. I introduced myself to Mr. A., the proprietor, and after snooping about a bit among the shelves, I asked him if he knew some insurgent young poet that I could meet, one who would lead me to the literary rebels of Athens. He reflected a split-second and then asked if I would keep shop for him for five minutes; of course, I said "yes" and he was off. In precisely five minutes he returned with a beautiful young Greek in tow—manuscripts dripping from beneath his nervous arm, his hair on end, a decidedly poetic look in his rebellious eye.

"I think this is who you are looking for," said Mr. A. and beamingly introduced us. "Madame Crosby, Monsieur Calamaris." I couldn't have been more gratified; he was far finer than I had hoped for. The shop was about to close up for the afternoon recess.

"May I take you and your daughter to lunch?" the poet invited. This was too good to be true—he was solvent as well as poetic. I accepted with a sigh of delight. During our stay, Nicholas Calamaris (Calas now) was our constant cavalier, and I was the envy of all my cruisemates, men and women alike.

While in Athens, I fed the flame of Nico's appetite for Paris to such good end that the following spring found him in France, a frequent visitor to the Mill, and soon an ardent disciple of that leader of surrealism, André Breton, whom he encountered at one of my aestival weekends. I remember pointing out André where he stood, fishing rod in hand, beside Valentine Hugo on that rustic bridge over the mill stream beyond the sheep pasture. André was ceremoniously dressed in dark double-breasted suit with high black button shoes, a stiff collar and a flowing tie. Valentine Hugo looked like a figure from Godey's *Ladies Book* in an elaborate black dress that swept the planks of the bridge, a high lace collar boned behind the ears, kid gloves and an enormous straw hat tied under her chin with a swathe of violet tulle. His leonine head and her fantastic headpiece etched the skyline hour after hour as they pontifically fished where no fish were—if there ever was a surrealist conception of the gentle art it was there portrayed—and quite logically, these arch surrealists were the only ones who ever *did* try fishing at the Mill.

CHAPTER 33

Midsummer. Jacques and I motored back to Paris from Cannes via Biarritz—to do this, one passed along the coast as far as Sete, then Carcassonne and on across the foothills of the Pyrennees through remote little Basque villages. We had friends at Biarritz and it was while visiting them that we decided to go across the Spanish border into St. Sebastian to see the American bull-fighter, Franklin, make his début in that arena. Ernest Heming-way had told us that he would be there too; he was writing a book on bullfighting and we arranged to meet at an appointed rendezvous near the bullring—a corner café frequented by toreadors, and one where Hemingway must have found much of his local colour.

Hemingway, Pauline and his eldest son, a boy of about six, were there already. The child Bumbi was being given lessons in the handling of the cape by one of the elderly fighters, already retired. When we arrived at the bistro, we found Hem-ingway straddling a chair in a far corner, the old Spaniard explaining an intricate manœuvre. The boy had to repeat it again and again; his father was a difficult taskmaster, and Bumbi's face was puckered with apprehension. He was very nearly ready for tears. Our advent seemed a happy interruption, to him at least.

Hemingway got up, arranged with the *torero* for another lesson, told his son that he would have to do better next time, and led us all out to the terrace, where Pauline was waiting and where we drank sherry, and ate what I think was a ragout of kid, cooked in Marsala wine. Ernest had engaged a box for the fight next to the President's, and every bit as good, and to my delight I found myself rubbing elbows with Charlie Chaplin, who was in the grand official box. When the ear was cut from the final bull, the torero offered it with historic ritual to the purposely flustered Chaplin, who waved and kissed his hands to applauding thousands in his most coy Chaplinesque manner. It was a wonderful day. We left Franklin and Hemingway waiting for Chaplin at the same corner bistro, where we had met earlier. We were sorry to leave, but there was to be a fancy dress ball that night in Biarritz.*

. . . "*Caresse Crosby a inventé le Soutien Gorge et Hemingway*," announced the headline in a Paris paper when I visited France in '48. I was on my way home from the Italian elections at the time. My readers by now know that I *did* invent the brassière, but for their peace of mind they should know that I did *not* invent Hemingway, although I managed to make him whopping mad . . .

I had already published *Torrents of Spring* in the Crosby Continental Editions, but that was a "first" for Europe only— it may be said that Europe was delighted not with the Hemingway alone, but with all the other American titles in the series, Faulkner's *Sanctuary*, Dorothy Parker's *Laments for the Living*, Kay Boyle's *Year Before Last*, etc., etc. However, I coveted a real honest-to-Hemingway original, a limited edition de luxe, just so many copies signed by the author, at an elevated price —the Press had done it before with Joyce, Lawrence, Crane, MacLeish—why not Hemingway?

It was on my return from Spain that I decided the Black Sun should have one legitimate Hemingway to its credit.

He and Pauline were stopping at a little left-bank hotel about halfway between the Press in the rue Cardinale and my apartment in the rue de Lille.

Narcisse and I walked over one fine noon and found the Hemingways still not up (much the best way to be at noon). On the big bed between them was propped a painting by

---

* Unwittingly we had driven away with all the Hemingway passports. See Appendix.

Juan Gris, of a guitar player, it was a beauty, and Ernest had just acquired it the day before. He ruefully remarked that it took nearly all the passage money for their return trip to the United States, scheduled for a few weeks later, they were hurrying to get back home, Pauline said, so that their next son could be born with the benefit of presidency.

With true publisher instinct I saw my opening, here was a fine gambit. "I could pay you for the story at once," I suggested, "if you do need money for the tickets." But Ernest was not to be taken that easily. "I'll have to know just what you want first, and see what I have to give you." I answered that I knew he was doing a book on bullfighting. "But it's not written yet." "What about writing some of it for me?' I could publish part of it as I did with Joyce's *Work in Progress*." This seemed to interest him. "How many words would you want?" (An echo of Joyce's voice in my ear) and I answered as Harry and I had answered Joyce.

"Whatever you care to give me, but enough to make a book, it will be a limited edition, and if you will sign a hundred copies I can sell them extra high so that we need not print over five hundred in all which can only delight your publishers."

"Scribners," he said.

"I know," I rejoined, "Perkins won't mind."

He wouldn't say yes, but he didn't say anything, so I only asked him to let me know in plenty of time before he sailed.

"Sure," he acknowledged, and put his arms protectingly around his Gris, as though to say "to hell with the B.S.P." Pauline kept very quiet. Narcisse and I stalked down the cabbage-perfumed stairs not quite as cockily as we had pranced up!

It was two days later that I received a rather frantic call. "I am here at the Line," he told me. "I'm having difficulty over the passage. The sailings are crowded, they want me to pay now, and I'm a little short. Could you let me have the advance this morning?"

"Then I'll get the manuscript," I answered.

"Sure you'll have it by the first of the week." He picked up the cheque at noon and I showed him *The Escaped Cock* by Lawrence, and Joyce's *Tales Told of Shem and Shaun,* so he'd have an idea of what I was planning. I said I would have the sub-title page set up before he sailed so he could sign a hundred copies, and he swore that I'd get the necessary text in less than a week. He had it written, he admitted, but he wanted to work it up a bit. It was part of the new book.

Monday came and no manuscript. I was not idle, however, for the edition was taking form in my imagination, and I believed that if de Chirico (I was being untrue to Grosz) could be persuaded to do a frontispiece (matador subject seemed right for him) the edition would leap in value. I went round to Le Divan, a small gallery near the Deux Magots Café on the Place St. Germain about two hundred yards from my office, for it was there that de Chirico exhibited his work from time to time—but the artist himself was rarely seen in Paris. I explained the idea to the lady in charge of the *boutique* and she was delighted, but thought it would be very difficult to make a rendezvous. Could I not write him? I was sure that my written French would be incomprehensible, I'd have to show de Chirico some of the Black Sun Books and also I guessed I would have to wave my hands a good deal to get the idea across. She invited me to return the next day at five and to bring Hemingway's text with me, she'd do her best to trap de Chirico at that hour. He was known to be unmanageable.

Tuesday came and no manuscript, and Tuesday was dwindling. I knew that the Hemingways had to sail on Saturday. I sent them round a note and waited, still nothing happened. Disappointed, but determined, I went to meet de Chirico. I was half an hour late, the voluble saleslady was beside herself with anxiety. She had, it seems, frantically shut the man up in her office. "He's dangerous," she hissed, and shaking her head she locked the street door behind her and prodded me ahead of her as though he were the bull and I was to be the toreador— when the office door opened, out burst de Chirico head down, tail up and charged me—he was in riding boots and corduroy jacket, his hair fell over his eyes like a forelock, he looked ferocious, and in his hand he held (and cracked) a short-thonged whip—the attack, God be praised, was only verbal—just what did I want and why?

I thought to myself what a fine pair of Miura (bulls)

Ernest and Giorgio would make, and what a miserable thing was a publisher after all! Luckily, Narcisse tried to bite my quarry and that calmed him down at once. I tied up my pet and he discarded his whip, and we both plopped down on the divan—in a few minutes I had an amenable collaborator in hand. His price would be lofty, but so were my ideas. We shook hands on it (the whip hand) and I promised to bring him, the story and the author together that Thursday.

I returned about noon and was waiting in fury at the Press when a messenger arrived. With agitated fingers I tore open a slim envelope to discover only a few pages of typescript, it seemed to be mostly one-word lines of four-letter words. The whole thing amounted to about one thousand words and had nothing to do with toreadors. It looked to me like a discarded passage from *Farewell to Arms*. I was so indignant and disappointed that I wanted to cry. Instead I sat down and wrote the author a red-hot letter in which, among other things, I said that a five-page edition de luxe of Hemingway, signed, at ten dollars a throw, would appear mighty "precious" to the public. With this letter the printer himself ran round to Hemingway's hotel.

The answer came back in a flash like a flash. "No one can call Hemingway 'precious' and get away with it." Would I please return the manuscript to him at once. He implied that any other publisher would offer a million on bended knees and he also added that he could not return the advance as they had to sail and their tickets were bought. I called Jacques Porel to my assistance and he was the bearer-back of the manuscript. He was to tell Hemingway that instead of the "precious" bit I would accept the Continental rights to one of his novels for the C.C.E. This he had offered before the special edition was discussed and he had suggested *Farewell to Arms*. I instructed Jacques to sign for *In Our Time* which I then considered (and still do) Hemingway's best. The barter was accomplished without too much compromise, but Jacques told me that as he left the hotel he could hear Ernest muttering a four-letter word and "precious" over and over as the banging of trunks grew to a mighty din.

I have never regretted my decision, but it makes it quite

obvious that I did *not* invent Hemingway : moreover, I like to think that it was Gris and not the steamship line that cashed that cheque, and I had already published this laudatory introduction to *Torrents of Spring!*

Paris, December, 1931.

Dear Ernest,

I have a confession to make to you. Do you remember that torrential day in Spain last August, "Torrents of Summer" when we all foregathered after the corrida, you, your wife, Jacques and I and the boot-black in the little posada behind the arena? I was feeling pretty sick after the fight and would have felt more so if it hadn't been that the matador now and then forgot his bull in admiration of Charlie Chaplin who was throwing gold cigarette cases from the box of honour to the pigtailed heroes. The place was full of English and Americans; you and Charlie were the focus of many admiring eyes and I felt very jealous of you. It must be thrilling to be famous and I wondered how to set about it. (Don't smile! There are, they say, a hundred gateways to the Temple of Fame and, woman-like, I fondly hoped to wedge my way in by one of them!) Above all, I wanted to do something as you two had done something; I wanted to make something out of all this Anglo-Saxon alertness and zest for discovery of new things in ancient lands. Every American fancies himself a new Columbus rediscovering Europe. And Europe seems to welcome their curiosity with open arms.

The barrier that separates us and always will (I am not Esperanto-minded, are you?) is the difference in language. Local colour, bulls and blood, are all very well, but one wants to know what the people are saying and thinking. You have told us and told us very convincingly how it all strikes you, but how about bull-fighting from the Spaniard's point of view? We are always hearing how Paris appeals to the American, or Berlin strikes the Briton—but Paris as the Parisians see it? Or Corsica as the bandits enjoy it and shoot it up? Or Lapland as the Lapps love it? (Do you know, for instance, that in proportion to its population Ice-

298

land publishes more newspapers than any country in the world?)

That is what I was thinking of, across the din and pageantry of that afternoon—my thoughts were revolving round a new idea, to give all these eager travellers a glimpse into the minds of the people they were visiting; something more than local colour, rather the racial consciousness that makes and mixes the colour, as the painter mixes the paints on his palette. I remember saying something to you about it after the second (or was it the third?) absinthe; and you answered "swell." You have probably forgotten, but that "swell" of yours was a prelude to a rising tide. Après vous, le déluge ... In other words the C.C.E.

As you know I have for some years been publishing de luxe editions at my Black Sun Press (for subscribers only!). Now I am venturing on something much less luxurious in form and at prices more in keeping with the times ... Cheap editions in English of the masterpieces of the modern world, books that will express the genius of every country in the language we all understand, at a price we all can afford.

I am beginning the collection with an American book, your book, because I admire it and because I know I am not the only one to admire what you write; a few million others do too ... The next book will be Kay Boyle's translation of "Le Diable au Corps" by Raymond Radiquet (Aldous Huxley has written the introduction to it), a masterpiece in its English form as well as in the original; and when I send you a copy I have an idea you will repeat that "swell." After the "Devil in the Flesh" will follow "Bubu de Montparnasse", that classic of the Paris underworld. I am amazed that our compatriots, for all their enthusiasm for Montparnasse life, have never been able to read in their own language this magnificent human document. Last month, during a voyage of literary exploration to Scandinavia, I was lucky enough to secure the rights to an amazing psychological crime story that has just won the Inter-Scandinavian prize contest, "Two Living and One Dead" by Christiansen—and also the rights to quite a different but very unusual type of work, stories of Corsica by Prince

Wilhelm of Sweden.

"Of the making of books there is no end" (*or so I am assured on good authority*) *and there are many beginnings, too many, far too many, as over-worked critics are fond of telling us, but of the re-making of really good books there can never be enough—or that is how I look at it. Europeans who wish to keep up with Anglo-American literature will be, I hope, delighted to find a supply at the same low prices as their own novels. Until now the prices of so many translations have been prohibitive.*

I am going to publish books that I like, that have merit, and that interest or amuse me personally, books for the serious reader as well as mystery stories to while away the hours on the Mauretania or the Ile-de-France, and fascinating cosmopolitan tales of adventure and travel for the Train Bleu.

I hope very shortly to secure books for this series by such leading authors as Lawrence, Joyce, Kafka, Colette, Maurois, Thomas Mann, Tozzi, Dos Passos, Sackville-West, Aldington, McAlmon, Huxley, Maugham, Kay Boyle, Katherine Mansfield, et al. —and I have just evolved a brilliant idea that the colours of the titles should match the countries, Red for Russia, Blue for Peru, but green for the "Torrents of Spring" in honour of Diana and the woods of Michigan!

Everyone tells me that I am lucky to begin my collection with a book of yours. If they only knew all that I have confessed in this letter, they would realize that you and those Miura bulls are, between you, responsible, not only for this edition of "Torrents of Spring" but for many C.C.E.'s to come.

Good fishing, and again many thanks.

Caresse Crosby.

CHAPTER 34

The next May a visiting publisher and I were heading south.
May would be like summer on the Riviera and I wanted summer. The car opened landau-wise allowing us to loll content-
edly in the cool sunshine en route. Lucien could drive that
road blindfolded and I could re-live each *étape* a dozen times,
but never so rapturously as the imagined trip with Harry (the
trip I never took).

I knew that D and I would have our first luncheon at Sens
behind the red and white checked curtains of the bistro under
the walls of our first Cathedral, the itinerary never varied.
The first dinner at Saulieu, of sole and truffles with a Chablis
sauce fit for angels, and then up to the corner guest room where
migratory headlights reflected in the cherub-laden mirror at
one's back and the *grande route* swung right, the lovely panorama of the castle at La Rochepot about noon next day, then
luncheon at Macon on the Quai de l 'Horloge, or maybe at
the Hospice de Beaune, the perfumed Burgundy and heady
Armagnac, the Inn at Arles with the stairs that creaked, the
stop on the landing and the four-poster bed on a slanting floor—
and on and on, a journey, where at every turn of the road I
remembered that Harry was not with me.

Each trip replenished the sweet with the sweeter. I had mapped myself a dream route so perfect that I hardly dared try
once again, but with a new companion some gesture, some word,
some unguessed delight might still be added to the summum of
perfection, and even twenty years later the joy of my first
glimpse of Arnay le Duc was augmented by a still more per-

301

fect thrill—the scene took on new magic, for my companion's response to La Rochepot, that fairy-tale castle, was as new as Monday and my hand clasped his while the road shone brighter. Perhaps I will never take that road again, but perhaps some measured mile still holds a rapture yet unknown. I never told them why but I believe that the spell was felt by each and every companion of *"la-route-enchantée."*

We had loitered in Arles, we had bathed in the sea at St. Maximes, we had corkscrewed the Corniche into Cannes, and now our road lay straight ahead along the Mediterranean to Nice, there we were to visit Kay Boyle and Laurence Vail in their villa high above the town. D had met neither Kay nor Laurence and was excited at the prospect and I as always was tense with anticipation for the renewed touch of their friendship.

About seven o'clock we climbed the last perpendicular, the sun had not yet set, Kay and her pinafored daughters, all but the baby, were setting a table in the garden overlooking the bay. Laurence had gone for ice, two enthusiastic puppies yapped our arrival. If you have not met Kay you cannot realize what delight awaits you. Of all the women I know she radiates more hapiness than any other, her appearance is electric, her hair is rampant like a craniere, her smile is from her heart and her fine humour shines in her eyes. Slim and *"tirée-à-quatres-épingles,"* her crispness is as pleasing to the eye as her warmth to the heart, and her little girls adorn her.

Laurence had just completed the translation of *Bubu of Montparnasse* for the C.C.E. Kay was writing a novel, *Gentlemen, I Address You Privately*—the house vibrated with work and fun and that garden supper was the pot of gold at the end of our trail. I loved them all so much.

After our al fresco meal friends began to drift in. Douggie back from Greece, Sacha and Effie Berkman, the soft-spoken anarchists who wore their hearts on their sleeves, Dorothy Harvey, precise in manner, rebellious in mind, and two boys from under the hill; that night, grownups and children were sprinkled haphazardly through the house—sleep found it difficult to woo us all. Next morning I awoke to the clicking of a busy Underwood and the aroma of chicorized coffee. In the kitchen I found

Kay tapping the keys with one hand while with the other she bathed the baby in the kitchen sink and scrambled eggs on a driftwood-burning stove. Laurence and Lucien had gone for the papers and the mail. D was taking a shower under the rain-barrel, the two elder girls were already off to school. I loved my privilege of inhabiting this special world of theirs so brim full of work, yet so free of toil, but it was evident that D's executive presence was a strain on the informal household, and that afternoon having all four lunched together at Carmellos on eggs *à la romeraie,* we went in search of hotel rooms in some water-front hotel. D liked the conventional set-up of the Beau Séjour, but I preferred La Voile d'Or where my suite was grandiose and very "Eugénie," and his cell-like, but with a secret panelled passage between and a wisteria hidden balcony built for break-fasts *à deux.* We stayed.

That afternoon D had a rendezvous with Frank Harris, who was on or near his deathbed, and I motored over to Cannes to talk with Jimmy Walker, who was honeymooning at the Negresco and supposedly writing his memoirs. Neither of these encounters bore very fine fruit, it was a case of the aggressors being even more apathetic than the aggressed, for D and I, alert publishers as we usually were, were both preoccupied with the battle of the balcony—nothing on earth seemed half as important as that predatory decision. I was not at all sure I had won it and he was very sure I must not. We whiled away a week in the southern sun and then one fine morning the *Europa* loomed up almost under our noses while we munched our *brioches* leaning on our con-troversial railing, she was due to sail from Antibes at 2 p.m. "The fastest route to New York in four and one half days" or so, the mammoth poster blazoned along the harbour front. Suddenly, the same thought struck us both.

"You can make it," I said.

"Come with me, Caresse."

I longed to say "yes" but delight had escaped.

I helped him pack, flinging my arms about him every other shirt. I hoped he believed it was due to delight postponed. I was inwardly turning handsprings—and yet I loved to say "yes."

Week after week that season the Surrealists gathered at the Mill. Jacques and Donald and René, the Ernests and the Dalis were regulars, and to these delightful and spirited gatherings were always added droppers-in. I welcomed and wined them with enthusiasm. I was Queen Mistress of my own small realm.

Harry and I never had seen very much of the Americans in Paris, nor did we frequent the Dôme and the Rotonde. Of course, we stopped by there from time to time, but en route to somewhere else. We usually gave rendezvous at the bodega on the corner of the rue Castiglione, or at the Ritz Bar for champagne cocktails, but most often we stayed at home and after Harry's death, I went out even less than before. I almost always managed to see my friends in the rue de Lille. I became integrated with the European *avant gardists* rather than with the American *escapists*. Kay Boyle and Laurence Vail and Jolas were the only American writers who ever visited the Mill then. (Bob McAlmon came with a flurry of snow once while I was publishing *Indefinite Huntress*.) Sam Putnam in his book *Paris Was My Mistress* mentions us twice. First, when he reports that Harry and I signed the *Surrealist Manifesto for the Revolution of the Word*—which is true—but the second report that "the Crosbys" were part of an expatriot colony at Cagnes-sur-mer is pure fiction. I have only once passed through Cagnes (last summer) and never stopped there, and Harry's aversion to "colonies" of any sort would have prevented our living in one, especially on the Riviera, and Malcolm Cowley's imaginative remarks in *Exile's Return* are myth. We did not know him in those days; nor he us.

After Harry's death I stayed from time to time with Meraud and Chile Guevara at Mougins, and with Kay and Laurence above Nice. Polleen and I had visited the Phil Barrys in Cannes and later Constance, but Harry and I used to spend our summers first in Normandy and then in Ermenonville, and always were at Deauville for the racing season. Many of the American writers and artists of the 20's whom I might have known I never met. My life reflected only one or two of the facets of that kaleidoscopic era.

CHAPTER 35

I love to entertain my friends and even at times my enemies—but entertain I must—I am very apt when someone calls on the telephone to ask me to lunch, cocktails, or dinner to reply, "Please come to me, instead." In Paris and Washington I reinstigated the habit of five o'clock tea complete with buttered scones in order to supply another outlet for this self-indulgence, and in New York in the 30's I even gave breakfast parties, because that was an added way to lure the busy business-man to my board. If one settled on the main stream that flows via the subway from upper Park to lower Wall, one can bait one's hook with eggs and bacon and entice many a fine fish to the lure—and in the 30's I did just that—and I breakfasted in Chinese pyjamas, which in the 30's was an innovation, too.

I don't like to go out very much, to a friend's house yes, but to a restaurant *no,* and this taste grows more and more acute with the years. A dinner party at 21 or at the Ritz I consider sheer torture—a combinaion of bedlam, broccoli and brandy—all of which I detest.

That, perhaps, is why in June '33 I decided to give a party at the Mill that would please Paris and afford me exquisite pleasure.

It was to be a ball, a costume ball and it was to be held *chez moi* on the outskirts of the forest of Ermenonville, in the rustic setting of mill and stream, it must not be elaborate. The main requisites in party giving are (1) guests, (2) drink, (3) en-

305

tertainment, in this case music—food is last, but should be as exotic as possible, so no one knows the difference, and copious.

No. 1 was the most difficult point because everyone would want to come. In Paris a party of this sort becomes a test of the *invité's* rating on the season's report card. To be invited and to attend is A plus. To be invited and not attend is A minus, but not to be invited at all is D minus.

I enlisted Max Ernst, Doyen of the Surrealists, to help with the food because he was a gourmet and could also make the preparation of a feast into a frolic, and Armand Count de la Rochefoucauld as "Emcee" due to his talent at entertainment. Evelyn Boirevain and an industrious American industrialist, who would do anything to be near Evelyn, were to take care of the decorations.

As to expense, I limited my helpers to the minimum—but point No. 2 was still to be dealt with—so I called cousins Nina and Melchior on the telephone and declared the party would be a failure without them, or the Polignac champagne. They'd let me know what could be done, they said—and soon the news got around—there was to be a fabulous party at Le Moulin— everyone was on tenterhooks, and the Polignacs wrote to say that they would transfer the necessary magnums of Pommery from their cellars at Rheims to my springhouse at Ermenonville. "How many people will there be?" "About a hundred," I guessed, and in true noble fashion they sent eighty fine magnums of Pommery Nature—as a family contribution!

Armand said if he possibly could he'd get Willie Lewis' orchestra, the hit of the Montmartre season, and as Willie was a friend of mine, the band was delighted to comply. Max said he would drive all the way to the Mediterranean if necessary to choose a *lotte* big enough and lively enough to concoct the true Marseilles bouillabaisse for which he was famous. Saffron was hard to come by in Paris, but he managed it and when he appeared the morning of the party the back seat of his "surplus property" Dodge was iridescent with mussel shells, crawling with lobsters and prawns and flopping with silvery fins fresh from a salty sea. Bushels of ripe tomatoes had been boiling in oil all morning following Max's instructions and were ready for their chef.

We had decided on "Matelot" and "Matelottes" as costumes for the party. As to point No. 1, of course, my surrealist friends were all invited, also the most amusing Parisians regardless of society's approval and a few friends from home. (These I recall included the Louis Bromfields and the Bunny Carters, he is now the president of Morgan and Company, but only Louis and Bunny turned up, their wives I was told later, were afraid to risk their Boston reputations.) But though the party was wildly successful, it was also wildly proper. My daughter, age fifteen, was there and no Peabody could have objected. We drank only champagne which is known to make for fun and not for ribaldry. One ghastly incident, however, occurred, when Bettina Bergery in a fit of jealousy, because of Maria de Gramont's subversive glances at Gaston, accurately extinguished her glowing cigarette between the Duchess's bare shoulder blades as she and Gaston danced by cheek to cheek—Bettina was and still is as jealous and as sudden as a viperess.

Another incident took place when several of my friends who had discarded their coats and handbags in my bedroom were ready to depart and the door would not open. No amount of knocking aroused whoever was within, until, after a polite wait and renewed banging, an agile guest climbed in my window to discover Cocteau, who earlier in the evening, a little bag in hand, had asked for a place where he could rest for a bit. If the door was locked, the bag was not and Jean with the smile of happy drowse upon his lips was tranquilly taking his dreamful ease, espadrilles neatly placed side by side upon the bedside rug. If heartless to waken, it was worth it, for his rest had enlivened his wit and enhanced his charm—it also enabled certain of my guests to depart in peace.

Elsa Schiaparelli won the first prize for her costume. Her maribou boa, knee-length skirts and fishnet stockings made of her a perfect Lady of the Cannebière. The men's prize went to André Dürst (*Vogue* photographer) as an 1890 dandy in yacht's clothing.

It was a lovely starry night, dark o' the moon, slightly fresh so that the huge bonfire provided a pleasant warmth for sitting out-of-doors. In the barn which was already equipped with trapezes and rings Armand had had a floor laid for dancing and while many danced, some swung and pirouetted overhead.

Paris was forty-eight kilometres away and as the Rochefoucauld Château, the Village Inn and my Moulin Tower could not bed them all, some of the guests were discovered at dawn wrapped in blankets and dreams, and interlaced for warmth, huddled about the smouldering embers of the fire.

I slept well that night and next morning awoke to quiet and order—everything had been tidied and garnished—Monsieur et Madame Henri had been up since dawn with mop and broom and suds and polish. The swimming pool was merrying in the sunlight beneath my window and when I leaned out and called, *"Bon jour, tout le monde,"* other heads appeared at other windows and soon were plunged beneath the cool waters that sluiced from the humming waterfall into the pool. Coffee in big bowls and croissants and strawberries were served as usual on matting rugs strewn about the courtyard and each guest, munching and basking in the sun, began to recount his special version of the party the night before.

Armand gave a luncheon at the Château that day and those who stayed assembled there—but by evening all had ebbed away.

It was a few weeks later. Max Ernst looked down from the upper berth through the strings of a gilded harp. We were on the night boat from Le Havre to Southampton, an unexpected trip—the harp was unexpected too, but there it stood beween us like a heavenly bundling-board.

The boat sailed about midnight, but at four that same afternoon I was still at the Mill in Ermenonville while everyone on the place tried frantically to get the village taxi going to take me into Paris to the boat train, but already the train was lost when Max and Marie-Berthe drove up in their vintage jalopy.

"You were nearly just too late," I called, "but now you are just in time." "We could never make Paris by five," answered Max, "but maybe we can make Havre by midnight." That was what I'd hoped he'd say and ordered Algerian Red to prepare for the trip. In a hilarious mood we finally decided it was time to be off, but when we had loaded all my bags and boxes aboard there was hardly room for me to squeeze in beside Max. Marie-Berthe luckily was delighted to spend the night with Polly at the Mill, Max and I were to go across country avoiding Paris and thereby saving fifty or sixty miles, and he said he himself could spend the night in Havre. Now, it was up to his ancient vehicle to bat out the necessary two hundred and fifty kilometres before midnight. Not too difficult, provided it held together, though it would be necessary to stop at almost every little village to fill the incontinent radiator with water. It was great fun, the night was clear and starry, and long ghostly lines of poplars marched on either side of the flat French highways that streaked across the countryside like silver ribbons unrolled before us. We steamed and ricocheted through the sleep-bound villages like outriders of some demon convoy. Max drove as though he were mounted and spurred for the Hades National. We leaped and rattled our way into Havre long before sailing time, in time actually for a late but copious dinner at a quayside bistro.

If I had arrived just in time to get on board, it probably never would have happened, but the fact that we'd made it and stowed my luggage, with two hours to spare, gave us all sorts of ideas and ample time in which to let them flower. I was on my way to the Surrealist exhibition that had so scandalized London when it opened the week before. Max had several exhibits in the show and he was even more allured than I was—he'd been invited to stay with Edward James for the opening, so why not now, and he actually had a thousand francs in his pocket, enough for a round-trip ticket, while I had an extra berth in my cabin—all he needed was a clean shirt and a toothbrush and, true to form, both were in his car.

I was as pleased as I could be, for Max was as wise and amusing a companion as one could hope for, and to arrive in London with the prize Surrealist would mean marks to my credit. Having decided all this after the third round of Calvados, Max went off to garage his car and to send a wire, and I went on board ahead, which was a fatal move for at the top of the companionway, I ran into Mildred Dilling, the world's foremost harpist—we had met at Etretat years before—and she accosted me now with a wave and a groan. Could I possibly help her out? She had so much luggage on her ticket that they said she would have to send the overweight by express. "But why not," I said, "it really is very quick." "No, no," she wailed, "it's my harp. I have to have it for a concert tomorrow, and I have to have my trunk, too." It seems it was a royal command performance. "That does put you on the spot," I commiserated, not very helpful, "I guess you'll have to get another ticket, my dear," and then fatefully I thought of Max. "But wait," I said, "I have a friend who is travelling light, perhaps he could check your harp on *his* ticket." At that minute, all smiles, Max appeared and her dilemma was explained to him. Very gallantly he went off with the lady to see to whatever was necessary. "I'll meet you in 28," I murmured, he nodded, and I went below to the cabin. The boat was moving, it was the stroke of midnight, and I was comfortably ensconced in my lower berth when the door opened and Max slid in, his face had lost its happy glow. "My God," he said, "I've got to bring the damn thing in with me." "Why not put it in the hold?" I was thinking fast. "Because it isn't packed, just draped, and she says the dampness is bad for it, it might catch cold in the hold!" There was a banging on the door and two surly porters lugged at the unwieldy object, but there just wasn't room. "You'd better get into the bunk, Monsieur," they suggested, "then we can stand it up." So Max, fully dressed, climbed in over my head and the porters pushed the great instrument bang across my line of vision and closed the door. "I'm not going to suffocate," I cried, and jerked off its black winding sheet to stare out in consternation as though from a gilded cage— the ridiculous object reached to the ceiling and there we were imprisoned behind bars, as chaste a set-up as ever was. I caught sight of Max's birdlike head between the aeolian strings and laughed until the tears ran into my ears.

"Le Jokey" was crowded. We were six. All of us old friends, sitting at the best table, receiving the best attention from the lofty proprietor, down to the lady of the lavabos. We always did receive the best everywhere, and we were the gayest, the most lavish, the most envied in Paris that season—1934—the very gizzard of the glamorous years. Extravagant in talk and in action, I was often the centre of an exhilarated group.

I was restlessly contemplating leading my followers to fresher fields for it was 2 a.m. of a balmy May morning, and we had not yet crossed the river to Montmartre—but just then I saw the boy! He was very young and browned a deep mahogany by some southern sun. He was dressed delectably in dark blue homespun, such as Breton sailors wear, his shirt and tie were blue too, and on his sunburnt feet he wore sandals. His short nose turned up disdainfully, wide, black eyes looked contemptuously around him. He drew a pipe from his pocket, lit it and flung the match beneath our table with the insolent gesture of a gamin, gazed over my head, then turned to leave, but M. Dupont had spied him and beckoned him with pleading gestures toward the bar. He hestitated, and in that moment he was lost . . . for quick as a flash I slipped away from the table and with the excuse of "telephone," was out in the starlit street calling for Lucien.

"Oui, Madame, ici."

"Lucien," I said urgently, "the young man in the blue suit, did you notice him just now?"

"Mais, oui, Madame."

"When he leaves, offer to give him a lift wherever he is going—I want to find him again tomorrow—then return right away."

I was back at the table in no time, unobserved, and with malevolent satisfaction, I saw the boy step forth again into the night—I wondered if he had even noticed me—but he had shown no sign—I lingered on long enough to give Lucien time to reconnoiter, and his *"C'est fait"* when he helped me into the car assured me that it was so.

The next day dawned (or I suppose) as if designed for love— I had Marcelle pack a picnic backet, not forgetting the Cointreau, and after Lucille had rubbed my back and finished my toes, I selected a blue denim apron-dress and a cartwheel straw from Lanvin, remembering D.H.L. I flicked "insouciance" behind my ears and seated myself in the Hotchkiss, the rear hood rolled back—then Lucien and I swung cheerfully into the sunlit traffic on the Boulevard and headed for the Rotonde—no kidnapper ever contemplated a manœuvre with such happy guile as I—I sat down at one of the café tables nearest the sidewalk—the car parked thirty feet to the left, and waited.

I'd had time for two coffee creams and one *brioche* when I saw the boy approaching. In the morning sun he looked even more charming than the night before—more as if made of mahogany and the sea—and to top the astonishing cynosuric effect, a handsome Dalmatian stalked close at his heels—my heart turned over. The dog made it simple for Lucien to say *"Ah, bonjour, Monsieur, quel beau chien."* The wicked deed was done and I stepped out in quiet fashion toward the car. I smiled. "What a graceful animal," I remarked louder than actually necessary, and stopped in the dead centre of the sidewalk swinging my hat by its ribbons.

The young man smiled back.

"Doesn't such a big dog miss the country on a spring morning like this?" I asked with casual interest.

"Excessivement," the boy answered, casting an amused sidelong look at the car at the curb.

"Perhaps he should be given a run by the river," I suggested.

"By all means," he answered, and we hopped in—Tojo, the Dalmatian sat proudly in front, Bobbie and I were swallowed up in the tonneau, now closed, as the car glided southward.

"I know a mill by a Roman bridge," said I.

"I know one by a pond with poplars," said he—so we tossed a silver franc piece to decide—Lady Liberté won.

The picnic was a success *à la limite.* I shall never forget the moist high grasses matted with poppies and with cornflowers, nor the drone of the ancient mill wheel—nor Bobbie— so reminiscent of mahogany and the sea—the fact that Tojo was not to be found until we finally gathered up our belongings at dusk in no way marred the perfection of the day.

In the summer of '34 while I was on a visit to "The Apple Trees," Emlen Etting stopped off for a week-end on his way to visit an aunt in Bar Harbour. Emlen and I were always contriving outlets for our surreal response to life. Just as The Black Party in Paris had been the nursling of our united brains and belief, so Poem 8 was born—but the achievement was Emlen's this time, I was only a prop, although a torrid one at that.

He arrived on 'the shore' laden with ciné camera, film, and fiction. Part One of his scenario had already been enacted in Philadelphia. The Poem was in three stanzas, each played by a different woman reflected in the lovelight of the poet's eye, which in this case, was the camera's eye. I gathered I was to be passion plus—and got into the mood at once.

That first afternoon—my mother-in-law having gone forth to a lady's lunch and bridge—Emlen and I set the stage on the front lawn, framed between box hedge and heliotrope bed.

We moved the guest room dressing table with its triple mirror out upon the greensward. We found a number of fine props in the Crosby living room and I, in a long low slinky evening dress, sat myself down before my looking-glass to register sultry desire—at any rate, that is what was registered upon the celluloid—in my desire I even crunched a dahlia between my teeth.

When Mrs. Crosby drove sedately up with Mrs. Beal by her side, the play upon their lawn was more than Bostonian sang-froid could accept. Everything was hustled quickly back into the house. I was requested to wash my face and cover up before tea, and Emlen was thereupon suspected of being some kind of a "Main line" Svengali.

Nevertheless, that piece of fantasy has endured and to-day Cinema 16 will rent you Poem 8 for home entertainment at the drop of a dollar. It was also shown successfully at the Paris Theatre on Fifty-eighth Street only last November, eighteen years after, thereby outliving my first movie appearance.

CHAPTER 36

When I stand on solid ground I lose my footing. There is something so unyielding in earth without tremor. Give me a firm foundation and I feel as though I were galvanized into public statuary and all monuments, public or private, I find depressing. The occasion on which, for once, I was palpably moved by statuary was a crisp eventide when driving back to Paris from the Mill, René Crevel asked me, his head comfortably on my shoulder, if I had ever visited the hidden garden of homeless statues? No, I never had, was it far? For already I was drowsily aware of approaching martinis, a sofa, and *A Season in Hell* (I was translating Rimbaud then). "It's here," René said, *"à gauche*, Lucien." We swung left from the Porte Clingniancourt into the boulevard exterior. We'd only gone a few hundred yards when he called, "Stop," the way the French love to, one hand upraised à la Hitler (this was before World War II) and the word pronounced as in opéra bouffe.

We screeched to a standstill in front of a long weather-beaten wall. I didn't really feel like it, but I got out, René's forever tousled head now erect. The doorway was unlatched, which was very unusual in Paris, so I followed him through, intrigued. When the gate clanged behind us, there took shape before us a dream vista of "marble men and maidens overwrought"—I gasped with amazement, for ahead there stretched row upon row of dusk-white forms—Aphrodite, Hermes, Ceres, Bacchus, Persephone, Atlas, Diana, Neptune, Louis XIV, Mirabeau, Bernhardt —and not only one Aphrodite or one Hermes, dozens of them,

314

but each slightly different according to the artist's vision. Every one of these figures had been removed from official life in some public square or civic hall to make way for newercomers, and then trundled off like displaced persons to be put in concentration behind barriers in this no-man's land of discarded pomp and nostalgic beauty. For in some miraculous manner these myriad "fair attitudes," which had once been honoured and then forgotten had recaptured, in this land of ghosts, a sense of the beauty that had invoked them—even forty-six Napoleons, each one more melancholy than his neighbour, wore a profound aura of nobility. Hundreds and hundreds of figures, flank by flank and breast by jowl, the nude and the noble, the statesman and the saint, all waiting for a Day of Judgment, when perhaps they would be reinstated, or else, in final submission, lay down their crushed and shattered limbs to pave some civic hall.

It was growing dark, so hand in hand we fled the lanes—only stopping a second to pat the fat little buttocks of a Pan, just in—his flute to his lips he seemed to grin and say, "They can't catch me, I'll pipe my way out!" René was faunlike too.

Back in the furlined fastness of the car we kissed for comfort.

There was another time we kissed for comfort, it was the last time, only a few days before his death. During the damp Paris winters René was forced, because of his lungs, to spend those dangerous months in Switzerland. His letters, illustrated with hearts and flowers and extravagant whirligig words, told me how impatiently, there in a Davos sanitarium, he waited for the spring. It was difficult for him to be separated from his friends and from the exciting contacts of Paris. His was a loving and lovable nature, but too easily hurt for happiness, and only Paul Eluard and I guessed that that spring he had fallen impossibly in love.

In the pages of the exquisite passage from *Babylone* "Mr. Knife and Miss Fork," which the B.S.P. published in 1932 three autumns before René died, one sensed the naive heart yet profound spirit that conceived them. Ernst, Crevel and I created that edition together. Max's fanciful illustrations and his Victorian cover-design made of René's text perhaps the publication that I am proudest of, for into it went not only our separate skills but our inseparable friendship as well.

315

One June morning in '35, René and I found ourselves in a Paris street in a spring down-pour, but we didn't notice, we were both shaken by the unexpected bitterness of a recent philistine encounter. He hailed a taxi and we slid in.

It was then that he turned to me and there were tears in his eyes and in his voice.

"I can't stand it," he said.

I knew what he meant, for Harry's same words were echoing in my ear, and once again as friends, we kissed for comfort, but at that moment I had a premonition of tragedy at my elbow—

"I can't stand it," must have been his cry against the stupid cruelty of the world—and who was there to comfort him at the last?

Not I, nor any other insufficient human friend.

June 18th, 1935, René Crevel committed suicide

That September, I decided to economize—I was feeling fine again, there was no need for a chauffeur. I sold the Hotchkiss and invested in a little Citroën, "citron" (meaning lemon) the French called them. I remember the day the salesman, the young Count de Gramont, delivered it. He spoke proudly of his wares. "Just try it yourself," he said and waved me to my purchase. I graciously turned the door handle with a flourish. It came off in my hand! He was terribly chagrined, and we agreed that "the lemon" had better be taken back to the factory for a thorough tightening up.

After I had driven the car for a week, I decided to accept Guido Sommi's invitation to visit him at Torre-Picenardi near Cremona. Guido, Marquis Sommi-Picenardi, spent most of his time in Paris where he had a bachelor *pied à terre* but in the summertime he returned for a few frugal months to his ancestral towers in Italy. He was a very dear friend and I longed to accept his standing invitation. Now the opportunity presented itself, Polleen was visiting a schoolmate, Billy was in America and I was *soi-disant* footloose.

I had replaced Lucien with Josef, a Czechoslovakian *valet-de-pied*—Josef did not drive a car but he was willing to do anything else. I decided to take him with me for ballast and protection. He could only speak a few words of French and no

English, and his Bulgar, Croat and Czech seemed confused, so I was sure I would not be bothered by conversation. It was only on traversing the Brenner Pass that I realized what a really timid protector I had chosen. At each corkscrew turn (and I admit I was not an ace at such things) he shut his eyes, prodded his head between his knees and began to moan. It really was unnerving—and the only time "the lemon" needed attention he burnt his fingers on the wrong gadget! The remainder of the trip he wore his hand in a becoming silk sling. That he was six feet two and in his twenties did not make him a bit more efficient. It was not until we arrived at Torre-Picenardi and slid through the great portcullis to halt in the ancient courtyard within crenellated walls that Josef showed his true worth. A castle acted on him like vitamin B. He bowed and smiled and toted bags, stood at attention and begged for orders, and like the best of Major Domos he at once took over the Service Department from Guido's female staff. That evening when dinner was ready he appeared in the Salon Doorway in Picenardi livery. *"Madame le Marquis est servi,"* he boomed getting us both into the announcement.

When after dinner the host like his fathers before him put on a denim apron and himself washed the precious India Company china from which we had eaten, Josef stood at his elbow to dry, like an acolyte at an altar—and Guido told me that on a tour of inspection the next morning he found Josef established in the butler's pantry sharpening knives with one hand and pressing my silk undies with the other! For him the joyous feudal days of his childhood had returned.

When I left Cremona after a giddy visit interluded with stuffy county nobility, I turned my wheels north toward Kitz-bühel—Kay Boyle and her family had been living there since the French Riviera sojourn and wanted me to join them for an October-Fest fling in Munich—I tried a different pass going back, it was no less hazardous but Josef's nerves had improved and we arrived in good form. I was delighted to see Kay and Laurence again, though Kitzbühel was a disappointment.

We left the very next day for Munich via Baden-Baden. I was supposed to follow their big grey Packard, but it was rainy and I couldn't always keep up. We did manage to meet at noon

317

for a showery lunch under a tree but by nightfall I was off the road hopelessly lost on a rain-soaked mountain, Kay and Laurence goodness knew where. The world seemed to have deserted us—no signposts, no real roads, no lights, only dripping forest. Then finally about nine I came upon an inn ablaze with lights and a dozen huge cars parked before its grilled entrance which strangely enough was closed. I told Josef to get out and try the gate. It was locked so he rang. The place looked very much alive and a signboard blazoned the fact that it was a first-class tourist hotel—meals at all hours. A doorman appeared and flicked on the postern lights. "Is this an inn?" I asked firmly. *"Ja,"* he answered, looking us over suspiciously. "I would like a room for the night and one for the chauffeur," I said clearly. *"Nein,"* was forthcoming this time. "Full up," he added. It was such a dreary evening it seemed strange to find this mountain chalet overcrowded. "Baden-Baden is fifty kilometres away," he continued. "Then I'll only need dinner," I answered pushing past him and mounting the steps, "I am very hungry." "No dinner," he almost yelled as a line of waiters bearing steaming dishes of Wienerschnitzel and Sauerbrauten streaked across the hallway and disappeared into the *Essenzimmer.* I was determined then and asked to see the proprietor. A little rolypoly man appeared, absolutely horrified when he caught sight of me. I hadn't believed I looked that bad. I insisted that I wanted to wash, to eat, to have a drink. "No, no, no," he insisted, practically pushing me down the steps. I decided to make a scene for it was a hotel for travellers and travellers we were.

Our argument became so heated that suddenly the door to the dining hall swung open and a big bald Nazi strode forth (one didn't know they were "Nazis" then). Over his shoulder I saw a long dinner table with about thirty brown-shirted Germans, all eating away with painful seriousness, their eyes glued upon the open door. I was explaining to their spokesman how hungry and tired I was and I added, "I am, you see, an American in distress."

"American?" His piggy eyes lit up. *"Augenblick bitte,"* he said and hastily went back to the head of the table and whispered something in the leader's ear—then hurried to usher me in.

Immediately the entire table rose to attention, clicked heels, and gave me a big concerted leer. A place was made for me at the right of the host. "American " they all chortled and then sat down as suddenly as they had stood up. I took my place and looked the company over—each one wore a sort of Siva sign on his armband, they were none of them young, they were hard and they were heavy, many wore monocles.

"I didn't mean to barge in on a private dinner," I apologized —my protest was waved aside—food was spread lavishly around me, *schnapps* was poured. I drank to them, they drank to me and to America. "Have any of you been there?" I asked politely. "No, but we all expect to get there soon." "All?" I replied innocently—"*Alle*," they fairly shouted and raised their glasses, chortling like mad. "*Alles in Amerika.*" And then "To the American young lady," and at that the table rose to its feet again and each took a folded sheet of printed verses from his breast pocket, one of them went to the piano and with a guttural burst the Horst Wessel song began, followed by others more and more martial.

I finished and hurriedly I thanked them all and said I must leave now, but they had no intention of letting me go, when to my great relief and to their utter amazement Kay and Laurence and Pegeen and Sinbad were ushered in—"friends of the American's," the word went round. *Schnapps* was pressed upon them too—but *they* were shown seats along the wall like retainers while I remained seated all unknowingly at the head of the German High Commandl!

Finally Laurence marshalled *his* forces, Josef reappeared and the six of us made a flying-wedge exit and I don't know whether it was Goebbels or Himmler who helped me on with my rubbers —but I do know that at the head of the table sat a gimlet-eyed man with a Charlie Chaplin moustache who didn't miss a *Heil*.

CHAPTER 37

At the back of the main building at the Mill, the one in which I lived, I had planted golden bantam corn, this I used to serve on-the-cob to the enjoyment of my European guests, for until the 30's corn in France was considered only as fodder for swine—the French grew a coarser grain than we do—and when my native corn ripened, not only our guests but the birds of the region flocked around to have a taste. In the morning and at sundown the cornfield below my window resembled an aviary, it was November, open season for pheasant, when I discovered that the fattest birds were daily visitors to my garden. All around in the forest you could hear the bang-bang of the sportsmen's weapons. I was never energetic enough to get myself up as a huntress, but one Indian Summer morning as I sat in my warm bubble bath, with the long windows of the bathroom flung wide, I watched two rolypoly birds pecking at my table dainties. I was about to say "shoo" but instead I thought "shoot," so I pulled the bell-rope and Marcelle came running. "Tell Henri to load the lightest shotgun and bring it here at once," I hissed, in order not to disturb the feathered trespassers. In a few minutes Marcelle handed me the firearm and my household crowded behind the adjoining window curtains, all French windows reach the floor, so I steadied my gun upon the tub's edge—the bath was a high old-fashioned affair like a landau. I sighted carefully and let blaze. With a roar of wings one jetted away, but one fine pheasant bit the loam. There was applause from the adjoining

51. The Haunted House, Virginia, 1940.

52. Bert, Caresse, and Cowboy at 'the ranch', 1939.

53. Dali enchanted the pond, Hampton Manor, 1940.

54. Polleen ready to sail for Finland, 1939.

55. 'Massa' Dali in Virginia, Hampton Manor, 1940.

room and Henri hobbled out to the field to retrieve our evening meal. Of course, I *had* shot a sitting bird (but I was sitting too) and at about a distance of twenty yards, but they were *my* yards and it was such comfortable hunting that I never again lacked game on the platter to go with corn on the cob.

I did put a stop to Henri's setting rat-traps for the birds when I was not there to provide—after all, I gave them a sporting chance, soap might have got in my eye! Thereafter, during the open season a shotgun lay handy on the shelf, along with the Floris talcum powder and the Roman Bath essence. To-day, I shiver when I think of such martial sport.

It was about this time that the Gilberts and the St. Exupérys came out to the Mill to talk over an English translation of *Night Flight,* and Mermoz, another great French ace, came with them. Antoine de St. Exupéry was a quiet, heavy man with a round, deliberate gaze, almost a stare. He talked little, his volatile wife talked most, but when he did talk, everyone listened. He had the great quality of suppressed drive and wonder too.

Mermoz, who was a sinewy "tough guy" in comparison to his friend, was full of activity and charm. He fell in love and romped with the schnauzer pups and begged to have one of them to take with him on his imminent flight over Egypt— so, later, with a ribbon through his collar, Sunday trotted happily away. I hated to part with one of my pets, but Mermoz was irresistible and Monday, the brother schnauzer, had been promised already to Juliette and Marcel Achard. Sunday's feelings, I surmised, had been hurt. So I was glad that he departed with his new-found friend ahead of Monday. A few days later Mermoz took off with a canine companion by his side, both smiling, it was a final flight—neither the man, nor his dog, was ever seen again.

That autumn Polleen and I again set sail for America. I had arranged to have her enrolled at Bennett School; there she could take dramatic courses under Edith Wynne Matthison and follow her heart's desire to become an actress. As soon as she was settled, I set out to find a furnished apartment in New York for the winter months. A friend of Mother's had prepared a list and hopefully led me from one ghastly prospect to another. The only possibilities according to my standards were about ten times more than my means and those within the budget were either small and dark and often smelly, or if high enough for fresh air, were walk-ups, arrived at by at least five flights of carpetless stairs, and I was still forbidden stair climbing. I was almost sure I would have to settle for unimaginative hotel rooms, which with my inclination to gather my friends and their friends around me, toss a salad or mix a martini, would be hades and ruination.

What *could* I do? Go back to Paris? I had too many irons in the New York fire to leave so soon, but I was in a spot. I asked Mother's friend if it was possible to sublet unfurnished apartments for a month or two. Quite impossible, I was told —then one October evening as lights began to go on in the swank apartment house opposite, I noticed from the River Club where I was having tea with friends, that two enormous windows over the way were completely dark and bare of curtains—empty, I thought, why not find out? I hurried across to ask the doorman point-blank what I wanted to know. "I am not so sure," he said cautiously, "but maybe so, a party just moved out instead of in." I asked to see the superintendent and heard that some "furriners" had taken a three years' lease in July, lived there without furniture until October, and then moved out in bankruptcy. It actually had been paid for through March, but in order to let it again the company must first break the lease and fix it up, he said.

"Let me have it until April," I suggested. "I'll pay a reasonable rent for it just as it is, and when I leave you will still have time to repaint and polish! What did those foreigners sleep on?"

"Oh, I let them sneak some beds and a chair or two," he grinned. "They're still up there. Would you like to see?" Indeed, I would.

The apartment was on the third floor overlooking the River House gardens; the entrance hall, the balcony dining room, the dropped living room and the kitchen were as bare as old Mother Hubbard's cupboard, but far more spacious—the windows were huge and ran right across the front from floorboard to ceiling, the stars were already twinkling through, and joy of joys, there was a big open fireplace as black as an oven.

Everything else was white, dead blessed white, except for the varnished hardwood floors. "Can I have it," I gulped, "for $150," naming my highest figure for rent, forgetting that it was competely unfurnished, and I to stay only a few months. "I guess for less," the superintendent beamed. "Give me the rent of the beds and it's yours." "How much less?" I nodded. "Half," he said. I'd even have enough left over to do some furnishing myself—I was turning mental cartwheels! The bedrooms were fine, big and airy, lovely baths, lots of closets and each room had twin beds, a dressing table and a chair. What more could I ask who loved space and hated clutter—to live in splendid emptiness is my ultimate desire, that is why in 1950 I was plunged in gloom when I had to leave the beautiful castle of Roccasinabalda in the foothills of the Italian Apennines.

I had lived in its 352 rooms, all empty, for over a year and was happier there than I ever had been anywhere. Alone at night, I could wander through the moon-drenched echoing halls and circle the deserted battlements and stand in the bare and brilliant solitude of the courtyard open to the sky in true beatitude. No other place has ever been so fair—or so empty, or so mine! I'll always long for Roccasinabalda—it is the one regret that proves my rule to "Never have any regrets."

There seemed to be no trouble at all with the superintendent. I paid him seventy-five dollars down and took a half-baked lease away with me. The next morning I moved in and began telephoning, I had relations who were storing grand pianos and I managed to borrow two. I ran over to Sherry's and persuaded them to rent me a dozen or more of their little gilt chairs. I went to a glazier and had him cut me a big square of glass for a dining room table, Bacchus only knew where I would find the legs! I bought two dozen large pillows at Bloomingdale's and green, white and red sateen to cover them with. I had the house carpenter knock together a long line of empty crates for a window seat. A Second Avenue upholsterer upholstered three long cushions in white imitation leather (£12-10-0) and to set the stage I invested in six flowering gardenia trees, entire cost of furnishing £40, and divided by four added only £10 a month to my rent. I could not afford curtains, thank goodness, though constant window-washing cost almost as much.

I now had one of the most sensational apartments in the choicest part of town, all for the price of a walk-up. With Virgil Thompson at one piano and Nicholas Nabakoff at the other and a Picasso over the fireplace, the room was immediately photographed for *Town and Country* (or was it for *Vanity Fair?*).

That winter with Virgil's help, I planned to stage Erik Satie's "Socrate" on my balcony. One day, I did. Ada MacLeish sang the role of the *Sybil*. Archie MacLeish did not appear that time, though I do remember an evening that same winter when Mrs. Crosby came down from Boston to take me to the opening of the Diaghilev ballet, *Union Pacific,* music by Nabakoff, libretto by MacLeish. She and I came home early, sipped some hot milk and went to bed, our hair in curlers. About 1.00 a.m., there was (it seemed) a great banging at my door which I was too deep in dreams to hear, but Mrs. Crosby, bless her, fearing some disaster, ran to open (barefooted) bristling with indignation and curlers. Three elated bards stood upon threshold. "We want Caresse," they chanted, "and her pianos." As Mrs. C. peeked out, she drew herself up. "I am her mother-in-law from Boston," she pronounced "she is sleeping, please leave quietly." They were so astonished that they retreated backward, shushing each other as they went. It was only under the rays of the hall light that she recognized the Stars of the evening—Archie, Nicholas and the maestro. If only I'd been awake, what a concert we'd have had !

When I had come to New York in 1932, hoping to sell the idea of paper-covered books to an American publisher,, I brought with me not only examples of those put out during '31 and '32, by the Crosby Continental Editions : Hemingway, Kay Boyle, Dorothy Parker, St. Exupéry, Raymond Radiguet, Robert Mc-Almon, among them. I also brought recent titles in French, Swedish and German. These all sold in their respective countries for the equivalent of one or two shillings and by their enormous circulation proved to me that more people would read more if books cost less. The board covers on current American editions did not seem to warrant the extra eight shillings involved. I called on Dick Simon of Simon and Schuster and on Bennett Cerf of Random House, on Doubleday, Rinehart and others, but just as in 1928, when no one had seen the possibilities of a pictorial magazine, which the French were successfully publishing during the '20's, and which *Life* has now become, so none of my prospects were remotely interested in paper-bound books.

The American public, they said, just won't buy paper covers. No matter how good or how cheap they are. To-day, I look with admiration at Simon and Schuster's dollar line of *Bees, Blossoms, Trees* and *Stars,* and at so many others as well. The New American Library, Pocket Books, etc., for only thirty-five cents. Unfortunately, the C.C.E. had been twenty years ahead of the market. I find it discouraging to have to wait on time. No matter how hard I tried to act independently, this book has proved to me that until I became fifty I never matured. My impatience with time, for instance—if an idea could not materialize at first trial, I moved on to another and another, getting no further in the end. Just as when I used to play golf, I would hit the ball, and run with enthusiasm to where it lay in earth, and then of course, by rules of the game, I had to wait fuming for my opponent to catch leisurely up. I always ran upstairs and I always pulled the calendar off by the twenty-fifth of the month, and stared impatiently at the first of the next for days. Now I can neither run up or down stairs and I have learned to say "this is going to take time." But I don't like to.

I remember during my first year in Paris how impatient I was when I called upon Stroobantz, the bookbinder, for a lovely order in grass-green leather, tooled in gold. I had left the book two weeks' before, and when I asked how long it would take, Stroobantz shook his head, looking at his calendar. "You can't have it before March," he replied. It was then the sixteenth of February. "No sooner?" I begged. "I have all that before me," and he waved toward the toppling recesses of his work room. "The first of March, then," I agreed, but when I returned on the dot, he looked at me as if I were demented.

"Not *this* March," he expostulated. I don't know which of us was the most astounded.

To my financial distress, I have never been able to cooperate

325

with another publisher. I hate to compromise. I'd almost rather give up. Twice in the '30's, I had the opportunity of making a profitable deal, but I didn't. First Random House suggested that I print my Black Sun Editions in Paris, and that they be bound and distributed by them under joint imprint. It sounded like an excellent idea.

Harry Marks was my distributor, and I was told he was doing me a disservice, because his specialty was erotica, and he was my only outlet in the U.S., but I pointed out that he had bought up the editions at my price, and had paid in advance which enabled the Black Sun Press to keep ahead of its costs. You are foolish, they said, and so I decided to speak to Mr. Marks about the offer.

When it came to the point, I found him at his office, in ecstasy over *The Bridge* (not erotica) and I didn't have the heart, or inclination, to mention the Random House offer. It might have been better for the B.S.P., but I believe it would have been a disaster for C.C.

The second offer was from Simon & Schuster. They made a valid proposal. I was to choose and edit a series of Black Sun modern novels. They would do all the rest. This delighted me. I had great confidence in Dick Simon and I went to his office bearing manuscripts. The first three titles were by Kay Boyle, René Crevel and Carnevali. Anne Watkins, Kay's agent, was present. Also Clifton Fadiman, Simon & Schuster's bright young man.

"Kay Boyle is okay," they agreed, "but here," said Mr. Fadiman, "are the other titles and authors for you to begin with." Katherine Anne Porter was first. I never have been as enthusiastic about *Flowering Judas* as others have. Willa Cather, too, was on their list. I protested. "This seems to be your choice, not mine," I wailed. "As far as I am concerned, it's Crevel or nothing, and Kay agrees with me."

Fadiman replied, "Later on you can slip in Crevel and Carnevali, but we've got to establish *you* first."

"Establish who?" I asked. "Mr. Fadiman, or Mrs. Crosby." And to the embarrassment of those present, I burst into tears. I had the agreement in my hand. This I tore furiously in two, and stalked sobbing out of the office. I kept my authors, but it is sad to say I've got them still, though I try perennially to wangle

Crevel and Carnevali into print, and have not given up hope. Anne Watkins and Simon & Schuster made a separate contract for Kay Boyle.

I did not linger in New York because I had several exciting publications pending, and I had to be in Paris to supervise them. On the press was *New Found Land,* the latest poems of Archibald MacLeish, in a limited edition, for which after my own B.S.P. sheets were run, I printed others on less fine paper for Houghton Mifflin of Boston, who bound and brought them out in their own regular edition. Archie told me that no poet could wish his poems more beautifully or satisfactorily presented. Then too I had started on a very special presentation of *Alice in Wonderland.* I knew that anyone having the audacity to do a modern "Alice" should present it in as opposite a manner to the original edition as could be managed. No one could emulate the perfection of Tenniel's work, or try to, but I believed that Marie Laurencin might create a very different and very lovely Alice to enhance the immortal text.

I made an appointment to call on her and when I was ushered into her apartment she was on the floor playing with a doll's house. Up she jumped (or rather bounced), cordial and utterly delightful—round smiling eyes, soft crinkly brown hair, an artist all ruffles and curves. She had always wanted to illustrate *Alice au pays des Merveilles,* she said, and ran to bring me the many editions in many languages that she had collected. She showed me, too, her collection of dolls and we had tea from doll-sized teacups.

Together we mapped out a plan for the book. Everything must be quite different—an oblong format, album size, I said and she agreed—She would do five or six full-page water colours and would choose the subjects herself from the text. There was to be a portrait of Alice as frontispiece—we worked over this edition together during that spring. It turned out to be a lovely thing—many of the copies were sold to French collectors but more than half were sold in New York by Harry F. Marks, Park Avenue bookseller, who before that had ordered and paid in advance for our entire editions of Lawrence, Joyce and Crane—thereby permitting the Black Sun to shine in sol-

327

vency. Frank Crowninshield, who was a Laurencin enthusiast and collector, bought twenty-five copies for Christmas presents, I believe all the *Vanity Fair* staff fared the same that year whether they liked it or not. The cost at the time was two pounds a copy. When Frank died in 1947, there was an auction of his treasures, pictures and books and his special copy of "Alice" inscribed by the artist was knocked down for £50, and so his investment paid off.

I had given up the rue de Lille apartment when I had returned from America the last time, it had been rented rather grandly during two weeks of my absence by the Lady in Waiting to the Duke and Duchess of York (it was the Duke of Kent who signed "George" on the Moulin wall) for their use during an official visit to Paris during the Colonial Exhibition, as a private retreat where the young couple could relax and receive their friends. They were officially guests of the British Embassy but unofficially tenants of Caresse Crosby. When I returned the rooms were smiling—I have the feeling that it had been a happy interlude.

Julien Levy, artist and art dealer, was in Paris looking for talent for his New York gallery. He was on the side of the Surrealists already, having shown to New York the works of Max Ernst, and a fur-lined teacup. He was by nature himself a Surrealist which endeared him to me. During his stay in Paris he had seen Salvador Dali's art and was contemplating a one-man show for him in the fall, but Dali was, in those days, difficult to approach and scared to death to meet the public. He had just married Gala, formerly the wife of Paul Eluard and before that the *belle amie* of Max Ernst. Now she had become the siren inspiration in the life of the young Spanish painter whom she had met the summer before on a lonely beach in Cadaques. She was searching for sea shells, he was wading.

During his visit Julien came out for a Sunday at the Mill and, as was usual, the Dalis and the Ernsts were there. Julien had just bought a superb ciné camera in Germany and it naturally followed that the week-end was spent in making a very surrealist picture. I think there was one shot when Max appeared to hurtle from the parapet of the sun tower, and then his shirt and trousers, empty of the body, went swirling through the air to lie limp upon the cobblestones below. The shirt was kicked aside into the pool while the trousers walked disconsolately away into the forest, presently Max's arm, back in the shirt, beckoned to us from a watery grave. Dali took part, so did I, and so did the eight donkeys that shared the dining room (they used to eat from a manger while we ate from upturned logs hewn from nearby forest oaks).

After Julien left for the States, Salvador lost momentum. He just couldn't pull himself together sufficiently to get across the ocean, especially with his precious paintings. It was not until a year later when I was about to travel to New York on the *Champlain* and offered to shepherd the Dalis safely to Julien's door, that he finally screwed up courage to agree to our plan. I remember well that morning when I arrived on the boat-train platform. I had promised that I would be there in plenty of time to help him stow himself and his paintings. The train had just backed into the station; only a few passengers were aboard, but Dali was aboard. In a third-class compartment next to the engine he sat like a hunter in covert, peering out from behind the canvases that were stacked around, above, below and in front of him. To each picture he had attached a string. These strings were tied either to his clothing or his fingers. He was very pale and very nervous. "I am next to the engine," he said, "so that I'll get there quicker." He refused to eat lunch on the way for fear someone would pick-pocket a "soft watch" or two.

I had rather grand quarters on the *Champlain*. It was my thirtieth crossing on the French Line and so they were particulary nice to me and I asked that the Dalis, who were travelling in third, might dine in first with me. I had run into Henry May on deck and we had decided that we would share a table in the dining saloon. In the bar before dinner the second night out I told him that I had some charming artist friends who were eating with us that evening. "How delightful," he said, "I must dress, I'll see you later." I guessed the Dalis would *not* dress, but I got into an afternoon silk by compromise and went to wait for them in the main saloon. Henry was there already. Presently there appeared two of the most fantastic voyagers I have ever seen. Dali, wrapped in sweaters up to his ears—I think I can remember mittens—Gala in true emigré style in trousers and a turban. Both wore long overcoats. "Here they come," I said to my companion. His jaw dropped. He bowed stiffly and politely but, which was very sad, most unexpectedly he developed a migraine and had to return in haste to his cabin to rest. We three, however, had a delightful dinner. Both of the Dalis that evening were so funny that I laughed until I, too, had migraine. It was so apparent that we were having a wonderful time that we rather scandalized the cautious passengers who were looking around surreptitiously to see who was to be courted and who was to be cut. After a brief interval in the bar we said good night and I insisted that they join me again the following evening. The next morning I had it out with Henry. I told him he had behaved extremely badly which he didn't believe since he is known on both sides of the Atlantic for his exquisite manners, and was and still is, the super American snob. I could not persuade him to share the table with me except at luncheon, so to the rest of the passengers I was a perfect lady at noon, and a perfect caution at night.

When we steamed up New York harbour, Gala and I hung over the rail while I pointed out Empire State and Lady Liberty but Dali would not quit the confines of his submarine cabin. He had been packed and ready to leave the ship since the third day out. When the pilot came alongside I recognized several of my reporter friends, one of whom approached me with the usual request for a photograph. I had my two black whippets on a leash, a number of diamond bracelets on my wrist and a very short black velvet skirt on my legs. They asked for cheesecake, and they got it. "But," I said when cameras and pencils had stopped clicking, "have you Salvador Dali on your list?" My friend fished out a bit of paper and ran his eyes up and down it. "Dali? No," he said, "who's he?" I looked over the names. "You can tear those right up," I answered, "but if you want a story, see Dali," and I gave him the number of his cabin. Two minutes later he reappeared. "Dali has a story all right," he said, "but I can't understand a word of it. Who is he anyway? French?" "Catalan," I replied, which seemed to bait him even more. "I'll go down with you if you like and do the interpreting." And to the others, cameramen included, I added, "Come along, boys."

Dali was indeed a sight for newsmongering eyes, again his paintings were attached to him and he attached to them. "They want to see some of your work," I explained, " these are the gentlemen of the Press and," I hissed in French, "they can take or leave you." He got the idea at once, untangled himself from his harness and began stripping the paper from the largest and most unwieldy of the paintings. They gaped at this one, they were convulsed at the next one. "This is important," I said, "let me tell you a little about surrealism." I gave a brief lecture and when they asked Dali which was his favourite picture he answered, "The portrait of my wife." "Yes," I agreed, "you see he has painted her with lamb chops on her shoulder." "Lamb chops?" they roared. That did it! The pencils began to move, the cameras to click.

I may have done Dali a good turn, but I am not so sure. At any rate I did not further my own special cause for Gala and the lamb chops took the place of cheesecake in all the morning editions.

It often is reported in print that I "introduced" Salvador Dali to Amerca and this could be interpreted to mean that I was responsible for bringing his work before the eyes of the American public, which is not exactly true. It was Julien who "promoted" Dali as an artist, while I only introduced him to the Press.

The "melting watches" and the lamb chops had an almost immediate success. The public was intrigued and "surrealism" became a household word. It was the following spring, while New York was keyed to this new interest, that we decided to give the Dream Ball as a farewell party for the artist who was about to leave New York for Europe a richer and much less timid man.

Dali and I organized the ball with the help of the manager of the Coq Rouge, the restaurant where the Dalis ate daily. We had gone there for luncheon direct from the boat and the proprietor had been interested at once. Now, six months later, he was full of enthusiasm to carry out our suggestions. The ball was to be by invitation, one exchanged the written card at the door for one link of sausage threaded out to each guest by means of an ancient sewing machine. There was a nominal entrance fee to cover expenses but every one paid for their drinks and supper. The guests were invited to come disguised as their most recurrent dream. This left tremendous openings for the mantic and the Freudian. There would be a prize for the best costume; a Dali drawing, of course.

Dali and I had scoured the five-and-ten-cent store for equipment for our surrealist ideas. I must say we succeeded delightfully. The waiters, who were all in dress suits, wore horn-rimmed spectacles and diamond tiaras from Kresge's. The barmen wore white coats to which each added a tie of auburn or blond hair knotted as a four-in-hand. I was able to exactly match the blonds and the redheads. The effect was absolutely disgusting. The doorman wore a wreath of pink roses instead of a cap and sat in a rocking chair on the side-walk waiting for the guests to arrive. Casually in the doorway, as though it had just been dropped there by mistake, was a hundred-pound block of ice tied up with a red satin ribbon. An empty bathtub was sliding down the stairs and the carcass of a cow wore a white wedding veil as it sat at the far end of the room, where its stomach once had been, a gramophone played the latest French tunes. All this was concocted in twenty-four hours. I hate to think what would have materialized if we had had a little while longer. The party was a tremendous success.

Every paper in town carried pictures and a story, some less sympathetic than the others. I had decked myself up in a very expensive disguise as the white horse of dream desire. The papers however reported that Mrs. Crosby looked charming dressed as a bunny rabbit. Gala had come as a baby doll to whose face clung bits of mold and leaves and around whose neck wound a procession of painted ants by Dali. Repercussions of this party reached Europe and even Russia, where a Sunday paper published it all complete with photographs showing, I suppose, the decadence of American culture. Could they have chosen a better subject? This was mailed to me by a Russian friend, *then*. But it was enormous fun and that first Dream Ball though often imitated has never been equalled.

When I boarded the *Ile de France* to return to the Moulin du Soleil, after that surreal winter in New York, I ran into

Mr. and Mrs. Bob Haas who were taking a trip to Europe combining pleasure and profit. The profit was in discovering new authors for Harcourt, Brace with whom Bob was then associated. He had in his hand, when we met on deck, a copy of *Waiting for Nothing* by Tom Kromer. Bob said it was an advance copy not yet on the market, but the author's eyes looked sharp out at me from the jacket and I knew I could not wait until publication date. "May I borrow it?" I asked. "Keep it," he answered, "I have already looked it through and I'd like to know your opinion."

That first evening at sea was spent in a bunk with a hobo. I took the jacket off so that I could prop his photograph before me as I read. I was completely overwhelmed by what he had to say and why, and quite unnerved by that desperate look. Not only did I read all through the night, but I answered the author by a letter written on French Line stationery.

I told him that if he could get to Europe I wanted him to come and live at the Mill, that I was sure he could write there and that his presence would be an inspiration to all of us and perhaps he'd find the reverse of the "nothing" he'd been waiting for. I thought about Tom Kromer all the way across the ocean.

It was not long before I received his answer and I realized that he terribly needed the help he asked for and so I took his book to Calman-Levy who agreed to publish it in French and to send the author an advance cheque large enough to enable him to take passage for Europe that summer. Kromer wrote wonderful letters; he was to sail in July and then a cable from Polly arrived for me saying that she had the chance of a lifetime to do a film for M.G.M.; the tests were already arranged for by Mr. Rubin if only she could get to Hollywood. "It means everything to me," she radioed. "Can't you come and take me?" So I did, first sending off a long cable to Tom Kromer to tell him that I was on my way west (he was living in Carmel, California) and asking him to wait there until I arrived. I would be motoring out, I would be motoring back, and would drive him east again. I had no answer to my cable and I set sail impatient to reach my goal, for I am afraid M.G.M. played second violin to that expedition. I was still journeying across duck ponds.

333

CHAPTER 38

I met Bert Young unexpectedly one unbelievable evening in Hollywood, and from then on, everything about our union was unexpected and unbelievable.

Our meeting was unbelievable because I was really waiting for Tom Kromer. Not at all "waiting for nothing" since I had built up in my mind, a mind obedient to my senses, the rôle half angel and half siren that I hoped to play in his life. I must have felt the absolute necessity of assuming responsibility for some baffled soul. I had heard through the grapevine that Kromer would be waiting for me at a certain house on a certain street on a certain night in August. The message had arrived mysteriously, I didn't know how, though I did know that he had spoken on the radio in Carmel the week before, the subject was controversial.

I had not heard that address, but I had issued my own private manifesto in Paris in '28 for a Caressive Community; it upheld the Marxian ideal of eighty years before and added many amenities—no one, I declared, should live well while another starved. But the masses, I insisted, should be helped to enjoy life, to work and to share, and emphatically to share the fun. I believe I advocated a compulsory working week from nine to one Mondays through Saturdays. Free enterprise, free education, free entertainment, from one to midnight. Picnics and parades on Sundays and lots of flags! (Harry was a self-declared anarchist.)

I was to be at the mystery address at midnight. Fred Healey, an embarrassingly good-looking boy was with me, I had to get rid of him. We had dined and gone to the cinema and had an hour to spare and so he suggested a drink at a Sunset Boulevard night club, the most fashionable in Hollywood. I was nervously watching my wristwatch in spite of music and Fred, when suddenly, I caught sight of a blond giant, handsome as Hermes and militant as Mars, who was evidently the host to a party at the table across the floor and surrounded by youths and maidens shrilly gay. Suddenly he caught my mesmerized gaze, got up and came across to our table. "You're Caresse Crosby, aren't you?" "Introduce me, Fred," he lorded. "Bert Young," Fred mumbled and gave me a warning kick under the table, but no warning served me then or ever after.

"Dance?" he invited and as though pierced by the fatal arrow, I rose and with a shiver was in his arms. I forgot Fred, I forgot Kromer—we danced our way out into the night. I remember, much later, a moon that dropped into the Pacific while we watched it sink under the waves from the sands of Santa Monica. He told me all the impossible, crazy things he longed to do, places he had been and places he would go some day. To me every word was intangible and spellbinding—I knew at long last I was falling in love again.

The stormy times we weathered, the impossible days and nights we spent on the impossible quest of an impossible future were unbelievable too. Bert obsessed me. I followed him from one world to another and he did the same. We feared and admired each other, we hated and we loved each other, until finally after months of frustration and longing we married each other. It was a dangerous road and yet the only destined road for me to take.

But Tom Kromer was deserted—I heard from him only once again and we never met. The need I had felt to plunge into an obliterating relationship had been satisfied. This I had been seeking and this I found.

I gave up the Moulin du Soleil at the end of 1936, I thought it was a good feeling to be footloose with the whole wide world before me. I might, I assured myself, proceed anywhere—but actually, I was already drawn back to my homeland where my children were becoming integral parts of the American scene,

335

or so I thought, for Billy was in Williams College making friends and Polly had "come out" in New York and seemed determined to follow a budding career in Hollywood. When I left her in California in October, I put her under the protective wings of the Ben Ray Redmans, Frieda Inescort (Mrs. R.) was a seasoned trooper and a charmingly civilized one as well. I had no qualms, though the Redmans may have had.

Later, with Bert at the wheel, I began to scour Virginia, looking for a bargain estate in which to invest.

In true emigrée style I plunked my dwindling bundle of securities in the Middleburg Bank—this gave the local landlords confidence and I was courted and touted from one borderline to another, but nothing I saw quite filled imagination's eye.

At the finish of an exhausting week we landed in a Fredericksburg repair shop while some major operation took place under the sputtering hood of the Ford. There would be hours to wait. I had time to kill—I wandered into a smoky and untidy little office and asked the equally untidy agent if he had any farm property to sell. "Farm?" he inquired, looking dubiously at my white doeskin gloves. Bert was not there so I launched forth on my own desires. "I'd like an old plantation house with columns"—I eyed him firmly—"smothered in roses and honeysuckle"—at this heresy he sat up like a ramrod—"a deer park, an avenue of elms, magnolia and tulip trees, open fields with lovely bramble hedges, and a pond with nénuphars." From his expression I guessed that he knew I meant "pond lilies." As my vision grew, his horror began to turn to cunning. This woman, he thought, is crazy but she may be solvent as well. His hand actually shook as he fished some dog-eared photographs from a bottom drawer. He handed them to me and I saw the figment of my imagining in all its beautiful reality. "It's perfect, where is it?" I asked. "About twenty-five miles from here." I looked downcast. "If you've got the time, Honey, I've got the transportation," he beamed, awakened to the full possibilities of the situation. "Let's go," I announced. Bert had said repairs would take several hours and I waved to him as we bounced by in a springless pickup—"Back later," I called as off we jounced.

"I better warn you," said my purveyor of dreams, "it has its shortcomings." "How many baths?" I asked—"There's a tin tub, and there's a nice clean outhouse," he grinned, but I wasn't daunted.

As we approached the house that Jefferson had designed for his friend and legislative colleague Colonel DeJarnette I knew that this was it. It was deep in honeysuckle, its elms stood like glorious sentinels, its magnolias loomed one hundred feet high, and spreading this way and that, the open uncultivated fields lay matted and soft with a weave of weed and creeper. Inside it was chilly and grimy, but I realized its perfect possibilities. Already my furniture was fitting itself into corners and my books were ranging themselves from floor to ceiling. There was a kitchen doorstep worn hollow by bare black feet.

"How much?" I asked. "$14,000," he said drawing a long breath. "I'll take it," I answered ($15,000 or £3,000 was my limit). He nearly fell backwards off the porch (the steps had tumbled away). Now he knew I was crazy. "Better get back to the office," he muttered. I remembered it was next to the police station and I think he was remembering this too, with comfort. I knew of course Bert would want to approve and I knew that he would get to work and bargain in proper style—that is why I insisted on closing the deal at once. On the return trip I cogitated. "I didn't see any barn"—"Nope," he answered. "It burnt to the ground, but there's a nice hen house out back." "Too bad," I said. "I dislike hens—I'll burn that too!"

Bert and I spent the night in Fredericksburg and drove over next day to our Virginia estate—for indeed it deserved all the glory that such rating could give it. Luckily Bert thought it wonderful too—only he must have guessed how costly it would be to do over—I hadn't an inking—and we started planning. Four baths, electricity from the source, telephone (three miles of wire), paint and plaster and brick—a new well and a ram a mile in the woods—it was fantastic how that place began to eat up money, but soon everything was humming. I took rooms at an inn in Fredericksburg to direct operations.

As soon as I bought Hampton Manor, everyone unwillingly, or willingly, seemed to desert me, that is, my closest and most needed did. Billy was working in New York in American Airlines, loading freight at LaGuardia Field. Polly was with my mother in New York, too busy with the social whirl to come to my aid. Bert went off to Florida for the season with some extravagant excuse, and I had the weeds and the mud, the plumbers, the plasterers and the electricians to deal with by myself, in the rain.

I lived in Fredericksburg at the hotel. It was comfortable enough and I had the Ford to drive back and forth in, but it was twenty-five miles each way each day and headaches at one end and backaches at the other. It would have been fun if I had not been alone. At first I was too proud to ask for help, but after a month of it I began putting in long-distance calls to New York.

Polleen dutifully came down supposedly for several weeks, but soon re-entrained for Fifty-seventh Street. She admittedly thought I was foolhardy to take on such a remote adventure. Billy could only get off on Sundays and a single day was not enough. Then, though I determined not to, I began calling Bert. He was having a fine time where he was. "If I come back it is for good," he said. I did not quite dare say "come." But one dreary night in February, up to my neck in problems, I broke down and wired, "Come back and stay." He did next day. And for two weeks we worked it out together. He was wonderful with contractors and labourers; things actually flew into shape.

By March we had moved into the new stable, the house would be ready by April. "After all, why not get married," we said. We were shopping in Richmond that afternoon. I was in jodhpurs, so was he, and we were eating Chesapeake oysters in Bob's Seafood Grill.

"I must be married properly," I said, "by a bishop, at least." "Of course, by a bishop," announced Bert. And in his amazing manner, he went to the telephone and dialed. I heard him mention "China."

"It's all arranged," he said. "And Bob will be best man!" Bob was the owner of the Grill. Overwhelmed, "I've got to change," I demurred, but Bert said the bishop promised he would be at the church in less than half of an hour, with his wife. They were on their way out to dinner. "We must meet them there with a ring, which I have," he added. And he produced it from his pocket. It was the same one he had bought two years before when we were in Barcelona, and the same one we had so nearly used the year before in Montgomery, Alabama, where Bert had taken me to meet his mother's family. We had gone hand in hand up the State House steps to gaze at the portrait of Rubin Saffold, first Governor of Alabama and Bert's great-grandfather. He hung in the place of honour as one entered the building, a handsome southern gentleman. It was from Rubin's grand-daughter, Bert's mother, Selberta Saffold Young that the name of "Selbert" was derived !

The bishop's wife did look startled when she saw how the bride was dressed, but it was Virginia, and in Virginia jodhpurs are correct for almost any occasion. The ecclesiastical knot was firmly tied. The bishop was judicious. I was a widow, Bert a bachelor. I don't remember any license !

We went back with Bob to the Seafood Grill for champagne and lobster, on the house—and rather startled at what had happened, we returned to Hampton Manor as man and wife.

Telegrams were sent off. My family was appalled and so were we for a time, but when we moved from the stable into the Jeffersonian Manor House with its floodlit pillars, we felt like very proper Virginians, broke and proud.

It had been during the long trek to and from Fredericksburg that I had decided I must have a dog for company and for protection too, and to my joy the Shaw MacKeans, who had met their first black Afghan Hound with me in France and who decided from that moment to raise Afghans instead of wire-haired fox terriers, told me that they had one black pup out of the first litter and it was mine if I wished—of course I did and Salar was shipped from Prides Crossing, Massachusetts, to Bowling Green, Virginia. He was frightened and ferocious when he emerged from the railroad crate but I started to woo him with soft words and venison. When he stopped between a gulp and a snarl to lick my ear, I knew that he was mine. Later there were red setters and beguiling beagles —and whippets.

The whippets came with the furniture, Harry's books too, four thousand of them, many from the Walter Berry library. Maple et Cie, world shippers, had packed the volumes in an

339

ark-like crate lined with heaviest paper, tarred on the outside and banded round with hoops of shining tin, it bore mammoth shipping instructions in French and it was a very awesome object indeed. We had to have a three-team vehicle to haul the thing from the railroad siding to Hampton Manor. The entire countryside turned out, and when the pie was opened the books began to sing—"Skylark," "Daffodils" and "babbling brooks."

Empty, "the Ark" now reared itself upon the lawn. I wondered what to do with it, it seemed so thriftless to break it into bits, and then Shep, our coloured head man, ambled shyly up to me and touched his cap. "If you all doan wan this box," his eye was pleading as he spoke, "I bin needin' to enlarge my house for some time." "But will it do?" I marvelled. "Jes fine," he enthused, "jes fine, me an' Sophie's expecting an addition to the fambly and an addition to the house will do jes fine." So he hauled it off to his shack beyond the corn fields and when I walked over a few weeks later to see how the new "addition to the fambly" was doing, I found a brand-new wing neatly nailed to Shep's "main house," and towering above it. The tarpaper top and silvery bands gave it a decidedly modern look and along its sides for all to see was painted in huge exotic lettering *"Prenez garde à l'eau de Mer"*!

I walked through the newmade door to find Mrs. Shep in her private bedroom, a minute kinky head upon her arm and tacked above the bed looking down upon them like some alabaster faun, the poetic eyes and naked torso of my erstwhile Parisian friend Johnny S. whose rakish likeness must have fallen in from between the books.

Another practical gesture turned out no less exotically. A quarter of a mile before arriving at the gates of Hampton Manor one came smack upon a fork in the country road and in the "V" of the fork stood a giant oak, the trunk menacingly solid. It was a real road hazard and difficult to see until one was almost up against it. I had a premonition that either our guests or ourselves in a rushing mood might at some dusky moment hit it, head on. In deference to my friend Michael Arlen I named it "The Green Hat" tree and I decided it should

340

56. Californian picnic—Billy, Kiki Preston and friend, Caresse, 1941.

57. Caresse and her son Billy Peabody, Summer, 1942.

58. Max Ernst shows horror at his own work as it arrives " chez Caresse "—Dorothe
Tanning (now Mrs. Ernst) looks ahead, Washington, 1944.

have a goodly band of whitewash around its waist for our future protection.

I entrusted the job to Ely, the handyman about the place. "Do your best," I instructed. "Yes, *Mam*" he said and interpreted it just that way. When I returned one evening from a day in Richmond the headlights suddenly caught and held an awesome sight—the great trunk for twenty feet up from the ground looked like the funnel of a White Star liner. (An outsized arrow barbed like a pin wheel pointed left.) Fifty dollars' worth of bath tub enamel lay thick and smooth upon the cylindrical surface of the oak, like porcelain upon a Kelvinator—it glistened like a Kelvinator too. No one ever hit it, I assure you, for everyone gave it the widest possible berth.

Bert loved being "Lord of the Manor" and looked the part, only it was a part which he play-acted to its fullest and to its finish too. I was left to sow the grain and winnow the wheat, calve the cattle and drive the tractor, that is, metaphorically speaking, for I had plenty of strong ebony hands to help me. If only I had started out with the idea that I was to be the one to mulch and dig and plant and harvest while Bert hunted or gallivanted, I would have planned it all properly, studied books, consulted experts, learnt *how* to farm; but during three whole years I procrastinated hopefully for the Lord of my Manor to take hold. He never did—it was I who on frosty nights, lantern in hand and Shep at my side, left a warm conjugal bed to help some princeling Domino enter the bucolic arena—and it was I who drove our harvest truck to market.

In spite of the fact that I had bought the finest lot of heifers in Texas at a Forth Worth cattle show along with Prince Domino II, the noblest and most expensive of bulls, Bert's devotion to cattle-raising lasted only as long as the neighbours came to "Oh" and "Ah."

The sartorial cowhand who arrived with the cattle jangling with silver spur and weighted lariat, whose brilliant neckerchief was changed every hour on the hour, thereby enthralling the village belles (I saw one being used as a *rebozo* later) was shipped back to Texas as soon as the cattle were duly inoculated and properly corralled. (That in Virginia they needed no branding rather upset him.) On arrival at the railroad siding (our second sideshow for the country folk) he had sauntered from his bed-sitting room at the head of the Hereford Association de luxe cattle car and had demanded very grandly, "Whar's the ranch?" and on arrival, already disillusioned, "and whar's the corral?" Bert and I were so embarrassed at our lack of equipment that we immediately set to work to build him what he asked for. I believe we boasted the only cattle-slip and cow-dip in the county. When he was ready to leave he insisted on making the return trip by air at our expense, we were moving into Hereford hierarchy. It was expensive.

Three years of marriage with Bert in which frustration and fascination both played their part, fled by. Bert had no wealth but had sworn his great ambition was to own a place of his own and to farm. Own we did and farm we tried to, and those years at Hampton Manor with its surrounding five hundred acres of woodland, stream and meadow hold many tender memories, some gay, some sad, some funny.

CHAPTER 39

Stuart Kaiser, one of Boston's literati and an India Docks tobacco merchant to boot, had been a close friend of Harry Crosby in the ambulance corps, and was one of our first guests. The tobacco business having gone up in smoke, Stuart was in need of a rest, my invitation to Hampton Manor seemed to fit the prescription and, for us, his visit could not have been more opportune. Our lawns needed attention, he needed exercise, and the singsong melody of our brand-new mower soothed everyone's nerves. Mornings at sunrise, I was awakened by the bladed music underneath my window, the least rest the most cure was Stuart's diagnosis of his need.

By the end of a month's diligence our greensward rolled out between the elms cropped and flat. It could have been used for a bowling alley, and was. At day's end when mowing machines and other implementi were laid aside, we gathered on the front steps, mint juleps in hand, to talk over the day's progression. Some had fished and some had hayed, some had mowed and some had played.

Our guests that first year were cosmopolitan and of varied ages—they ranged from Mother and her contemporaries to Billy and his—and from Turkey to Texas. One amenity that amazed Paris visitors was the rare quality of the French wines served at our table—better than they could get in France, they declared.

In Virginia no wine or liquor was sold in shops, all had to be bought from the A.B.C. stores (Alcohol Beverages Control).

Most of the citizenry stuck to spirits, but after World War I, some sophisticated legislator had with perspicacity engaged a French nobleman to replenish the state's wine list. This Frenchman happened to be Comte Boni de Castellane, one of the greatest connoisseurs of the era, and thus the Count's choice was placed modestly at the foot of the A.B.C. list in the heedless little town of Fredericksburg. Here I found listed such delectable cuveés as Chambertin '29, Corton '28, Chablis '34 and even Perrier-Jouët '28 at a price commensurate with the local purse.

When in astonishment I asked the clerk if they had any of this treasure left—"The whole lot," he answered, "no one round here drinks that French stuff"—and so as quietly as possible I bought "the whole lot" up. Constance, who came to visit, smuggled some Mouton Rothschild back to France for special dinner parties in Paris.

Bert and I vied with each other for embellishments. I said I would build a stable and Bert said he would build a barn. We both set to work with rule and pencil to map our projects. I designed a low four-stall building, loose-boxes and office and tack room with open fireplaces as pretty as a doll's house. Bert's barn looked mammoth on paper and was to be bright red, with white trim and a handsome Hereford weathervane on top.

We each hired our own labour and each set to work. Lumber was cut at the sawmill down the road and Ely our handyman-carpenter teamed up with Bert—I had an intelligent Negro bricklayer and his impish son to hustle for me. The place hummed, we whistled while we worked. Both buildings grew with the speed of an animated cartoon. The cost was so low that none of our neighbours believed us, "Noth'n liahs" that we were! But Bert was born in Alabama and managed to pass muster, I "damnyankee" (ten-letter word) that I was, sometimes slipped up.

It was while the coloured bricklayer was helping me lay the chimney that one evening on entering the Bowling Green drugstore to pick up the evening paper I ran into a dozen or more citizens waiting for the mail. The bricklayer was there too, in a corner. I knew him best so my first greeting was for him. "Good evening, Mr. T—" I said—then nodded to the others. There was a sudden freezing, a shuffling of feet and a hollow silence—no one responded, not even Mr. T—. I didn't know until Bert explained later that to call a Negro "Mister" in Virginia was considered an insult to the whites. I did not change my ways.

When I had departed for my eight weeks' sojourn in Reno where I took a course in Animal Husbandry at the University of Nevada, I already suspected a house divided among guests —Salvador Dali on one side of the Jeffersonian hallway, painting from dawn till dusk, and Henry Miller on the other, while he completed his book *The Colossus of Maroussi*—and when I returned I found Dali ankle deep in the pages of his autobiography while across the hall in a room whose walls were tacked with fresh-made water colours sat the erstwhile scribe at an easel! (I later helped edit Dali's *Secret Life* for publication by the Dial Press and gave Miller his first one-man show of painting at The Crosby Gallery of Art in Washington.)

The New Yorker that season reported in its pages that as a Virginia hostess I found it far easier to swing a piano from a tree top than to provide a fourth at bridge. That was quite true, for Hampton Manor was way off the beaten track, and besides I don't play bridge. But when Dali insisted to Pathé Newsmen that pianos were just as fitting in trees as in parlours, they scoffed and said, "But of course, you can't *put* a piano in a tree." "Why not?" I parried, and in no time at all, there it hung. We had a truck on the place with a great steel cable, used for pulling farm machinery out of waterholes, or station wagons out of ditches. Shep and Len and four of the younger generation of "hands" made light weight of bearing the grand piano from the front room to the front lawn, a coil of cable hurled over a sturdy upper limb was belted round the instrument's waist, then the cable attached to the truck which, in lowest speed, majestically advanced swinging the mahogany music box into the magnolia branches forty feet overhead— and half an hour later, our truck was again carrying grist to the miller.

I also prodded my prize heifer into the library where she

chewed a contented cud in front of the fire while the celluloid reeled. The trouble with Hampton's Pride was that she didn't want to go back to the barn and had to be pushed in sitting position down the front steps.

It was the month of February, and in Virginia it was a very dreary month. During our first spring, Bert and I had discovered the abandoned house a mile or two down the road, past the little DeJarnette post office at the fork, where the Green Hat Tree divided the ways that led, on the left to "Hampton Manor," and on the right to "Oak Grove," another DeJarnette homestead.

The first day that we rode through that deserted property, it was a tangle of hawthorn and honeysuckle, the fresh green leaves formed a lacy garment to hide the mansion's bursting seams and cupolas out at the elbow. It looked mysterious and inviting that spring afternoon—we had heard it was for sale —for a song—had been for a long time, and in the back of my mind I stored the idea that some day some friend of ours might like to sing for it, and make it livable again. So when the Dalis inquired about a possible place in the vicinity, I drove them over one February afternoon to Oak Grove.

The road in from the highway through the woods to the house had been passable for our mounts before, but a car was something else, and it looked as if no car had come that way for many moons. We floundered in red Virginia mud up to our hub caps and halfway to the lonely house the overhanging boughs, denuded of foliage, caught and held the station wagon tight. Even backing seemed impossible. We got out and walked. The wood was wet, the sun was about to set when we reached the mouldering steps, and looked up at the cockeyed windows with blinds flapping in the rising night wind; we shuddered and then laughed amazed. It seemed impossible that any one could envisage the purchase of such a dilapidated manse, but we were curious to investigate, and since I had the big iron key from the owner in Bowling Green, we gingerly mounted the rotting steps and turned the key in the lock; the door swung wide with the proper creaking sighs—the room on the left of the hall had a fireplace but no roof, and mice scuttled and bats flew at our ingress, what a place for a murder or a surrealist adventure, we exclaimed. The rest of the place was drearier.

We noticed it was just five as the sun dropped like a great glob of blood behind the cemetery fence that edged the bramble-matted lawn and we decided to leave then and there "but we must stage a return" we agreed as we locked the door upon the watchful ghosts.

The next week I went to New York to bring Mother back for a visit and while there I talked with Fulco de Verdura about using some of Dali's designs in his jewellery business. The Duke was interested and I invited him to come down for the following week-end at Hampton Manor where he and Dali could discuss the project. "Is your place far?" asked the Sicilian nobleman. "Is it difficult to find?" "It's remote, but we love it. It is really old-time South," I said brightly. "Have you never been to Virginia?" "No," he answered, still undecided.

"I'll meet you in Fredericksburg," I promised. "The Florida express stops there. You get on at Penn Station and off in Virginia, it's easy." He said he would love to come.

"The Duke de Verdura believes he is coming to some outlandish spot," I said on my return. "He is sure we are quite uncivilized in these parts"—and then the big idea dawned on us simultaneously.

Why not? I was delighted and Dali beamed, *"Perfect."*

That night we made our plans, and next day we set the stage for the adventure of the haunted house. Fulco was to arrive the following afternoon, the train reached Fredericksburg at three, but I promised to delay our arrival until 4.30 for the setting of the sun. That morning we had a dress rehearsal and I arranged that Shep, our major-domo, should drive Gala and Dali over to Oak Grove with all our props. They said by four they would be ready for our arrival.

I met Fulco in jodhpurs and riding jacket and I carried a wicked-looking whip under my arm. I noticed with satisfaction that he was immaculately dressed, and carried a very large and handsome leather bag, which must have contained the proper clothes for every occasion, except perhaps the one awaiting him.

The wind was rising, he drew his overcoat about him, I

347

knew he was looking forward to the promised warmth and comfort of Hampton Manor. I had to delay our arrival until the appointed hour, so I stopped at the market in Fredericksburg. I exchanged a book at the library. I dawdled, and drove first very fast and then very slow. He was as fidgety as a pheasant by the time we reached the Green Hat Tree. We swung to the right through the wood leaving the open macadam. " Is it much further?" he groaned. "Not if I don't lose the way. It's always hard to find the entrance. It is very overgrown," I unassured him. With that I lurched the car sidewise across a wicked ditch and we entered the driveway of Oak Grove. We crashed and lunged along over gullies and under wicked boughs. It was gloomy in the wood.

"Here we are at last," I cried heartily, as we careened to a full stop in front of the most dismal objective I have ever aimed at. I timed it right. The blood-red sun was about to set. The damp wind was rising. The sighing of shutter and creaking of hinge had begun and to my satisfaction I heard an owl hoot nearby in the copse. (Garfield Upshur was doing his best!)

"Isn't it beautifully romantic," I said, as I leaned on the claxon. "Nobody home?" He replied dismally. "Lots of people," I calmed him as the front door opened and the Hampton Manor retinue appeared single file. Shep and Monroe and Garfield—in white jackets wearing cotton gloves, very well trained, they all bowed low and helped us out. "Be careful of the steps, sir," Shep warned, "likely to break a leg." Fulco jumped sideways. The step under Garfield gave way with a crash (more good work).

"Take the Duke's things to the north room," I instructed, "and see that there are no broken panes." "The north room," queried Shep. "Better put the gentleman in the tower." "Yes," I whispered back, "that's wiser, but set the rat traps."

"Do come in," I continued to our guest, "but better keep your overcoat on."

We turned into the roofless parlour. Gala was warming her hands before a crackling fire on a chimneyless hearth. As she got up she caught her foot in the rotting carpet and fell to her knees, but said gaily *"Ce n'est rien"* and smiled at the discomfited guest. "Dali is in the library. Do come along." And we

348

continued on into the most sinister chamber imaginable—cracked plaster had fallen, old volumes lay about covered with mould, the paneless windows were boarded up, and in the midst of this gloom, Dali was crouched before an easel, working by the light of one guttering candle. Before him was an ancient cradle, and tucked in it, its legs dangling over the end, his subject, a leering skeleton.

After ohing and ahing very graciously at this work, we repaired to the salon, where we gathered round the windy hearth. I pulled a bellrope, it came off in my hands, but with its clatter, as if by magic, in marched the retinue again. First, Shep with an enormous silver tea tray and tea set, polished and perfect, then Garfield with caviar and canapes, and then Monroe with a bucket of iced Pol Roget, and crystal goblets. "Garfield, please put on the Berlioz records," I said. "Yes'm," he answered, and as he disappeared we heard the hoot owl very close at hand. Fulco was frozenly polite. He told us afterwards he was trying desperately to think of some way of escape.

"I must show our friend around the park," said Dali, "before the sun sets. The drinks can wait."

"I hope you have some sweaters with you," Gala warned Fulco. "We have arranged dinner in the summerhouse just for you." "How good of you," he quavered. "Yes," said Gala, "it is so quaint there overlooking the burying ground."

We left the appetizing spread and led our shivering guest out into the night. As we descended the steps a piece of the roof slithered by our shoulders and we heard what sounded like a pack of bloodhounds baying in the woods. Fulco tottered and clutched Dali's arm. "Good God" he yelled. At this, we exploded. His expression of loathing was too magnificent. "Cheer up," I said, "we don't really live here!" "My God, I hope not." Seigneur that he was, it took him some time to recover his equilibrium. We went back to snatch a sandwich or two and then hustled him into the station wagon. "We'll find sustenance at Hampton Manor," I promised, and indeed we did. Two miles away we came to our own manicured driveway. The great colonial pillars of the Manor house were floodlit; it was warm and bright and in the library Mama was waiting with a shaker full of driest martinis.

After a hot bath and a Southern dinner, which included canvasback, wild rice and hot biscuits, the guest relaxed. Garfield and Monroe, delighted with their act, fairly danced around the table. That evening, Fulco and Dali planned the strange and beautiful jewels, which were exhibited in New York later that spring; the best pieces were a gold and onyx hoot owl, and a resplendent spider caught in a surreal web.

I was very busy now the full responsibility for herd, farm, and genius was on my shoulders—actually I was much happier, for my life was all mine again. Gala departed on a motor trip to the coast at my instigation to carry the *Secret Life* written in pidgin French to the translator Haakon Chevalier at the University of California and Dali and I were left to our own devices, they were many, it was fun. Both of us worked all day, talked at once during mealtime, played chess in the evenings, and went to bed early. Dali was always up by seven. Mother came down to visit, which she had loved to do even when Bert was there—now she was completely happy, knitting on the cool screened piazza, overlooking the busy life of kitchen doorstep and kitchen garden. She pottered in the flower garden and took frequent walks around the stables and barns. I was able to enjoy her visits without the tension of Bert's eruptive presence. Mother played chess, too.

The winter raced by—I was writing again and planning my new life—I had no regrets, either about marriage or a future without marriage. There was still so much to see, to learn, to tackle.

The Dalis left for Williamsburg. Billy was in the Navy, Polleen was overseas and in uniform. I realized then how fully another chapter of my life was ended.

I finally trucked the costly Herefords over the mountain into Staunton for a much advertised, but wholly unrewarding sale. Later I spread my surplus property out upon the lawn for a county auctioneer to cry. Although I was moving on I felt I was not losing but gaining a lap on life.

I regretted leaving the friends I had made in Virginia, they had proved good neighbours and good company—but actually I sold out with hardly a qualm. I was a lady alone, a war was on and when my farmhands began to appear in uniform, I knew it was time to leave. Tranquil little Bowling Green with its one cinema and one café had become a mecca for noisy trainees. So, piling all that was left into two monstrous moving vans, I at the wheel of a leftover Ford, with Salar at my side, headed out on Route 2 for points north, toward the lieu where once upon a time I had originated.

In Fredericksburg I stopped at the vanman's office to estimate his bill, I found that it had mounted considerably. "You see," explained the mover, "every time we cross a state line it costs you more." Rapidly I calculated, "Cross one and stop!" And that is how, with goods and chattels in tow I came to halt in the District of Columbia and how wartime Washington became the Holocene branch upon which I so frugally lit. To the bending of its twigs I was soon eager to apply my imagination and my determination. When General and Mrs. Spaatz (the Chief was moving his family nearer to the Pentagon) suggested that I take over their little Georgetown house, my answer was "Yes."

"Yes" is both epilogue and prologue to the things I will never forget. With the Second World War my life took on a clearer pattern. The things that I loved gave colour to that pattern, those I had learnt gave form. My contribution to the "war effort" was to open the Crosby Gallery of Modern Art, and as a projection of a world ideal I plotted the publication of *Portfolio, Intercontinental Review of Art and Literature*. I was not without a plan. Such exciting undertakings drew me far afield. From then until now as a Citizen of the World I have travelled and worked for a world without wars.

I have learned that personal life is the individual's only means of expression in a cosmos forever mysterious. It is the right to this life itself that must be made secure for the unborn citizens of a challenging universe. Like Harry, I believe there can be no compromise. The answer to the challenge is always *"Yes."*

351

1,115,674.

Patented Nov. 3, 1914.

2 SHEETS—SHEET 1.

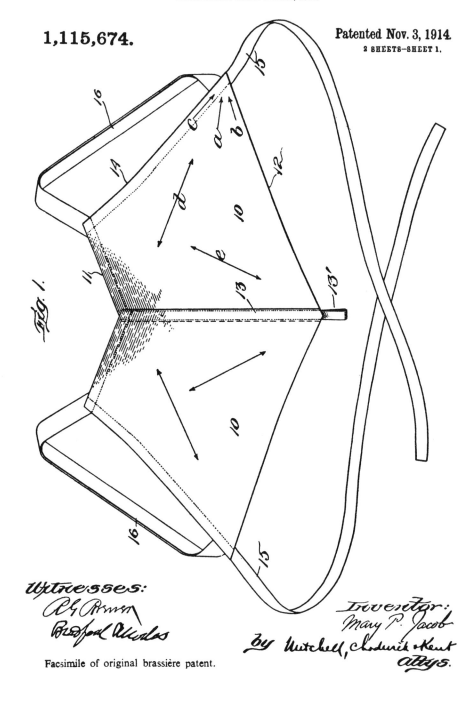

Facsimile of original brassière patent.

Letter addressed to
Harry Crosby,
19 Rue de Lille, Paris.

Paris 6 April '29

Dear Harry,

The packet of sweets just come—awfully nice of you &
Caresse. We've thought of you a lot, these two pregnant days.
But keep a little sun spot of insouciance somewhere inside you.
I'm sure one of the great secrets of the Sun is a strong in-
souciance, in the middle of him, where no-one breaks in on him.

We leave in the morning—via Orleans & Toulouse. I
do hope we shall like Spain, & perhaps find a place a bit like your
mill, with sun in the courtyard, & very still.

I shall write you as soon as we really arrive anywhere—
meanwhile Thomas Cook & Son.

Calle Fontanella, Barcelona
will find us.

Pax, then ! the sunny sort.

D.H.L.

Gᵈ HOTEL ESKUALDUNA
HENDAYE (B.P.)

9th Sunday —

Dear Connosse:

Pauline left her — in the back of your car with our three passports in it. The hotel and I took a taxi after you but couldn't catch up with us —

If you stopped at Perjes — kept taxi at spanish border crossed French frontier and came back to hotel but you were already —

---

②

Could you telephone us tonight at Hotel Aspendis Ses Selasbieme that you are sending the 3 passports by Express — registered mail to that hotel —

Imagine it would be to much trouble to bring them — Regret terribly making you this trouble —

Ernest Hemingway

WHAT FAMOUS AUTHORS SAY ABOUT
CROSBY EDITIONS

● "Paul Valéry has rightly said : 'The real League of Nations should be a League of Minds.' But how create this when Anglo-Saxons and Latins misunderstand each other? To widely diffuse —as does the CCE—the best books of the two civilisations, is to lead towards the formation of a new Europe."

André MAUROIS

● *"The Crosby Continental Collection* fits easily in the pocket, can be carried everywhere, ready to give life and hope—in fact, the opposite of a revolver."

Jean COCTEAU

● "Paris will perhaps play, in the history of books and American culture, the same rôle in the XXth Century as that which Amsterdam played for European "Belles Lettres" in the XVIIIth Century. The *Crosby Editions* are leading the Vanguard of this emancipation and doing most useful work for a closer contact between French and Anglo-Saxon literature."

Paul MORAND

● "Caresse Crosby is doing a work for which we should all, readers and writers alike, be grateful and which is certain to make her name as well known with future generations as those of the list of writers she has chosen to publish. Her choice continues to be excellent. The writing of Dorothy Parker is unmistakably American and inevitably human, of that order which is new and stands entirely on its own. It is as American as Cocteau is French and Morand cosmopolitan."

Louis BROMFIELD

● *"Modern Masterpieces* . . . added to all the reasons for which we can congratulate Mrs. Crosby on her happy initiative, must be added still this other, namely that thanks to her we can at last become acquainted with the masterpieces of Contemporary Literature. As for the authors of the past, we know them pretty well already, but the moderns . . . we had to have someone to decide on a list for us. Courageously Mrs. Crosby is doing it : bravo !"

Edouard BOURDET

● "Two problems confront us at the bookstalls to-day : how to choose in such a plethora and how to buy in circumstances so reduced. The *Crosby Continental Editions* (to judge by the advance programme which I have just perused) will solve both problems; its publications are not only absurdly cheap but, above all, admirably selected. The purchaser of any or every volume in the series is assured—*mirabile dictu* in this year of disgrace, 1932 —of making an investment which he will not regret."

Stuart GILBERT

● "I cannot think of any two modern French novels that I have read which I should be more interested to see translated than the "Diable au Corps" and "Bubu de Montparnasse."

T. S. ELIOT

● "English speaking people are great travellers in the body but stay-at-homes in the mind. They carry their island and their distant continent with them wherever they go. By publishing translations of the best European literature, you are—at last— making it possible for tourists to go abroad mentally as well as physically. I hope they will be grateful and that the series will be a success."

Aldous HUXLEY

● "I read Radiguet's book for the first time in manuscript thanks to Jean Cocteau. What a joy to see, at last, that psychological masterpiece so well presented to a vast English-American public ! And what a service your series is going to render since, from the start, it offers to the intelligent reader who does not know French, such examples of pure French beauty !"

Joseph KESSEL

● "A good book is often of more value than a long trip. So, let us confidently make our reservations at the new Tourist Office opened for intellectual voyage between France, America and England by the *Crosby Continental Editions.*"

Guy de POURTALES

Paris, 1932.

INDEX

362

Johns Manville (*New York firm*), 68, 75
Johnson, Hallet (*of U.S. Embassy, London*), 62
Jolas, Eugene, 165, 167, 191, 248, 304
Jolas, Maria, 192, 248
Jones, Mr. (*patent lawyer*), 73
Josef (*valet*), 316–7
Joyce, James, 191–7, 283, 294, 327
Joyce, Nora, 191, 192
Julian's Academy of Painting, 123

Kaiser, Stuart, 343
Katie (*cook*), 23, 26, 27
Keefer's wharf, 25, 28, 36
Kelleher, Pat, 104
Kent, George, Duke of, 328
Keyport, New Jersey, 30
Kimber, Blanche (*Author's governess*), 33–4, 36, 42, 43, 44, 45, 48, 53, 54
Kiss (*pet whippet*), 178, 180
Kitteredge, Ben, 114
Knickerbocker, Cholly (*columnist*), 120
Kobbé, Gustave and Carol, 98
Kromer, Tom, 333–5

" Lady in the Yellow Hat, The," 256
Lafayette Escadrille, the, 88
Lane, Kay, 258
Lanes, the (*of Brooklyn*), 41, 42
Latin, Quarter the, 123–5, 143, 156
Laurencin, Marie, 283, 327
Lawrence, D.H., 160, 200, 212, 227–32, 252, 264, 294, 295, 327
Lawrence, Emma, *see* Jacob, Emma
Lawrence, Freda, 230, 231, 232
Lawrence, Riker, 19, 20
Lawrence, T. E., 223
Lazzari, Pietor, 234
Lee, Canada (*actor*), 277
Léger, F., 125
Len, Uncle, 19
Lescaret, Roger (" *the perfect printer* "), 156–61, 197, 227, 264
Levy, Julien, 328–91, 331
Lewis, Miss, 56
Lewis, Rosa, 269–271
Lewis, Willie, his orchestra, 306
Life, 41, 325
Lilac Time (film), 100
Lily, Aunt, 32
Lindbergh, Charles Augustus (*aviator*), 151–3
Lisa, Aunt, 15
London, 241, 267–71
London, Jack, 223–4
Longchamps races, 114 183
Longworth, Alice, 47
Lou Dillon (*thoroughbred filly*), 35–6
Louisville races, 35, 36
Lowell, Amy, 222
Lowndes, Miss, 56,

Lucien (*chauffeur*), 249–57, 272, 301, 303, 311–312, 316
Lucy, Aunt, 42
Luichon (*bookbinder*), 130
Luxor, 200–4
Lymington, Gerard (Earl of Portsmouth), 128, 141, 235, 241, 262, 267, 269, 271

McAlmon, Robert, 248, 304, 324
MacKean, Shaw, 339
MacLeish, Ada, 170, 192, 324
MacLeish, Archie, 170, 192, 257, 283, 294, 324, 327
MacMullen, Johnny, 288
Mad Queen, by Harry Crosby, 218, 264
Madame Butterfly, 48
Madison Avenue Gazette, 44
Mahlstead, Robbie, 43
Mallarmé, Stéphane, 144, 224
Malraux, André, 192
Man on the Eiffel Tower, The (film), 168
Manifesto for Individual Secession . . . , 278
Manifesto : The Revolution of the Word, 165–7, 304
Maquis, the, 115
Marcelle (*maidservant*), 238, 246, 262, 311, 320
Marie (*French maid*), 71–3
Marie (*the Count's maid*), 186, 189
Marks, Harry (*New York bookseller*), 326, 327
" Marno, Valerie " (*Author's film name*), 101, 104
Mars, Mary (*gardener's daughter*), 75
Martel, Constance (*scavenger*), 131
Martinez, Carlos, 247, 248
Mary (*nursemaid*), 112, 113, 114, 115
Mathias, M. (*nudist secretary*), 175
Mathison, Edith Wynne, 321
Maurois, André, 233
" Maxixe Maidens," the, 99
May, Henry, 329
Mayflower, the, 20
Mazuchi, Vera, 287
Mendl, Lady Elsie, 288, 290, 291
Mermoz (*French air ace*), 321
Merry del Val, Mme., 61, 62
Messin (*Paris publisher*), 221, 222
Mexican Border affair, the, 76–77
Mexico, 220
Meyer, Dick, 272
Mifflin, Houghton (*Boston publisher*), 222, 327
Mike (*iceman*), 24–5
Milford-Haven, Marchioness of, 241, 243, 244
Milford-Haven, Marquis of, 241
Millbrook, N.Y., 106
Millar, George, 285
Miller, Henry, 222, 345
" Mirage," 223
Monday (*pet whippet*), 178, 321
Monnier, Marie, 191
Montgomery, Tony, 288, 290, 291
Montparnasse cemetery, 126

365

his return from France, 83–6 ; out of uniform and frustrated, 88 ;
divorced, 91, 106–7 ; his reform, 91–2 ; forerunner of " Alcoholics
Anonymous," 92 ; death, 92
Peabody, William Jacob (*Author's son*), 75, 79, 88, 92, 110, 112, 113,
115, 136–7, 169–70, 241, 262, 264, 267, 272, 276, 316, 337, 338, 343
Pepio and Chico (*S. American playboys*), 213, 216
Perse, St. J. (*poet*), 284
Phelps, Eliza (*Author's grandmother*), 20
Phelps, Mary, *see* Jacob, Mary
Phelps, Walter (*Author's grandfather*), 20–1
Picasso, Pablo Ruiz, 136, 193–4, 225, 233, 234, 284, 286, 324
Pisa, 172–3
Plumed Serpent, The, 200, 203, 218, 227
Poe, Edgar Allan, 144, 159, 223, 224
" Poem 8 " (*film*), 313
Poems for Harry Crosby, 192, 223, 263, 271
Polignac, Nina de, 262, 264, 306
Polo, le (*dog-racing club*), 228
Porel, Jacques, 273–5, 278, 286, 287 293, 304
Porter, Cole 53–6, 287
Porter, Katherine Anne, 326
Portfolio (*Review*), 45, 224, 351
Postman (*bull terrier*), 27–8
Poteau de Perthe, the, 252
Pound, Ezra, 172, 264–266
Powel, Peter and Gretchen, 128, 146, 152, 153–4, 199–200, 226, 228, 262–3
Proust, Marcel, 116–9, 133, 135, 160, 192
Proust's Forty-seven Letters to Walter Berry, 117, 160
Punch, 19
Putnam, Sam, 304

Quaker Ridge, 75, 76
Quatre Arts Ball, the, 141–3
Quorn Hunt, the, 38, 102

Radiguet, Raymond, 324
Radziwill, Prince Loch, 174–5
Rainey, Paul (*big game hunter*), 121–2
Random House (*publishers*), 325, 326
Rauch twins, the, 65
Rea, Henry, 53
Red Skeletons, 159, 222, 284
Reid, Mrs. Whitelaw, 61
Reisner, Dr. (*archaeologist*), 204–6
Rejane, Gabrielle Charlotte, 273
Reynal, Eugene, 114
Rigaud, Jacques, 232
Rigby, Douglas, 167
Rimbaud, Jean Nicholas Arthur, 144, 202–3, 204, 221–3, 314
Rimbaud, by Rickword, 221
Roccasinabalda, castle of, 323
Rochefoucauld, Count Armand de la, 174–7, 213, 306, 308
Rochelle, Drieu la, 232
Roosevelt, Alice, 47–8
Roosevelt, President Theodore, 47
Roosevelt Hospital, 47

Varda (*Greek painter*), 231
Varin-Bernier, M. (*Proust's landlord*), 118
Vechten, Carl van, 234
Venice, 108
Verdura, Duke de, 347–50
Verlaine, Paul, 221
Versailles, 114
Vert Gallant, Le (barge), 162–5
Virginia, 336–42
Vogue, 41
Voronoff, Dr. (*gland specialist*), 216–8

Wailing Wall (Jerusalem), 210
Waiting for Nothing, 333
Walker, Jimmy, 303
Warner Bros. Corset Co., 74
Warren, Bayard, 66
Warren, Lily, 66, 90, 91
Washington, 351
Waterbury, Conn., 98
Watertown, Conn., 70, 98, 109
Watkins, Anne, 326–7
Weeks, Ted, 229
Wharton, Edith, 119, 120, 221, 226–7
Wheatland, Florence, *see* Peabody, Florence
Wheatland, " Mouse " (*Author's grandfather-in-law*), 79
Wheelright, Miss (*teacher*), 49
William (*Cavendish doorman*), 269, 270
Williams, William Carlos, 257
Windsor, 60, 63
" Windward " (*Barnums' home*), 33–4, 42, 45, 49 68, 69, 70, 75
Wood, Christopher (*painter*), 287
Worcester, Dr. George (*psychologist*), 92
Work in Progress, 193
World War I, 61, 63–4, 66–7, 77, 270
World War II, 277, 350–1

Young, Bert (*Author's 3rd husband*), 335–42, 344, 346
York, Duke and Duchess of, 328

Zulu (*pet dog*), 147, 150, 199, 228